AN **END** OF **INNOCENCE**

The Watershed Season of
1959/60

AN **END** OF **INNOCENCE**

The Watershed Season of
1959/60

TIM QUELCH

First published by Pitch Publishing, 2021

Pitch Publishing
A2 Yeoman Gate
Yeoman Way
Worthing
Sussex
BN13 3QZ
www.pitchpublishing.co.uk
info@pitchpublishing.co.uk

ISBN 978 1 78531 758 3

Typesetting and origination by Pitch Publishing
Printed and bound in India by Replika Press Pvt. Ltd.

Contents

In memory of David Hughes
and Michael Jennings

THANKS

THIS BOOK is dedicated to two late friends who suffered with an incurable lung disease. All my royalties will be donated to the British Lung Foundation, a particularly worthy cause in these critical times.

Thank you to everyone who has helped me in writing this book. Many former players and managers have assisted, including Ray Pointer, John Collins, Bob Seith, Jimmy Robson, Lawrie McMenemy, Jimmy McIlroy, Keith Tucker, John Angus, Ken Ballard, Brian Pilkington, Alan Ballard, Trevor Meredith, Adam Blacklaw, Martin Dobson, Geoff Nulty, Arthur Bellamy and authors, Ivan Ponting, John Doherty, Dave Thomas, Mark Metcalf and Jonathon Wilson. Thanks also to all at Pitch – Paul, Jane, Gareth, Dean, Duncan and Graham. Your help has been invaluable. Thanks to website owners Tony Scholes of Up the Clarets, the Mighty Whites and Chris Fort of York City South supporters' website www.yorkcitysouth.co.uk, plus national and local press and a wide range of books, journals and video footage. All sources are listed in the reference section at the end of this book. Where possible I have sought copyright clearance but, in a few instances, it has not been possible to identify ownership because of the age of the material or image. Please accept my apology if I have inadvertently breached copyright. If anyone wishes to pursue this further, please refer this to my publishers in the first instance.

This is Pitch Publishing, A2 Yeoman Gate, Yeoman Way, Worthing, Sussex BN13 3QZ.

INTRODUCTION

IN HIS autobiography *Greavsie*, Jimmy Greaves suggested that the 1959/60 season brought football's age of innocence to an end, with open, attacking football giving way to defensiveness, aided and abetted by specialist coaches and tacticians. In *An End of Innocence*, the author looks at English football in the '50s and '60s: the management styles; tactics; coaching and training methods; with a wide range of illustrative games reflecting upon how open or insular we were. Some of the questions considered in this book are:

- How did England change as a country in the '40s, '50s and '60s?
- Did any of these changes affect English football?
- Was the '50s a time of innocence for English football or a time of naivety, insularity, myopia, prejudice, and complacency, hastening the decline of the national team?
- Was English football slow to learn its World Cup and Hungarian lessons?
- Was coaching, training and tactical awareness good enough in the '50s?
- How and why did English football shift its emphasis from attack to defence?
- How did '60s coaching and tactics turn England into World Cup winners?
- How did British clubs conquer Europe? Did Euroscepticism ever impede them?
- How did the minnows beat the biggest and best English clubs in the '50s and '60s?
- Did English professional football change forever and for the better in the '60s?

- Did some liberated 'soccer slaves' become well-paid celebrities during the '60s?
- Did this change have any impact upon rising hooliganism?
- How did the English youth movements of the '50s and '60s generally affect football?
- Did '60s football become too rough? Was this worse than in the '50s?
- How did '60s economic decline affect the health of once famous English clubs?
- Was television a force for good or bad for English football clubs?
- Who were the main movers and shakers in '50s and '60s English football and why?
- Was the 1959/60 English football season the watershed Jimmy Greaves claimed?
- How healthy did the English game appear to be at the end of the '60s?

Tim Quelch
May 2020

PART ONE

Absolute Beginners

THE WAY WE WERE BEFORE THE 60s SWUNG

1.

LOST SUPREMACY 1945–1950

GREAT BRITAIN concluded its part in the Second World War battered, barren and bankrupt. After suffering six years of trauma and hardship its working people were eager for something brighter and fairer, with greater protections against want and disease, better standards of living and improved educational prospects. It was this deep-seated sense of entitlement, aroused by the bleak deprivation of the hungry '30s, which brought about the Labour landslide of 1945.

On the back of the excited VE Day celebrations, the British public flocked once again to our sad, neglected seaside resorts and turned up in their thousands to watch five vibrant 'Victory Tests' of 1945 in which a creaking England cricket side took on a scratch Australian Services XI. Brilliant England batsman Wally Hammond recalled the occasion with uncharacteristic euphoria, 'There was a feeling of peace and happiness in the air that was very delightful to me. It seemed as though after years in the shadows England was marching into the sunshine again.'

Our cinemas, dance halls, race tracks, athletics stadia, boxing arenas and football and cricket grounds became packed, too, as the grim war years were cast aside with almost febrile glee. Writer and former diplomat Bruce Lockhart exclaimed in 1945, 'Never have I seen a nation change so quickly from a war mentality to a peace mentality. The war [in the Far East] has disappeared from the news. Sport and the election now fill the front pages.'

But the carefree mood did not last long. The country was £3bn in debt. Capital and overseas investments had taken huge hits. The nation's infrastructure was in tatters. Bombed-out housing had to be replaced. With servicemen returning to their estranged families and the first wave of 'baby boomers' voicing their needs, an enormous and urgent housing shortage had to be addressed.

As an emergency response, 30,000 prefabricated dwellings were erected from kits financed by United States subsidies under the Lease-Lend programme. When that programme ceased in 1945, Britain had to cadge another £4bn loan to meet its 'financial Dunkirk', as John Maynard Keynes aptly put it. This was not charity. With the Cold War pressing ever closer, the Americans needed Britain to maintain its position as head of the Commonwealth to help stem the spread of international communism.

In a statement resonant of Britain today, Labour minister Herbert Morrison declared, 'We are in danger of paying more than we can afford for defences that are nevertheless inadequate, or even illusory.' Yet it was in this anti-communist capacity that Britain obtained additional American funding, via the Marshall Plan, to pay for its Welfare State reforms. This loan was not repaid until 2006.

Pumped up with wartime heroics, Britain professed to be a world power still, despite its increasing reliance upon US financial support. While its leading politicians attended world summit conferences, its servicemen undertook global policing duties in Malaya, the Mediterranean and the Middle East. The Berlin blockade was defied, and a further global conflict was in prospect in Korea.

Meanwhile, Britain struggled to make and pay its way. Industrial production needed to be modernised, diversified, and expanded to deal with the vast balance of payments deficit. The state of British agriculture was dismally primitive. Almost 80 per cent of West Country farms lacked electrical power. Milking was done mostly by hand. The situation was scarcely better closer to London where only 50 per cent of farms had electricity. With home-produced food needed for export to help repay the huge national debt, a depressingly long list of rationed items was retained until the '50s.

The railway network was in a decrepit state. But the railway companies found the remedial costs too high, so the government stepped in. As radical as the Welfare State reforms were, they had to be delivered on the cheap. The ascetic-looking Stafford Cripps seemed to epitomise the Labour government's grating exhortations of self-denial. David Lean's *Brief Encounter* was on-message. Family duty came before affairs of the heart. Morale was worse than during the war years, not helped by the arctic winter of 1947. Coal was short, so were other fuel and food supplies. Production halted, household pipes and geysers froze, and the shivering occupants went to bed in heavy clothes and balaclavas.

This was the scene as the country returned to its sporting life. If the VE- and VJ-celebrating crowds thought that a British military victory would translate into sporting success they were much mistaken. After all, the war had not been won by Britain's efforts alone. Without the colossal resources supplied by the USA, USSR and, indeed, the British Commonwealth, this nation's brave, lone stand in 1940 would not have been converted into collective victory. Unabashed, London successfully laid on a cheap and cheerful 'Austerity' Olympics in 1948 in which 'Team GB' gained four medals. As if there was any doubt that taking part took precedence over winning, one of our sprinters replied to a question about his training regime with, 'Train? I just stubbed out my cigarette and ran.'

Not that such self-deprecation inhibited the jaunty Pathé news team who flew the patriotic flag in Britain's smoky cinemas. Their message was that Britain was best at manufacturing, design, fashion, military actions, and sport. At least the England football team did their best to raise public morale as they thrashed world champions Italy 4-0 in Turin in 1948, albeit after a shaky start. Crushing victories were also achieved against Portugal (10-0), the Netherlands (8-2) and Switzerland (6-0). But this was a deceptive interlude of success.

With a full resumption of the Football League programme on a stormy late August afternoon in 1946, the fans returned to their grounds in droves, oblivious to the soaking many of them had to endure. During the 1946/47 season 35.6 million people watched English Football League games, 15 million in the top tier. But not all were excited by what they saw. One British journalist carped, 'The game is currently being played by large numbers of young and not so young men who know little about the game, watched by large numbers of others who know practically nothing about it. It is being administered in many instances by gentlemen whose attitude to a tough profession is unrealistic and directed in its performance by too many men who are nearly two wars behind its development.' So much for the 'Golden Age of Football'.

On 9 March 1946, a horrific disaster occurred at Burnden Park, Bolton. Thirty-three people were killed and over 400 injured when crush barriers gave way. This tragic incident emphasised the dangers of accommodating huge crowds in Britain's decrepit stadia. Incredibly, the two teams played on amid the carnage.

British cinemas were packed too in these pre-TV times. In 1946 there were 1.6 billion admissions although what was shown did not appeal to everyone as this sour gentleman illustrates, 'Whatever picture is on, whatever drivel it is, the queues are there. Dogs, pictures, tobacco, drink, football pools, crooners – what an indifferent lot of pastimes there are for our people. To do a monotonous repetitious job you loathe, and to use these anodynes to help you forget tomorrow's work!'

Outside the football grounds disenchantment was spreading virally. During the winter of 1948–49 the nation's big cities became engulfed by filthy, sulphurous smog. In London it lasted for six consecutive days. The capital's coughing citizens shuffled through the grimy shroud with scarves wrapped around their downcast faces trying to filter out the noxious fumes. These were indeed the dark ages. Railway signalmen were depicted peering hopelessly into the impenetrable gloom. Trains collided, so did cars, buses and lorries as street flares failed to disperse the murk. Worse was to follow. The pound was devalued by 30 per cent in September. Feted novelist Doris Lessing recalled 'London was dull and grey. Clothes were still "austerity", dismal and ugly although clothes rationing ended in March 1949. Everyone was indoors by ten, and the streets were empty. The dining rooms served good meat, terrible vegetables, and nursery puddings. The war still lingered, not only in the bombed places but in people's minds and behaviour. Any conversation tended to drift towards the war, like an animal licking a sore place.'

A familiar cry in Great Britain was, 'We're so short of everything.' So, when the England Ashes squad arrived in Australia in the late autumn of 1946 they were amazed at the array of 'goodies' available. An Australian broadcaster commented, 'In between meals the English cricketers were forever eating fruit, cakes and chocolates.' Fast bowlers Bill Voce and Dick Pollard put on two stones, while another admitted eating more in one day than in a week in his heavily rationed homeland. Although completely outclassed by the

Australians, the English players admitted that abject defeat had never tasted so sweet.

With the Home Nations tournament accepted as a qualifying process, England headed for the World Cup finals in Brazil after beating Scotland 1-0 at Hampden Park. At the instigation of FA secretary Stanley Rous, the organisation decided to participate this time having refused condescendingly to participate in the two pre-war tournaments. Just as Churchill realised in 1946 the importance of Britain joining a newly formed European community in the interests of enhancing mutual prosperity and peace, the FA realised that it would be better if it was on the inside of a rapidly growing FIFA if it was to maintain its presumed global standing. Continued insularity was no longer viable. Meanwhile, the jingoistic Pathé news reels whipped up a belief that England could, should and would demonstrate their world supremacy at football by bringing back the FIFA Jules Rimet Trophy.

Walter Winterbottom had been appointed as England's team manager and FA head of coaching in 1946. He was a thoughtful, innovative, and engaging man who had briefly played for Manchester United during the '30s. Although he was well regarded, he was strangely marginalised in the FA's World Cup preparations. The FA decided it would continue to conduct often difficult negotiations regarding the release of players from their league clubs. Chairman Arthur Drewry also took it upon himself to select the teams in Brazil. Talk about buying a dog and barking yourself!

Incredibly, the FA also arranged a simultaneous tour of Canada with Stanley Matthews and Jim Taylor selected to take part. So, when FIFA demanded that each country name 22 players 21 days before the finals, these two players appeared unavailable. Seemingly, so were Aston and Cockburn of Manchester United, their club having unilaterally arranged a summer tour of North America. And to cap it all, England's best centre-half, Neil Franklin of Stoke, excluded himself by joining a Colombian club in Bogota for a lucrative fee. He had played in all of England's 27 previous games and his loss was keenly felt. Charlie Mitten followed him a little later, giving an early indication of footballers' mounting frustrations with their capped wages.

It was a relief, though, when Matthews, Taylor, Aston, and Cockburn were released just in the nick of time. Despite these difficulties, England won their opening World Cup game against Chile, 2-0, but their victory was not as comfortable as the score suggests, The South Americans had only one full-time professional, Newcastle's George Robledo, but had the better of the game before Mortensen headed in Mullen's fine cross in the 39th minute. The longer the game went on the more likely it seemed that Chile would equalise. However, Mannion saved English blushes by scoring England's decisive second goal with only 20 minutes remaining. Chile still strove hard to get back into the game and were unlucky when Robledo's scorching 30-yard free kick smacked against the post. It was a close-run thing.

Wilf Mannion found the going very tough, explaining, 'We needed to have been there for a few weeks to acclimatise, especially after having had a hard season. It would have been better if we were given time to just walk about maybe. But we were immediately pressed into training in that sizzling heat. It was all against us. We beat Chile but it felt as if we had weights on us, despite having oxygen ready for us at half-time.' Tom Finney added, 'We had a three- or four-day get-together in London. It had been a tough season. The grounds were particularly hard at that time of year, and then when we arrived in Brazil, we were put in this hotel on the Copacabana beach. We were fortunate to get any sleep there with the noise that was going on. In the early hours there were car horns blaring and of course we went from a temperature here of about 60°F into something like 90°F and bone hard grounds.' Years later, Stanley Matthews recalled, 'The food wasn't good at all. Tom Finney, Wilf Mannion, and I shared our rooms and we were eating bananas mainly. There was no preparation as there is today.'

Just as England were preparing for the Chile game, the sombre news reached them that communist forces were streaming across the 38th Parallel separating North and South Korea. Clem Attlee responded by dispatching a British military force to assist the United Nations' peace-keeping effort. He also put British Far Eastern naval forces at the disposal of Second World War hero General Douglas MacArthur, who led the combined force. The bellicose MacArthur was soon threatening the North Korean invaders with the atomic bomb. It was a dismal prospect with the previous war still painfully fresh in peoples' memories. Meanwhile, the House of Commons considered a complaint that nylons laddered too easily and indignant clergy in Brighton condemned the town as 'morally dead' for allowing cinemas to open on the Sabbath. A fiddle for Mr Nero please!

With the Chile result in the bag, the England squad were confident of qualifying for the later stages with the USA team to play next. The American side comprised players who had settled either temporarily or permanently in the USA, originating from six different countries. Captain Eddie McIlvenny was a Scot who had been given a free transfer by Wrexham 18 months before but would be signed later by Manchester United. Clearly, he was no mug. Moreover, just two weeks before, an England XI struggled to beat this team in New York, ragging a 1-0 victory. Spain found them no pushovers either. For in their opening World Cup game against the Americans they were 1-0 behind with only ten minutes left. However, a chastened Spanish team belatedly got their act together, scoring three times to win.

With the USA game planned for Belo Horizonte, the England squad moved from the Copacabana beach to the British-owned Morro Velho gold mine in the mountains above the city. Here they luxuriated in the generous hospitality provided. There was no intensity of preparation. Meanwhile, the Americans' Scottish coach from Pennsylvania allowed his team to stay up late enjoying themselves, believing their defeat to be a formality.

Winterbottom's examination of the narrow ground on which they were to play revealed it to be totally unsuitable for a World Cup game. The pitch was rutted and stony and the dressing room was dimly lit, and rat-infested. Winterbottom took issue with the dressing room, obtaining leave to change at the Minas Athletic Club, a ten-minute coach drive. Strangely, though, he did not complain about the unsuitable pitch, which caused the American centre-half Colombo to wear protective leather gloves throughout the game. Winterbottom wanted to rest some of his best players in preparation for the harder tests ahead. Drewry would have none of it, believing the game to be a light work-out. Neither Matthews nor Milburn were selected which was odd given the efforts made to bring about Matthews's release.

From the off, England poured forward. The American defenders were at sixes and sevens. Mullen was presented with an open goal but at the crucial moment the ball bobbled badly, resulting in his shot sailing over the bar. At first, pratfalls like this were amusing but soon exasperation crept in when the England team realised their superior skill counted for little.

Urged onwards by the 20,000 Brazilian crowd, the Americans began to grow in confidence, believing they could keep England out. US inside-left John Souza set his ambitions higher, having already scored against Spain. Shaking off his late-night hangover, Souza forced Williams to make his first save of the game.

Mannion's brilliance was nullified on this unpredictable surface where the ball suddenly stood up or diverted crazily, leaving the England ball players floundering. It was almost impossible to pass accurately. Then suddenly Finney struck the post with goalkeeper Borghi helpless. England struck the woodwork 11 times in this bizarre match. But with their spirit shrinking, and their forwards becoming increasingly hesitant, the re-energised US defenders eagerly dispossessed them.

Then, in the 38th minute, Gaetjens, a naturalised Haitian, scored. It was a freakish slice of fortune. US wing-half Bahr unleashed a shot 25 yards from goal. Williams had it covered before Gaetjen's ear intruded, defecting the ball past the stricken Wolves keeper. Although England were left with over 50 minutes to save the game, they could not find a way to do so, despite making several positional changes. They nearly salvaged a point in the final seconds when Mullen's header appeared to have crossed the line before being hooked away. However, the referee was unconvinced, and in a blast of firecrackers, shame-faced England slouched off the pitch. American wealth and culture already dominated British lives. Now their ragbag team had beaten England at its favourite game.

Drewry considered appealing against the result on grounds that the USA had fielded an ineligible player. However, there was little support for this action and the matter was quickly dropped. While the American team were jubilant, they received little or no acclaim from their indifferent countrymen. Tragically, Gaetjens was arrested by Tonton Macoute thugs on his return to Haiti during the '60s, never to reappear.

Walter Winterbottom commented afterwards, 'America, let's be fair, had held Switzerland to a 2-2 draw. It was a team of Europeans who had been over there for three months and allowed to play.

It was a game that we dominated. They scored by a deflection and from then on, they did everything to stop us playing, but you cannot blame them. We missed our chances, striking the woodwork 11 times. That is ridiculous! The South American teams were in mid-season. They are fresh. We are at the end of an exhausting season. And the refereeing was not as good as it is today. The South Americans can push you off the ball with impunity but if they are brought down by tackling, they get furious. Our game is based on fierce tackling.'

Tom Finney added years later, 'We had probably 85 per cent of the game. It was like when North Korea beat Italy in the 1966 World Cup. It is just one of those things that happens in football. It was a poor pitch, but it was the same for both sides. We have no excuses. We should have beaten them comfortably.' Billy Wright reckoned, 'We didn't play badly. We could not hit the target. It was a disaster. I think it was the worse result I ever had playing for England.'

Journalist Bryon Butler carped, 'Walter Winterbottom got the blame, but he didn't pick the team. He was just the manager and carried the can. We had about 23 selectors capable of going into a geriatric ward that used to pick the team, but on this occasion, it was left to one man, Arthur Drewry. He did his best, but it was an awful result.'

On Thursday, 29 June 1950, the English football and cricket teams suffered grave humiliations. While its football team were losing to a lowly side of part-timers, its cricket team was being routed at Lord's, set up by the bludgeoning blades of the three Ws, Walcott, Weekes, and Worrell. The bewildering spin of those 'pals of mine' Ramadhin and Valentine did the rest, sharing 18 English wickets. West Indies won this Test by 326 runs. It was their first victory on English soil. They went on to win the series emphatically, much to the pleasure of the *Windrush* immigrants who had been greeted so shabbily by their 'mother country'. At Lord's and Lancaster Gate, the respective homes of MCC and the FA, one could imagine a tattered Union Jack hanging limply at half-mast.

England's footballers still had a slim chance of reprieve, but only if they beat Spain in their last group game. Changes were made with Milburn and Matthews selected but to no avail. Despite dominating the first half, England were once again unable to score. Soon after the break Zarra scored for Spain who then barred all routes to their goal. England lost and were shown the door. Spain were then obliterated by Brazil 6-1, underlining how far England were from global supremacy.

The South American expedition was not entirely in vain, though, as the England players and manager were given amazing masterclasses in football skills by the Brazilian children on Copacabana beach. Tom Finney commented, 'There were hundreds, literally hundreds of kids playing on the beach, and not with footballs. Some had small rubber balls, but some had brown paper parcels tied together with string. One youngster kept up his parcel one hundred times. This is where they learn their skills. I am a big believer in that. Look at the number of players from poorer countries like Pelé who have come from very humble beginnings.'

Southampton Football Club's summer tour of Brazil in 1948 was an eye-opener, too. It was meant to be an English masterclass for the supposedly inferior Brazilians, but the roles of teacher and pupil were rapidly reversed. Southampton player Ted Ballard said, 'Every player in a Brazilian team was an accomplished footballer. In British football this was not the case. Players were confined by their position. The full-backs were good kickers of the ball but had difficulty in beating a man. This was true of other players too. The Brazilians paralysed Saints. Even a reserve goalkeeper could perform outstanding acrobatic ball skills.'

First Division table (6 May 1950)

	P	W	D	L	F	A	Pts	Goal ave.
1. Portsmouth	42	22	9	11	74	38	53	1.9
2. Wolverhampton W.	42	20	13	9	76	49	53	1.6
3. Sunderland	42	21	10	11	83	62	52	1.3
4. Manchester United	42	18	14	10	69	44	50	1.6
5. Newcastle United	42	19	12	11	77	55	50	1.4
6. Arsenal	42	19	11	12	79	55	49	1.4
7. Blackpool	42	17	15	10	46	35	49	1.3
8. Liverpool	42	17	14	11	64	54	48	1.2
9. Middlesbrough	42	20	7	15	59	48	47	1.2
10. Burnley	42	16	13	13	40	40	45	1.0
11. Derby County	42	17	10	15	69	61	44	1.1
12. Aston Villa	42	15	12	15	61	61	42	1.0
13. Chelsea	42	12	16	14	58	65	40	0.9
14. West Bromwich Albion	42	14	12	16	47	53	40	0.9
15. Huddersfield Town	42	14	9	19	52	73	37	0.7
16. Bolton Wanderers	42	10	14	18	45	59	34	0.8
17. Fulham	42	10	14	18	41	54	34	0.8
18. Everton	42	10	14	18	42	66	34	0.6
19. Stoke City	42	11	12	19	45	75	34	0.6
20. Charlton Athletic	42	13	6	23	53	65	32	0.8
21. Manchester City	42	8	13	21	36	68	29	0.5
22. Birmingham City	42	7	14	21	31	67	28	0.5

2.

'BACK TO THE FUTURE': PUSH AND RUN, 1950/51

BELIEVE IT or not, there were English complaints about defensive football during the late '40s. Heaven knows what these critics would have made of *Catenaccio* employed by the Italians and by Joe Mercer's Sheffield United in the late '50s. The defensive blight that became commonplace after the Chile World Cup of 1962 would surely have dismayed them more.

Arthur Rowe was determined not to succumb to such sterility. He, like compatriot Jimmy Hogan, coached on the continent during the '30s. Hogan, from Burnley, made a huge impact upon the development of Austrian and Hungarian football that would flourish so splendidly during the '30s and '50s, respectively, at least before the Soviets crushed the Hungarian Revolution in 1956. Rowe must have made a strong impression with the Hungarians too, because he was offered the post of manager of their national team in 1939. Alas, war broke out and Rowe turned to Tottenham where, in the late '40s, he revived a creative style of football not seen since the early 20th century, as practised then by Newcastle and the Corinthian teams. In 1949/50, Rowe helped lift Spurs out of the Second Division with a tactic commonly known as 'push and run'. In the following season, Spurs soared even higher, to the top of the First Division, employing the same tactic.

Rowe's inside-forward, Eddie Baily, commented, 'Arthur insisted that football was a lovely passing game. He used to have little sayings like, "make it simple, make it quick" and "he who holds the ball is lost". If you made a pass, the objective was to get it to someone quickly and get the return. We used to work in triangles and squares. You pushed it and you moved. It was a simple principle. We used to do this all over the field.' Left-winger George Robb added, 'Arthur was shrewd. He saw something different from strong tackling and get it into the box for a Lawton or Lofthouse to head. What impressed me was that after doing the track work, the other players would make for the car park for six-a-side. The blokes loved it.'

Rowe modestly dismissed the notion that he was the originator of this tactical plan. He explained, 'I merely evolved the idea after watching kids running down the street flicking a tennis ball against the wall and collecting the instant rebound in full stride. The "wall-pass", "one-two", "touch play", "push and run", call it what you will, we developed at Tottenham from the rear, from the goalkeeper up to the front, right through the team. Eddie Baily with his instant reactions and accuracy was made for it and with Medley as his wing partner and Ronnie Burgess behind, we had an outstanding left flank. Played well from tight positions, "push and run" put a defender out of the game at a stroke.'

Alf Ramsey, signed from Southampton, was a crucial addition. At £21,000, Ramsey was the most expensive full-back of his time. Although somewhat slow on the turn he read the game astutely, timing his interceptions with rare foresight and defending with the instincts of a wing-half or inside-forward. Walter Winterbottom recalled, 'Tottenham played beautiful football. Alf Ramsey had an uncanny knack of judging a chip pass just above his opponent into the direction of an on-running forward. Arthur's great contribution was to weld a team together capable of playing silky football in which everybody had plenty of time on the ball and yet were running into space.' Bill Nicholson, a late, great, double-winning Spurs manager, recalled, 'We called Alf Ramsey "The General" because he was so cool, calm, and collected and seemed to have everything under control. He had excellent control of the ball and passed well. Alf's only weakness was a lack of pace but he compensated for that by his shrewd reading of a game. He was probably Arthur's favourite player although Arthur liked most of us. Arthur got the best out of Ronnie Burgess too. Ronnie had been inclined to run with the ball too much. Arthur sorted him out. We did have one or two who occasionally ran with the ball. Les Bennett was capable of that, but emphasis was placed upon passing, and in Eddie Baily we then had the best first-time passer in the English game. The Leicester players once told us, "We hate playing against you. It's like trying to catch pigeons."'

Sports journalist Ivan Ponting wrote, 'The spine was sound too. Ditchburn in goal was a terrific shot stopper with uncanny positioning. Clarke was a formidable centre-half and Duquemin, from Guernsey, was a reliable, no-frills striker who scored 134 goals in 308 senior games for his solitary Football League club. Despite his lack of extravagant natural ability, Duquemin was considered a key man by both manager and team-mates as he helped his side reach the very top. His honest sweat was an important lubricant to the smooth running of Rowe's captivating machine.

'It was a fresh, swashbuckling approach which lit up the post-war soccer scene and won lavish plaudits not only for the ball-playing Eddie Baily, Les Bennett, the wing-half and skipper Ronnie Burgess, but the wingers Les Medley and Sonny Walters, too. But there was a place, too, for players who would run ceaselessly when they were not in possession, providing extra passing options for their artistic colleagues.

'They did not always get the ball and rarely took the eye, but without them the system would have foundered. One such player was rugged wing-half Bill Nicholson, destined to become the most successful manager in Spurs history, and the other was Duquemin. They remained close friends for life. In the first two decisive seasons of "push and run", Spurs were the division's highest goalscorers: 81 in 1949/50 and 82 in 1950/51. No wonder the fans poured into White Hart or "Hot" Lane.'

The year 1951 was a better one for Britain despite the enduring Korean War. Petrol rationing ceased, as did curbs on canned and dried fruit, and certain sweet items. The Conservatives returned to power pledging to build 300,000 houses a year. Meanwhile, the Festival of Britain raised spirits, showcasing the best of British manufacturing, engineering, aeronautics and science, also featuring a futuristic, cigar-shaped structure called the Skylon, which seemed to float without any visible means of support. 'Just like Britain' quipped one wag. Yet then British manufacturing produced a third of the national output, employing 40 per cent of its workers and commanding a quarter of world exports. Sixty years later, British manufacturing produced barely a tenth of the nation's GDP, employing just eight per cent of its workforce and accounting for a mere two per cent of world exports.

First Division table (5 May 1951)

	P	W	D	L	F	A	Pts	Goal ave
1. Tottenham Hotspur	42	25	10	7	82	44	60	1.9
2. Manchester United	42	24	8	10	74	40	56	1.9
3. Blackpool	42	20	10	12	79	53	50	1.5
4. Newcastle United	42	18	13	11	62	53	49	1.2
5. Arsenal	42	19	9	14	73	56	47	1.3
6. Middlesbrough	42	18	11	13	76	65	47	1.2
7. Portsmouth	42	16	15	11	71	68	47	1.0
8. Bolton Wanderers	42	19	7	16	64	61	45	1.0
9. Liverpool	42	16	11	15	53	59	43	1.0
10. Burnley	42	14	14	14	48	43	42	1.1
11. Derby County	42	16	8	18	81	75	40	1.1
12. Sunderland	42	12	16	14	63	73	40	0.9
13. Stoke City	42	13	14	15	50	59	40	0.8
14. Wolverhampton W.	42	15	8	19	74	61	38	1.2
15. Aston Villa	42	12	13	17	66	68	37	1.0
16. West Bromwich Albion	42	13	11	18	53	61	37	0.9
17. Charlton Athletic	42	14	9	19	63	80	37	0.8
18. Fulham	42	13	11	18	52	68	37	0.8
19. Huddersfield Town	42	15	6	21	64	92	36	0.7
20. Chelsea	42	12	8	22	53	65	32	0.8
21. Sheffield Wednesday	42	12	8	22	64	83	32	0.8
22. Everton	42	12	8	22	48	86	32	0.6

3.

A LION ROARS IN
VIENNA, 1952

IN THE spring of 1952, the FA arranged a tour of Italy and Austria for the England team. Only two wide men were selected, the vastly experienced Tom Finney and uncapped Burnley winger Billy Elliott. Billy had an intimidating presence. His reputation was scary. Much like Sunderland hardman Kevin Ball during the 90s, Billy took few prisoners. On 25 December 1951, his fiery clashes with Preston firebrand Willie Cunningham raised the heat so high that North End's captain, Tom Finney, felt compelled to switch his full-backs to maintain 'peace and good will'.

In March 1952, Billy was dismissed at Maine Road for a 'look of intent'. He could certainly summon a menacing stare. Billy was the only Burnley player to be dismissed during the '40s and '50s. Their distinguished playmaker, Jimmy McIlroy, recalled Billy losing his rag with him and his fellow forwards in one game. McIlroy said, 'Having softened up his marker, Elliott proceeded to send over a series of head-height crosses at rocket-like speed. The ball was like concrete in those days, and, when wet, weighed a ton. The laces left a nice imprint on your forehead. Who the hell wanted to head the ball when it was driven with the power that Elliott imparted? Elliott became thoroughly fed up with this in one game. Glowering menacingly at us midget forwards he demanded, "Which one of you f***ers keeps f***ing ducking? I'm wasting my f***ing time here."'

Sports writer Ivan Ponting described Billy as a 'study in high-velocity pugnacity laced with deceptively subtle skills'. He added, 'His attacking speciality was racing beyond his marker to reach the goal line, then driving a low cross into the penalty area, often through a tangled forest of legs, for conversion by lurking marksmen.' This ability led to his selection for England's European tour in the summer of 1952. His debut came in a 1-1 draw with Italy in Florence. It was an insipid England performance, though. A Reuters correspondent wrote, 'This game was one of the poorest internationals seen in years.' The *Daily Express* reporter Peter Wilson added, 'Each year we hear from the players complaints that the season is getting more and more congested and that the strain of the domestic season is becoming more excoriating.' How little has changed in 64 years.

Although inside-right Ivor Broadis gave England an early lead, their attack relapsed into sterility. Had Walter Winterbottom been able to call upon another winger in his squad, Elliott might not have played in Austria. Fortunately, Billy survived, contributing to a notable victory. Austria were powerful and sophisticated opponents, featuring the immaculate, multi-faceted Ernst Ocwirk, who starred in the 2-2 draw at Wembley earlier that year. Although dubbed an attacking centre-half, he could play anywhere in midfield. He was tall, authoritative, precise, graceful, and inventive, often probing at the heels of his forwards, capable of unlocking opposing defences with long, raking passes. Once seen, he commanded attention. As proof of their strength, Austria had thrashed Yugoslavia, Hungary, Denmark, Belgium, and Scotland in an unbeaten 16-game run, amassing 57 goals.

On an overcast Sunday afternoon, the open-bowled Prater Stadium was heaving with around 60,000 people present. The arena was spiced with dissent. For many Austrians railed against the British Army's occupation of their country. They roared their side on, hoping that their gifted players would inflict a humiliating defeat upon the English team just as they had upon Scotland (4-0) and Belgium, Yugoslavia, Republic of Ireland, Hungary and Denmark against whom they had scored eight, seven, six, five and five goals respectively.

The British squaddies' presence in the crowd only heightened the political tension. But Billy Elliott was not fazed by this, helping set up the opening goal. In the 21st minute Baily broke up an Austrian attack on the halfway line. His pass to Elliott was transferred immediately on to Jackie Sewell whose cross found Lofthouse in front of goal. The Bolton centre-forward's shot was instant, fierce, and true. England led 1-0 although it was much against the run of play. Their joy was brief as Dienst was brought down by Froggatt in the box and Huber beat Merrick from the spot. Portsmouth's centre-half made amends though by initiating a move which led to British record signing Sewell outwitting the Austrian defence with a feint and a shimmy followed by a crisp shot that evaded goalkeeper Musil. The squaddies were jubilant but not for long as dangerous centre-forward Dienst made a fool of Wright and slammed in an equaliser on the brink of half-time.

Perhaps provoked by the crowd's abrasive mood, the second half was a rugged, tetchy affair. This did not bother battling Billy Elliott one bit. Forced into helping his under-fire defence, he conceded a corner. But Merrick claimed the ball safely above the mass of heads in a congested box. He instantly hurled it towards Finney whose eyes lit up at the space in front of him with most of the Austrians caught upfield. Finney's superbly judged through ball evaded centre-half Happel but found Nat Lofthouse who took it in his stride. Lofthouse recalled, 'There was about eight minutes left as I raced half the length of the pitch with the ball at my feet and a pack of Austrian defenders at my heels. Austrian goalkeeper Musil hesitated about coming out and was a split second too late to stop me shooting when he raced out of his goal. We collided head on and I went out like a light. Our trainer Jimmy Trotter brought me round with the magic sponge, and it was he who told me that I had scored. I had a splitting headache, but it was well worth it!'

Although groggy and in need of further treatment, Lofthouse refused to come off. Instead, he returned to slam another chance against the post before the referee whistled time. The squaddies poured on to the pitch, ecstatically lifting Nat and the others on to their shoulders. England had recovered a semblance of pride thanks to Lofthouse. The watching pressmen celebrated his brave determination by dubbing him the 'Lion of Vienna'. Alf Ramsey remarked, 'The courage that Nat showed in Vienna was typical of him as a man and as a player. He lifted the heart of every Englishmen in that stadium and made us redouble our efforts at keeping the Austrians out.' Creative inside-forward Johnny Haynes added, 'Nat was not all muscle like his reputation suggests. He had a lot of method. His positional sense made him an ideal centre-forward who was always finding room so that his colleagues could pick him out with passes.' Tom Finney concluded, 'Nat was perfectly named as the Lion. He roared through every game, giving defenders a nightmare with his non-stop probing and tremendous power. Nat never knew when he was beaten, and continually popped up with vital goals.'

Afterwards, Lofthouse remarked modestly, 'If Musil had not come, then checked before coming again, I'd never had got there first.' On such a slender slice of fortune does an everlasting reputation survive.

First Division table (5 May 1952)

	P	W	D	L	F	A	Pts	Goal ave
1. Manchester United	42	23	11	8	95	52	57	1.9
2. Tottenham Hotspur	42	22	9	11	76	51	53	1.9
3. Arsenal	42	21	11	10	80	61	53	1.5
4. Portsmouth	42	20	8	14	68	58	48	1.2
5. Bolton Wanderers	42	19	10	13	65	61	48	1.1
6. Aston Villa	42	19	9	14	79	70	47	1.2
7. Preston North End	42	17	12	13	74	54	46	1.0
8. Newcastle United	42	18	9	15	98	73	45	1.0
9. Blackpool	42	18	9	15	64	64	45	1.0
10. Charlton Athletic	42	17	10	15	68	63	44	1.1
11. Liverpool	42	12	19	11	57	61	43	1.1
12. Sunderland	42	15	12	15	70	61	42	0.9
13. West Bromwich Albion	42	14	13	15	74	77	41	0.8
14. Burnley	42	15	10	17	56	63	40	1.2
15. Manchester City	42	13	13	16	58	61	39	1.0
16. Wolverhampton W.	42	12	14	16	73	73	38	0.9
17. Derby County	42	15	7	20	63	80	37	0.8
18. Middlesbrough	42	15	6	21	64	88	36	0.8
19. Chelsea	42	14	8	20	52	72	36	0.7
20. Stoke City	42	12	7	23	49	88	31	0.8
21. Huddersfield Town	42	10	8	24	49	82	28	0.8
22. Fulham	42	8	11	23	58	77	27	0.6

4.

'WHEN THE LEGEND BECOMES FACT PRINT THE LEGEND': THE MATTHEWS FINAL

WHEN PRINCESS Elizabeth succeeded her deceased father in 1952, she was overwhelmed by a tide of public goodwill. At her coronation in June 1953, an estimated 27 million British people watched on TV as heavily bejewelled Elizabeth solemnly dedicated herself to a life of regal duty. The euphoric occasion was talked up by Winston Churchill and the press as representing the start of a glorious new Elizabethan era. It was claimed that it would be characterised by patriotic pride; revived economic vitality; freedom from want; stirring successes at work and play; and greater contentment for everyone oppressed by years of austerity.

A litany of proud achievements were showcased: Britain's launch of the world's first jet liner, the de Havilland Comet; the conquest of Everest by a Commonwealth team; Roger Bannister's sub-four-minute mile; plucky Randolph Turpin's recovery of the world middleweight title; Len Hutton's recapture of the Ashes from the previously invincible Australians; the Korean War coming to an end with brave tales of the valiant 'Glosters' at the Battle of the Imjin River. On the home front, luxuries such as family saloons and televisions became more affordable while the hated meat rationing began to peter out, albeit unofficially.

Central to the new Elizabethan myth was the presumed exceptional qualities of the British people – brave, humane, resourceful, determined, fair-minded but tough. The nation's courageous, lone stand against other Armadas, the Luftwaffe, and the U-boat menace, epitomised these qualities. Our nation's defiance of overwhelming odds was celebrated by the cinematic release of self-reverential war dramas, showcasing heroic feats with stiff-upper-lipped or jaunty conviction. These included: *The Cockleshell Heroes*; *The Desert Rats*; *Reach for the Sky*; *Battle of the River Plate*; *The Dambusters;* and *The Cruel Sea*, all emphasising the gallantry of this small island. As wartime cartoonist David Low put it in his depiction of 'Tommy' shaking his fist at waves of oncoming bombers, 'Very Well, Alone'.

The sunny 1953 FA Cup Final was swathed in sentiment, too. For this was probably 38-year-old Stanley Matthews's last opportunity of winning the competition. With exception of those with an allegiance to Bolton, just about everyone else was rooting for a Blackpool victory. At first the script did not go to plan.

Just 75 seconds after kick-off, Bolton were ahead. After an exchange of passes outside the Blackpool box, Bolton inside-left Hassall found right-winger Doug Holden, who immediately pushed the ball into Lofthouse's path. Although 20 yards from goal, Lofthouse had a pop. It was not a clean strike. Blackpool's Scottish international goalkeeper, George Farm, appeared to have it covered. But as Farm dived to his right the ball sat up just in front of him, before slipping through his fingers and into the net. Lofthouse said, 'That was lucky. I didn't know what to do, so I just swung at it.'

Blackpool's centre-half and captain Johnston looked aghast, giving Farm an accusatory stare. Twenty minutes later, Lofthouse muscled through Blackpool's diffident defence to poke the ball goalwards, at full stretch. Farm was beaten but to his relief the ball hit the left upright and bounced away safely. By this time, Bolton left-half Eric Bell had realised his foolishness in declaring himself fit. The muscle strain that he had been carrying flared up after just 17 minutes. He became a passenger, left to hobble on the left wing.

In the 35th minute, Mortensen, who had recently recovered from a cartilage injury, burst through on the left of the Bolton box. His cross-shot was on target but just as goalkeeper Hanson was about to field the ball, his team-mate Hassall intervened, inadvertently deflecting it into the opposite corner of the net. Hanson said ruefully, 'That was an easy catch before Hassall's deflection.' Two goals scored, two blunders, and the sides were level.

Three minutes later the blunder count rose to three. Langton lobbed the ball into the Blackpool box. Farm dithered, before belatedly racing from his goal and leaping for the ball. Moir out-jumped him, though, finding goal with the slightest touch of his head. The Blackpool fans groaned again, and it was about to get worse for them.

In the 56th minute Shimwell's inattentiveness allowed the injured Bell to climb above him, and score Bolton's third with a thumping header. Having taken off on one leg, Bell crashed to the ground in ecstasy and pain. Right-back Shimwell berated himself for taking his eye off Bell, wrongly believing him to be out of the action. No side had overturned a two-goal deficit in 71 FA Cup finals. Blackpool looked doomed.

However, Bolton were down to nine fit men when Ralph Banks succumbed to cramp. He explained, 'My shins started to ache, and I couldn't shake off the cramp. I had to go off four times for treatment, but it was no good. Taylor kept pulling me out of position, leaving Matthews free on the right wing.'

The day was hot and enervating and the grass lush and sapping. Blackpool manager Joe Smith had prepared his players by training in Blackpool's Stanley Park where the turf was green and grassy like Wembley. Matthews said after the game, 'I wasn't happy with the park surface. For that reason, I was a bit hesitant and slightly pulled a muscle. On the Saturday I got the club doctor to inject it. I felt much better then, but I still worried that my leg might let me down. That was, until I got on to the pitch when I felt fine.' It was surprising that Matthews was in Stanley Park. He had leave to train alone each day on Blackpool sands, practising his explosive bursts that dumbfounded so many full-backs.

Bolton tried to ride out the final 30 minutes, relying on long clearances into touch. Arguably, Bolton's manager, Bill Riddings, made a grave tactical error. Their left flank was horribly exposed with Bell a hopping passenger, Banks blighted with cramp, with only winger Langton left to defy Matthews. It might have been better had the Bolton full-backs been swapped with the fleet-footed Holden also assigned to stopping Matthews. But neither manager was inclined to give tactical instructions. Joe Smith tried to relax his Blackpool side by cracking jokes. He rarely presented a game plan. Bolton boss Bill

Riddings did not see any point in preparing his men, either, confining himself to a vague exhortation, 'Do your best lads,' as did Chelsea manager Ted Drake, according to Jimmy Greaves.

Blackpool's playmaker Ernie Taylor was the true man of the match, revelling in the spaces left by the indisposed Bolton players, providing the re-energised Matthews with a gold tap service. Prompted by Taylor, the previously subdued Matthews began to out-strip his depleted markers and pump a succession of dangerous crosses into the Bolton box. Perry blazed one gilt-edged opportunity wide and Hanson blocked a fierce effort from Mortensen. As if Bolton didn't have enough woes to contend with, Lofthouse became injured too.

With their attacking capacity removed, Bolton were sitting ducks. But Blackpool needed another blunder to achieve a turnaround. In the 68th minute, Matthews looped a high cross towards the far post. Hanson leapt for the ball but found it just out of his reach, and the ball dropped for a lunging Mortensen to prod it in with his studs.

Bolton continued to blast the ball into touch while Blackpool continued to gobble up possession, turning up the heat on their opponents' ragged, flagging defence, to no avail, apparently. Yet with only seconds remaining, Bolton conceded a free kick on the edge of their penalty area. Mortensen grabbed the ball. Taylor reproached him, 'You are not bloody well going to shoot from there, surely?' Mortensen retorted, 'Just watch me!' but in truth he was undecided. Bolton set up a long wall. It looked impregnable. Mortensen wondered whether a chip might be better. But just as he was about to take the free kick, Shimwell shot off towards the right-hand post, taking a Bolton defender with him. This left a chink in the wall. Mortensen decided to blast it, hoping to find that small gap. His shot was fierce and true. The ball flashed through the wall and found the goal high to Hanson's right. The brutality of the shot left the Bolton goalkeeper motionless. Blackpool were level.

Mortensen attributed their victory to a pier soothsayer, quipping, 'A gypsy on the Golden Mile was the match-winner. Every time she threw it in, I got the credit.' And two minutes into injury time, Matthews's sinuous run enabled him to reach the goal line. Despite slipping, his cut-back found Perry, and with Bolton's centre-half pulled out of position, he decisively struck the winning goal to ended the so-called 'Matthews Final' in which Mortensen was a hat-trick hero and Taylor the most influential player on the pitch. Taylor commented, 'My job was to get the ball to Stan how he wanted, when he wanted, where he wanted. That is what Joe Smith brought me to Blackpool for. I was always under pressure to perform because if I didn't do my job, Blackpool would not be successful.'

Matthews was quick to deflect the acclaim, insisting, 'There was not one match-winner. There were 11!' According to today's Opta statistics, Matthews was only the fifth best player in that game. He had been largely anonymous for an hour. But Stanley did not mind. He had the medal he craved. As his eyes welled up, he said quietly, 'This is something.'

As a postscript to this game with a misleading sub-title, when Stan Mortensen died in May 1991, a *Guardian* reporter suggested that his burial should be renamed the 'Matthews Funeral'. This FA Cup final continues to be touted as the best of them all and yet it was an error-strewn affair, mostly mediocre. However, it featured a stirring fightback, notwithstanding Bolton's depletion. Importantly, it pleased most of those watching because Stanley Matthews had his just reward. When passion competes with objectivity, the former often triumphs.

First Division table (May 1953)

	P	W	D	L	F	A	Pts	Goal ave
1. Arsenal	42	21	12	9	97	64	54	1.5
2. Preston North End	42	21	12	9	85	60	54	1.1
3. Wolverhampton Wanderers	42	19	13	10	86	63	51	1.4
4. West Bromwich Albion	42	21	8	13	66	60	50	1.1
5. Charlton Athletic	42	19	11	12	77	63	49	1.2
6. Burnley	42	18	12	12	67	52	48	1.3
7. Blackpool	42	19	9	14	71	70	47	1.3
8. Manchester United	42	18	10	14	69	72	46	1.0
9. Sunderland	42	15	13	14	68	82	43	0.8
10. Tottenham Hotspur	42	15	11	16	78	69	41	1.1
11. Aston Villa	42	14	13	15	63	61	41	1.0
12. Cardiff City	42	14	12	16	54	46	40	1.2
13. Middlesbrough	42	14	11	17	70	77	39	0.9
14. Bolton Wanderers	42	15	9	18	61	69	39	0.9
15. Portsmouth	42	14	10	18	74	83	38	0.9
16. Newcastle United	42	14	9	19	59	70	37	0.8
17. Liverpool	42	14	8	20	61	82	36	0.7
18. Sheffield Wednesday	42	12	11	19	62	72	35	0.9
19. Chelsea	42	12	11	19	56	66	35	0.8
20. Manchester City	42	14	7	21	72	87	35	0.8
21. Stoke City	42	12	10	20	53	66	34	0.8
22. Derby County	42	11	10	21	59	74	32	0.8

5.

'AN ENTIRELY DIFFERENT GAME': THE MAGICAL MAGYARS

IN 1953, a year of patriotic pride, heady jingoism and deluded hubris, the fatal crash of Britain's ground-breaking Comet jet liner was a horrific, shattering blow. Furthermore, the humiliation heaped upon the England football team in November by the 'Magical Magyars' confirmed it was no longer supreme either abroad or at home. The illustrious Tommy Lawton, an old-school England centre-forward with a new-look attitude, commented, 'We forgot that the continentals were all the time perfecting the art of the game, advancing the tactics and the moves. We did not think that anyone had anything to teach us, at least while playing at home. We didn't want to learn that our tactics had become out-of-date.'

The irony was that the emergence of two leading continental sides during the '50s – Hungary and Sweden – owed much to the coaching skills of two Englishmen – Jimmy Hogan from Burnley and George Raynor from Barnsley. Talk about 'a prophet is not without honour save in his own country'.

Hogan favoured the 'pass and move' game which often caught opposing defenders ball-watching and helped evade their crunching tackles. He championed the techniques employed so successfully here: by Arthur Rowe's 'push and run' Spurs side of the early '50s; by Alan Brown and Harry Potts at Burnley; and by Bill Nicholson's Spurs sides in the late '50s and early '60s. Hogan preached the advantage of the short corner to keep possession and to draw tall defenders out of the penalty area. He advocated the short free kick to keep the momentum of the game going and prevent the opposition recovering the ball. He insisted goalkeepers should throw the ball out to a colleague rather than launching it down the middle. He would demonstrate the art of the 'drag back' with the sole of his boot, perfected so exquisitely by Puskas at Wembley in 1953. Hogan was frustrated by the 'Victorian ideas' impeding English football.

He commented, 'Our former intelligent ideas are gradually fading out. We have developed an "up-in-the-air", "get-the-ball-if-you-can" game. We are continuously kicking the ball down the middle to the marked centre-forward, hoping for a defensive error and not exploiting the wing play as we used to.'

Scottish international Tommy Docherty took note. During the '50s he became a convert to Walter Winterbottom's new gospel of coaching, alongside Alan Brown, then of Burnley, Ron Greenwood, then of Arsenal, Bill Nicholson of Spurs, Malcolm Allison, then of West Ham, Joe Mercer, then of Sheffield United, Don Revie, then of Manchester City, and Alf Ramsey, then of Ipswich, among others. He could see clearly how Hogan's influence had manifested itself in Hungary's victory at Wembley. It was small wonder that the Hungarian people dedicated their famous 1953 victory to Hogan. Docherty remarked, 'Hungary's passing and movement made us British players feel as if they were from a different planet. They'd lull you into a false sense of security with a procession of quick, short passes that took them nowhere, and then suddenly unleashed a paralysing long pass that would arrive in space a split second ahead of one of their tuned-in team-mates. They realised the importance of supporting runs. Every time they had possession, they had between two and five men ready to receive the ball.'

On a grey winter afternoon at Wembley on 25 November, Olympic champions Hungary beat England 6-3, combining elegant short passing and the English long-ball game, knitted together with exact control and speed of movement and thought that crushed the home side long before the end of this one-sided fixture. The Hungarians moved the ball swiftly along the ground with delicate flicks, also showing expansive vision with their array of long, raking, pitch-perfect passes. They constantly changed their point of attack with mesmerising speed and intuition and shot with blistering force and accuracy.

From the first minute the writing was on the wall. A quick central thrust by Bozsik, Zakarias and Hidegkuti left the latter to sell a dummy and lash home. Out-paced and out-maneuvered, England were never in this game despite a spurt of hope when Sewell equalised after 15 minutes. Hungary restored their lead just five minutes later. Puskas, dubbed 'the Galloping Major', sent winger Czibor racing down the left flank. His swift cross found Kocsis, whose deft flick set up Hidegkuti to evade Eckersley's desperate lunge and score from close range. From the restart Kocsis regained possession and released the speedy Czibor once again, this time on the right flank. He flashed past Eckersley and found Puskas with a diagonal ground pass. Wright moved in to block Puskas's path but in one sinuous moment, Puskas dragged the ball back from Wright with the sole of his right foot, swivelled and smashed it high into the net with his left. Goalkeeper Merrick and captain Wright gaped at one another in amazement. Eminent *Times* journalist Geoffrey Green wrote, 'Billy Wright rushed into the tackle like a fireman racing to the wrong fire.'

Minutes later Puskas used his heel to deflect a free kick by Bozsik past Merrick to make it 4-1. With the interval almost nigh, Mortensen seized upon a throw-in and bulldozed through the middle, first losing the ball, then regaining it, before beating Grosics with a savage shot. Was a stirring revival still possible?

Not on your life! Ten minutes after the resumption, Merrick turned Czibor's header on to the post only for Bozsik to be set up to score Hungary's fifth with a rising drive. Hidegkuti then grabbed a hat-trick when he volleyed in Hungary's sixth from Puskas's lob. The sun suddenly emerged from the London mirk, trite but apposite. Before the curtain went down on this immaculate display, Ramsey put away a penalty devoid of consolation.

England were beaten in every respect, on the ground, in the air and tactically, by a side with superior skill and nous. Hidegkuti, a deep-lying centre-forward, continually prompted, probed, and provided, leaving England centre-half Johnston isolated and utterly bemused. Matthews and the absent Finney apart, England were a team of anachronistic artisans ravaged by a company of artists. It was time to set aside a proud past and look to the future.

A Hungarian journalist said many years after the game, 'We lived under Stalinist control. I was then president of the Hungarian

FA but I had no power. That is why I said then, "To win at Wembley is not as hard as getting there." My team MTK was the best club in Hungary then. We always had an English coach. Jimmy Hogan came to my club. He was one of the most successful coaches in Hungary.'

Hungarian right-back Jeno Buzanszky explained that the deep-lying centre-forward idea arose when playing Switzerland in 1952. He said, 'Hidegkuti replaced Palotas as centre-forward but was told to stay back to neutralise the Swiss centre-back. Having been 2-0 down before he came on, we won 4-2. This move set the pattern of our future play, until the Soviets crushed our revolution in 1956. We attacked with six players. We had to reassure our defenders that if our opponents get a goal, we will score two.'

Buzanszky also drew attention to their preparations for this game initiated by their shrewd coach and manager, Gusztav Sebes, 'We widened one of our pitches at home because Wembley is wider. We imported English balls because these were harder than our softer and more sensitive ones. When we first kicked an English ball, it felt as if it was made of wood. The Austrians told us that the grass at Wembley was like a sponge, soggy and dense, so it required more energy to lift our feet. One gets tired quickly doing this. To deal with this we decided to make the ball do the running. We had to pass the ball.'

An exhausted Jackie Sewell said, 'I don't think I've run about so much in my life. They worked triangles all over the pitch. It was just clockwork to them. They did not even have to look. It was something that we weren't told about.'

But surely Sewell was conversant with 'push and run' initiated by Arthur Rowe, an English coach who had cut his teeth and gained a vaunted reputation in Hungary? Presumably, team manager and FA head coach Walter Winterbottom did not see fit to liaise with Rowe in his preparations?

Sewell continued, 'I remember that England's preparations were very relaxed,' admitting that 'what was missing was that we didn't know a thing about them.'

This is an incredible admission because Winterbottom said he had watched Hungary play before the Wembley game.

Winterbottom admitted, 'I saw Hungary win the Olympic Games. It was almost the same team that played at Wembley. Before they came here, they were granted a fortnight away from their clubs for special training. I saw them draw 2-2 with Sweden at home. I knew they were a strong side, but we had to make many changes with two new players. It wasn't on to expect us to jell together in one match without any preparation at all.'

What Walter omitted to say was that Sweden achieved their impressive 2-2 draw in Hungary on the back of George Raynor's coaching. It was Raynor's tactical innovation to put a man on Hidegkuti and stall the Hungarian supply line. He was astute enough to know that this would be an exhausting task and therefore detailed two Swedish players to undertake this task in turn, swapping them over during the game to ensure that the marker always remained fresh. Bewilderingly, England failed to follow Raynor's lead, despite Winterbottom being an onlooker in Budapest.

Raynor, the international coach from Barnsley, like Jimmy Hogan, the international coach from Burnley, were lone voices crying in an English football wilderness, because in Europe they were respected, warmly greeted, and richly appreciated. After Raynor had masterminded a depleted Swedish side's victory over England in 1959, he said, 'I feel like a football fifth columnist. I got some sort of satisfaction out of this result but not enough. I would much rather have been doing the same sort of thing for the country of my birth. I want to work in England – *for* England. They want me in Ghana, in Israel, in Mexico and in Sweden. I am a knight in Sweden and have a huge gold medal of thanks from King Gustaf. I have a letter of thanks and commendation from the Prime Minister of Iraq. My record as a coach is the best in the world. I don't smoke. I don't drink. I live for football.'

It would take a determined, Raynor-like tactician to sweep away the 'club amateur' fustiness and assert winning tactical disciplines; to prepare better; to develop squad stability and cohesion; and to turn a group of talented English players into a world-beating team, with its whole seeming greater than its collective parts. His name was, of course, Alf Ramsey.

6

MANAGEMENT STYLES AND METHODS DURING THE '50s

MANCHESTER UNITED boss Matt Busby was one of the first leading managers in England to prioritise skill over power and fluency over method. While he had a pattern based on the long-established 'WM' or 3-2-2-3 formation, his instructions were usually short and simple, allowing his talented players the freedom to express themselves. Busby's simple message was, 'Just make sure you pass to a red shirt.' And given the talent he accumulated before and after the tragic Munich disaster, this was often enough as the victories piled up. As *Times* journalist Geoffrey Green observed, in the period 1947 to 1959, Manchester United were the masters of English football. Even after the trauma of Munich, United incredibly seized the runners-up position to Wolves in the season which followed.

While Busby's methods seemed uncomplicated, according to Stanley Matthews he was not devoid of tactical nous. Matthews recalled how his Blackpool side was outwitted during the second half of the 1948 FA Cup Final against Manchester United, having bossed the first period. Matthews attributed this turnaround to Busby's tactical change. While Blackpool manager Joe Smith was enjoying his 'reet good' half-time cigar, Busby was busy reorganising his side, instructing his defenders to push up to harry and hustle their opposing half-backs, Johnston and Kelly, to cut off their supply lines to wingers Matthews and Rickett. Matthews believed Busby's instruction enabled United to turn a 2-1 deficit into a 4-2 victory. Stan told Jimmy Greaves, 'At the time it was very unusual to encounter a manager who paid so much attention to tactics as Sir Matt Busby did during that final. It completely flummoxed Blackpool.'

Nevertheless, John Doherty, a former Busby Babe said, 'Matt was never a great tactician. He did not talk deeply about the game. His view was that if he had to tell his players how to play, then he would not have signed them. Sir Matt's attitude to the game was so simple it was frightening. His instructions, if you could call them that, were no more than, "All the best. Keep playing football. Make sure you pass to a red shirt and enjoy your game." However, he had a certain presence which I have never encountered with anyone else, an aura of quiet dignity and authority. He seemed to be in command of every situation. He was always immaculately dressed, invariably with his pipe and would dominate effortlessly every room he entered. Incredibly, he remembered everyone's name, even casual acquaintances.'

Charlie Mitten, an FA Cup winner in 1948, added, 'Sir Matt was the best man-manager that I've ever come across, and I've been round the world. He knew his players inside out and he knew what to say at the right time and in the right place. He'd go up to the lads and he'd say, "Now, come on. Wake yourself up." Or he would put his arm round the old boys, and say, "Come on, you can do better than that," or, "Well done son, come on now." It would make all the difference in the world.

'Neither Busby nor Murphy knew the game in a technical sense. Jimmy had guts and he imparted that to the players. The confidence that Busby and Murphy gave their players was the belief they could manage what was being asked of them. As the game changed in the '60s with coaches having greater prominence in determining how the game should be played, being more analytical and setting more specific instructions for their players, Busby's and Murphy's methods began to be questioned by some of their players. There seemed to be a division of opinion among their players as to whether Busby's approach was profound or facile. There was an alternative perspective, suggesting that given the calibre of players Busby developed and increasingly bought, perhaps it was sensible to allow them their head.'

Esteemed *Guardian* journalist and scriptwriter Arthur Hopcraft believed Busby was content to allow his star players a loose rein when they were on the field. He rarely gave tactical briefings or instructions on team organisation. However, he insisted that each player needed to know what was expected of one another. Much as he did not like to distract players before a game, a poor performance was always followed by a quiet intense talk with detailed instructions 'to get an under-performing player back to where they were'.

John Doherty continued, 'What a marvellous combination it was, Matt and his assistant Jimmy Murphy. A pipe-smoking Scot with the air of nobility and a cigarette-gasping Welsh dragon who would have your guts for garters. But Jimmy was always there for us. He might give us a bollocking, but you could talk to him about anything. He reckoned some players needed a cuddle while others needed a hard word. He gave both.

'I remember one game in which Albert Scanlon had a nightmare first half at Preston. Jimmy told him, "Well played, Albert." Scanlon was a different player after the break, full of confidence. Jimmy got us playing "shadow football", playing against nobody, always passing and moving, getting it back and laying it off and moving again. We would finish with a shot at goal and then start again. Jimmy explained if we passed and moved enough it would become second nature. As for Bert Whalley, the third member of the United triumvirate, he was a lay preacher and one of the nicest fellows to work on God's earth.'

Sir Bobby Charlton also spoke highly of Murphy, 'Jimmy Murphy turned me from an amateur schoolboy player into a professional player and it took about two years. Whenever he got the opportunity, he used to pull me to one side and try to teach me the folly of trying to make impossible passes, when there was something more realistic that you can do, more beneficial to the team. He made me think more as a team player rather than an individual, but nevertheless always encouraged me to make the best of the assets I had.'

Busby's biographer and former Republic of Ireland footballer Eamon Dunphy concluded, 'The best test of a manager is how he uses his resources. Given the spectacular results Busby drew from his 1948 team by switching their positions and from his novice youngsters in winning the 1955/56 league championship, there is little doubt that Busby was a genius.'

But that judgement needs to be set against the criticisms of the shambolic nature of training sessions, voiced publicly by Wilf McGuinness and Noel Cantwell: the insanitary and ragged training kit; the filthy communal baths that required a subsequent cold shower to remove the black residue; the dreadful lights on the training pitch, dimmer than a Toc H lamp; the feral 20-a-side games that separated the survivors from the weak. Unlike Cantwell, McGuinness recognised the value of recreating the rough, improvised, massed games of the players' childhood in building their resilience. Games could not be won on superior skill alone.

Johnny Giles was at Old Trafford from 1956 to 1963 when he was sold to Leeds for a bargain fee of £33,000. He added, 'Matt was a charming man. He never lost his temper. He had a belief in young players, hence the Busby Babes. His great attribute was patience even after heavy defeats. If we were winning by a solitary goal with ten minutes left, he preferred that we went for the second goal. He would say, "It was the right thing to do." He was crushed by Munich. But he got the right players in and they worked their individual magic. Yet there was more to Busby than charisma and a bent for adventure and innovation. He could be ruthless. If someone needed to go, they went. A lot of players talk up his man-management skills, but I honestly thought they were poor.'

According to John Doherty, Giles and Busby clashed over Busby's insistence that Giles played on the right wing when Giles' greater skill was in midfield, as he proved at Leeds where he became a world-class performer in that role.

John Carey played under Busby in Manchester United's first great post-war side. He was an elegant footballer, captaining their superb 1948 FA Cup-winning team. After his playing days ended, he managed Blackburn, guiding them to promotion to the First Division in 1958, whereupon he became Everton's manager. Remaining true to Busby's mantra which prioritised constructive, attractive, attacking football, Carey believed that a studious, creative move was much better than a 'bang-it-anywhere' clearance. Like Busby he gave few instructions other than to exhort his players to 'fizz it about' and 'give and go'. Although widely respected, he lacked Busby's authority, and despite leading Everton to fifth place in the 1960/61 season, their highest post-war position, he was sacked in the back of a taxi by director John Moores. As a result, the jibe 'taxi for …' has become a staple terrace insult directed at any manager facing the sack.

Carey's faithful lieutenant at Everton was fiery, pint-sized, Scottish midfield dynamo Bobby Collins. Collins was concerned that discipline standards were slipping, and other players were taking too many liberties. He believed that Carey should have cracked the whip more but that was not his style. Therefore, it was left to Collins to fire up his recalcitrant colleagues on the pitch. Collins's influence was crucial as Everton narrowly avoided relegation to the Second Division in 1960, before he helped revive Leeds under Don Revie.

Carey was better when paired with his snarling assistant Eddie Baily, a First Division title winner with Arthur Rowe's Spurs. At Leyton Orient in 1961/62 Carey's choice of Baily, as his coach, was an inspired decision. Whereas Carey was laid-back, measured, and urbane, like Joe Murphy, Baily was excitable, confrontational, and profane. But Baily was also astute, skilful, and vastly experienced. Carey was wise enough to buy a terrier and let it bark for itself. Baily was given the scope to hone his players' technique and sharpen their tactical awareness, geeing them up with choice vernacular. He was equally prepared to put his arm around their shoulders, too. Baily was a man after their own hearts. The pair guided unfancied Leyton Orient to promotion to the First Division in 1962.

Meanwhile, another former Manchester United star, Charlie Mitten, was about to cut his teeth as a manager at St James' Park, Newcastle. Mitten, like Neil Franklin and George Mountford, suffered ostracism after returning from their ill-fated Colombian adventure. These three had gone there in search of better pay but were punished heavily for their illicit action. Mitten was fined six months' wages and banned for the same period. A piqued Matt Busby transferred Mitten, the supposed 'Bogata Bandit', to Fulham. However, Mitten subsequently made his peace with Sir Matt and sought his advice about applying for the vacant Newcastle management post. Busby tried to dissuade Mitten, saying, 'It's not a job I'd take laddie. There's already too many managers there.' It was alleged that the directors tried to involve themselves in team selections and tactical changes during a game.

Mitten appeared to be grasping a poisoned chalice. He soon understood the extent of his task as the 1959/60 season opened in swooning heat with a 5-1 home defeat by Spurs. After Newcastle's first three games, they were bottom of the First Division with no points. But Mitten soon turned the team around, winning much approval on the terraces and in the stands while the boardroom bickering continued. The fans loved watching the goals stack up with adventurous play. Everton were thrashed 8-2 and Manchester

United 7-3. Unlike pre-Munich Manchester United, Newcastle were too reliant upon imported, experienced players, several of whom were coming to the end of their careers. But Mitten stamped out the dressing room squabbling, brought the team together and began selecting younger players, including his son, in place of the ageing or departing former stars.

He also introduced Highland dancing into their training repertoire, seeking to improve his players' balance when twisting and turning with the ball at their feet. Old-school warriors like Jimmy Scoular were not impressed. Scoular protested that it made him look like a 'Sissy'. He was equally critical of Mitten's introduction of a white strip sewn along the bottom of their black shorts. It was intended to improve players' recognition of one another during a game. But it resulted in cat calls of, 'Your slip is showing.' Mitten's successes were in vain. With the internecine boardroom warfare continuing, Newcastle's disunity resulted in relegation just 12 months after challenging for the title in 1959/60.

Stan Cullis at Wolves took a contrasting approach to Busby, Carey, and Mitten. He adopted a direct, physical, schooled style of play. His goalkeeper was instructed to 'launch' the ball long and his wing-halves were told to 'hit the corners', giving the wingers something to chase. This was not mindless, ill-considered force for Cullis was a thinking manager who fashioned a game plan based upon what he believed to be irrefutable statistics. Wing Commander Charles Reep's analyses had revealed to him that 50 per cent of goals came from no more than one pass and 80 per cent from not more than three passes. So convinced was Cullis by the greater efficacy of the long-ball game that it was this aspect of the Hungarians' play which impressed him while he sat watching their mauling of England at Wembley in 1953.

His former captain, Billy Wright, said, 'The newspapers didn't like our style. They wanted to see us play like Tottenham, but Stan produced great players – Hancocks, Mullen, Broadbent, Wilshaw, Swinburne, Clamp, Flowers, and Slater – all of whom played for England, so he was not producing rubbish.' Cullis added, 'Our play was designed to hit continental teams with passes they weren't used to. In other words, we tried to hit long balls over their heads for our forwards to run on to, we were not happy inter-passing. But long passing was only part of our game.'

National coach Walter Winterbottom said of Cullis in 1960, 'His theories of playing the long ball, pouring incessantly into the opposing penalty area, have produced a specialised type of player. Cullis himself would be the first to tell you that there are certain types of player, talented though they may be, that he simply does not want and cannot use at his club. He "typecasts" his players. They must be physically strong; they must be prepared to accept severe training; they must be fearless; they must be mentally indomitable; they must be prepared to fight and chase and harry and tackle; to snap at the merest crumb in front of goal; to defend remorselessly in front of their own goal. Cullis consumes pace, devours it with far-flung clearances and passes.

'Arthur Rowe, of Tottenham, on the other hand, embraced space, married it to his purposes with a shimmer of short, quick passes. Cullis to some extent has modified his method of the past two years, because he knows the value of surprise and variation against a team that will have calculated his style and devised tactics to upset it, but his own team still bears the strong imprint of his personality.'

Jimmy McIlroy, then of Burnley, felt bound to recognise Cullis's achievements while firing off a broadside at 'fighting soccer', epitomised by Wolves' style of play. Jimmy wrote in 1960, 'I should like to see manager Stanley Cullis aiming his sights even higher by trying to out-match the leading continental exponents in the pure skills of soccer. Wolves' success does Mr Cullis great credit, but it has also done much damage to the game in general in England because so many lesser managers have attempted to ape the Wolves–Cullis technique. Artistry with the ball is not all-important with Wolverhampton Wanderers. Therefore, it is now treated as something of an expendable luxury by managers all over the country. These managers to their eternal shame are breeding a race of footballers who would be more at home in a wrestling stadium than on a playing field.'

There were several football journalists who agreed, citing Wolves' alleged 'spoiling' tactics against Red Star of Belgrade in the European Cup of 1959/60, and against Leicester in the FA Cup quarter-final during the same season.

While Wolves achieved prestigious victories against some of the best continental sides, such as Hungary's Honved, these were in friendlies. Once they began competing in the European Cup in the late '50s, they were not nearly as successful.

Although Alan Brown, Burnley's manager in the mid-'50s, and his successor, Harry Potts, favoured skill over power, placing them closer to Matt Busby, their tactical preparations, such as their dead-ball routines, had a greater affinity with Cullis and Spurs manager Bill Nicholson. Nicholson was formerly a member of Arthur Rowe's title-winning 'push and run' side, whose fluid, creative, short-passing style mirrored the principles of international master-coach Jimmy Hogan. And yet Nicholson, like Cullis, was not averse to employing 'spoiling' tactics. For example, he helped Walter Winterbottom devise a successful plan to stop the fluent Brazilians from expressing their suave talents, notably those of their playmaker Didi, against England in the 1958 World Cup group fixture in Gothenburg. The result was a satisfying 0-0 draw. It was the only game in the tournament in which the Brazilians failed to score.

In his book *The Sixties Revisited*, Jimmy Greaves acknowledged that Alan Brown, Burnley's manager between 1954 and 1957, was responsible for introducing quick, short corners and a variety of dead ball routines at Turf Moor. Nicholson also practised dead-ball routines at White Hart Lane. He claimed to be the first English boss to instruct his centre-half to join the attack at corners or set pieces. That might have been true among '50s teams, but the Austrian 'Wunderteam' of the '30s appeared to be the originators. Incidentally, this crack Austrian line-up were also coached by nomadic Jimmy Hogan of Burnley, the Hungarians' guru.

Nicholson explained his interest in set plays, 'Statistics have shown that between a third and a half of the goals scored by a football team come from restarts, corners, free kicks or throw-ins, so we spent hours rehearsing our tactics.'

According to FIFA statistics derived from 2006 World Cup and UEFA Champions League games, 28 per cent of goals were scored from set pieces. Bill recalled, 'We had five or six free-kick routines with each player knowing his role. One of the best is the chip over the wall for the man standing on the end of the wall to run around and pick it up. I believe we were the first club to put a marker on an opponent taking a throw-in.'

Bill might be wrong here. I believe it was lowly Bournemouth who first experimented with this ploy. Veteran Cherries forward Olly Norris caused mayhem by standing right in front of a thrower.

Ironically, Spurs were among Bournemouth's victims when they were dumped out of the FA Cup at Dean Court in 1957. Spurs seemed to have heeded their giant-killing lesson well, though.

Although the arguments ranged back and forth as to who were the innovators and who were the disciples, it is undeniable that there was a new breed of tactically astute coaches and managers emerging during the mid-to-late '50s, typified by Alan Brown, Bill Nicholson, Ron Greenwood at Arsenal, Vic Buckingham at West Bromwich, and Joe Mercer at Sheffield United and Aston Villa. Others such as Tommy Docherty, Don Revie and Dave Sexton would soon join them. The time of the true 'tracksuit' manager was nigh.

But progress was exasperatingly slow for some 'young Turks'. Looking back at his final playing days at Highbury, 20 years on, Docherty lamented the lack of tactical preparations when playing under Arsenal manager George Swindin. He commented, 'I liked George. He was a good guy but by now completely out of step with the revolution that was taking place in English football. I guess he knew that, too, which is why he brought Ron Greenwood to Highbury.'

Against Fulham in April 1960, Arsenal were trailing, but according to Tommy, 'George had little constructive to say' at half-time other than "keep it going" or "play your normal game". Fulham's right-wing pairing of Johnny Key and Graham Leggat was causing us problems. Leggat, usually a left-winger, was using his pace to run from deep but George did not remark upon this pair at all. I sat in the dressing room looking at George and thinking, "I could do your job, I can manage."'

Arsenal fell by ten places in the 1959/60 season, ending in 13th position. They were also humiliated in the FA Cup by Rotherham. This was not just the product of bad luck with injuries, although the regularity of these impeded continuity. The seeds of Arsenal's decline were sown earlier in the '50s when former manager Tom Whittaker failed to prepare for the impending departure of his ageing stars. He neither invested in youthful talent nor bought accomplished replacements. As a result, the stalwarts of his successful side – Joe Mercer, Walley Barnes, Archie Macaulay, Denis Compton, Laurie Scott, and George Swindin, were left to retire without being adequately replaced.

During this hiatus, Whittaker was not a well man. After his death in October 1956, Arsenal were forced to use the cheque book. After watching Denis Law's stunning performance against West Ham in an FA Cup replay, the Gunners joined the race for the young Scottish star's signature. However, Law was not impressed that Swindin sent his assistant, Ron Greenwood, to discuss terms. So, he opted for Manchester City instead. Ironically, City were in a similar fix to Arsenal. Even more strangely, Arsenal were prepared to offer their leading scorer, David Herd, as a makeweight in the Denis Law deal. This was despite Herd's prolific scoring record at Highbury – 107 goals in 180 senior appearances with 14 league goals coming in this injury-ravaged 1959/60 season. Arsenal were not flushed with natural goalscorers and Law had yet to prove himself in this capacity.

Swindin already regretted selling fiery Derek Tapscott to Second Division Cardiff after the Welsh international scored the goals that helped propel the Bluebirds towards promotion. Here, he seemed to show scant recognition of Herd's abilities as a top marksman. Herd was a tall, powerful, direct centre-forward with a ferocious shot. He was an effective target man, too. Although not particularly good in the air, once into his stride Herd was difficult to shake off the ball as many defenders testified. If Arsenal did not appreciate his worth, then Matt Busby did, unhesitatingly paying £35,000 for his services in 1961. Although Herd took a little time to settle at Old Trafford, he proceeded to score 145 goals in 265 senior appearances, with 14 of these coming in European competitions, which included the 1967/68 European Cup-winning campaign.

There were tensions between Docherty and Swindin as there were between Swindin and Greenwood. Upon Greenwood's appointment in 1959, after Arsenal finished in third place, Swindin said, 'I leave Ron free to get on with his football coaching while I get on with the administration of the club's affairs.'

Twelve months later, the strain in their partnership was evident as the two argued over tactics and selections. This is unsurprising. With the game becoming increasingly tactical, the coaches began to assume greater responsibility for team affairs, causing conflict with the general managers. This occurred at Burnley where shrewd tactician Jimmy Adamson usurped his former manager, Harry Potts, amid much grief and recrimination. At Highbury, Swindin's days were numbered, not on account of Greenwood's promotion but following Billy Wright's accession. Instructively, Arsenal's double-winning side of 1970/71 comprised just three imported players. Suddenly, youth development, as practised successfully at Burnley, Chelsea, Wolves and Manchester United became more important.

Jimmy Greaves pointed out that most managers in the '50s were figureheads, largely concerned with administrative and secretarial duties as they had been in pre-war times. They did not have the time and possibly the inclination to supervise training or consider tactics. Their duties could involve matchday catering. Although many were largely desk-bound, Aston Villa boss Joe Mercer made time for two hours of coaching each day while still dealing with the welter of administrative tasks. This was only possible because he was prepared to arrive early and work long into the night. Few had his dedication. And few had the public profile or status they command today.

Bill Shankly, writing in *Charles Buchan's Football Monthly* in 1960, moaned about the lack of recognition of managers' efforts in achieving team success. Remuneration was a sore point, too. Top bosses were rarely paid much more than their players, which, until 1961, was restricted by the maximum wage ruling.

Ted Drake was appointed manager of First Division Chelsea in June 1952. Upon his arrival he made sweeping changes, ridding the club of its previous amateurish, music hall image. He discarded the club's Chelsea pensioner crest and with it the 'Pensioners' nickname, and insisted a new one be adopted. From these changes came the lion rampant regardant crest and a new nickname, 'Blues'. He introduced scouting reports and a new, tougher, training regime based on ball work, a rare practice in English football at the time. He was then often seen at the club's training ground, but that practice diminished as the years passed.

Under his management there was a greater emphasis placed upon finding promising young players in the lower divisions and amateur football. The development of the club's youth policy became a priority, too, with a productivity rating that rivalled Burnley. The first wave of new talent included John McNichol, Frank Blunstone, Derek Saunders, Jim Lewis and Peter Sillett plus Spurs' double-winning stars, Bobby Smith and Les Allen.

Within three years of his arrival, Drake led Chelsea to their first league championship triumph. He became the first person to win the league title both as player and manager. However, Drake never came close to repeating this impressive feat, despite the influx of highly talented youngsters such as Jimmy Greaves, Peter Brabrook, Terry Venables, Bobby Tambling, Barry Bridges, Tony Nicholas, Charlie Livesey, Ron Harris, Micky Block, Ken Shellito, Albert Murray and Eddie McCreadie.

The press dubbed Chelsea's second wave of vibrant talent 'Drake's Ducklings'. But by the time these youngsters began playing for the senior Chelsea side, Drake had become a more remote figure, Albert Tennant having a prominent coaching role. Performances and results became very erratic, leaving the club customarily stranded in lower mid-table. During the late '50s and early '60s, the club was largely reliant upon Greaves's prodigious goalscoring in avoiding relegation.

Jimmy Greaves came to regard his Chelsea manager, Ted Drake, with a mixture of disparagement and fondness. He claimed that Drake was nicknamed the 'all the best manager' because that was the sum of his pre-match instruction. Meanwhile, standards were slipping. In the 1959/60 season, Greaves's 29 goals were once again crucial in keeping Chelsea just above the drop zone, although their 18th position gave only a four-point cushion. Only relegated Leeds conceded more than the 91 league goals that Chelsea let in. When Tommy Docherty was asked what he thought of the Chelsea defence, he replied, 'A jellyfish has more shape.' A *London Standard* newspaper carried a cartoon in which one man is saying, 'I see Chelsea have won,' to which the other replies, 'They can't have. They won last week.'

Chelsea's embarrassing FA Cup losses to Fourth Division sides Darlington (4-1) and Crewe Alexandra (2-1) weakened Drake's position, and early in the 1961/62 season, he was sacked and replaced by Docherty. By then Greaves had left for Italy. It was no surprise when Chelsea were relegated at the end of this season, whereupon Docherty revitalised his young charges, achieving promotion in his first full season in charge.

As an amusing aside, Greaves recalled that Joe Smith, the Blackpool boss, was once accused of falsifying his expenses by the club treasurer. Joe was alleged to have claimed expenses for entertaining a fictitious Scottish scout. Wily Joe retorted, 'I've been had. The man is clearly an imposter. I shall cease entertaining him immediately.' Even desk-bound managers could still be quick on their feet.

Not that everyone was pleased to see the back of the desk-bound boss. Although Stan Matthews acknowledged the benefits a tactician could provide, he and team-mates Bill Perry and Ray Charnley enjoyed the freer hand they had with the 'old-school' Joe Smith. Perry recalled, 'In our day we had no coach, rarely had team talks or discussions. Joe Smith never did much talking because he trusted us to go out and do our best. He was a fatherly figure. He once screwed up a newspaper article on the talents of Jimmy Greaves, telling us, "Just go out and play your own game."'

Don Revie's obsessive preparations, particularly before critical games, might have been counterproductive. Leeds coach Syd Owen was instructed to prepare detailed dossiers on their opponents but considered them over-cautious. So did Lorimer and Hunter, who believed they created too much respect for sides they should not fear.

Bob Stokoe, a former Newcastle centre-half, and an FA Cup-winning Sunderland manager, once declared, 'It's easy to be a good manager. All you have to do is sign good players.' This was said in the early '70s when English football had become much more tactical. Bob Seith, Burnley's championship-winning wing-half, and a former Preston and Hearts manager, agreed, stating, 'A manager is only as good as his players.'

Judged by Stokoe's criterion, Joe Smith was among the best. Before the wage cap was abolished, Smith may have enticed many talented players to Bloomfield Road by waving a stick of Blackpool rock in their faces. After all, when there was equality of monetary rewards, Blackpool, the resort, might have helped to clinch the deal.

But Stokoe over-stated his point. Even the desk-bound managers needed to know how to look after their staff. The Blackpool experience illustrates this. Smith may have been blunt, but he was canny, too. He knew exactly how to respond to Stan Matthews at a time when his star winger was facing a crisis of confidence. Stan was considering a return to Stoke City after experiencing the intense disappointment of two FA Cup final defeats. Stan never forgot how Joe found the right words to re-inspire him. A year later, Stan became a Wembley winner. Thereafter, Joe was always held in fond regard by Stan. Several Burnley players were indebted to Harry Potts and Alan

Brown for their sensitive support at times of personal crisis, bonding them closer to the club and its manager.

The emergence of the new breed of tactical, coaching managers was not universally welcomed by leading sides. A further example can be drawn from Blackpool. Bill Perry was critical of Ron Suart who replaced the much-loved Joe Smith. He explained, 'Ron was full of the new ideas of the day and had studied as an FA coach. Instead of players being left to do their own thing on the field they were taught set plays and tactics. I was 28 years old and being asked to do things I had never tried before. I was not capable of this. I told him, "Look Ron, it is all right talking to a young kid of 18 to 20 about something like this because they are at an age when they can adapt but I'm too long in the tooth to change my style."'

Another leading manager of the time came in for greater criticism from his players for neglecting to engage their 'hearts'. This was Cliff Britton, Preston's boss between 1956 and 1961. He had also managed Burnley and Everton. Cliff had an excellent track record. He led Burnley to promotion to the First Division in 1947 and achieved two top-three finishes there while with Preston. He also took Preston to the top of the First Division table during 1959/60. He helped revive Tom Finney's career, by converting him successfully into a centre-forward, resulting in Finney gaining further England caps. But Cliff was not popular with his players. Although Finney believed Britton to be a master tactician, he described him as 'ridiculously over-strict and unsympathetic', citing several examples of over-zealous discipline. Finney thought Britton to be a 'cold man'.

Bruised by various confrontations with Britton, Docherty moved to Highbury in 1958, tersely calling Britton 'a tw*t'. This prompted his ex-Preston colleague, Frank O'Farrell, to remonstrate, 'Don't beat about the bush, Tommy. Tell it the way it is.' Britton might have been heavy-handed, but he did not expect his best players to necessarily agree with him. He explained, 'The greatest difficulty experienced by a manager after he has laid down what he expects from his staff, is getting an outstanding player to accept the team plan. After all, he wouldn't be outstanding if he hadn't his *own* point of view.'

In the late '50s, managers varied greatly in how much licence they were prepared to grant to their teams in deciding the pattern of play once on the pitch. Stan Cullis was not in favour of delegation, and neither was Harry Catterick, then at Sheffield Wednesday. Their players worked to a pre-set plan whereas Bill Nicholson at Spurs allowed team captain Danny Blanchflower to be the leader on the pitch. Harry Potts took the same line with his captain, Jimmy Adamson. The freedom they granted was crucial to their teams' success.

Peter Swan, a former Sheffield Wednesday and England centre-half, described his former manager Harry Catterick as a 'hard man who took no prisoners'. He explained that if you did not do what Catterick wanted, you were in trouble. Catterick was said to be a big man who spoke with authority. No one messed with him. If anyone retaliated to a challenge on the pitch, gave away a penalty or got sent off, there would be trouble. But Swan also said, 'When you had a good game, he'd congratulate you. Catterick was not bothered if any one of us attracted bad press during our own time, but made it clear that if we did not perform well in the next game, we would suffer the consequences.' Catterick was said to use a clenched fist to make his point. Swan added, 'He also threatened us that we would never play again if we fouled up.' While his man-management was forces-style, Catterick was described as a shrewd tactician, whose game plans were carefully prepared.

The training under Catterick was different to that under the previous manager, Eric Taylor. Catterick was said to be much more thorough. Although the Owls' training facilities were then basic, a schedule was drawn up with trainer Tommy Eggleston. Catterick told each player to take this seriously and make every effort to improve their ball skills. Before Catterick came to the club, all the players did was lapping and sprinting, finishing off with a game of football. There was no work on set pieces. Swan said, 'Taylor would tell us to go out and enjoy ourselves before a game, but Catterick would talk to each of us one by one telling us what he wanted us to do.'

Catterick gave information about their opponents, 'telling us if a player we were expected to face had a particular trick, which he liked to use', said Swan. They worked a lot on set pieces. Swan was part of a 'swivel' formation at the back with Tom McAnearney and Tony Kay providing defensive cover. He added, 'If any one of us attacked on one side, another would stay back, usually in the centre of the park so that we were never caught square. Before that we were too flat at the back, making it easier for a winger to race on to a through ball.'

Vic Buckingham left West Bromwich Albion in the summer of 1959, having been in charge at the Hawthorns for six years. He guided the club to an FA Cup triumph in 1954 with the double only eluded after a late loss of form. From 1932 to 1949 Buckingham had been a classy wing-half with Spurs. He gained a reputation as a deep and original thinker on football as a coach with Oxford University and at crack amateur club Pegasus. He helped Pegasus win the FA Amateur Cup at Wembley in April 1951, before embarking upon football management at Bradford later in the same year.

Buckingham introduced a version of Arthur Rowe's 'push and run' style of play at West Bromwich. He made an important modification, though. He used a long ball as a swift and shrewdly timed spring. Ronnie Allen, his nimble, deep-lying centre-forward, provided the outlet. Allen frequently tracked back at speed to pick up a ball from one of his defenders, taking his marker with him. Having received the ball, Allen would pivot and look to slide a pass through the vacated space in the centre of the field for one of his breaking colleagues to pick up in full stride. Buckingham insisted that all his players should attack and defend, depending upon the state of the game. He also encouraged his goalkeeper to begin an attack by throwing the ball to one of his defenders, who in turn were expected to move forward using exchanged passes rather than launching the ball downfield more in hope than expectation.

In 1954 he wrote, 'Football is an easy game. Its exponents make it appear difficult. I began coaching amateurs Pegasus in 1950/51, guiding them to victory in the FA Amateur Cup. I realised when I first met them that, Pawson apart, they were not very skilful ball players and some lacked ball control under the pressure of match conditions. But they had the intelligence to realise that it does not require excessive ability to push a pass and move into position for a return.

'It was these straightforward tactics which took my club West Bromwich Albion to victory in the FA Cup Final in 1954. Our wingers George Lee and Frank Griffin play deep. The wingers and the full-backs remain in close touch as they move up and down the field. When in possession, only two players come into the picture –

the man on the ball and the man to whom he passes, although there may be decoys. I want our centre-forward to come back for the ball and not to run away up front on his own, like so many do, waiting for a long pass.

'We have not abandoned the long pass, but we differ from Spurs in how we use it. Spurs use the long pass diagonally. We use it straight, as when our full-back finds our centre-forward Ronnie Allen, having the effect of elongating us. Although we place an emphasis upon teamwork, Allen is the key man in our system. He tries to buy space by pressing up against our opponent's defence. He is "the wall". He receives a ground pass from one of our defenders, having run back from his marker to receive it. He then moves it first time to another forward racing up in support. This move not only gains us 30 or 40 yards, it turns our forwards around, so they are facing our opponents' goal, not ours.'

Buckingham broke new ground by taking his side on tours of the USSR, Canada, and the USA, to fly the flag, flex their muscles and improve their game. He left Albion to manage Ajax, steering them to the Dutch title in 1960, in his first season in charge. Albion's chief scout, Gordon Clark, took over from him in June 1959, inheriting a strong squad comprising Bobby Robson, Derek Kevan, Graham Williams, and Maurice Setters, all of whom had been recruited by Buckingham. Albion had the knack of picking up gems in the lower divisions. Allen, Kevan and Setters were good examples.

At West Ham the 1959/60 season opened with so much style and promise but ended in a wretched rabble. It was a huge disappointment for such a forward-thinking, enterprising club. For West Ham were one of the first top-division outfits to fully embrace the modern game, readily absorbing the latest continental ideas on coaching, fitness training, positional play and tactics. Their choice of kit reflected their beliefs. Following the Hungarian example, they adopted lightweight boots, trimmed-down shin pads, lighter, cooler, V- and polo-necked short-sleeved shirts, and shorter shorts. Their away shirts had a swish continental design – twin hoops across the chest, one in claret and one in sky blue.

Although Ted Fenton was the manager, he permitted his players to discuss potential tactics and formations at a local café owned by the Cassettari family. Here, the likes of Malcolm Allison, Noel Cantwell,

John Bond, Dave Sexton, Frank O'Farrell and Jimmy Andrews debated and formulated new ideas with passionate intensity, using salt and pepper pots to set out their plans. But the contribution of club manager and former player Ted Fenton was important too. He had managed West Ham between 1950 and 1961, establishing 'the Academy' which spawned a wealth of vibrant talent including Bobby Moore, Martin Peters, and Ken Brown.

The teams that Fenton developed reached the FA Youth Cup final twice in the late '50s. With the help of his chairman Reg Pratt, Fenton encouraged his players to qualify for their FA coaching badges, not only helping spread the gospel of skills development but enabling them to have something to fall back upon when their playing days were over. Above all, Ted was prepared to allow his players their heads. When the members of the Cassettari café society wanted to try something new, he listened.

Malcolm Allison recalled, 'I brought in weight training, heavy weight training. Bill Nicholson said it was wrong and at first Ted Fenton did not want to do it. But I found that our jumping became better. We became stronger and quicker.' The inclusivity demonstrated at West Ham was revolutionary at a time when many club owners and managers still clung to the past.

Like West Bromwich's former manager, Vic Buckingham, Manchester City boss Les McDowall was also willing to experiment with a deep-lying centre-forward, as was one of his leading players, Don Revie. Revie explained, 'Along with every thinking footballer, I was motivated by the performance of the Ferenc Puskas-inspired Hungarian team that took England apart at Wembley in 1953. The player who really took my eye, though, was their centre-forward, Nandor Hidegkuti, who wore a number nine shirt but played a withdrawn role. He came through from midfield to steal a hat-trick. The England defenders could not cope with him. Until then, we always thought of centre-forwards as battering rams who led from the front. We decided to try the system at Manchester City with me in the Hidegkuti role. It was not my copyright although the press called it "the Revie plan".'

Revie was right. McDowall eagerly championed this approach, too, perhaps hastily at first. McDowall was an inveterate innovator. He was captivated by new tactical and formation ideas. He was the first English manager to come up with the idea of wing-backs. But he was not a tracksuit manager; he left the implementation to his coaches. He was a 'tinker man' as much if not more than Claudio Ranieri, frequently trying out his players in different positions. It drove Revie wild with exasperation. Revie wanted stability. He wanted to be the deep-lying centre-forward, producing diagrams of possible game plans. His obsession with dossiers when managing Leeds began here.

Having watched the Hungarians at Wembley and seen his reserve side achieve considerable success with a withdrawn centre-forward, neophiliac McDowall was keen to introduce the plan at the start of the 1954/55 season, calling in his players early from their holidays to rehearse the system. Although excited by the idea, Revie was more cautious. He feared being left adrift by balls pumped over his head. A 5-0 opening-day thrashing by Preston hardly helped. The tactic needed rebooting as did the cast.

But McDowall was intent upon giving the method a fair crack. He wanted to allow the new formation at least a one-month trial. The idea clicked into gear when reserve wing-half Ken Barnes was selected to help with its implementation. His stamina and passing skills gave Revie the support he craved in adopting his new role. Barnes was like the Hungarian Bozsik to Revie's Hidegkuti. The pair combined forces to devastating effect as the Blades were put to the sword 5-2. City began to climb the table, also progressing towards Wembley. A succession of injuries halted their quest for the league title, but they reached the FA Cup Final where they met Newcastle. Alas they were shot down by a 45th-second goal from Jackie Milburn and a serious injury to right-back Jimmy Meadows, losing 3-1.

However, they returned to the Twin Towers a year later where the 'Revie Plan' was triumphant. By this time Revie's relationship with McDowall had soured. Revie took a summer holiday when McDowall wanted his squad to be preparing for the new season. Revie was suspended for two weeks. Although he returned to first team action, the rift remained and festered, souring the atmosphere at the club. For a while, McDowall chose the speedy Bobby Johnstone for the Revie role but reverted to Revie shortly before the 1956 final. Revie amply repaid his manager's change of heart by running the show, setting up two goals in City's 3-1 win.

In the third minute, City snuffed out a Birmingham City attack. Right-back Leivers seized upon the loose ball and passed it to Revie, positioned well inside his own half. Revie counter-attacked at speed, his fast strides taking him deep inside the Birmingham half. Drawing the opposing defenders towards him, he released a perfectly weighted 40-yard pass into the path of his left-winger, Roy Clarke. Revie then made for the Birmingham box anticipating Clarke's centre which came in, fast, low, and true. Revie essayed a dummy only to re-route the ball deftly with his left heel as he hurdled it. This wrong-footed the Birmingham defenders, allowing Joe Hayes the space to pick his spot, driving the ball into the right-hand corner of the net. It was a goal that Real Madrid would have been proud of. Revie set up their second goal, too.

That final was also memorable for the outstanding, if misguided, bravery of Manchester City goalkeeper Bert Trautmann, who remained at his post despite sustaining a broken neck in an accidental challenge with Birmingham's Peter Murphy.

Regrettably for City, Revie moved to Sunderland in November 1956 whereupon the FA Cup winners began a protracted decline, awaiting an eventual rescue in the mid-'60s by Joe Mercer and Malcolm Allison. Trautmann played an important role in the development of the 'Revie Plan'. He was an accomplished handball player, enabling him to hurl the ball 50 yards or more, thereby launching a counter-attack with speed and great accuracy. But with the City squad depleted by age and key departures, without adequate replacements, a wistful Trautmann concluded, 'The "Revie plan" is only a good system if you have the players to work it.'

Unlike Busby, McDowall appeared uninterested in youth development, telling his new signing, Denis Law, 'We don't have kids here.' McDowall continued to experiment with diminishing returns. He once proposed filling his forward line with inside-forwards, to the bemusement of his players. With his attacking potential withering after Law's departure, McDowall concocted a 2-5-1-2 defensive formation for the 1962/63 season, comprising two centre-backs, five half-backs, a lone playmaker and two strikers. It was a disastrous plan. West Ham thrashed them 6-1 at home and away while Wolves won 8-1 at Molineux. City conceded 102 goals and were relegated, resulting in McDowall's dismissal.

City's 1956 FA Cup Final opponents, Birmingham, were also in a dicey position at the end of the '50s, not helped by a strange managerial move. In January 1958, Pat Beasley joined the club, believing he had been appointed as assistant to manager Arthur Turner. However, chairman Harry Morris announced to the press that Beasley had been appointed as joint manager. When Turner found this out, he threatened to resign. He was persuaded to stay 'for the time being' but left in September 1958, whereupon Beasley took over. As for Turner, he took Oxford into the Football League.

Beasley's first season in charge seemed to be going well. Fiery forward Bunny Larkin top-scored with 18 goals in 31 league appearances and Birmingham achieved a respectable ninth position. But tragedy struck in April 1959. Jeff Hall, a young England international full-back, died suddenly of polio, only 14 days after his last appearance for the club. The national campaign for polio immunisation had attracted few takers but after Hall's untimely death, the take-up rate increased prodigiously.

This sad loss seemed to rock Birmingham because the 1959/60 season almost resulted in relegation. Eighty goals were conceded compared with 68 in 1958/59 with 21 fewer goals scored. Larkin managed just four. Midfielder Johnny Gordon with 16 goals and winger Harry Hooper with 13 strived to fill the gap but it was barely enough. Beasley made repeated attempts to sign a centre-forward to no avail. Their season was saved by four critical wins in their last seven games, including an unexpected 4-2 victory at Hillsborough. Beasley did well to hold his fragmented team together, particularly after their disastrous 7-1 drubbing by visiting West Bromwich on a not-so-good Good Friday. He was relieved to tender his resignation at the end of this troubled season.

Blackburn Rovers and Nottingham Forest were threatened by the possibility of relegation in the closing stages of 1959/60. The season ended disastrously for Blackburn when their maverick centre-forward Derek Dougan submitted a transfer request on FA Cup Final day just before his team were due to meet Wolves at Wembley. Dougan compounded his crass behaviour by declaring himself fit to play when he was not. Blackburn lost full-back Dave Whelan during the final to a broken leg in a challenge with Deeley. With Dougan also incapacitated, Blackburn lost 3-0.

Disaster almost befell Forest, the 1959 FA Cup winners. Within months of achieving Wembley glory, most of their side was broken up. Days after the final, Forest manager Billy Walker told Wembley hero Stewart Imlach that he wanted him to go to Second Division Sheffield United. Stewart and his team-mates were dumbfounded that their efforts counted for so little. In the event, the move fell through, but the players' previously cordial relationship with Walker began to fracture.

According to author Gary Imlach, Stewart's son, Walker was miffed when the players unanimously rejected his offer to act as their agent in commercial matters. Walker had apparently responded by speaking out against players' acquisitive tastes – cars and 'nice suits' – which he regarded as excessive. An ensuing spat over alleged cup final ticket profiteering stirred up further animosity. On top of this, the players found that the club's 1959 summer tour of Spain and Portugal was poorly organised, excessively arduous, and exploitative as the club attempted to cash in on their status as FA Cup holders. The team did not approach the new season in the best frame of mind. Additionally, Jimmy Greaves accused some Forest players of attempting to bribe his Chelsea team to concede the points when they met on Easter Saturday 1960. At that time Forest were in grave danger of relegation. According to Greaves, the Chelsea players unanimously refused.

Syd Owen, the 1959 Football Writers' Association Player of the Year was equally disenchanted with life at Luton Town, FA Cup finalists in 1959. Having ended his playing career after the Wembley defeat, he accepted the post of manager at Kenilworth Road. But the experience proved to be a sour one. A string of poor results and declining crowds were aggravated by his board of directors' insistence that they had the right to buy players for the club without his involvement.

Whether managers led from the front or not, they had to be arch diplomats in dealing with their board. Some directors liked to involve themselves in playing matters. At Newcastle and Bolton, it was not uncommon for their directors to visit the dressing room at half-time to give their advice. Occasionally, Newcastle directors attempted to select the team. The '50s and early '60s were still the heydays of the 'club amateur' – whether in sport, business, or politics. A club amateur was a dilettante without the necessary qualifications or experience but an out-sized sense of entitlement. While Burnley's domineering chairman, Bob Lord, understood it was not his job to check out possible recruits or determine how his team played, he did not allow his managers a free hand in football matters, as Alan Brown and succeeding Burnley bosses found.

The degree to which directors invested in their club, not just their team, separated the best from the rest. While Lord was often abrasive and sometimes offensive during the '50s and early '60s, he and his board gave Burnley the calibre of support which enabled them to thrive, as club captain Jimmy Adamson and leading player Jimmy McIlroy confirmed before they fell out with him. What marked Burnley out as the top English side in the 1959/60 season was the degree of balance it achieved. It was a family club but an ambitious one. It was well-disciplined but generally caring about its staff and their families. It was close-knit but with a modern, outward, and forward-looking perspective. It imposed routines but allowed individual expression and improvisation. It was focused on success but encouraged fun, too. It was a thrifty club but one prepared to invest strongly in its future, as evidenced by its comprehensive scouting network, advanced coaching, modern training facilities, and strong youth policy.

There were similarities between Burnley and Fulham. Like Burnley, Fulham appeared to be a family club with a tactile manager in Bedford Jezzard who readily hugged his players when they played well. There were questions raised about his authority, though, when players Langley and Mullery arrived late for Fulham's league game at Leeds. They became lost while walking around Leeds. By the time they had arrived, Jezzard, a former England international centre-forward, had changed and was ready to fill one of the missing positions. With Fulham winning 4-1 there were no repercussions apparently. However, Jezzard resigned in 1964 when Fulham sold prize asset, Alan Mullery, to Spurs without consulting him. Disillusioned, he never returned to football.

7.

TEAM FORMATIONS AND TACTICS IN THE '50s

BURNLEY AND Northern Ireland playmaker Jimmy McIlroy observed, 'In the '50s, most teams adopted a similar formation, although there was room for experimentation if the club was so inclined. Many were not. Normally, there would be two wingers, one tricky like Stanley Matthews and one more direct with pace like our John Connelly or Preston's Tom Finney. The most forward player was the centre-forward. He would be a spearhead such as the late Tommy Taylor of pre-Munich Manchester United, Nat Lofthouse of Bolton or Bobby Smith of Spurs. There would be two inside-forwards: one would be a midfielder, like me or John White of Spurs, Johnny Haynes of Fulham, or George Eastham of Newcastle; the other would be a striker like Jimmy Robson or Jimmy Greaves, then of Chelsea.

'One of the wing-halves would be an attacking midfielder. In our case, this role was undertaken by Jimmy Adamson, our captain. Other notable examples include Danny Blanchflower of Spurs, Bobby Robson of West Bromwich, or Ken Barnes of Manchester City. The other wing-half was more like a second centre-half, like the late Duncan Edwards of pre-Munich Manchester United or Bill Slater of Wolves. At Burnley, Brian Miller frequently played as a defensive left-half, although he would bomb forward, too, at times. Bobby Seith of Burnley also played here.

'There would be two full-backs. Possibly one would be a hard man like Roy Hartle at Bolton or Don Megson of Sheffield Wednesday, and the other more of a ball player like Jimmy Armfield of Blackpool, although everyone had to be a capable footballer. At Burnley, full-backs John Angus and Alex Elder combined both qualities. Although Burnley extemporised with a fluid "WM" or 3-2-2-3 formation, with their players regularly exchanging positions, many clubs utilised it with rigid orthodoxy. It was for this reason that "Don Revie's plan" caused so much confusion once its substantial teething problems were sorted out.'

Captain Jimmy Adamson suggested that his Burnley sides of 1959 to 1963 played a version of 'Total Football' as Spurs appeared to do also. This flexible, fluid system of play is commonly, but wrongly, attributed to a Dutch innovation during the early '70s. Arguably, the playing patterns adopted by Sebes's Hungarian teams pre-dated the Dutch by two decades. Adamson explained, 'At Burnley, we like to keep our game fluid. We do not believe in sticking to numbers on our backs. If the full-back suddenly finds himself in a momentary role of a winger, then he gets on with it, and someone else takes over his job at the rear. Burnley play their football "off the cuff". There are few hard and fast rules. Obviously, we try to vary our tactics according to the opposition and state of the pitch. But "off the cuff" fluid football is the aim.'

Not that this innovation found universal favour among the Burnley supporters. After a 4-1 home defeat by Blackpool in October 1959, the disgruntled home fans voiced their objections to a 'confusing system of play' which was blamed for the Clarets' heavy loss. Of course, experimentation is fraught with risks as Don Revie and his Manchester City colleagues found, but Tommy Docherty asserted, 'Even in these cautious, conservative times these setbacks should not and did not halt the march of progress.' Helped by increasing continental club competition and wider television coverage, British clubs began to look at tactical ideas being developed abroad.

The Italians had introduced *Catenaccio*, the 'bolt' system of defence, based upon a 4-4-2 formation, as early as the late '40s. Its principal aim was to defend the scoring zone in and around the box by employing tight man-to-man marking of the opposing forwards supplemented by a sweeper who would seal off any gaps and pick up opposing players breaking from a deep position. Joe Mercer's Second Division Sheffield United began experimenting with a *Catenaccio* system during the 1958/59 season. Mercer deployed the immaculate Joe Shaw as his sweeper operating behind a back four of Cec Coldwell, Tommy Hoyland, Gerry Summers, and Graham Shaw. Over 17 Second Division league games, bridging the 1958/59 and 1959/60 seasons, 'the Blades' conceded a stingy seven goals. At the other end of the spectrum, Les McDowall's 'gung-ho' Manchester City were scoring and conceding in copious quantities, aggregating 90 goals in their first 20 league games of the 1959/60 season.

Cliff Britton, the Preston manager, agreed with Mercer. Britton said in June 1960, 'I have long held the belief that all teamwork has to start from defence. Unless you have a workable defensive system, goalscoring can be futile.' He achieved promotion with Burnley in 1946/47. Their often impregnable 'iron curtain' defence bore testimony to that philosophy. Britton observed, 'The Brazilians proved themselves better with a defence in depth while being equally adept at gaining a quick advantage on seizing the initiative.'

The experimenters were not just the 'leading edge' tacticians. Although not given to trenchant tactical analyses, the Blackpool side under Joe Smith experimented with a 4-4-2 formation en route to their Wembley triumph in 1953. Stan Matthews explained, 'During the '50s, managers began to realise there were different systems of play. We played what was in many respects a 4-4-2 system with me and Bill Perry playing wide but coming up from deep.' Although regarded as a conventional winger, Stan was quite prepared to go a-roaming rather than hugging the touchlines if the game merited it. Stan demonstrated this vividly at Turf Moor in October 1960 when young Burnley left-back Alex Elder gamely tracked him everywhere, causing Matthews to say to Elder at half-time, 'Would you like to come in and have a cup of tea with me since you have followed me everywhere else?' But as Walter Winterbottom found, Stan was less keen on tracking back. Perhaps a violin maestro is less inclined to do the washing-up?

Towards the end of the '50s, a wider and more informed debate was taking place about team formations and styles of play, encouraged by the work of the FA School of Coaching at Lilleshall under Winterbottom. Once that centurion of English caps, Billy Wright, had retired at the beginning of the 1959/60 season he was free to express his reservations about the 'hit the corners' dictum of

Stan Cullis, his former manager, despite Wolves' success with this approach, at least in domestic competitions.

In advocating the 4-2-4 formation adopted loosely by the Hungarians of 1953/54 and Brazilians of 1958, Wright attacked the received wisdom of transferring the ball from the centre of the field to a winger who makes as much ground as he can on a flank before crossing into an over-crowded penalty area. He said, 'That such an obvious drill can produce goals regularly is one of the fallacies of our modern game. Such centres are effective only when there is a forward of the huge ability of Lawton or Dean in the centre.' Wright claimed, 'Even the more imaginative sides have a problem in beating a well-drilled defence employing a 4-2-4 system. The four-man defence drops back, allowing their opponents unchallenged possession in midfield. Then they take up position on the edge of the penalty area, where space between the last line of defence and the goalkeeper is minimised. They will be joined in seconds by the two midfield link men. Six men who know what they are doing should be able to bolt and bar the penalty area to all-comers.'

While Wright indicated that the 4-2-4 system was not 'a golden panacea for all ailments', his unbridled enthusiasm for it suggested otherwise. Meanwhile, Gusztav Sebes, coach of the 'Magnificent Magyars' and architect of their 1953 victory at Wembley, was about to break new ground. While addressing British football's cognoscenti – Cullis, Shankly, Mercer, Nicholson, Stein, and others – at Lilleshall in the summer of 1960, he said that at his Ujpest club, he was experimenting with a 'circular system'. 'With this system attackers became defenders and vice versa so that during a game each outfield player fulfilled every position.' Just as we were coming up to speed with the Brazilians' 4-2-4 system, the goalposts appeared to be moving again.

Sebes placed skill ahead of method, though. He insisted that 'more attention should be given to raising the quality of coaching at all levels'. He recommended that British clubs should involve young people at an earlier age, dedicating more time to improving their ball skills. As testament to the success of his recipe, he explained that his deep-lying centre-forward, Hidegkuti, practised ball control for two hours or more every other day. The groundwork Sebes undertook prior to his Wembley victory had been meticulous, practising extensively on a Wembley-type surface using a British ball, supported by detailed intelligence of the English approach.

The legacy of his influential address was to open the minds of our top managers and coaches. They were left pondering whether they had better chances of success at home and abroad by employing skill more than power, creativity as much as strength, patience as well as pace, short passes as much as long ones, by working the ball rather than the player, by using short, accurate clearances rather than long, hopeful ones, and by playing to feet rather than going aerial. The ways that Burnley and Spurs played their football at the beginning of the '60s suggested that they might be on the right path.

Burnley inside-forward Jimmy Robson said, 'The European Cup had a big bearing upon how the game came to be played in the mid- and later '60s. Up until then, our teams played to win home and away. It did not matter whether the team we were playing was any good or not. After exposure to the continental style of play, teams gradually became more cautious. By the time I had moved to Blackpool in 1965, the English game had changed a lot. It was much harder to score goals as defences became more packed. The Bloomfield Road pitch did not help. It was quite narrow, giving opposing defences greater opportunity to snuff out our attacks. At the end of the 1966/67 season we went down. We could not win at home for love nor money. We had just one victory at home, a 6-0 thrashing of Newcastle, whereas on the road we won five times.

'I think we benefited at Burnley from our summer tours, notably in the '50s, taking on foreign opposition. It gave us early experience of continental styles like the sweeper system. We used to try to combat this by putting a man on the sweeper, reducing his freedom to play. We did well. On one summer tour we played against seven good European sides, including Atletico Madrid, Charleroi, and Servette. We won four and drew three of these games. We also played the Polish, Czechoslovakian and Austrian national teams only losing these three games by a solitary goal. They liked playing us because it gave them the opportunity to practise against the British style of football, although I'm not sure that we were then a typical English side.'

In his 1961 book *Striking for Soccer*, Jimmy Hill implored English teams to adopt a more fluid, fluent style of play. Hill maintained, 'The refinement of positional play is the fundamental lesson we must learn from the continentals. The reason we shall have difficulty in digesting the lesson is that it is always the man who makes the pass and fails who is blamed; whereas very often it is the idiotic position his colleague takes up that brings about the bad pass.'

Burnley right-back John Angus recalled, 'When we had our weekly discussions about our next opponents, we would examine their particular strengths and weaknesses. We would know which goalkeepers were confident about dealing with high crosses and which were not. We would know which players were good in the air and which were better on the ground. We would identify the danger men. We would not alter our basic style of play to combat these threats but as individuals we would prepare to adjust our game. I cannot remember ever being told to change the way I played whether at club level or when playing for England, either at under-23 or at senior level. The national coaches, Walter Winterbottom and Ron Greenwood would attempt to build upon our strengths, making some suggestions about how we might improve our game. But there was never any attempt made to alter the basic way we played. With Alan Brown and Harry Potts, at Burnley, it was the same.'

Angus's colleague, left-half Brian Miller, added, 'At Gawthorpe we didn't spend hours looking at blackboards and discussing tactics. Harry took us through the opposition before a game, went through our responsibilities. But there was no need for tactics as such. You had 11 good players, they had their positions and formation, they played to their strengths, and went out to score goals. The team picked itself. "Worry about you, not the opposition," is what he said. The tactic was simple – move forward and score. In training at the end of the day he loved the five-a-sides. He loved to win. So no, we were never bogged down in theories.'

Jimmy Adamson confirmed Brian's view. He wrote in 1962, 'We don't do a lot of talking at Turf Moor. Of course, we held team talks but these lasted only five or ten minutes. They are a free-for-all with every player saying his piece. We prefer to concentrate on our tactics and teamwork on the field. In talks you can tell a winger to "go or come back". He walks away not knowing exactly what you are talking about. On the field he sees in a flash when it is best to go and pick up a short pass from his half-back or go inside or forward or run on to receive a pass. Every player is encouraged to put forward ideas. I was with the England World Cup party in Chile. Naturally, I picked up lots of ideas. The same applies with Jimmy McIlroy or Alex Elder when playing for Northern Ireland.'

8.

COACHING AND TRAINING METHODS IN THE '50s

WRITING IN 1961, Jimmy Hill questioned, 'How is it that Uruguay with a population of three million, has twice won the World Cup? Could it be, perhaps, that at a certain period all the best players in the world happened to be born there? Or could it be that their training and coaching systems squeeze the last ounce of talent out of their material?'

Burnley manager Alan Brown required no persuasion about the value of coaching. He was an exacting coach himself and his players were encouraged to maximise their coaching knowledge and skills by obtaining their badges at the FA School at Lilleshall. However, Burnley's playmaker Jimmy McIlroy cautioned against an uncritical acceptance of new methods, pointing out that these should focus on developing strengths rather than eradicating errors. Nevertheless, an increasing number of managers and players in the '50s began to heed the importance of coaching.

Arsenal's Ron Greenwood eulogised, 'Walter opened our eyes. He would give you an insight into how to teach. We could all play, but we did not know how to present it. Some had reservations like self-coached Stan Matthews. And some took the p*** like Tommy Banks. When Walter Winterbottom said that he wanted his players "to feel joy", Banks turned to Billy Wright, who had just married Joy Beverley, "Bloody hell, that's one bonus I never expected playing for England. Reet sporting of you is that Billy lad."'

Journalist Brian Glanville thought, 'The decent, well-educated, honest and unassuming Winterbottom had difficulty in relating to his players, other than England captain, Billy Wright, meaning there was always a barrier between them.' But there were many players who accepted Winterbottom's ideas.

Among those drawn to exploring new methods was Malcolm Allison, who had returned from National Service in Austria excited by the training methods adopted by their top teams. His club colleagues, Noel Cantwell, John Bond, Dave Sexton, Frank O'Farrell and Jimmy Andrews, were kindred spirits. Nat Lofthouse was a disciple, too. He said, 'I used to go to Lilleshall and Walter would bring coaches over from countries like Italy, Spain, Germany, France, Holland and Belgium, and we used to listen to them. However, Walter put the onus on us to realise the benefits of their ideas. I mean, a coach can only go so far. If the player does not take it in or says he cannot put it into practice, it's not much point in him trying to talk the player round.'

Winterbottom found this when introducing 'shadow training' to the national squad during the mid-'50s. This idea involved simulating an attack without any defenders to stop them. The benefits were that it helped develop rhythm, movement, accuracy, and weight of passing before being employed in a real game. But the purpose was lost on some. The 'Clown Prince of Soccer', Len Shackleton, asked Walter, with weary sarcasm, in which side of the goal did he want his unmolested attack to score. Some leading players such as Stanley Matthews and Tommy Lawton were sceptical of the benefits of coaching per se, believing they should be left to develop their game.

Winterbottom saw more value in gearing training to a coming match by choosing specific opposition for practice matches. If he wanted to practise against a hard-tackling side, he would try to enlist the help of someone like title-winning Chelsea. If he wanted to practise against a fast-ball, continuous movement style of play he might approach Spurs. Because he had much less time to mould his team than a club manager, he had to be judicious in his use of the limited time with a constantly changing group of players.

Walter was not sold on the value of five-a-side routines, though. He said in 1960, 'The danger of five-a-side play in training is that it involves almost no tackling and can develop a leisurely, almost dilettante attitude in the minds of players. Although it is good fun, it can degenerate into pointless larking.' This description did not apply to the five-a-side games organised at Burnley and Spurs. Jimmy McIlroy took issue with Walter over this, saying, 'Every footballer likes to have a ball at his feet. That is why I have always regarded five-a-side practice games as the finest form of soccer training ever devised.'

Burnley's Jimmy Robson added, 'It helped keep our ball skills sharp, developing instant control and quick passing. They were competitive affairs – everyone got stuck in.' Spurs trainer Cecil Poynton, concurred, saying, 'I consider that five-a-side games have tremendous value. Because they are played on a field which is less than half the size of a real pitch, the boys have to run, think and act twice as fast as they normally would and this helps to give them a fine edge when they transfer their activity to a full-size pitch. Mastery of the ball is the first thing that you must achieve if you want to be a professional footballer. Fitness and knowledge of tactics can be instilled later.'

While new ideas were emerging in the '50s concerning how the game should be played and how the necessary skills might be developed, there were strong 'luddite' factions, notably at Leeds. In the late '50s the club was in chaos. The huge fee they obtained from John Charles's move to Italy had to be set aside for the rebuilding of the burnt-down West Stand at Elland Road which had been under-insured. The club was strapped for cash.

When Eric Smith joined Leeds shortly after their relegation in 1960, he commented, 'The club was fifth rate and the players were undisciplined. Manager Jack Taylor had let things go. We would go on long training runs and some players, quite senior players, slacked, walking in with ice lollies in their hands.' Bob English, the club physiotherapist, remarked, 'There wasn't much enthusiasm. Jack Taylor, was a nice man but he did not crack the whip enough. Training was slack although Don Revie was one who really did train.' Young Billy Bremner agreed, 'Training was just doing laps, a kick-about with a ball, no ball on Fridays, just sprints.' Bremner was impressed by Revie's vision on the pitch, though. 'It was tremendous and after he had struck the ball, he would pose, as if for a photograph.'

Bremner was contemptuous of the unprofessionalism, in marked contrast to the club that Revie subsequently built. Bremner illustrated Leeds's shortcomings during 1959/60 by citing the build-up to a critical game at Blackburn. He said, 'Towards the end of that season we were playing at Blackburn Rovers. I remember thinking, "I wonder where we're going to eat." In the end, we stopped off at a cafe and had beans on toast. It was all a bit of a rush. Nothing had been arranged. And this was our most important game of the season. We lost 3-2. Even as a young fellow, I thought, "We haven't really prepared well for this game."'

Ex-Manchester United player Freddie Goodwin was horrified at what he found at Elland Road in 1960. He commented, 'At United, we had played for the team, whereas at Leeds, so many of the side seemed to play for themselves. And Jack Charlton was part of that. He was an undisciplined player when I joined.' Don Revie was enraged by Charlton's behaviour in practice matches which Jack seemed to treat as a joke. Even Charlton admitted later that his habit of racing about all over the park was 'totally unprofessional'.

Charlton recalled that there was little coaching in his formative days at Leeds. He remarked that his first manager, Raich Carter, was not a coach and did not employ coaches. The only training was said to be a run down the long side of the pitch, a jog along a short side and a sprint along the other long side followed by five-a-side or eight-a-side games on the cinder car park. He said, 'There was no practising of free kicks or corners, no team talks, we never had a run-down on the opposition. It wasn't a professional club.' Bill Lambton, who replaced Carter, was said by Charlton to be a 'fitness fanatic'. Charlton continued, 'The balls we used for training were too hard,' causing the players to hobble off after a session.

Although 1959/60 manager Taylor brought along his brother Frank, who was a coach, Charlton said, 'The players didn't respond. They weren't interested in developing skills.' Charlton did acknowledge Frank Taylor's help in learning to 'kick the ball properly'.

Norman Hunter was also startled by the indiscipline. He said, 'Jack Taylor was manager when I first joined Leeds. The team were well down the First Division and he felt it was time to call a meeting to thrash things out. It was just before Christmas and all the players were there, from the first team down to the newcomers. He was a very polite man but to my surprise no one took a blind bit of notice of what he was saying. Several first-team players were throwing Christmas streamers across the room while he was talking. The training staff had set up circuit training on the Elland Road pitch. They had carefully placed cones in strategic places with mats, footballs and skipping ropes. Unfortunately for them some of the older lads didn't fancy circuit training one little bit so they promptly gathered together all the cones and threw them down the banking at the corner of the ground.'

Denis Law was also appalled by the quality of coaching and training at Manchester City when he arrived in March 1960. He said, 'The training under Jimmy Meadows was poor. It was just running and more running. There was nothing to inspire the younger players and no work on developing skills or tactics. When I went to Italy, it was a different world. The training was excellent, completely different from anything I had experienced in England, and everything was done with a ball at your feet, even the running.

'We hardly ever saw a ball at Manchester City. It was not just at City. Many other English clubs, Manchester United among them, prepared their players in this way. The weak theory at the time was that if the ball was kept away from the players during the week, on a Saturday they'd be more eager for it. Speaking personally, I needed the ball to work with to improve. My career was not in athletics; when I trained for football, I wanted to do it with a ball. Things didn't really change until Joe Mercer and Malcolm Allison arrived in the mid-'60s to breathe life into the club.'

Ironically, at Southern League Guildford City, four or five divisions below Manchester City, their manager Albert Tennant, the former Chelsea full-back, had already heeded the call. Tennant explained, 'There cannot be too much emphasis on the importance of ball work in training. Even when running my players have a ball at their feet.'

The slackness described here lasted at some clubs until the later '60s. Former Burnley goalkeeper Adam Blacklaw recalled disappointment at finding much less disciplined training regimes after moving to Blackburn and Blackpool. He said, 'When I went to Blackburn in the later '60s there was no discipline at all about the training. We just messed around. When I was at Blackpool, too, I can recall a morning spent larking around in the dressing room while Freddie Starr was making us laugh.'

A BBC reporter made a visit to Gawthorpe, Burnley's training facility, in the mid-'60s and observed, 'Perhaps one of the major attractions at Burnley has been the marvellous training facilities provided by the club. The visitor, who might be forgiven for expecting something primitive at such a small club, would be amazed by the magnificent training grounds, two miles out of town. There are three full-sized pitches, a weather-proof shale pitch and a huge outbuilding which serves as a gymnasium. At Turf Moor itself, an extra training pitch has been provided, and the superbly equipped gymnasium is as big as the playing area, and full-scale practice matches can be staged there.' Winger Brian Pilkington confirmed, 'Burnley was the best-organised club that I played with. They introduced an all-weather pitch during the '50s so we could practise our ball skills on a firm surface. That was very unusual then.'

John Collins, once of Queens Park Rangers, remembered visiting Gawthorpe in 1966. The training ground was just over ten years old then. John said, 'The facilities were quite a bit better than anything I'd seen before. I had grown up training at Loftus Road in the late '50s and early '60s. In good weather you would get on the pitch but in bad weather you had to run around the perimeter or use the weights. They might set up a bit of head tennis under the stands, but you did not get much chance to practise ball skills. It was mostly stamina work at the start of the week and sprints at the end. They would keep the ball from you especially at the end of the week.

'Looking at what went on at Gawthorpe it was easy to see how much better things were. You could see how you could do some proper skills training there. At QPR the players were interested in developing their skills, but we did not have the facilities. You could not use the local parks, so we were a bit stuck. You would come in most days at 10am, do a couple of hours and then clear off. There wasn't any incentive to do more really.'

The training facilities at First Division Blackpool were no better than at Third Division QPR. Their international winger, Bill Perry, recalled that the team had to train on the Bloomfield Road pitch or the cinder car park because they did not have an extra training pitch or an indoor gym and training facilities. Perhaps it was small wonder that Stan Matthews was often allowed to train on his own on Blackpool sands.

During the '50s the role of the goalkeeper was beginning to change, inspired by ideas developed in Europe. For example, Billy Wright noticed how Hungary's Grosics operated as a sweeper, frequently sprinting from his area to intercept through balls when his back four pushed up. He was also aware of the offensive role adopted by Grosics, helping to start an attack by bowling the ball out to the unmarked backs or retreating wingers. This was a ploy advocated by respected nomadic coach from Burnley, Jimmy Hogan.

Grosics said, 'Starting by hand is important for a goalkeeper because a quick and precise hand-thrown ball can gain time and space from the opponent. In the '50s this was not widespread, but I thought it was safer than kicking the ball, which might or might not reach its target. My team-mates were told to move to a position so that I could easily throw them the ball. Puskas and Hidegkuti very often came back to a space 20–25 metres from goal so I could throw the ball to them.'

In the late '50s, Manchester City's Bert Trautmann could hurl the ball with accuracy much farther than Grosics. Trautmann said, 'Using my handball experience, once I caught a ball, it was already on its way. Our players were prepared, running into spaces. By delivering the ball by hand, I could eliminate three, four or five opponents. We were like a military machine. Unfortunately, when a lot of good players left this method ceased to be as effective.'

During the 1959/60 season, emerging Leicester star Gordon Banks demonstrated the greater accuracy of a thrown clearance compared with the lottery of the long kick. Burnley's Adam Blacklaw confirmed that he was expected to play in this way, too, although he also kicked from hand. He said, 'Fortunately, I have big hands. You need big hands as a goalkeeper. It helps with bowling the ball out as I was encouraged to do to help get an attack going.'

However, the Wolves manager, Stan Cullis, did not want his giant goalkeeper, Malcolm Finlayson, to hurl the ball out. Finlayson was told to launch the ball long towards the opposition's penalty area with the minimum of fuss. But it seems that not even Cullis's men were bound by an unswerving rule, for there were times when their brilliant inside-forward Peter Broadbent dropped back to collect a short ball from Finlayson, before prompting an attack.

When Banks broke into the Leicester team in the late '50s, he was surprised to find no specialist training for goalkeepers. So he designed a supplementary training regime himself. He said, 'Sometimes, after training and on Sundays, I'd ask some young lads to hammer shots at my goal from a variety of angles and at different heights and distances.

I would ask them also to chip or lob the ball towards goal, making me run backwards, so I improved my positioning. I worked hard at everything, footwork, handling, punching, positioning, and reflex saves. I would repeatedly practise clearing out of both hands, building my stamina and strength, improving my body suppleness and ability to ride a challenge. I studied angles, the flight of the ball and how to organise defences in front of me.' Even as a novice goalkeeper, Banks was the consummate professional – setting a benchmark of excellence for the new breed of top goalkeepers who minimised the necessity of spectacular saves by judicious positioning.

At the start of the '60s, England's incumbent goalkeeper, Ron Springett, 'trained' by throwing himself into five-a-side games as an outfield player. Former Queens Park Rangers colleague John Collins remembered that the London-based Springett was given licence to train at QPR, his former club, by Sheffield Wednesday manager Harry Catterick. 'Ron would stay in London for most of the week and then travel up to Sheffield on a Thursday or Friday,' he said. Collins remarked that there was little evidence that Ron worked on his goalkeeping skills while joining in with the QPR players, 'He seemed keener to pepper shots at goal rather than spend time trying to stop them.'

While there were no goalkeeping coaches as such in Blacklaw's playing days, he did not feel deprived of practice in team training sessions. Adam explained, 'I didn't need special training. I would get the boys to belt balls at me. That was enough to keep me on my toes.' In the '50s and early '60s little thought was given by any of the professional clubs about how best to prepare their goalkeepers for action. Even clubs with advanced coaching ideas like Burnley and Spurs seemed deficient in this respect. Ron Reynolds, a reserve goalkeeper at Spurs, was unimpressed with his club's goalkeeper training, believing that what was offered did little to enhance his ability.

Regarding general fitness requirements, Walter Winterbottom was sceptical about the value of long-distance running. He said, 'Soccer is not rhythmical and therefore it is important that the footballer should practise the kind of running needed in a game. He must break up his running into short bursts of sprinting, jogging, and walking, moving off at different angles.'

Jimmy Greaves agreed, remarking, 'I didn't like long-distance running because I didn't think I benefited from it. Where I did apply myself was in sprinting and shuttle runs.' Burnley's Jimmy McIlroy shared that view. He said, 'Pressure training, and by that, I mean the really strenuous stuff, is good propaganda for clubs, but quite unnecessary. Once an athlete has reached peak fitness, he finds it a simple matter to remain in that desirable state by simply doing routine lapping and sprinting. When I tried my hand at weight training, I noticed nothing more beneficial than an ache in my limbs and a loss of balance. Also, my nippiness was suffering, and I was losing my speed off the mark.'

Although Winterbottom thought weight training was of value, there have been recent instances where excessive use of heavy weights bulks up muscular strength but diminishes speed as McIlroy claimed. Ade Akinbiyi testified to this during his time at Sheffield United in 2005 and 2006. Burnley's Jimmy Robson added, 'We were very fit. Even when several of us did our one-year National Service at Bank Hall Colliery we stayed fit. I guess we were all naturally fit. That may have something to do with the way we were brought up. I remember playing football for hours on end as a kid, growing up in a mining community. I don't think today's kids are as well prepared in that respect.'

At many clubs in the '50s and '60s the apprentices were treated as skivvies but not all younger players were treated so dismissively. For example, former Burnley captain Jimmy Adamson said in 1962, 'Our youngsters learn by watching and copying the senior players. An inside-forward will watch Jimmy McIlroy; study Jimmy's positional play, his ability to find the open space, his pacing of a game.

'Training at Turf Moor generally takes the same pattern. The idea is to have all players thinking and playing along similar lines. Then, if a reserve player is introduced into the first team, he slots into the pattern without too much effort. Obviously as far as the younger players are concerned there is a bigger emphasis on basic skills. The first team is more concerned with tactics.'

9.

SET PLAY RUSES

JIMMY GREAVES remembered, 'In the season that took us up to the '60s, Burnley were writing poetry on their way to the First Division championship. They played smooth, skilled football that was a warming advertisement for all that was best about British football. Harry Potts was the Burnley manager, inheriting a squad that had been shaped and fashioned by his predecessor, Alan Brown, who was mainly responsible for introducing the success-breeding tactics, particularly the quick, short corners and mesmerising variety of free-kick scams.'

In 1961, Billy Wright opined, 'In the case of clubs such as Burnley or Spurs, it is apparent that a great deal of thought and practice has gone into taking free kicks.' Jimmy McIlroy added, 'Burnley have often been labelled the 'gimmick team' because we concentrate more than most on gaining maximum advantage from free kicks, corner kicks and throw-ins. We have made progress, too, but only after months of monotonous practice on a single idea. To perfect a "gimmick", a minimum of three men must do the right thing at the right time. Such tactical planning could not be seriously attempted only two or three days before a vital game.'

Two examples of Burnley's skill in executing these smart plans came in their European Cup tie with Reims, in November 1960.

Burnley were awarded a free kick just outside the Reims box. Jimmy Adamson and Jimmy McIlroy retreated five yards behind the ball. It looked as if one of them would go for goal with a power drive. With the French defenders apparently preoccupied with this possibility they ignored centre-forward Ray Pointer, who had slyly moved into position to the right of their wall. Meanwhile, defender

Brian Miller was prepared to do a blindside sprint on the left. Both Adamson and McIlroy ran towards the ball. At the last moment Adamson peeled away leaving McIlroy to slide a pass to Pointer, who unhesitatingly deflected it behind the wall into the sprinting Miller's path. Without hesitation Miller struck the ball firmly against the underside of the Reims bar. Ever-alert Robson capitalised on Reims' bemusement and stabbed the loose ball in, putting Burnley 3-0 ahead on aggregate.

Shortly afterwards, Burnley were awarded another free kick in an identical spot. This time McIlroy was joined by Miller. It looked like a repetition. Both took an extended run-up, but Pointer was merely a decoy. Miller peeled away at the last moment, leaving McIlroy to clip a lofted ball towards the penalty spot for Jimmy Robson to head in. This ruse was rumbled though, with the French centre-back just managing to beat the leaping Robson to the ball and clear the danger.

Sunday Times reporter Brian Glanville saw a similar routine in Burnley's 2-1 victory at Chelsea in December 1961. Here, he described Adamson and McIlroy huddled together at the end of their run-up as if in an NFL set play. This time, Adamson ran up to take the kick but hurdled the ball and curved around the left of the Chelsea defenders. McIlroy followed immediately, prodding the ball towards Pointer, who once more flicked on the pass. But this time Adamson could not capitalise on the clear opening and blasted his shot over the Chelsea bar. Glanville was impressed. He said, 'Burnley nearly equalised with the most sophisticated movement of the game, one of an infinity of free kicks which they surely design in a private drawing office. It was worth a goal.'

To keep the opposition guessing Burnley developed further variations on this free kick routine. Journalist Ivan Sharpe witnessed one example. He recorded, 'At a free kick 20 yards out, McIlroy conferred momentarily with Miller before loping towards the ball, as if he was intending to run past it, but upon arriving at the ball he proceeded to scoop it over the wall of defenders and into the top corner of the net.'

Robson confirmed, 'A lot of time was given to practising dead-ball routines – corners, free kicks and throw-ins. Tuesday and Thursday afternoons were dedicated to set play practice. These innovations came in principally during Alan Brown's time as manager in the mid-'50s when we had the smallest forward line in the country. We knew then that it was a waste of time pumping over high balls for forwards who were little more than 5ft 6in tall if that. This is where the short corner came in.

'We used to come up with a variety of moves to fool defenders. I remember we had this corner routine where the taker would wait until Jimmy McIlroy had trotted over with a defender close behind him. Jimmy and the corner taker would then start a mock argument over how the kick should be taken. With Jimmy turning on his heels in apparent disgust, the marking defender was momentarily put off guard, expecting a long corner to follow. The corner taker would then push the ball quickly along the goal line and Jimmy would dart round the back of the defender to pick it up. We had similar routines at throw-ins, too, where we tried to throw markers off the scent.'

Burnley employed a series of coded signals at throw-ins to demonstrate what move was to be used. Two ploys typified Burnley's inventive approach. Both involved McIlroy. In the first set play he would come over to receive a throw-in but the ball would be thrown to someone else, whereupon McIlroy would complain to the nearest opponent, 'He never gives you the ball when you want it.' So, when the next throw-in was awarded to Burnley the defenders were less focused on McIlroy, who immediately became the receiver of the ball. In the second set play, McIlroy would bend down, apparently to fasten his boot laces. The defenders' attention re-focused on other Burnley players but the ball would be thrown to McIlroy who would be off in a flash.

Such deceptions are commonplace these days and are more easily countered but during the late '50s, when the game was being played along largely conventional lines, the range of subterfuges practised by Burnley and Spurs, but few others, were indicative of greater planning.

John Connelly remembered, 'All of the throw-ins and free kick routines on the right-hand side of the pitch Jimmy Adamson would organise. Manager Harry Potts would do them on the other. Even at that early stage, before Jimmy Adamson became coach, he had a large input. He was a natural and a good captain, good at talking to the younger players.'

10.

BALLS AND PITCHES

DURING THE '50s the football's uncoated leather material would easily absorb any surface moisture, doubling its weight so that in wet conditions it became more like a medicine ball. Using the modern, lighter ball, one shot by David Beckham was recorded as reaching a speed of 100mph. However, David Herd, a centre-forward for Arsenal, Manchester United and Stoke City, managed to hit the much heavier ball of the '50s at speeds of almost 75mph. Given the greater heaviness of the ball in Herd's day, it is probable that his shooting was the fiercer of the two. Although the '50s ball was more difficult to strike with as much force as the lighter ball of today, Burnley's Brian Pilkington commented, 'You could master it with practice. It was all a matter of timing.'

Burnley's Jimmy McIlroy remembered, 'In our day no one was expected to score from outside the penalty area. In fact, the goalkeeper would get a right rollicking if anyone did. Today, it is so different. The ball is so much lighter. It bends and dips, too. The first player to bend a ball in my day was Newcastle and Sunderland inside-forward, Len Shackleton, known as the "Clown Prince of Football" for his showy skills and his forthright views on football's inadequacies, particularly club directors. He could make the heavier ball swerve by as much as four feet. It was amazing.'

Jimmy recognised that the heavier ball of the '50s posed a health hazard for those who had to head it frequently, notably the centre-forwards and centre-halves. He added with an ironic smile, 'Not that it caused me a problem because I rarely produced a header.'

Regarding the state of pitches in the '50s, McIlroy observed, 'The pitches are so different today. I regret not playing on such pitches. I remember walking on to the Turf Moor playing surface a few years ago after a period of heavy rain. I was astonished to find how firm it was. I was listening to the Arsenal groundsman recently. He reckoned that the quality of the modern grass surfaces and the lighter weight of today's footballs accounted for the biggest changes in the present game.

'I am sure these factors also contribute to the greater number of injuries experienced today, too. The bounce of the modern ball is so much steeper. You see more players clashing heads as they converge on the higher bouncing ball, their eyes focused upwards rather than upon one another. When we played, referees would allow games to go ahead on surfaces that would not be fit for play today.'

Brian Pilkington added, 'We were at our best in the early season games before the autumn and winter rain. The pitches were firm and smooth at the start of the season. We could play our passing game better then. But by winter most of the pitches had become ploughed fields and once they began to dry out in the early spring, they were horribly rutted and bumpy.'

McIlroy commented, 'We played on some icy surfaces, too, that would not have been allowed today. We were playing Swansea in the FA Cup. There was a sudden change in the weather. It had been wet, but the temperature plummeted overnight causing a sharp frost. The pools of water on the pitch iced over. It was difficult for us to keep on our feet. So, our trainer, Billy Dougall, came up with this idea to help us retain our balance. He replaced our normal studs with ones he had fashioned himself. He tipped the nail with a narrow strip of soft leather that would easily rub off once we were on the pitch. This left us with small spikes which helped us to keep our footing. It might be considered dangerous now although I don't remember this causing any harm!'

11.

A FOOTBALLER'S DIET IN THE '50s

BURNLEY'S JIMMY McIlroy recalled the food players would consume 70 years ago, 'In those days there was a different view about an ideal diet. A typical pre-match lunch consisted of steak, chips, and peas. I used to find this a bit much although I would often have quite a large breakfast. I would watch Ray Pointer, our centre-forward, tuck into a large steak lunch and point out to him that I would be sick after five minutes of the game starting if I had eaten as much as him. Ray would retort that he wouldn't get through the game without it!'

Jimmy Robson added, 'It was left largely up to you what you ate. On matchdays I would normally have a regular English breakfast but would only eat toast before a game. I remember Willie Irvine getting stick for eating fish and chips before a game but then went on to score a hat-trick, so I wondered whether I should do the same.'

The received wisdom in the '50s and early '60s was that a player needed a substantial pre-match meal to build up his energy levels. Gordon Banks recalled that as a Leicester City player in the early '60s a typical feed would comprise a large steak, boiled and roast potatoes plus peas to be followed by a large bowl of rice pudding. Jimmy Greaves remembered that he would often eat a pre-match meal of roast beef and Yorkshire pudding 'with all the trimmings' or pie and mash followed by blackcurrant crumble and custard.

Steak was the Holy Grail, though. No one knew that it took as much as 36 hours to digest steak and that its benefits – protein, strength, and energy – would only be experienced after a few days. It is incredible to think that players managed to get through their games without being violently sick or falling asleep.

McIlroy continued, 'When we were travelling with the club, eating out in those days could be very regimented. I recall a player at another club telling me that their manager had told the coach driver to pull into a café on the way home from a match and, without consulting with the team, ordered fish and chips for all of them. Apparently, one member of his team had requested double helpings of fish, to be told in no uncertain terms by his manager that he would have the same as everyone else!'

12.

FOOTBALLERS' MEDICAL CARE IN THE '50s

IN THE '50s fractures generally took longer to heal and cartilage injuries were much more serious than now. Medial or cruciate ligament injuries were generally career-ending, as with Bolton's Nat Lofthouse and Burnley's Frank Casper and Brian Miller, although another victim, Burnley's Tommy Cummings, eventually returned to the fray.

Burnley's Trevor Meredith remembered that Billy Dougall, the club physio, would use ultrasound to help heal muscle and ligament damage. During the 1959/60 season, Jimmy McIlroy kept Billy very busy indeed as he continued to play through the pain of a persistent groin injury. Jimmy added, 'In those days, injured players often had to play on. There were no substitutes, so you had to get on with it as best you could. In December 1959, we were playing at Arsenal and during the first half my groin went. Instead of being taken off, I played deeper, virtually standing on one leg, but I still managed to dominate the game, fanning passes out to either wing.'

Jimmy explained that he was rarely fit during that season, with either shoulder, groin, or thigh problems, although he missed only 11 games and three of these were because of international commitments.

Meredith added that Dougall also used a hot waxing machine to boost the healing process for muscle, hamstring, and ligament injuries. He said, 'It was an earlier version of the heat and ice treatment. Billy would use this waxing machine to apply a heated mould around the injury and then you would take it off and apply ice.'

Jimmy Robson said, 'The medical back-up was good. We had quick access to a consultant surgeon at Colne Clinic if someone had a serious problem, with a doctor on call, as well. I had reason to be grateful for this because once I bent my large toenail back having kicked a stake when we were playing an impromptu game under the terraces. It hurt like hell, but I kept playing. You did in those days.

'When I'd finished, I could feel a horrible squelching feeling. The boot was full of blood. Billy Dougall suggested taking the nail off, but Dr Iven came in and bent it back into position. Had he not done so I would have been out of the team for the important game on Saturday. If I were to make one reservation about the medical care, I suppose we were propped up too often with cortisone injections. It was the same everywhere. That could not have done us much good. But in those days, without substitutes, you had to play on if you were injured during a game.'

John Angus agreed with his best man. He commented, 'For the most part I stayed pretty fit although I did have trouble with my knee ligaments. That was what brought my career to an end in 1972. There were many occasions when they would pump cortisone into you just to get you going. I am sure that has not helped in the long run. I still get a bit of soreness around my knees. But that was the way it was back then.

'You would often play when not completely fit. There were many times when I found I could not stretch because my muscle injury had not healed properly. Billy Dougall had his heat treatment and ultrasound appliances but I'm not sure they did us much good.'

John Connelly of Burnley and Manchester United remembered this was an era when players played when injured. He said, 'Cortisone injections were commonplace. You played even if you were unfit or injured. Just about the only player who refused to play, if he was not fit, was Denis Law, "The King". He could stand up to Busby. He wouldn't play if unfit although that wasn't very often.'

13.

FOOTBALLERS' PAY AND CONDITIONS OF SERVICE IN THE '50s

JOHN ANGUS said, 'Soon after I started at Burnley I was apprenticed as a joiner. One of the Burnley directors sorted that out for me. We were all encouraged to take up a trade. It was hard going in those early years, particularly when I started doing my national service at Bank Hall Colliery. I was employed as a joiner there. Although the Coal Board were good about letting us players have time off for football, we still did almost a full day's work with training and night school to fit in during the evenings. It was slower getting around then. It took around an hour to get from my digs in Brierfield to Gawthorpe on the bus. Then there was a tidy walk from the bus stop down the long drive to the training ground. There was not much time to yourself.

'In those days I was earning around £7–£8 per week as a part-timer with Burnley. That compared well with what most working people were getting but it was not a huge sum. I didn't get my first second hand car, an Austin Somerset, until 1957 or 1958 when I was 19 or 20. By that time I was established in the first team and earning around £15 per week with a win bonus of £2 and a draw bonus of £1. Once I got the car, I could drive to Gawthorpe or Turf Moor. On matchdays I would park further up Brunshaw Road and walk down the hill to the ground. Having the car cut the journey times but I did not mind mixing with the supporters on the bus. They would chat away to you and ask you how you thought the last game went or how the next game might go. It kept you in touch and helped keep your feet on the ground.'

To put these pay details into context, in 1959, the national average weekly wage was £11 2s. Consequently, a professional footballer's maximum weekly wage was £20, 80 per cent higher than the national average, although considerably lower than what top entertainers might gain. For example, Fulham's chairman, comedian Tommy Trinder, was paid around £100 per week as the compere of ITV's *Sunday Night at the London Palladium*. Also, £20 per week would be paid only to the top performers. Stewart Imlach, Nottingham Forest's Scottish international winger and man of the match at the 1959 FA Cup Final, was offered £20 per week for the 1959/60 season, but only while he remained a first-team regular. This figure fell to £15 per week if he was dropped. As was the custom then, summer-season wages were paid at a lower rate. For him, this was also £15 per week.

Jimmy McIlroy recalled, 'You were at the club's mercy over what you could earn. There was always the possibility of doing a bit of coaching on the side or some summer work, like helping out the groundsman but it didn't add up to much. Some of the team had work with the National Coal Board but that was part of their National Service. Those on National Service often received preferential treatment, as did Brian Pilkington during his period with the RAF.

'As a professional footballer on a full-time contract you were committed to the club. Your freedom to earn more was limited. It was made clear to me that if I wanted to increase my income, I would need to join one of the London clubs, where I could use the higher public profile to secure advertising deals. Denis Compton, of Arsenal and Middlesex, was one of the first top sportsmen to cash in on this opportunity when he advertised Brylcreem. Jimmy Greaves of Chelsea advertised Bovril. But Burnley would not let me go. I wasn't resentful, though. After all, I was getting £20 per week while local tradesmen were earning around £7.

'In 1957, I was sufficiently well off to buy my first car – an Austin 7. Not many players had cars then. A few had second-hand ones, like mine, but most of us were still reliant upon public transport or upon lifts given by better-off supporters. A son of a local businessman would drive me to some of the local games, such as at Blackburn. I can also remember shelling out for our first continental holiday – a week in Ibiza for £52! That seemed quite an outlay then.

'We were helped also by the club housing policy. As a married couple we were allocated a club house in 1954 for which we paid a rent of £1 per week. At that time, my earnings would have been around £15 per week. We were also given an allowance for decorating the house and I recall one of the Burnley directors creating a bit of a fuss when he thought we had been a bit extravagant.'

Trevor Meredith agreed that it was difficult for players to supplement their income. He said that during the summer months when he was at Shrewsbury he worked in a nursery and hoed sugar beet but at Burnley opportunities were more limited. He agreed with McIlroy that there was the possibility of helping the groundsman, but these jobs were not very lucrative. He was not surprised, therefore, that there was solid support for the action mounted by the Professional Footballers' Association (PFA) to challenge the maximum wage cap. He recalled that the senior players at the club led the action locally and Tommy Cummings was the Burnley players' PFA representative.

14.

STARTING OUT AS A PROFESSIONAL FOOTBALLER

IN 1962, Burnley captain Jimmy Adamson said, 'Care was taken in bringing young players to the club. As soon as a youngster arrives at Turf Moor, he is made to feel part of Burnley Football Club. He is assured of his place here. Every young player arriving at Turf Moor is guaranteed four or five years on the staff. In that time, he gets the chance to learn the game. He is not tossed out if he fails to live up to expectations in one season. The only reason he may go is if he does not measure up off the field. If he wants, the lad can be apprenticed to a trade [this was mandatory in the '50s when National Service still applied] or he goes on the ground staff, doing all the odd jobs. There is always one ground staff lad with the first team – looking after the kit.'

John Angus recalled his introduction to the life of a professional footballer, 'Charlie Ferguson, the Burnley scout, spotted me while I was playing for Amble. Newcastle was the nearest league team, but I knew I had no chance there because they bought many of their players. So, off I went to Burnley. It was quite a journey in those days, involving a change of train at Newcastle, York, and Leeds and two bus journeys. It took ages. I remember finally getting off the train at Manchester Road Station in Burnley. That is the station halfway up the hill above Burnley town centre.

'I looked down on this town with its many mill chimneys and smoggy atmosphere. It was quite unlike anything I had experienced – coming from a small Northumbrian fishing village. When my wife and I were first married we lived on the hill overlooking Turf Moor and on matchdays we'd frequently look down on this thick smog engulfing the town and ground and think, "There's no chance of the game being played today." But usually we would be wrong. Once you got down there it would be okay to play, though it was very murky.

'I started off in digs in Brierfield with Jimmy Robson, who later became my best man. Although we were made to feel welcome there, I was always pleased to get home. As soon as the season ended, I would return to Northumberland. That is where I met my wife. Most of my team-mates married Burnley girls. Perhaps that's why so many stayed here after they finished playing.'

Bob Seith remembered, 'I started as an apprentice at Burnley in 1948. Cliff Britton was the club manager. He was a dour, censorious man who warned us not to use the snooker halls in town, instructing us to use the table at the club. He thought public snooker halls were occupied by "neer-do-well" types. One day he asked me to accompany him on a walk to the top of an adjacent hill. He said nothing until we arrived.

'Looking down at the town below there was a heavy pall of industrial pollution engulfing it, the product of many tall mill chimneys and nearby pits. With a sweep of his arm Cliff Britton said, "Remember, down there are hard-working folk who labour for five and a half days a week. It is our DUTY to entertain them on a Saturday afternoon." This biblical-like instruction remained with me to this day. We then returned to the club, not saying a word to one another.'

Jimmy Robson added, 'When I first came down to Burnley, I was dreadfully homesick. Remember, I came from a small mining village. I had not seen much life outside. A lot of us were like that. Those first three months here were hard. The digs were good, but I knew that the big test would come after I went home for the first time. Anyway, I came back and stayed here since – apart from a spell when we moved to Blackpool, which was nice. A lot of us stayed here because we married Burnley women. It really is not as bad as Jimmy Greaves made out. He must have arrived from the wrong direction. There is so much lovely countryside around. Life in Burnley has been good.'

Tommy Cummings recalled, 'I arrived by train in a place called Todmorden and I hadn't been on many train journeys before. I was like a little boy looking out of the window and taking everything in. There was somebody from the club to meet me and we caught the bus to Burnley where they had arranged digs for me. There was another lodger, a Pole, who was working at the pit, but when the landlady proposed taking in a third, it would have been too cramped, so I was moved to lodgings near the ground.'

These were the pre-celebrity years when footballers did not have expectations of lucrative lifestyles and remained grounded with family values they had inherited from their working-class parents. Spurs' brilliant inside-forward Eddie Baily, a star of the championship-winning 'push and run' side and an England international, described his modest '50s lifestyle thus, 'After a home game I would meet my wife outside and we would walk home together, perhaps picking up some fish and chips on the way.'

15.

SO MUCH FOR THE 'BEAUTIFUL GAME'! HARD MEN IN THE '50s

BURNLEY WINGER Brian Pilkington thought full-back Don Megson of Sheffield Wednesday was one chap he disliked playing against, stating he could be reckless. A Wednesday fan described Megson as 'built like a Sherman tank, a master of the sliding tackle'. Another of Brian's bete noires was John Sillett, of Chelsea. Pilkington said, 'You didn't get much protection in those days.' Trevor Meredith agreed, remarking, 'You had to use your skills to evade the punishment these players dished out. If you were quick, you were mostly okay because these full-backs would dive in and you could nip around them. But there were always a few who would hurt you if they caught you. Bolton's Roy Hartle would whack you down.'

Burnley's John Connelly singled out Megson and Hartle, too, as particularly tough opponents. He said, 'I scored goals from the wing and that meant going in where it hurt. Probably the hardest opponent I faced was Megson. When he walloped you, it shook you up. Bolton had a big side as well with Tommy Banks at full-back. He was hard but I was lucky he was just ending his career as I was starting. He was never fast and when I played against him, he was even slower.

'Mind you, there was one game when I thought I would switch wings with Brian Pilkington to get away from him. Then I looked across and saw it was Roy Hartle on the other side, so I stayed where I was. You knew you were going to get wellied, but you got up and got on with it. The boots we wore in those days were like concrete. They were so stiff, you had to break them in and wear them a few times at Gawthorpe to soften them before you could ever wear them for 90 minutes in a game. And we didn't get a new pair every couple of weeks. They were repaired repeatedly at Cockers in Burnley.'

Pilkington reckoned that Blackpool's Jimmy Armfield and West Bromwich and Arsenal's Don Howe were the best full-backs that he faced while at Burnley. Both were England internationals and were renowned for their creative play. Trevor thought Huddersfield and Everton's Ray Wilson was the best full-back he played against. Like Armfield, Wilson possessed great pace as well as supreme ability.

Jimmy Robson added, 'There were a lot of tough defenders in those days, who were happiest if they could engage you in a physical battle. We were a naturally fit side and we had players with real pace – Ray Pointer, John Connelly and "Pilky". So, we tried to pull these defenders around to create the spaces to exploit. We did not play with a target man as they do today. There was no point trying to play with your back to goal, trying to screen the ball. You would just get one of those hefty centre-halves come clattering through the back of you, sending both you and the ball back as far as you had come. There was little protection from referees. They allowed tackles from behind. No, you had to learn to lay the ball off first time before you got hit. That was not easy, though.

'The pitches were generally poor – they were either thick with mud or, like at Easter time, when they were often bone hard and bobbly. Either way, the ball bounced erratically giving defenders a big advantage, so you had to perfect your technique in these difficult conditions. I remember when I first started at Burnley as a kid. I had this big guy up against me – Eric Binns. He went straight through me as soon as I got the ball – totally flattened me. There I was lying in the mud thinking "this isn't right" but there was no one to protect me. You had to look after yourself. None of my team-mates said a word, but I knew what they were thinking, "This is part and parcel of the game and you'd better get used to it!"'

In reflecting upon the toughest opponents that he faced during his career, Robson commented, 'Looking back, I guess the most difficult players I have had to face in my career were Bobby Cram of West Bromwich and the Sheffield Wednesday and Bolton defenders. When I was at Burnley, I found a real problem in getting the better of Bobby. The funny thing was that when I moved to Blackpool, I started to get more joy in my tussles with him – it's strange, that. Sheffield Wednesday and Bolton were tough teams to play against. Wednesday had Peter Swan, Tony Kay, and Don Megson. They were a handful – very physical. Bolton had Tommy Banks, Roy Hartle, John Higgins and so on. Roy Hartle was well spoken, but on the pitch he was tough. Generally, I thought all these players played fairly. I cannot remember getting the sly punches or kicks that players have doled out since.'

Burnley's Jimmy McIlroy was less sanguine about the standards of fairness. He recalled, 'I was playing against an England under-23 defender. I anticipated a hard match against a skilful adversary, but my illusions were soon shattered. In the first minute, this future England ambassador had whipped my legs from me! Later, as the two of us went up to head a centre, he hit me, by no means accidentally, across the face and sent me reeling. I was livid as I struggled off the ground, but the referee, an experienced official, took me on one side and said, "Keep cool, Mac. I saw what he did." Coming off at half-time, considerably bruised, I said to the referee, "What chance has England of ever winning anything when clowns like that are honoured?" He said simply, "I've thought that for some time now."'

It was not just the outfield players who took the hard knocks. In the '50s and early '60s, goalkeepers were often charged by opposing forwards. They needed to be hardy souls. Adam Blacklaw confirmed this, 'You had to look after yourself as a goalkeeper. They would shoulder charge you, so you had to be prepared. I was a big lad, about 15 stone, so I always reckoned I could give as good as I got. The funny thing was that one of the worst offenders was Jimmy Greaves. He was such a gentleman off the pitch, such an amusing man, but he would scrape you across your shins if you didn't look out. I used to warn these fellas, "Any funny stuff and you'll get more than you bargained for." I took smelling salts out with me along with my string gloves and flat cap. You had to be prepared.'

In his book *The Life of a 1950s Footballer*, Spurs' reserve goalkeeper Ron Reynolds detailed the many horrific injuries he sustained during his career when most forwards called open season on the guys between the sticks. An article in the *1959 Big Book of Football Champions* posed the question, 'Is Football Too Rough?' This followed eight top goalkeepers sustaining serious injuries after incidents of rough play.

International stoppers such as Colin McDonald, Jack Kelsey, and Bill Brown suffered nasty injuries. Lower-division Accrington Stanley had been forced to field right-back Bob McNichol in goal after all three of their keepers had been injured by over-robust challenges. Referees did not look after those between the posts back then as they do now.

Just like Adam, many goalkeepers were prepared to ward off potential aggressors. Villa's combative Irish left-winger Peter McParland confirmed this, recounting how Chelsea's England international Reg Matthews once 'decked' him to make sure he stayed his distance. Of course, McParland's charge on Manchester United's Ray Wood in the 1957 FA Cup Final represented the other side of the coin. The collision left Wood with a fractured cheekbone, torpedoing United's chances of winning the double. Nat Lofthouse's challenge upon Harry Gregg in the Wembley final of the following year left Gregg in pain for several minutes although he was not injured as badly as Wood.

Despite the disastrous consequences of shoulder-charging goalkeepers, '50s players seemed divided about its legitimacy. Sam Bartram, who was an outstanding goalkeeper with Charlton during the '40s and '50s, thought that forwards should be allowed to charge the custodian, claiming, 'Soccer is a man's game and goalkeepers should not be wrapped in cotton wool.' Trevor Churchill, an FA coach, added, 'If the shoulder charge is outlawed, we'll see the undesirable practice of goalies bouncing the ball to waste time.'

Former Birmingham and England man Gil Merrick disagreed, maintaining that shoulder-charging was not beneficial to goalkeeping or to the game. West Bromwich's international centre-forward Ronnie Allen supported Merrick as did Burnley's Ray Pointer. Pointer commented in 1963, 'I'm sometimes asked why I don't indulge in the traditional British centre-forward practice of charging goalkeepers when they are in possession. Well, to begin with I do not like the idea. And secondly, with my weight of under 11 stones, I should often come off second best. Some of those goalkeepers are hefty fellows and if I did much charging, I should find myself crocked in no time. No, I keep close to goalkeepers in possession so that if he drops the ball or misses his kick, I am on the spot to take advantage of it, but otherwise I leave him alone. I don't find myself penalised for it by foreign referees as some of our centre-forwards do.'

Pointer remembered his clashes with Spurs with affection, 'We knew how they would play and vice versa. So, we knew we had to do something different if we were to get the better of them. Maurice Norman, the Spurs centre-half, was probably the most difficult defender I faced during my career. He was a hard player but not dirty. To be honest I do not think there were outright dirty players although there were certainly many hard tacklers. There was not any nastiness that I can recall. After all, they were your mates. We would talk to one another, sometimes during the game.'

The 1962 FA Cup Final between Burnley and Spurs was a shining example of sporting behaviour. It was an enthralling exhibition of fast, cut and thrust, attacking football, played with skill and determination but devoid of niggling fouls or antagonism that sully so many games today. Although the Burnley players were deeply disappointed, having come second in both the league and FA Cup, their behaviour was exemplary, warmly congratulating the victors at the end of the game. Both sides set a challenging standard for the pampered and petulant modern stars.

The main teams to beat in 1959/60 were Spurs and Wolves. As indicated by Pointer and Greaves, the Spurs games were remembered with fondness. The Wolves games were physically tougher, though. Brian Pilkington recalled, 'Wolves were difficult to break down. They played to a strict plan. Stan Cullis, their manager, was as much of a disciplinarian as our Alan Brown had been. They had these powerful six-foot defenders. When we played them at Molineux in March 1960, they hammered us 6-1. I am not sure what happened. I think they caught us on an off day. It did not shake us up too much, though.'

Bob Seith added, 'At Burnley we didn't fear anyone really. Wolves were difficult to beat. They were not necessarily the most skilful side we faced but they played to their strengths. Their wing-halves, Flowers and Clamp, would hit balls into the corners for their wingers to chase. Peter Broadbent, their inside-left, had skill, capable of hitting accurate 30-yard passes to his wingers, but their success relied heavily upon a physical, direct style of play. As for individual tough opponents, Jimmy Scoular, the Scottish wing-half, was about as tough as they came. Blackburn Rovers had this Scots winger called

Alistair MacLeod. He was certainly one for shooting a line as he did when taking Scotland to the World Cup finals in Argentina in 1978. MacLeod reckoned that he was a bit of a hard case himself and claimed that he would sort out Scoular. When Bob told this story to Sir Alex Ferguson, Fergy treated it with withering contempt. "Oh aye," Fergy said, "I believe if Scoular had been at the OK Corral then Wyatt Earp wouldn't have turned up."'

Bob reckoned that among the most skilful players he faced while at Burnley were Tom Finney, Jimmy Greaves, then of Chelsea, Bobby Charlton and Jimmy Hagan of Sheffield United. Of Greaves, Bob said, 'Jimmy was so quick around the goal – a brilliant finisher, so composed.' He thought that Charlton was the more complete player, though. He said, 'Bobby had two great feet and, boy, did he have a fierce shot on him. I recall Billy Dougall telling me that it was better to make a clearing header in two stages – the ball was so heavy in those days. He told me to head the ball up in the air and then complete the clearance with a volley. Billy was always bringing you down a peg or two – he was loath to give you any credit. Anyway, I followed his advice. The trouble was that my partial header reached Charlton before I could hack the ball clear. Without hesitating, Charlton unleashed this volley. It caught me square on my left thigh. The shot was so powerful that an imprint of the ball's panel remained on that thigh for a week. Had the shot been slightly to my right, I'd have been turned into a soprano.'

John Angus reckoned, 'One of the most difficult opponents I had to deal with was Cliff Jones, Spurs' left-winger. He was very direct and very quick. He was a good finisher, too. He developed this knack of getting in behind you and rising to head in right-wing crosses at the far post. While I was preparing for such a cross, it was difficult to keep track of Jones. In training I was instructed to position myself, so my body was turned around more to the right. This enabled me to track Jones's runs but at the same time to keep an eye on the balls coming over from the opposite flank. Then, there was only three defenders. Both full-backs needed to cover the centre-half, watching for the high crosses which might go over his head.

'Peter McParland, the Aston Villa left-winger, was one of the most physical opponents I faced. He never gave any quarter and was the hardest player of my era. Tom Finney and Stan Matthews were coming to the end of their careers, although Stan went on to play until he was 50 years old. Finney was two-footed, very skilful, and direct whereas Stan was tricky with that wonderful burst of speed over 15 yards.

'The fastest player I saw was Blackpool's winger, Bill Perry. Bobby Mitchell of Newcastle was another difficult winger, although, like Stan and Tom, he was coming to the end of his career in the late '50s. It was a privilege to play against these stars that I had looked up to as a 15-year-old playing for my local side, Amble. Of course, George Best was a real handful but one winger who always gave me a difficult time was Clive Clark of West Bromwich. Peter Thompson at Liverpool was some winger, too, a right-footed left-winger!'

16.

PLAYERS' CONTACT WITH SUPPORTERS AND THE PUBLIC IN THE '50s

BURNLEY'S JIMMY Robson said, 'There was not any of this celebrity thing in the '50s. We would mix with the Burnley public on the bus or in the shops. We did not think we were that special except that we were being paid to do something we loved. Working with the miners at Bank Hall Colliery helped keep our feet on the ground. They'd give you some stick if you hadn't come up to scratch and rightly so – they'd paid their money and were entitled to their opinions.'

His club colleagues Brian Pilkington and Trevor Meredith remembered that life as a footballer in the late '50s and '60s was different from the remote, celebrity life of their modern counterparts. Brian said, 'We just blended in. We would travel on the buses alongside other local people. I remained living in Leyland, so I would catch the 8am bus to Burnley each day to get to training. So, supporters would come up to me for a chat and that was fine.

'There were some days when you wanted a bit of peace and quiet. Some days I would be riding home on the top of the bus just as one of the local shifts was ending. If I felt a bit tired and didn't fancy talking, I would hide myself behind my paper. But that was rare. You just got on with your life just like everyone else.'

Trevor added, 'Burnley had a reputation for being an accessible team. When the first team travelled to London, the autograph hunters made a beeline for us because they knew we would sign. They would be waiting at the platform as we boarded the train home.'

17.

CODE OF CONDUCT

BURNLEY'S BOB Seith remembered, 'Burnley was so small. You could not get away with anything without the whole town knowing. Everyone knew if you broke the rules, so there was no point in trying.'

Jimmy Robson continued, 'Life here was settled and pretty well disciplined. The discipline was mostly self-imposed. We knew the rules. Nobody had to read the riot act to us. We knew how to behave. We went out but rarely drank much. We were in at sensible times. We looked after ourselves. It was a good club to be at, a family club where both the players and their wives were close with one another.'

18.

RELATIONSHIPS
WITH THE PRESS

A BENEFIT of having a lower profile in the '50s was that the players were not continually preyed upon by the media. Burnley's Jimmy McIlroy remarked, 'Despite Bob Lord's criticisms of press intrusions, the relationship we had with the press was good. In the '50s and '60s they were primarily sports writers. Their main interest was what was happening on the field of play. They were often our friends, regularly coming out with us, playing snooker, for example. We were not worried whether we would be exposed or misquoted. You could trust them more. They would respect confidences. From that point of view, it was better then. We may not have earned as much as modern players, but we had more freedom.'

19.

MOVING ON

WHILE THE Burnley players remembered the strong family atmosphere at the club with great fondness, they were very aware of their status as hired hands with a limited shelf life. Ray Pointer spoke of his sadness about leaving, saying that he would have accepted reserve football to stay, but ultimately accepted moving on with equanimity. Trevor Meredith spoke in similar terms. Jimmy Robson added, 'When it came to it, I didn't really want to leave. I was prepared to play in the reserves, too, but the club was right. They had other players coming through like Willie Irvine. That was often the case then, if you were replaced, it was because younger players were coming through the ranks.'

Although his chances of progression were restricted on account of the strength of the first team squad, Trevor said that he always felt an integral part of the Burnley team, while accepting that there was always going to be tough competition for first team places. He said that it was only when he reached his late 20s and when new stars like Willie Morgan and Ralph Coates were coming through that he decided he would move on. Trevor was satisfied with his transfer in April 1964. He explained, 'Shrewsbury was a bit like going home. You see, I grew up on a farm in Shropshire, so this was familiar territory. I knew I was coming to the end of my career, so I was quite prepared to move down a couple of divisions. I was happy to be offered a contract by player-manager Arthur Rowley, the brother of Manchester United's Jack Rowley, and a scorer of a record 434 goals in 619 league games. This contract determined that my wage would increase according to the size of the crowd at Gay Meadow. Not that there was too much scope for major increases at Shrewsbury.'

Brian Pilkington had greater misgivings about his departure, though. He commented, 'I had chances to move on before I was transferred to Bolton in February 1961. Manchester United were interested in me after the Munich crash but the club would not let me go. So, it came as a big surprise when Harry Potts told me that I was going to Bolton, particularly after I had just scored two goals in our European Cup win over Hamburg. Before we played the second leg in Germany I was gone.

'It did not really make sense at the time. I was in the first team, I was playing well, I was scoring, I was doing everything right. However, Harry Potts called me in to the office. He says at first, "There's some teams interested in you." There was Everton, Preston North End, Blackpool, and Bolton Wanderers. He said I had a choice where to go. I replied, "Oh, well no, I'm all right. Everything is okay here. But do you want me to go or what?" He then said, making it clear there was no choice, "Well put it this way, the chairman's agreed terms with Bolton. It is out of my hands. You will have to speak with him." So, I tried to get hold of Bob Lord but every time I attempted to contact him, I was told he wasn't available. In the end I had no choice. I had to go to Bolton.

'With hindsight, I should have called his bluff and said, "I'm not moving," but at that time there wasn't the player power that there is now. There was no freedom of contract. In those days they could just retain you and you could do nothing about it. I was only 26 or 27 at the time. I had probably another six or seven years in me. I should have stopped here. Bob Lord and Harry Potts said afterwards, "We should never have let you go." But they had Gordon Harris coming through. He was a good player. So, I ended up at Bolton. I was not very happy there, though. They played a different game to what I had been used to at Burnley. They kept pumping long balls over the top of me. My head was forever swivelling back and forth.'

There was little security for a professional footballer then. Contracts were for one season only and, as Stewart Imlach found at Nottingham Forest, clubs often dictated terms. Gordon Banks said, 'If a club decided to sell a player, he had to uproot and move home and family to wherever he'd been sold. If the club did not want the services of a player anymore, he was never told in person. He simply received the dreaded "not retained" letter at the end of the season – the signal for him to pack his bags and leave. Even if we had a voice in these matters, no one would have listened. Players were seen by the clubs as commodities, to be hired and fired, bought, or sold. There were no agents or personal advisers to look after our interests, no heart-to-heart chats with the manager and certainly no mollycoddling.'

Under the 'retain and transfer' system, a football club could then keep hold of a player's registration – his licence to play – when his contract had expired, irrespective of his or his family's wishes. If a player refused to comply and pushed for a transfer, as was the case with George Eastham at Newcastle in 1960, the club could prevent him from playing for another club by refusing to relinquish his registration. It was small wonder that the Professional Footballers' Association complained that the system represented 'soccer slavery'. Eastham contested this practice, claiming it was on 'unlawful restraint of trade'. In 1963, the High Court agreed.

20.

HOW THE '50s GAME COMPARES WITH TODAY

BURNLEY'S JIMMY Robson observed, 'When I look at the modern game and see so few English players playing at the very top of our game now, I start to wonder whether this is because life nowadays is generally much more comfortable. I see youngsters in the academies. There are a lot of youngsters below the age of ten who look as if they could make it – loads of talent, brilliant skills – but somewhere along the line, before the age of 16, a lot fall by the wayside.

'I wonder whether it is because so many of them have had easier lives than we had – things are laid on for them, they are less fit having been carted around so much and stuck in front of computers for hours. They do not seem so hungry as we were, brought up in hard times during and after the war. Our hunger for success and the good things that went with it was possibly greater. We probably had more knocks, too, so we learnt to cope with distressing or disappointing circumstances.

'I wonder whether we have more Africans playing at the top now because more of them have that hunger we had to drive them on and build up their skills – the hunger that makes you play and practise for hours on end.'

Brian Pilkington lamented what he saw as the negative style of play adopted by modern club and national sides. He said, 'There's too much focus on what the opposition is doing. They should concentrate more on their own strengths. I cannot understand all this bunching that goes on, either. When a goalkeeper is taking a goal kick, you see both sides grouped in one small part of the field. Surely it makes better sense for at least the wingers to spread the play by moving away from the crowd?'

Jimmy McIlroy agreed. He said, 'I cannot imagine that current top sides have the same thoughts about winning as we did. Keeping possession seems to have disproportionate importance. Stopping the other side from scoring seems more important than scoring themselves. In my playing days, if a bottom team faced a top team, the emphasis was on, "Let us get this lot licked," not, "Let us stop this lot from scoring." Today's managers are much more frightened of losing their jobs.'

Regarding match officials, Bob Seith said, 'Yes, it is different. Referees give the ball players more protection than they did in my day, but I think the degree of regulation now is excessive. What it has done is to drive tackling underground. I am sure that is why there are more niggling, nasty fouls today. It was a physically harder game in my day, but I think that generally it was played more fairly, too.'

There have been vast changes in the rewards gained by the top professionals. The top teams today appear better equipped to defend a lead. The leading Premier League strikers are probably more ruthless in converting chances despite having a slightly inferior ratio of goals to games than their predecessors in 1959/60. The modern strikers are not blessed with the open spaces afforded to the forwards of 50 years ago. They must contend with massed, tactically astute defenders. Nevertheless, most goals are still scored from three or fewer passes. Also, between a quarter and a third of goals still arise from set plays (see page 82).

21.

THE SNARL OF THE UNDERDOG IN THE '50s

BRIAN PILKINGTON told me, 'An ordinary player needs three touches to control the ball, a good player requires two, but a great player needs only one. I moved to Fourth Division Barrow towards the end of my playing career. I enjoyed my time there, but the players at this level did not think quite as quickly as those in higher divisions. They did not see attacking opportunities as sharply as I did nor spot the potential dangers soon enough. Their touch was not as good; their passing was less accurate and timely; their positioning was not as reliable; their shooting was not as precise; and their running off the ball was not as smart.'

If Brian's assessment was correct, surely top-flight teams should always prevail over sides two or three divisions below them. And yet during the '50s there were extraordinary FA Cup feats performed by lower-division teams, repeatedly overturning supposedly superior opposition. Incredibly, three Third Division clubs, Port Vale (see opposite), York City (see page 120) and Norwich City (see page 161) progressed as far as the semi-finals during this decade. Previously, only one unfancied lower division side had managed to go as far, Millwall in 1937. Third Division Swindon went one step further in 1969, beating Arsenal at Wembley in the Football League Cup Final (see page 357).

22.

VALIANT VALE: PORT VALE'S AMAZING FA CUP RUN, 1953/54

DURING THE austere post-war period, Burslem, like so many towns and cities in bomb-cratered Britain, recognised the urgency of restoring full industrial production to recover local and national prosperity. There was no time for anything that did not meet this objective. And yet here, amid the noxious fumes from the clustered chimneys and vast, domed kilns, an ambitious plan was being hatched to provide its nomadic football club, Port Vale, with a new stadium. It would be described fancifully as a 'Wembley of the North' with a projected 70,000 capacity.

While many fans were excited, calling the plan 'brave and visionary', others saw this as an act of lunacy given this time of want. Unabashed, the Vale supporters' club launched a major fund-raising effort, attempting to generate £30,000 towards the mega-project. Despite the scepticism, 12,000 turned up in torrential rain to see the nascent construction. But progress was slow, despite a £50,000 investment. There was a shortage of necessary materials on account of priority being given to post-war reconstruction. By the time the ground opened on 24 August 1950 for a Third Division fixture with Newport, it was still uncovered, and had only temporary dressing rooms. Nevertheless, a record crowd of 30,042 witnessed the longed-for new dawn.

Yet disillusionment spread as a succession of teething problems bugged the development. The promise of 70,000 seats was way off the mark. Only 1,000 were installed and there was a frustrating wait for covered accommodation. Some fans longed for a return to the Old Recreation Ground in Hanley, which was tight and compact, helping generate a febrile atmosphere, whereas the wide-open spaces of Vale Park dissipated the raucous cheers. Vale Park was exposed, too, on a hill, making it the second highest Football League ground in England. West Ham fans have had similar misgivings about leaving their compact Boleyn Ground for the London Stadium. Moreover, Vale were hardly ripping up trees. By the end of the '40s the club was in the bottom third of the lowest division.

Then came the catalyst for a remarkable change of fortunes as Vale appointed Freddie 'Nobby' Steele as their player-manager. Steele came with a huge reputation. He had played six times for England, scoring eight goals. He had scored 140 times for bitter rivals Stoke City and, more recently, 39 for Mansfield. The partisan Valiants swallowed their pride and prejudices for Steele's impact was huge and immediate. In his first full campaign, he guided his new club to second spot in the Third Division (North).

In that 1952/53 season, his side raised their goals for quotient by 17, or 34 per cent, while reducing their goals against figure by 31, or 53 per cent. Something special was happening. In the following season, Port Vale were runaway winners of the Third Division (North) amassing 67 points, 95 with today's scoring system, and conceding only 21 goals in 42 games, with just five at home. This was a new club and Football League record low.

Goalkeeper Ray King might have gone before the season started. It was just as well that Steele changed his mind for King kept a club record 39 clean sheets, protected by an almost impregnable iron or 'Steele' curtain. Vale's defence was one of the best in the land.

Their defence was founded upon a pioneering flat back four, comprising captain Tommy Cheadle, Reg Potts, Stan Turner, and formidable giant Roy Sproson. They lost only three league games, one of which was at Workington, then managed by Bill Shankly. Their phenomenal success was achieved without any recognised stars. The local newspaper, *The Sentinel*, put that right, acclaiming the whole team as stars. Who would disagree?

How did they manage to achieve this improbable success? Firstly, everyone became incredibly fit, setting a standard not seen before in English football. Pre-season training, led by assistant manager Ken

Fish, included daily 10km runs from Burslem to Hanley and back with a swift half-pint of shandy at the end. After returning, Fish organised a practice game. When the winter rain set in, turning every ground in the Football League into a quagmire, Vale were better equipped to deal with this than most.

Secondly, Steele was a tactical wizard. Fish explained, 'Steele was light years ahead of anyone else. He played a 4-4-2 formation, just as Alf Ramsey did in winning the 1966 World Cup. Both wingers, Askey and Cunliffe, were withdrawn, bombing forward when possession was gained, but hastening back whenever it was lost. Nobby expected his wide men to put in the tackles, helping shepherd their opponents away from the danger zone. We always had eight to ten players behind the ball when possession was lost. The stamina we built up in pre-season meant that everyone could run and run without stopping, whether attacking, or defending. We had scorching pace, too. Our counter-attacking game worked a treat.

'Then there was our versatility. We had defenders who could score. Right-back Cheadle had played up front before, scoring seven times in 16 games. We had midfielders who could score. Our two forwards, Hayward and Leake, were good defenders as were our wingers. Our centre-forward, Basil Hayward, was previously a centre-half and an accomplished right-back. Roy Sproson could play in several positions: at centre-half; left-back; and left-half. Moreover, when he completed his career in 1972, he had scored 30 goals for us.

'But fitness and versatility are not enough without togetherness. Everyone was hugely committed. There were no prima donnas here. Everyone grafted for one another. I should mention another matter, superstition. This really mattered to Steele. He ensured that the team stuck rigidly to their pre-match rituals such as how the kit was laid out and the order in which players left the dressing room.' Don Revie must have been watching.

In 1953/54 Port Vale not only ripped up records in league football, they threatened to do the same in the FA Cup. In the first three rounds they disposed of Darlington 3-1 at Feethams, having come from behind, overcame Southport 2-0 after a 1-1 struggle at Haig Avenue, and squeezed past QPR 1-0 at Loftus Road with a second-half goal. Their biggest test thus far came in the fourth round when they were drawn against well-placed First Division side Cardiff City.

In the Ninian Park snow, Port Vale skated to a fine 2-0 victory. Fish remembered, 'Cardiff were impressed with our right-winger, Colin Askey, who murdered them on that snowy afternoon. First, they offered a £30,000 fee, a massive figure, worth about £30m today. Jackie Sewell's transfer fee of £35,000 in 1951 had raised eyebrows! But this offer was incredible! "Too good to miss," some said. Not for us though. We turned Cardiff down. It was said they then sent us a blank cheque to prise him away. It made no difference. We knew Colin's worth. We turned them down again. Colin remained at Vale Park.'

In the next round, Vale faced holders Blackpool. It was a nostalgic journey for Blackpool's famous winger Stanley Matthews, who was born in neighbouring Hanley. Saturday 20 February 1954 was a sparkling day, enticing an enormous 42,000 crowd to Vale Park. Despite the popularity of Matthews, most there were rooting for a Vale victory and how they made themselves heard! Blackpool's exuberant 'Atomic Boys' were there in force, with their huge rosettes, comic hats and suits, webbed feet, rattles, bells and bags with 'Matthews Soccer Ambassadors' written on them. One Port Vale fan with a gigantic black and white umbrella unsuccessfully attempted to block their circuit of the ground. In the dazzling February sunshine, it was the only contest that went Blackpool's way.

Some fans, unable to get hold of or afford tickets, perched on the roofs of the adjacent houses. The pitch was a mess, boggy, grassless, and heavily sanded in the middle although the wings were grassed and firmer. Steele wanted to stop Matthews using the drier flanks. He instructed his players to drive him inside, where the mud would impede his explosive sprints. Left-back Reg Potts was told to hug the touchline to stop Matthews bursting through on his left side. Meanwhile, rugged centre-back Sproson and withdrawn left-winger Dickie Cunliffe created a roadblock in front of Matthews when he ventured inside. Frustrated, Matthews returned to the right flank, hoping to evade Potts with his nifty footwork and speed off the mark. But he was no better off here. While he was held up by Potts, Cunliffe nipped in to dispossess him.

At the other end, sought-after winger Askey set up several chances with his smart dribbling and defence-splitting passes. He remembered, 'I could hardly believe I was seeing Stanley Matthews, let alone playing against him. Thankfully, it was not one of his best games. We knew how much damage he could cause if he got to the goal line. Our plan to drive him into the mud worked superbly. Without Matthews doing his tricks, Blackpool were toothless. Winning was such a brilliant feeling. I was walking on air for days after.'

With Port Vale pressing pugnaciously, Blackpool struggled to get into the game. Matthews stood up an oblique cross for Mortensen at the far post. Immediately hemmed in by Sproson, Mortensen's header was weak and easily snatched by King.

Vale broke with menacing speed despite the oozing mud. Having forced a succession of corners on the left, Cunliffe crossed his fourth effort long and high towards the far post where Leake easily out-jumped Hugh Kelly and headed across Farm and into the far corner of the net. Culpably, Blackpool right-back Shimwell deserted his post. Ten minutes later, Griffiths and Cunliffe combined to send speedy Hayward away on the left. Hayward crossed low, fast, and true into the goal area, where Leake out-paced three hesitant defenders and prodded in.

Although Blackpool had an hour to turn the game around, they never seemed capable, such was the strength of Vale's grasp on the game. Blackpool were restricted to four attempts on goal: a long-range effort which King grabbed with comfort; a drive from centre-forward Stephenson which King tipped over; a speculative effort by Matthews which was blocked on the line; and a misplaced shot from shackled Perry, after his marker had slipped. In short, Blackpool were out-thought, out-fought, out-paced, and out-classed.

Vale were next drawn against Leyton Orient at Brisbane Road in the sixth round. It was a dour affair for the 30,000 crowd. Orient's only attacking stratagem was to pump long balls into Vale's box which Steele's defenders dealt with nonchalantly. The game seemed to be drifting towards a tedious stalemate when Vale won it with a rare attacking sortie. Askey crossed from the right, and Leake steered the ball past Groombridge in the Orient goal. In the final minutes, Orient belatedly found some fire when Poulton's powerful drive was on target but clean sheet supremo King pushed it away safely.

Vale's ecstatic fans could hardly believe it. Their side were in the FA Cup semi-final. The tie was to take place at Villa Park where it would be watched by a 68,000 crowd and their opponents were First Division leaders West Bromwich Albion, whose centre-forward Ronnie Allen was a former Vale hero. Despite being massive underdogs, Vale could not count on the customary sympathy vote as many regarded their style of football as a stain on the 'beautiful game'. There was a fear that if Vale's methods were widely adopted, it would kill interest in the game. The '50s fans demanded open, attacking football.

Vale centre-forward Basil Hayward recalled, 'They were saying that we were killing the game. But we were simply well-organised, that is all. We worked and ran for one another. We defended in great numbers, broke quickly, and developed the habit of limiting our opponents' chances while making the most of those that came our way. We worked all the time.'

Little did the carping public know that the Port Vale method would become commonplace in the decades which followed. Sean Dyche's Burnley attract similar criticisms today from bigger clubs thwarted by their dogged defence and productive counter-attacks.

The pitch was dry and firm, better suited to Albion's ball players. It came as no surprise that the top-flight side had more possession in the first half. Adopting Vic Buckingham's twin-pronged attack, Albion persistently knocked at the door. But Vale barred entry. Vale's defence sat on Albion's twin centre-forwards and denied them space. The few shots Albion mustered were competently handled by King. Albion's frustrations mounted.

Then, out of the blue Port Vale broke away, and in the resulting goalmouth scrimmage, Leake scored. A roar went up not only from the Valiant partisans, but from a Birmingham contingent pigging out on *Schadenfreude*.

At half-time Vale were still ahead and it took a freak second half goal to undermine their self-belief. Albion's Dudley floated a long swinging cross into the goalmouth. Cheadle and Allen leapt for the ball, but it eluded them. Unfortunately, it eluded the partly unsighted King, too, and plopped into the net.

Lifted by this huge slice of luck, Albion began to play with confidence and style. Somehow, Vale clung on. Allen hit the post but with only a few minutes remaining an Albion forward was felled in the penalty area. A spot-kick was awarded, and Allen scored.

The decision was challenged, to no avail. Albion were through to Wembley where they defeated Preston North End 3-2.

As for plucky Port Vale their amazing journey was over. I imagined them 12 years later watching England's World Cup victory together, saying to one another, 'Didn't we once play like that?'

First Division table (May 1954)

	P	W	D	L	F	A	Pts	Goal ave
1. Wolverhampton Wanderers	42	25	7	10	96	56	57	1.7
2. West Bromwich Albion	42	22	9	11	86	63	53	1.4
3. Huddersfield Town	42	20	11	11	78	61	51	1.3
4. Manchester United	42	18	12	12	73	58	48	1.3
5. Bolton Wanderers	42	18	12	12	75	60	48	1.3
6. Blackpool	42	19	10	13	80	69	48	1.2
7. Burnley	42	21	4	17	78	67	46	1.2
8. Chelsea	42	16	12	14	74	68	44	1.1
9. Charlton Athletic	42	19	6	17	75	77	44	1.0
10. Cardiff City	42	18	8	16	51	71	44	0.7
11. Preston North End	42	19	5	18	87	58	43	1.5
12. Arsenal	42	15	13	14	75	73	43	1.0
13. Aston Villa	42	16	9	17	70	68	41	1.0
14. Portsmouth	42	14	11	17	81	89	39	0.9
15. Newcastle United	42	14	10	18	72	77	38	0.9
16. Tottenham Hotspur	42	16	5	21	65	76	37	0.9
17. Manchester City	42	14	9	19	62	77	37	0.8
18. Sunderland	42	14	8	20	81	89	36	0.9
19. Sheffield Wednesday	42	15	6	21	70	91	36	0.8
20. Sheffield United	42	11	11	20	69	90	33	0.8
21. Middlesbrough	42	10	10	22	60	91	30	0.7
22. Liverpool	42	9	10	23	68	97	28	0.7

23.

THE WINTER OF OUR CONTENT: YORK CITY'S INCREDIBLE FA CUP RUN, 1954/55

IN THE harsh winter of 1954/55, the coldest since 1947, a remarkable FA Cup run by lowly York City gave the shivering football fraternity a warm glow, just as 'Typhoon' Frank Tyson did in skittling the Aussies on their own turf in cricket's Ashes series. Clips of fearsome Tyson and York's amazing march towards Wembley were covered by Pathé and Movietone news at our local cinemas.

York had an early-season setback. A dispute between manager Jimmy McCormick and his board over team selection resulted in his resignation. McCormick would never manage a Football League side again. Meanwhile, City were left managerless for the next 18 months. Undeterred, trainer Tom Lockie and club secretary Billy Sherrington took over team affairs and what a fantastic job they did.

Before he left, McCormick did a great service for his club by signing several players who would collectively drive York towards the FA Cup semi-final and fourth place in Third Division (North). No one envisaged this managerless team with four part-timers would progress so far, bettering what their pre-war predecessors achieved in reaching the FA Cup fifth round in 1938. A key factor in York's unexpected success was the team's sense of togetherness, which prompted them to name themselves the 'Happy Wanderers' taken from a popular song of the time, sung, appropriately, by the Stargazers.

McCormick sold the club's prize asset, centre-forward David Dunmore, to Spurs for a £10,750 fee. But what a return he achieved with a fraction of the proceeds. He was permitted to sign five new players, strengthening his attack and defence. His choice of recruits was inspired. In came goalkeeper Tommy Forgan from Hull City for only £500. Forgan had been kicking his heels at Boothferry Park for five years, making only ten appearances as understudy to the revered Billy Bly, who racked up over 400 appearances on Humberside. To make matters worse, Forgan had to put up with the fans' catcalls, having been dubbed 'Fumbling Forgan'. At Bootham Crescent he would serve his new club with distinction, playing 428 senior games in an 11-year stay. Those derisive Hull fans had no idea what a gem they had lost.

It seemed as if McCormick regarded Hull City in the same way as many of us think of Aldi, loads of bargains at decent quality. Full-back Ernie Phillips was the second Hull player to be dropped into his trolley, this time with no fee required. Phillips had played regularly for Hull and had previously made 80 appearances for Manchester City, mostly in the First Division. He would notch over 160 league games in three years at York. George Howe, another tough and experienced defender, came from Huddersfield on a free transfer. He would represent York in over 300 league matches.

To complete his Hull shopping, McCormick signed their 21-year-old part-time inside-forward Norman Wilkinson for a ridiculously low fee of £10. Wilkinson became a star at Bootham Crescent. Although he was not quick, he had an instinctive grasp of the game, consistently putting himself in positions where he would inflict damage. He was terrific in the air too. In a 12-year stay at York, Wilkinson made 354 appearances, scoring 157 goals. Norman maintained his cobbler business throughout his career, ensuring he always had the best boots on show.

McCormick struck pure gold, too, when he signed 25-year-old centre-forward Arthur Bottom, from Sheffield United. Arthur had been kicking his heels, managing only 24 appearances at Bramall Lane, scoring seven goals in a six-year stay. As with his other signings, McCormick had a much better sense of his recruits' value than the clubs they had left. Bottom was heavily reliant on his right foot but what power and trickery he could wield with it. Bottom had a thunderous shot, aggressively contesting any challenge, and getting himself into a bit of bother with the officials sometimes. On the pitch he was a firebrand, or a 'bit of a bugger', as he described himself, whereas he regarded his strike partner Wilkinson as 'such a nice man'. Enigmatically, away from the heat of battle, Arthur was a quiet, private person.

Bottom scored 92 goals for York in 137 league appearances before leaving in February 1958 for Newcastle, for a £4,500 fee. That figure would be around £4.5m today. He stayed on Tyneside only briefly, but long enough to establish himself as a hero there. When he signed for Newcastle, the Magpies were in mortal danger of the drop. Bottom hammered home seven goals in eight games, two on his debut, to help United avoid relegation by the narrowest margin, thanks to the old goal average system. Although he was soon moved on to Chesterfield for £5,000, his performances at York and Newcastle suggested that he could have thrived at a higher level. However, the First Division's loss was certainly York's gain.

York's established wingers, Billy Fenton and Billy Hughes also had an eye for goal. During their lengthy stays at Bootham Crescent they scored 118 and 55 goals, respectively. Hughes had retired to his native Scotland at the end of the 1953/54 season but fortunately was persuaded to return. His re-appearance had an important bearing upon York's upturn in form. Sid Storey was a highly rated, part-time inside-left. He managed 40 goals in a nine-year stay, laying on countless chances for others. Storey was also a miner while Fenton was an engineering draughtsman. Wing-half Gordon Brown, who also provided Bottom with excellent service, was a storekeeper.

Thanks to McCormick's canny dealings in the transfer market, this team packed a formidable punch as Wrexham found to their cost in the opening fixture at their Racecourse ground. York won 6-2 with Bottom scoring three times and Wilkinson twice. Two days later Hartlepools United were defeated 1-0 at Bootham Crescent but any hubris aroused quickly evaporated. An eight-game winless run followed before Hughes and Storey were restored to the side, heralding improved fortune. Suddenly, the team clicked into gear playing in a more expansive, attacking style which drew in many more visitors to Bootham Crescent. During this renaissance, York won seven of their next ten fixtures with the other three drawn. Stockport County and Chester City were put to the sword, 4-0 and

5-0 respectively, while a nine-goal thriller at Brunton Park, Carlisle went York's way, just.

Their FA Cup run began at home on 20 November, when non-league Scarborough were the visitors. Scarborough were far from pushovers and York were twice behind before two second half strikes gave them a tense and a probably unmerited 3-2 victory. Scarborough's vociferous fans were well represented in the 10,155 crowd, often out-shouting the home support. Many York followers thought this was the hardest match in the run to the semi-finals.

In round two, City had a 300-mile journey to Dorchester Town, a Western League side. Thoughtfully, York arranged a two-night stay for their team and directors in a Bournemouth hotel, ensuring that the players would be fresh and well-prepared. The small contingent of City fans were greeted loudly by the Dorset Regiment band who played 'On Ilkla Moor Baht At' in their honour, while the York directors were entertained in a specially erected marquee. This was Dorchester's first competitive fixture with a Football League team. But here the niceties ended as the home side swept into an early lead. Stoked high on adrenaline, Dorchester competed hard. But with the break approaching, City snatched an equaliser. Once again, the supposed minnows were putting up a brave fight.

The game turned on a bad injury to Dorchester's centre-half which forced him to leave the field. Although he returned later to make a nuisance of himself on the right wing, by then City were in control, crushing their game hosts 5-2 with Bottom grabbing a hat-trick. City were beginning to attract the attention of the national press. Ex-England international David Jack wrote, 'York played some really brilliant football and performed like world beaters in a devastating spell.' The Dorchester secretary was very complimentary, too, eulogising City as 'continental Yorkshiremen'.

They seemed a better prospect than the languishing England side who were thrashed 7-1 by Hungary before the 1954 World Cup finals in Switzerland. Although England played spasmodically better in this tournament, they were eliminated 4-2 by defending champions Uruguay, who were reduced to eight fit men in the second half.

York then went on another unbeaten run in the league, leading up to the Blackpool tie. After a home 3-3 draw with improving Wrexham, Mansfield were defeated twice over the Christmas period,

3-1 at Bootham Crescent on Christmas Day, and 2-1 in the return fixture two days later. Scunthorpe were also overturned 2-1 at their Old Show Ground on New Year's Day.

On 8 January York travelled to Bloomfield Road for a third-round tie with First Division Blackpool. The 'Pool were having a miserable season. Since the beginning of the '50s they had become accustomed to a top-ten finish or better. They were third in 1950/51 and sixth in their FA Cup winning year, 1952/53. But this season they were struggling. Their final position was 19th, two rungs above the relegation zone. It was they who were nervous about this game, not York.

Before the match, the York players spent two nights in a Southport hotel. Because of a colour clash, both sides wore change kits: York in blue shirts and white shorts; Blackpool in white shirts. In those days, both teams were required to change their shirts if there was a clash of colour. They tossed coin to decide who had first pick.

George Howe did a sterling job subduing Stanley Matthews as the hosts made the early running. Then, in the 37th minute City struck. Storey received the ball from a throw on the left flank and made for the goal line, but before he arrived, he had a sudden change of mind, electing to chance his arm. His 20-yard shot lacked pace and conviction, but it caught goalkeeper George Farm by surprise, just as Nat Lofthouse's scuffed effort had in the 1952/53 FA Cup Final. And once again Farm allowed the ball to slip through his fingers. Turning his head sharply, he was horrified to see the ball rolling gently into the net. As if to save his blushes the goal was awarded to Storey but, unlike the 1953 FA Cup Final, there was no way back for him or Blackpool.

With their confidence already low this goal was a hammer blow to the hosts. They found it hard to respond. Their attempts at mounting an attack were just huff and puff. Their heads dropped. York pounced gleefully on their opponents' litany of errors and with only 20 minutes remaining they struck again. Wilkinson found space near the right corner of Blackpool's box, and seeing winger Billy Fenton closing in on the left, he released the ball into his path. Without hesitation Fenton side-footed his shot into the Blackpool net from 16 yards.

This second setback did spur a belated reaction, forcing York to retreat. This left Blackpool greater space in which to pick a pass and line up their crosses. At last Stanley Matthews rid himself of Howe's shackles, revelling in the space available. He produced a series of testing crosses, but the dogged York defenders managed to scramble these away. Blackpool did manage to find the back of the York net, but to their great dismay, the goal was disallowed. Blackpool continued to pour forward though, causing York's 5,000 travelling fans to become increasingly anxious.

Under an incessant bombardment a foul was committed inside the penalty area and the referee pointed to the spot. Jim Kelly strode forward for what was surely Blackpool's last chance. Kelly went for placement rather than power and the magnificent Tommy Forgan guessed correctly, flinging himself high to his left to punch the ball away and preserve York's two-goal lead. Kelly reacted by holding his head in his hands. It was another shutout for Forgan, who achieved a club record 120 clean sheets in his 428 games for York.

This win remained the only time York beat a top-flight side away before defeating Manchester United 3-0 at Old Trafford in the League Cup in 1995.

The City fans were beside themselves with joy while the downcast Blackpool team sauntered off silently. For the second year running, the 1953 FA Cup winners were eliminated by a third-tier side. Not a squeak was heard from the 'Atomic Boys', Blackpool's flamboyantly dressed supporters. But York's smug smiles were soon erased when they lost 3-1 at home to Third Division (North) leaders Barnsley a week later.

Next up was the battle of the giant-killers at Bishop Auckland on 29 January. The Durham side were the best amateur team in the country, shortly confirming that status by winning the 1955 FA Amateur Cup at Wembley in front of a 100,000 crowd. Over the next two seasons they would register a hat-trick of Wembley victories. With professional footballer's wages capped at £20 per week, the amateur game still flourished, supplying some amateur players for Football League clubs, such as Mike Pinner and Warren Bradley who both played for Manchester United, although Bradley later turned professional. After the professional wage cap was removed in 1961, public interest in amateur football began to decline.

When York headed north they knew a fierce contest awaited them. In the previous round, Bishop Auckland eliminated Ipswich

AN END OF INNOCENCE

in a blizzard. Some 15,000 were crammed into The Bishops' Kingsway Stadium which they shared with the town's cricket club. Although Storey put York ahead in the sixth minute, Bishop Auckland equalised soon after, and hung on to parity until the break. However, York enjoyed greater possession in the second half. The amateurs were flung back in defence, but they were powerless to prevent Arthur Bottom scoring two late goals. Before the home fifth round tie with Spurs on 19 February, York had two league fixtures to fulfil, both against mid-table opposition – Oldham Athletic and Halifax Town. City won the former, 2-1 at Bootham Crescent, while drawing the latter 3-3 at The Shay, keeping them in with a shout at promotion.

While Spurs were not yet the formidable side that won the first 'double' of the 20th century, they had a strong team featuring seven members of Arthur Rowe's championship-winning side – Ron Reynolds, Tony Marchi, Harry Clarke, Alf Ramsey, Sonny Walters, Eddie Baily and Len Duquemin. They also had recent signing Danny Blanchflower, a sublime half-back. Unfortunately, ex-City centre-forward Dave Dunmore was injured.

There had been eight days of snow and frost in Yorkshire, putting the game in doubt. A local building firm helped, levelling the frozen ridges, and rolling tons of sand into the playing surface. On the morning of the match, York ground staff had to shovel away further falls of snow. The pitch was awful, a treacherous combination of ice, snow, and slush but the referee had no qualms and deemed it fit to play on. But a further heavy snowfall obscured the pitch markings. Once again out came the ground staff to paint all markings in blue paint. Yet more snow arrived at kick-off, but the referee was not for turning and with the sun soon appearing, it was all systems go. The subsequent flurries were stoically ignored by everyone, including the hardy official.

Despite the hideous weather, the ground was full to bursting with 21,000 squeezed in. Spurs soon swept away any anxieties about the playability of the surface by scoring a splendid team goal. In the 11th minute, Ramsey strode forward purposefully on the right, Sonny Walters intercepted and quickly found roving centre-forward Len Duquemin in space. Duquemin did not tarry, producing a low centre that fizzed across the York area allowing speedy winger George

Robb to steer the ball home from five yards. The *Times* correspondent pronounced this goal to be 'the beginning of the end for York'.

It was such a beautifully executed goal that most watching believed it might be repeatable. Not so. These York lads refused to be intimidated by Spurs' elegance and in the 29th minute they hit back. Winger Fenton seized the ball in midfield and with Ramsey in pursuit, he made a 30-yard diagonal run, evading all attempts at dispossessing him, before back-heeling the ball to Hughes wide on the right. Hughes centred immediately to find Wilkinson whose thumping header sent the ball flashing past Reynolds and into the top-right corner. Bootham Crescent erupted.

Neither the York people nor their players were present to admire Spurs' sophistication. They were there to foment a scrap. The raucous invective which poured down from the terraces inspired City's combative strength and their nifty skills. Driven on by their deafening fans, York turned the game upside down. Bottom pounced upon a loose ball, and instantly found Wilkinson in space. The cobbler's scorching cross-shot was too hot for Reynolds to handle, forcing him to parry the ball. Unfortunately for him, it ran right into the path of Fenton who tucked away the gift. There was a split-second pause while the huge crowd digested the enormity of what had happened before an incandescent roar broke out. York were beating Spurs.

City went in at half-time buzzing, although there were some who doubted whether they could maintain their blistering assault. It was soon clear that they would. Spurs, in their white kit and shrouded by the persistent flurries, seemed no more substantial than apparitions. Their attack had become toothless, well mastered by Brown and Howe. The visitors were hounded out of their neat, passing game by York's determination, intensity, and pace.

The only surprise was how long it took them to deliver the *coup de grace*, but in the 81st minute Fenton flashed past the lumbering Ramsey and crossed for Wilkinson to slide in the third and final goal. At the final whistle, an enormous war cry went up. This was football at its tribal best, devoid of the stain of violence, throbbing with adrenaline, fast, skilful, pugnacious, and dogged, where players and their community come together as one.

Daily Express reporter Henry Rose stated, 'No fluke, it might have been six. The humiliation, the unmistakable cup blitz of London's aristocrats was achieved by a team who played Spurs' own immaculate stylish soccer but played it more quickly, more accurately and with more urgency and spirit.'

The *York Evening Press* reported, 'York City today showed Tottenham Hotspur the way to play the traditional, classic style of football, come to be regarded as Spurs' own style. On such form as this City could go even further in the Cup because they out-smarted them. So complete was York's mastery that Tommy Forgan handled few difficult shots.'

The gross takings were £3,845, the equivalent to £100,000 today, £933 of which was paid in entertainment tax, the forerunner of VAT. The remaining receipts went to Spurs as their share. City netted £906 profit, worth around £25,000 in today's values.

Two days later, York were at Stockport County for a Monday evening game. They won that, too, 2-1. On the following Saturday they defeated Gateshead at home by the same score. But a week before the quarter-final at Notts County they lost by the only goal at Darlington. Their chances of overtaking Barnsley were fading.

However, York were still in the FA Cup. On a brilliantly sunny 12 March, York travelled to Meadow Lane, to face their upper Second Division opponents. With 14 special trains laid on there was a heavy York presence in the 47,301 crowd, shoehorned into the ageing ground. This attendance figure remains County's club record. How nostalgic it is to see the Pathé footage, featuring the men with their flat caps or trilbies, collars and ties; women with head scarves and schoolboys with school caps and gabardine macs – the train-spotting fraternity, for this was still the age of steam. The game was hardly a classic, but you would never know that from the footage which captures both sets of supporters in high states of excitement with many rattles revolved furiously.

While the game was largely scrappy, City's defence excelled, with goalkeeper Tommy Forgan and captain and right-back Ernie Phillips earning most plaudits. Both sides had a goal disallowed. But as the game wore on, County's Gordon Bradley became the busier keeper. The Pathé footage shows Bradley hurling himself one way and another in desperate attempts to keep the City attack at bay.

With 12 minutes left, Storey took a shot following Hughes's free kick. The ball was fortuitously deflected into the path of Arthur

Bottom who made no mistake, smashing his effort high into the net at close range, whereupon he immediately embarked upon a jolly jig, joined by his ecstatic team-mates, a commonplace reaction now but curiously out of place in these more restrained times. On the Pathé coverage, the Notts County players are shown contesting the legitimacy of the goal, presumably believing it was offside, but the referee just ignored them.

Fenton could have quelled the York fans' mounting anxiety by converting a late chance as County threw everyone forward. But it proved unnecessary as Forgan had kept yet another clean sheet and little York were one game away from Wembley. Back in York, hundreds congregated along Blossom Street and Tadcaster Road to welcome the team coach on its return. A police escort was needed to ensure the coach made its way through the crowd.

For the semi-final against Newcastle United at Hillsborough, 21,000 fans travelled from York. Twenty special trains and well over 70 coaches made their way to Sheffield for the game of their lives. City's preparations were hindered by an injury to magical inside-forward Sid Storey, who had played in every match so far this season. His place was taken by the inexperienced Sam McNab, playing his most important game for the club. Tommy Forgan said, 'It was a big blow to lose Sid before the first semi-final. He was an important player with the ability to hold on to the ball and set up play. Sammy McNab was capable but no Sid Storey.'

The weather was awful and so was the pitch. But despite the quagmire, 65,000 saturated supporters saw an enthralling game. Remarkably, both sides played stylish football on this mud heap. York fell behind in the 14th minute when Vic Keeble slipped the ball past Forgan, who said, 'I do not think Vic Keeble's 14th-minute goal was a classic and, on another day, I might have got to the ball.' Keeble also went close again before the underdogs levelled after half an hour.

Master marksman Arthur Bottom scored his eighth goal of the cup run when he robbed Jimmy Scoular in midfield and ran 30 yards before drawing Ron Simpson out of his goal and placing the ball into an empty net. Bottom remembered, 'There was a bad pass by Newcastle's full-back Alf McMichael. I picked it up and made for goal, getting past Jimmy Scoular and Bob Stokoe, leaving me with only Simpson to beat. He came out, so I chipped the ball over him.

He managed to get his fingertips to it, but only deflected it into the goal.'

Forgan added, 'I think perseverance was then the reason for Arthur Bottom's equaliser. Once he got on to the ball, he took a lot of knocking off and was reliable in scoring goals. In the second half, Milburn shot over from point-blank range and Billy Fenton shot straight at Simpson before an almighty 80th-minute scramble saw Bottom's header scooped away by the Newcastle keeper's despairing one-handed save. We came close to winning the game, but it could have gone either way.'

The replay at Roker Park, Sunderland, was played on a firm surface in bright sunlight Storey returned but Newcastle were clearly the stronger team and went ahead again through Keeble after just three minutes. City strove hard for an equaliser but struggled to get a serious shot on target. Early in the second half, York's commanding centre-half Alan Stewart sustained an injury following a clash of heads with Keeble. He had to leave the pitch for 12 minutes and had five stitches put into the wound. When he came back on, he could only add nuisance value on the wing in the days before substitutes were allowed. Although City continued to compete gamely, the tie was over a minute from time when Len White scored the Magpies' second. Newcastle went on to win the FA Cup, beating Manchester City in the final.

Forgan summarised, 'We were all proud of what we achieved in the cup run. It was a lifetime ambition to play at Wembley in a cup final but, while we did not quite make it, it is nice to look back on the good things we achieved and not what could have been. As for the semi-finals, it was the first time I had played in front of 65,000 people and, when we ran out of the tunnel, the noise was unbelievable. After the warm-up and the whistle blew to start the game, the noise was just as loud, but it was all about concentrating on the game.'

Some 47,916 fans saw City's cup run come to an end and the club's share of the gate receipts was around £8,000. Throughout the later stages of the run, updates were broadcast in York's cinemas and at rugby league games while a loudspeaker in the marketplace provided live commentary for the semi-final replay.

As for York's remaining league fixtures, they completed their season with seven wins, three draws and three losses, earning them fourth place, seven points behind champions Barnsley. Arthur was their leading goalscorer with 39 goals in both competitions. The season concluded with two crazy games with lowly Barrow, who won 4-1 at Bootham Crescent on 2 May, yet three days later at Holker Street, York won 5-1.

It was quite a season. It would have been interesting to know what Jimmy McCormick thought about York's incredible achievements. His dealings in the transfer market played such an important part in York's success. He is a hero, too.

First Division table (May 1955)

	P	W	D	L	F	A	Pts	Goal ave
1. Chelsea	42	20	12	10	81	57	52	1.4
2. Wolverhampton Wanderers	42	19	10	13	89	70	48	1.3
3. Portsmouth	42	18	12	12	74	62	48	1.2
4. Sunderland	42	15	18	9	64	54	48	1.2
5. Manchester United	42	20	7	15	84	74	47	1.1
6. Aston Villa	42	20	7	15	72	73	47	1.0
7. Manchester City	42	18	10	14	76	69	46	1.1
8. Newcastle United	42	17	9	16	89	77	43	1.2
9. Arsenal	42	17	9	16	69	63	43	1.1
10. Burnley	42	17	9	16	51	48	43	1.1
11. Everton	42	16	10	16	62	68	42	0.9
12. Huddersfield Town	42	14	13	15	63	68	41	0.9
13. Sheffield United	42	17	7	18	70	86	41	0.8
14. Preston North End	42	16	8	18	83	64	40	1.3
15. Charlton Athletic	42	15	10	17	76	75	40	1.0
16. Tottenham Hotspur	42	16	8	18	72	73	40	1.0
17. West Bromwich Albion	42	16	8	18	76	96	40	0.8
18. Bolton Wanderers	42	13	13	16	62	69	39	0.9
19. Blackpool	42	14	10	18	60	64	38	0.9
20. Cardiff City	42	13	11	18	62	76	37	0.8
21. Leicester City	42	12	11	19	74	86	35	0.9
22. Sheffield Wednesday	42	8	10	24	63	100	26	0.6

24

ANGER AND AFTER:
TEDDY BOYS IN THE '50s

IN 1955, the Comets' rockabilly was streaking across the firmament to crash into conservative Britain with meteoric force. In the British cinemas, crowds of teenagers were literally ripping it up as 'Rock Around the Clock' provided the rowdy soundtrack to the film *Blackboard Jungle*. It was the first film to link rock and roll with juvenile delinquency. By 1956, the Comets had begun to splutter out, exposing Bill Haley, their avuncular-looking, middle-aged vocalist, as the 'Great Pretender', an improbable adolescent hero, whereas Elvis not only sounded, but looked like, the real deal. So did the gender-bending Little Richard, with his raunchy shrieks and key-bashing excitability; the leathered Gene Vincent, with his sultry Virginian whispers; and the manic, deranged, piano-pummelling Jerry Lee Lewis. This insurgent quartet blasted a giant crater in the grey conformity of the times.

In 1956 came the rise of the 'Angry Young Man', when, with a growing swagger, restless adolescence barged into the narrow confines separating childhood from adult life; when the British working class flexed their muscles in response to rising prosperity; and when their children began seizing the educational opportunities granted by the Butler Education Act. It was the year when despotic Soviet rule crushed the Hungarian Revolution, and when Britain ceased to be a world power, following prime minister Anthony Eden's abject humiliation at Suez.

While the so-called 'angry young men and women' seemed more peeved than outrightly hostile, anger did course through the veins of the rebellious 'Teddy Boys' who became involved in serious public order offences during the mid-'50s, as occurred at rabid cinema showings of *Blackboard Jungle* in 1955. The 'Teds' were largely unqualified early school leavers, destined for a life of manual labour, whether as roadworkers, van boys or market porters. Their style first emerged in the working-class communities around Elephant and Castle in south London but spread quickly to the provinces, where 'Teds' were to be found in council estates and run-down areas. Their style celebrated or satirised a period when Britain was said to be 'great' when its empire was still intact before the ruinous legacy of two wars.

When it came to self-improvement, the 'Teds' were largely on the other side of the tracks to working-class grammar school pupils. But they too displayed the growing assertiveness of British youth, defying establishment mores, rejecting deference. Their defiance was often associated with alleged unruly behaviour. The press seized upon this, whipping up a moral panic, feeding public concerns about the supposed 'unmanageability' of youth. The 1958 race riots in Nottingham and Notting Hill brought these festering worries to a head, exacerbated by the increasing gloom about Britain's place in the world after the 1956 Suez fiasco, not helped by drubbings by Hungary's brilliant football team. Like other rebellious youth movements, the 'Teds' liked their music, too, not only rock and roll but Johnny Ray, Guy Mitchell, and Frankie Laine.

Meanwhile, a re-emergence of football hooliganism in the mid-'50s caused the national press to denounce Merseyside fans, citing incidents of train vandalism and assaults upon opposition players. A *Times* editorial on 5 September 1958 attempted to sweep the alleged villains into one sack, declaring, 'We should ask ourselves whether the time has not come to deal with hooliganism severely in all social classes: the university students who wreck theatrical performances; the football spectators who seem to feel that their afternoon's enjoyment is not complete unless they rip up the railway carriages that take them home; the Teddy Boys who, whether harmlessly or lethally, are obstreperous in public; are manifestations of a strand in our social behaviour that an adult society can do without.'

The *Times* correspondent had yet to meet the Mods and Rockers, and Skinhead gangs. Their story comes later.

First Division table (May 1956)

	P	W	D	L	F	A	Pts	Goal ave
1. Manchester United	42	25	10	7	83	51	60	1.6
2. Blackpool	42	20	9	13	86	62	49	1.4
3. Wolverhampton Wanderers	42	20	9	13	89	65	49	1.4
4. Manchester City	42	18	10	14	82	69	46	1.2
5. Arsenal	42	18	10	14	60	61	46	1.0
6. Birmingham City	42	18	9	15	75	57	45	1.3
7. Burnley	42	18	8	16	64	54	44	1.2
8. Bolton Wanderers	42	18	7	17	71	58	43	1.2
9. Sunderland	42	17	9	16	80	95	43	0.8
10. Luton Town	42	17	8	17	66	64	42	1.0
11. Newcastle United	42	17	7	18	85	70	41	1.2
12. Portsmouth	42	16	9	17	78	85	41	0.9
13. West Bromwich Albion	42	18	5	19	58	70	41	0.8
14. Charlton Athletic	42	17	6	19	75	81	40	0.9
15. Everton	42	15	10	17	55	69	40	0.8
16. Chelsea	42	14	11	17	64	77	39	0.8
17. Cardiff City	42	15	9	18	55	69	39	0.8
18. Tottenham Hotspur	42	15	7	20	61	71	37	0.8
19. Preston North End	42	14	8	20	73	72	36	1.0
20. Aston Villa	42	11	13	18	52	69	35	0.8
21. Huddersfield Town	42	14	7	21	54	83	35	0.7
22. Sheffield United	42	12	9	21	63	77	33	0.8

25.

THE BUSBY BABES

MATT BUSBY was undoubtedly the top manager of the '50s. When he became Manchester United's manager in 1946, the club was on its knees. Old Trafford was blitzed beyond recognition. They had an overdraft of £15,000, around £0.7m today and yet by 1956 when United won their second First Division championship since the war, the club had £60,000 in the bank, worth £2.6m today with playing staff valued at £300,000, probably around £1bn or more now.

Within two years of taking over, Busby fashioned a team comprising captain Johnny Carey, Crompton, Aston, Anderson, Chilton, Cockburn, Delaney, Morris, Rowley, Pearson and Mitten, who won the FA Cup with a glorious display of attacking football. The brilliance of their 4-2 victory over Blackpool is still appreciated today. United finished the 1947/48 season second in the First Division, behind champions Arsenal.

A year later they emulated that feat, this time finishing just behind Portsmouth. In the 1949/50 campaign, they slipped slightly in coming fourth, but in the following year they were back in second place behind 'push and run' maestros Spurs. It was no surprise when the 1951/52 season ended with United in pole position, a triumph achieved with seven of the 1948 FA Cup-winning team, supplemented by those who would play a prominent part in Busby's future successes, notably Roger Byrne and Johnny Berry.

After coming eighth in 1952/53, Busby knew it was time for a major reshuffle. The accent was placed on youth with strapping 17-year-old Duncan Edwards debuting and playing 24 league games at left-half. Twenty-year-old Jackie Blanchflower, brother of Danny, who made his debut in 1951, was granted a run of 27 games in 1953/54 and scored 13 times.

Brawny 21-year-old Tommy Taylor, a £29,999 signing from Barnsley, was given a primary striking role having served notice of his tremendous ability at the end of the previous season, when he scored seven goals in 11 games. In 1953/54 he became top gun, scoring 22 times in 35 appearances. Another prolific goalscorer in the making, 20-year-old inside-forward Dennis Viollet, showed his capabilities with 11 goals in 29 appearances. Nineteen-year-old left-winger David Pegg played in nine games while sturdy 21-year-old full-back Bill Foulkes made 32 appearances. Meanwhile, 22-year-old goalkeeper Ray Wood became number one between the sticks, completing 27 games.

Just two years later Matt Busby won the First Division championship for the first time with a group known as the 'Busby Babes', helped by the canny experience of Byrne and Berry. By then Edwards, Taylor, Foulkes, Viollet, Blanchflower, Pegg and Wood were established first team players, with 22-year-old centre-half Mark Jones and dazzling 19-year-old wing-half Eddie Colman joining them.

Reflecting upon the youth policy he inaugurated at Old Trafford, Busby had this to say in 1954, '[Saturday] 31 October [1953] was one of the most important days in the history of Manchester United and in my career as a football manager. We fielded that day, in an away match at Huddersfield, who were then second in the table, seven youngsters of 21 or under. It was one of the youngest teams ever to take part in a First Division game. The seven were Ray Wood, forthright Bill Foulkes, Duncan Edwards, fair-haired Jeff Whitefoot, Tommy Taylor, Irishman Jackie Taylor, and former office boy Dennis Viollet. Edwards was only 17. Of the other four, only two, Allenby Chilton and Jack Rowley, remained of the fine side which carried off the [FA] Cup in 1948.

'We were 13th and on a bad run. It seemed a good idea to give some of the bright youngsters a go. I have known them since they were schoolboys and helped them develop into accomplished footballers. I was confident about their ball skills. But the test is to see what they can do under pressure, playing in the first team in front of a large crowd. Temperament counts here, too, because a young man can go to pieces under pressure. I wanted to know how they would react when we are a goal down and the defence is being given a hard time. I have known wonderful reserve players who flopped in the senior side. Would some of these boys come through, survive the test, or have the necessary stamina. I was sweating over this for the first four or five games.

'We forced a goalless draw with Huddersfield. It was an excellent game. However, the stamina concern arose again in the next home match. On a very heavy surface, we were held to a 2-2 draw by Arsenal after we had taken a two-goal lead. But in the next game we went to Cardiff, and on another difficult pitch, won 6-1. I slept well that night! We went six matches before being beaten, finishing fourth in the table.

'There was a time when Tommy Taylor was not enjoying much luck. He had set up chances for others but had little success with his own finishing. Seeing this I patted him on the back and said, "Well played." He looked up and said, "Well boss I'm improving. I twice hit the post today." This told me that he refused to be satisfied with his performance and was ready to learn how to improve.

'As for courage, outside-left David Pegg gave ample proof of this. In the first few minutes of one game, the opposing right-back came in hard on him. He took the lot, the ball, Pegg and himself. Soon after, he repeated this. Some might have lost their nerve. Not David, though. We won both points from that game with David instrumental in the victory.

'We search relentlessly for young talent. Murphy and Bert Whalley are two of the finest spotters in the land. We look for boys who have decent ball control, who can pass, and shoot, show ball sense and some form of positional play, and are useful with their headwork. These are the bare fundamentals and we look for a boy's qualities that will enhance his development, namely keenness and love of the game. These will ensure he will spend hours perfecting his ability, and ride the inevitable disappointments, and avoid arrogance.

'We cannot keep our prodigy, Duncan Edwards, away from training. He returns every afternoon of his own accord and asks trainer, Tom Curry, for extra work. If given the opportunity he enjoys joining the junior practice games on Tuesdays and Thursdays at Salford. Although Duncan represented England Schoolboys nine times, a record, and has assisted England B and the Intermediate sides, and is tipped to gain a senior England cap soon, he is completely unspoiled and aware he still has a lot of room for improvement.

'Our greatest asset is the floodlit practice ground at Salford [notwithstanding the criticisms about the calibre of United's training facilities expressed by Noel Cantwell – see page 150]. Here, on Tuesday and Thursday evenings we coach the youngsters who have just left school. Jimmy Murphy and Bert Whalley are in charge. I take over when I have the time. In the practice matches here, the lads get an early sense of our system and tactics. Other clubs have them around the league pitch and charge a fee for staging attractive friendlies. We do not do that here. We prefer to produce a few new players.

'When the youngsters have developed sufficiently, they join senior practice sessions on Tuesday mornings with a few old hands there to help them fit in. This ensures that the young players are ready for the big day when they play in the first team. Our older players are extremely helpful to their younger colleagues. I'm certain this is the best way to find players for our senior team, so we do not have to use the transfer market. I estimate that around 80 per cent of our "Babes" turn out well. Nevertheless, there are occasions when it has been necessary to use the transfer market. Tommy Taylor is a case in point. We agreed with Barnsley, his parent club, that we would pay £29,999 for him because I was concerned that he might find a £30,000 fee too onerous to live up to.'

Manchester United's 1955/56 First Division championship triumph was an irrefutable endorsement of Busby's faith in his young stars, but the season started rather erratically. When United completed the first half of their league fixtures with a 3-2 defeat at Portsmouth, their record from the opening 21 was ten wins, six draws and five defeats. But in the second half of the season they bulldozed to the title with 15 wins, four draws and only two losses.

The top sharpshooters in this surge were Viollet with 15 goals and Taylor with 12, although Taylor had the best record overall with 25, five more than Viollet. The 83 league goals they scored was the best seasonal tally since their previous title victory in 1951/52 when they had a much more experienced squad.

Having won the First Division, Matt Busby set his sights not only on winning the title again but also competing in the new European

Cup. This was a vexed issue for the Football League management. At the instigation of the organisation's blunt, blowhard secretary, Alan Hardaker, Chelsea were 'persuaded' to withdraw their application after winning the championship in 1954/55. Football journalist Brian Glanville remarked, 'Hardaker was a powerful man. He didn't like getting involved with football on the continent.' According to Glanville, Hardaker disparaged Europeans, couching his antipathy in offensive terms. Glanville explained Chelsea's withdrawal thus, 'Unfortunately for them, their chairman, Joe Mears, was a leading light on the Football League management committee and when Hardaker said, "I don't think you should enter," he meekly kow-towed to him and didn't enter. But Matt Busby would not accept that as a manager of Manchester United. He was a far-seeing and with an internationalist outlook.'

Given the seniority of Hardaker's position and the degree of power he wielded it is unsurprising it took so long to rid ourselves of the insularity which had hampered the development of English football in the post-war years.

Thank goodness for Matt Busby. He probably deserved his knighthood for that stand alone. In the mid-'50s there was little public appetite for closer links with Europe, despite former prime minister Winston Churchill's earnest wish that they were developed. Clem Attlee, the man who deposed Churchill in 1945, sneered at the prospect of a stronger bond, stating, 'Very recently this country spent a great deal of blood and treasure, rescuing four of 'em from attacks by the other two.'

However, incumbent PM Harold Macmillan became converted to Churchill's view, having initially snubbed an offer to join the European community. But in 1957, when Macmillan assured us that we have 'never had it so good', a national poll revealed that most Britons were indifferent or hostile to joining the European Economic Community. Hardaker was dismissive, high-handed, and discriminative towards European competition but his 'little Englander' mentality was prevalent in this period, as attested in a national poll and in the 1958 race riots.

Manchester United started the 1956/57 Football League season in a rich vein of form, remaining unbeaten in their first 13 games with 11 wins and two draws. However, the eight European Cup matches they played between September and April caused their form to wobble periodically.

Busby admitted that the strain of competing in Europe, on top of Football League and FA Cup commitments, was greater than he anticipated. The Football League suggested that the club should withdraw if the European ties were compromising their domestic commitments. Busby was not to be bullied, replying that he would have considered that option if he did not have sufficient reserve strength at his disposal.

United did very well in Europe, progressing as far as the semifinals where they were eliminated by a peerless Real Madrid team. Busby suggested that the present domestic fixtures should be reduced to give English sides a better chance of progression in Europe, proposing that the First Division be slimmed down to 18 clubs. Presumably, he knew this riposte would have been an anathema to Hardaker.

Unabashed, Busby insisted that European competition should go on, drawing the line at a European League though. His case for supporting knockout European competition was based on his belief that the public liked it, and that it was good for British football, bringing in fresh ideas. He reminded those listening that the Hungarian thrashings had driven home how far our football had slipped, adding that his club had tightened their training routines and other preparations in response, adopting lightweight kit and low-cut boots.

United won the First Division title at a canter after a burst of mid-season victories and another on the final stretch. In his debut season Bobby Charlton scored ten of their 103 league goals in 14 appearances, although Billy Whelan headed their goalscorers with 26, followed by Taylor (22) and Viollet (16).

26.

TOTTENHAM HOTSPUR v MANCHESTER UNITED: FIRST DIVISION, 24 NOVEMBER 1956

TOMMY TAYLOR picked out United's 2-2 draw at Spurs on 24 November 1956 as a key game in the Busby Babes' second triumphant season. He said, 'This was a needle match. We were top of the table and they were two points behind. After only eight minutes they were two goals ahead. We were not disheartened because there was so much time left. Our defence was magnificent after this early setback and we did most of the attacking, but somehow, we could not put the ball into their net. I should have scored. It was a near miss but a miss all the same. Roger Byrne made a tremendous surge forward and hit a screamer. Alas it only shook the crossbar, whereupon Duncan Edwards, following up, slammed the ball back towards goal only to find the upright. We were not disheartened, though. At the break we were of the same mind. We knew we were playing well. That led us to believe that we would get our rewards.

'Sure enough, straight after the resumption, winger Johnny Berry scored a fine goal. Now we were truly back in the game and poured forward in search of an equaliser. But Spurs defended magnificently. This was football at its best. The crowd certainly got their money's worth. But our chances kept slipping away. It looked like Spurs would hang on, but with only three minutes left, up popped Eddie Colman to blast the ball into the net. It was the right result. We left the field wearily but shook each of the Spurs' players' hands heartily. It was a razor-keen competitive match, and yet it could not have been played in a more friendly spirit.'

27.

ASTON VILLA v
MANCHESTER UNITED:
FA CUP FINAL, 4 MAY 1957

UNITED SEEMED sure to seize the first double of the 20th century on 4 May 1957, but after Peter McParland crashed into United's goalkeeper Ray Wood in the sixth minute of the FA Cup Final, the game irrevocably turned in Aston Villa's favour.

Here are extracts from an unattributed cutting in one of my 63-year-old scrapbooks: 'Manchester United were robbed of the cup. The robber-in-chief is the FA who has steadfastly resisted all attempts to introduce much-needed and long overdue reforms into laws of the game. One is to allow substitutes in all matches, at least for an injured goalkeeper like Wood. The other is to make it illegal to charge a goalkeeper.

'McParland's robust charge which broke Wood's cheekbone was a foul, but the penalty – a free kick – was not commensurate with the damage he did. United were left with ten men and compelled to put Jackie Blanchflower, one of their best outfield players, in goal through no fault of their own. To add insult to injury, McParland smashed home two goals that won the game for Villa. Although Tommy Taylor managed a late goal it was too little, too late.'

Blanchflower, who played well as a substitute goalkeeper, recalled, 'Peter McParland was a naïve lad. Villa told him that Woody was suspect and "to get in and let him know you are there". Unfortunately, McParland did as he was bid, excessively so.'

Wood remembered, 'I had the ball in my hand when the charge came. McParland had no chance of getting the ball. I ran three or four yards before he charged. Next thing I found myself lying on the grass covered in water. Somebody said, "I think his jaw is broken, he'll have to go off."'

It was an awful game. If United's exciting draw at Spurs represented the best of English football, this game was among the worst. Had Michael Oliver re-refereed the 1957 showpiece as he did with the controversial 1970 FA Cup replay, surely, he would have shown McParland a red card. Yet commentator Kenneth Wolstenholme insisted it was a 'fair challenge' and castigated the United fans for booing McParland whenever he touched the ball. To add insult to injury, those jeers inspired McParland's powerful finishing.

Fifty years later, professional football analysts with modern tracking monitors re-examined this game with their devices for measuring possession, ball control, passing accuracy, tackles, aerial duels and interceptions, comparing this data with that of the 2007 final. Here are some of their findings:

- In the 1957 FA Cup Final there was little build-up play and no playing from the back unlike the 2007 final
- The ball was often hit high and long for the centre-forward and wingers in 1957
- The game was fast, physical, and direct in 1957
- Possession was easily lost but regained quickly, often through error
- Passing accuracy was less than 30 per cent in 1957 compared to 90 per cent in 2007
- Stamina was much higher in 2007. United ran out of puff in the second half in 1957
- In 1957, there was no specialist medical care for injured United goalie, Ray Wood
- Wood's jersey was yanked off oblivious to the risk of causing permanent damage
- Despite McParland's reckless charge, there were fewer fouls given in this game compared to 2007. Tom Finney said fouls on goalies were rarely given in the '50s
- In the '50s football was predominantly a working-class game, played by the working classes for the working classes. This changed during the late '50s and '60s.

First Division table (May 1957)

	P	W	D	L	F	A	Pts	Goal ave
1. Manchester United	42	28	8	6	103	54	64	1.9
2. Tottenham Hotspur	42	22	12	8	104	56	56	1.9
3. Preston North End	42	23	10	9	84	56	56	1.5
4. Blackpool	42	22	9	11	93	64	53	1.5
5. Arsenal	42	21	8	13	85	69	50	1.2
6. Wolverhampton Wanderers	42	20	8	14	94	70	48	1.3
7. Burnley	42	18	10	14	56	50	46	1.1
8. Leeds United	42	15	14	13	72	63	44	1.1
9. Bolton Wanderers	42	16	12	14	65	65	44	1.0
10. Aston Villa	42	14	15	13	65	55	43	1.2
11. West Bromwich Albion	42	14	14	14	59	61	42	1.0
12. Birmingham City	42	15	9	18	69	69	39	1.0
13. Chelsea	42	13	13	16	73	73	39	1.0
14. Sheffield Wednesday	42	16	6	20	82	88	38	0.9
15. Everton	42	14	10	18	61	79	38	0.8
16. Luton Town	42	14	9	19	58	76	37	0.8
17. Newcastle United	42	14	8	20	67	87	36	0.8
18. Manchester City	42	13	9	20	78	88	35	0.8
19. Portsmouth	42	10	13	19	62	92	33	0.7
20. Sunderland	42	12	8	22	67	88	32	0.8
21. Cardiff City	42	10	9	23	53	88	29	0.6
22. Charlton Athletic	42	9	4	29	62	120	22	0.5

28.

ARSENAL v MANCHESTER UNITED: FIRST DIVISION, 1 FEBRUARY 1958

THE TRAGEDY that befell United in the following season was prefaced by a remarkable game at Highbury, which became an epitaph for the Busby Babes.

United were on top form the start and after only ten minutes they took the lead. A neat pass from Viollet found Edwards in space just outside the Arsenal box. His shot had too much speed and power for Arsenal's goalkeeper Jack Kelsey, a Welsh international. The ball scudded through his helpless grasp and tore into the net. After 30 minutes, United were two-up following a lightning counter-attack. Gregg had just made a brilliant save to protect United's lead. He quickly released the ball to left-winger Albert Scanlon who flew up the left wing and centred crisply for Bobby Charlton to lash in the second. The *Manchester Guardian* reporter was compelled to pen, 'Charlton has grown from a limited left-side player of little pace into a brilliant inside-forward.'

Just before half-time, Scanlon crossed from the left wing to Morgans on the right who set up rampaging Tommy Taylor to burst through the middle of the Arsenal defence and stroke the ball past Kelsey.

Even at the end of the '50s teams were not well equipped to defend a lead, even one as big as this. Having little to lose, Arsenal took the game to United in the second half. David Herd, a future championship winner with United, slammed in his riposte after receiving Bowen's lobbed pass and a minute later Arsenal were within touching distance of the visitors as Groves headed Nutt's centre down for Bloomfield to score elegantly.

Highbury recovered its voice as the fans urged the Gunners on and in next to no time, Arsenal were level as Nutt crossed for Bloomfield who scored with a deft, glancing header. Pandemonium ensued. Bowen was controlling the game, threading passes through the porous United defence which Herd, Tapscott and Groves tried to capitalise upon.

United weathered the storm, however, and began probing the home defence once more. A swift exchange between Scanlon and Charlton resulted in a cross that Viollet headed emphatically past Kelsey to restore the lead, then a breakaway by Colman and Morgan enabled Taylor to score from a tight angle, only for Bowen and Herd to combine forces to send Tapscott through the middle and pick his spot calmly to bring the score back to 5-4. It was an unforgettable, thrill-a-minute game.

29.

PEN PICTURES OF THE BUSBY BABES BY JOHN DOHERTY

JOHN DOHERTY was a former Busby Babe, whose career was truncated by injury. He had this to say about his fellow players who died or survived the Munich disaster:

Roger Byrne (died), 'He had exceptional pace and a good right side, but he had no left side and wasn't much of a tackler or a header of the ball. Despite that, I haven't seen a better full-back.'

David Pegg (died), 'David liked to do a bit on the ball, dip a shoulder and send his man the wrong way, very intricate, clever and exceedingly quick.'

Tommy Taylor (died), 'A magnificent centre-forward. He was brilliant in the air. He could head the ball harder than some could kick it. He had an amazing strike rate, and was brave too, a superb athlete who was prepared to chase lost causes. He was a tough target man as well.'

Duncan Edwards (died), 'He wasn't as tall as some people think but my God he could play. He had a presence, a supreme self-confidence, that never strayed into arrogance. He was fearsomely strong, gifted with both feet, majestic in the air and very, very hard, a genuinely great player.'

Geoff Bent (died), 'He was in Roger Byrne's shadow as a reserve left-back. He was quick, tidy on the ball and prepared to put his foot in. There was talk about Roger moving to right-back, allowing Geoff to take the left-back berth. It never happened. He was only on that plane as cover for Roger.'

Billy Whelan (died), 'His goals to games ratio was phenomenal for an inside-forward but he had lost his place after United had suffered a bad run before Munich. He scored a wonderful goal on Bilbao's mud heap which gave us enough scope to get through in the second leg.'

Eddie Colman (died), 'An effervescent lad from Salford. He pulled off all sorts of tricks swivelling his hips, dipping his shoulder in entertaining the crowd. He didn't score many goals as an attacking wing-half, but he was a beautiful passer.'

Mark Jones (died), 'Mark was a gem. His giant stature, his strength, and his courage made him a natural in the old-fashioned centre-half role.'

Jackie Blanchflower (survived), 'He suffered terrible injuries at Munich and never played again. Before that, he was a fine all-round player who played as a wing-half, inside-forward, centre-half and as Ray Wood's replacement in the 1956/57 FA Cup Final. He had no pace but was excellent in the air and a great reader of a game.'

Harry Gregg (survived), 'A genuinely great goalkeeper. Bought from Doncaster in 1957 for £23,500. He was taking over from Ray Wood who was a line goalkeeper, whereas Harry was ahead of his time as a box keeper. He fiercely dominated his area. The United defenders were used to dealing with crosses outside the goal area, but this big, fractious Irishman began punching and catching anything that moved. He was generally popular but upset a few at the club. He once dangled Albert Scanlon out of a hotel window several floors up for smoking in their room. However, his bravery at Munich is legendary, when he rescued fellow survivors, re-entering the crashed plane.'

Bill Foulkes (survived), 'Bill was a big fellow and a fitness fanatic whose greatest attribute was strength. He took some beating in the air, he was not slow on the ground, and though he was very right-sided, he coped with it. No one was more focused on the job. After Munich, Bill became centre-half, the rock at the heart of United's defence.'

Albert Scanlon (survived), 'He will go down as a dashing, crowd-pleasing winger who on his day was frightening. He must have driven Matt mad with the scrapes he got into, but his saving grace was that he could play.'

Bobby Charlton (survived), 'When he drifted past his marker and hammered the ball into the net from 25 yards, it was exciting and beautiful. He started as an inside-forward, then became an outstanding left-winger before fulfilling a deep-lying playmaker role. Probably the greatest faux pas of Alf Ramsey's reign as England manager was substituting Bobby with Colin Bell in the 1970 World Cup quarter-final against the Germans. Beckenbauer did not give a monkey's about Bell whereas he was terrified of Bobby. Bobby could not tackle a fish supper, though.'

Dennis Viollet (survived), 'At a time when England were crying out for a proven marksman to play alongside the centre-forward, how could they ignore a man who averaged more than a goal every game in Europe, and far better than one in two over all competitions? He was all skin and bone but was as fit as a flea and had tremendous pace, lovely control, and a sharp brain. He was not a brilliant striker of the ball but was an instinctive and deadly finisher who preferred to pass it into the net.'

Kenny Morgans (survived), 'A pacy, tricky right-winger who replaced John Berry after United's disappointing start to the 1957/58 season. Suffered concussion and fractures at Munich. He never recovered his early momentum after the plane crash.'

Johnny Berry (survived), 'Johnny was the hardest flankman I've seen in my life. He was brave in an era when we were not used to brave wingers. Sadly, his injuries at Munich prevented him from playing again.'

Ray Wood (survived), 'Woodie was a magnificent shot stopper, with outstanding agility and very quick feet. However, he was never the soundest judge of a cross. He was outstanding against Borussia Dortmund away in the European Cup.'

30.

POST-MUNICH
MANCHESTER UNITED

MIRACULOUSLY, A heavily patched-up United side comprising a clutch of young reserves and new signings – Ernie Taylor, a wily playmaker from Blackpool, and Villa's midfield enforcer Stan Crowther – reached the 1958 FA Cup Final. But, despite fashioning several chances, United were beaten at Wembley by a better Bolton Wanderers side who were more robust in defence and more incisive in attack. However, Bolton's second goal should have been disallowed as Nat Lofthouse later admitted.

United even beat AC Milan 2-1 at home in the European Cup semi-final but lost the away leg 4-0. Moreover, they challenged for the 1958/59 First Division championship fired by goals from Charlton (29), Viollet (21) and Scanlon (16), with expensive recruit Albert Quixall pulling the strings in midfield. Creditably, they finished as runners-up to Wolves.

Thereafter, United's fortunes declined. In 1959/60 they racked up 100 league goals for the second successive year, but their suspect defence leaked 80. In 1960/61 they finished seventh, as they did in 1959/60, but once again they were hampered by a dodgy defence. A year later, they slumped to 15th and in 1962/63 they were perilously near to relegation, despite winning the FA Cup with style. This victory prompted a vigorous upward trajectory.

In November 1960 Irish international full-back Noel Cantwell arrived from West Ham for £29,500. He was dismayed at what he found, comparing his experience at United unfavourably with what he left behind at West Ham. He shared Denis Law's concerns about the poor state of preparations at Manchester United. He disparaged the apparently limited training routines. 'Is that it?' he once asked Eamon Dunphy, a fellow Irish colleague, shaking his head with disbelief. 'A bit of running, head tennis and "round the back" for a bloody free for all!' Cantwell was referring to the 20-a-side games on the cinder car park.

At West Ham, the enthusiasm of Malcolm Allison rubbed off on Cantwell and others. Cantwell recalled, 'After finishing our lunch, Allison would say, "We should practise for hours more." Teams didn't warm up before games, but we would go into the gym at quarter past two and have a good workout.' Cantwell missed West Ham's greater professionalism.

Former Burnley and England winger John Connelly had similar reservations after he joined Manchester United in April 1964. John said, 'At Old Trafford it was great players rather than great coaching or training that won trophies. Matt Busby was rarely seen at The Cliff training ground. He would give a short team talk on a Friday and that was largely it. The Cliff was frequently waterlogged, so makeshift training took place at Old Trafford, very often under the stands or around the pitch when an impromptu obstacle course was laid out.

'At Burnley, the Gawthorpe training facilities were then ahead of their time. There was a coach to collect the players at Turf Moor and take them to Gawthorpe. At Manchester United we had to pile into our cars in muddy kit.'

It seemed as if the trauma of Munich had blighted so much that was good, thoughtful, and effective during the '50s. Busby was no longer relying upon his youth policy to build a new club. United began trading prolifically in the transfer market, something Busby had set his mind against in the '50s.

31.

CHARLTON ATHLETIC v HUDDERSFIELD TOWN: SECOND DIVISION, 21 DECEMBER 1957

I HAVE a soft spot for Huddersfield Town. My first Chix bubblegum card was one of Ron Staniforth, their cultured, international full-back. In a scrapbook there is a cutting describing a Second Division match at a wet Valley. Huddersfield were two-up at half-time, Charlton having been reduced to ten men after centre-half Derek Ufton was carried off with a dislocated shoulder. Massie had opened the scoring with Bain making it 2-0.

Charlton winger Johnny Summers ditched his old boots at half-time. Sporting new ones, he pulled one goal back with a miscued shot, causing Bill Shankly to lambast his team. Spurred by his tirade, Huddersfield instantly added three more goals, one from Bain, another from future Wolves boss Bill McGarry, from a penalty, with winger Bob Ledger banging the final nail into Charlton's coffin or so it was thought.

Four goals had been scored in a wild seven-minute spell. When Huddersfield scored their fifth, Charlton fans left in droves, casting a spectral silence upon the cavernous Valley. However, Summers refused to throw in the towel, helping Charlton pull two back. Summers laid on Charlton's second goal for centre-forward John 'Buck' Ryan before thumping one in himself, again with his weaker right foot.

Shankly was beside himself with rage. With Charlton having reduced the deficit to two goals, their few remaining fans suddenly sprung into life. Huddersfield were rattled. Pugnacious Summers was dashing everywhere, lunging into tackles, forcing distributional errors, seizing upon the second balls, while screaming at his colleagues to get stuck in. Overturning possession time and again, he made straight for goal. But with time ticking by, the Charlton fans became subdued.

Yet, with 16 minutes left, a scorching Summers drive flashed into the Huddersfield net for his hat-trick. Summers ignored the fans' acclaim, urging them to give more encouragement. With his adrenaline pumping, Summers hammered another shot home to equalise. If that was not surreal enough, he instantly scored again, giving Charlton a stupefying 6-5 lead.

Christine Lawrie, a long-standing Charlton supporter, remembered, 'We went absolutely berserk. No one had seen anything like this. It was once-in-a-lifetime stuff.'

But the action was not over. With exhaustion taking a hold, Charlton dropped their guard momentarily, allowing Huddersfield to race through their makeshift defence and equalise, helped by a wicked deflection from defender John Hewie. Summers was apoplectic and instantly set off on another swashbuckling raid. There was less than a minute left as Summers made for goal, creating mayhem in the Huddersfield defence. Seeing Ryan in space on his right he put him through on goal. Time seemed to stand still as Ryan carefully took aim and hammered the ball past Sandy Kennon for an astonishing 7-6 victory.

As exhilarating as this game had been, I felt sorry for Huddersfield. To have been 5-1 up against ten men only to lose must have been devastating for them. It was their grave misfortune to run into a five-goal cyclone called Johnny Summers. Pitch invasions were rare in those days, and always frowned upon, but nothing could stop the hoarse Charlton fans pouring on to the pitch to embrace their heroes. These fans then gathered in front of the directors' box demanding that Summers return to take a bow.

Meanwhile, a seething Shankly was laying into his players in the dressing room. Huddersfield left-back Ray Wilson described the train journey home as 'wretched', with an inconsolable yet furious Shankly prowling up and down the carriage, muttering loudly, 'How could they throw that game away! How! How!'

Sadly, Summers died of cancer five years later, aged only 34. However, his legacy remains with those remaining team-mates and fans fortunate enough to have been there on that damp winter afternoon.

32.

MORE WORLD CUP
DISAPPOINTMENT: 1958

IN 1956, England captain Billy Wright hailed an impending revival for the national side. Prestigious victories had been achieved at home and away against world champions West Germany, while Brazil, soon to take over the Germans' crown, were beaten 4-2 at Wembley in 1956.

But when it came to the 'real thing', at the next World Cup finals, England faltered again, although they weren't helped by the tragic loss of key players at Munich in the shape of Roger Byrne, Duncan Edwards and Tommy Taylor.

After Manchester United's First Division title ambitions were lost in the air disaster, Wolves were the next English side to compete in the European Cup, buoyed by their success in friendly contests with some of the continent's best European clubs including Honved, Spartak Moscow and Real Madrid. However, Wolves stumbled at the first hurdle, losing to Schalke in their first taste of European Cup football in 1958/59. As England found in the 1950 World Cup, their prospects were talked up before being tested in an international tournament.

England's performances in the 1958 World Cup finals in Sweden were once again gravely disappointing, while recognising the loss of three Manchester United men and an unfortunate injury to Tom Finney, arguably England's best outfield player. Walter Winterbottom's misfortune did not end there, though. Fulham's Johnny Haynes was exhausted after a hectic promotion race. So were Ronnie Clayton and Bryan Douglas of Blackburn. Much was expected of playmaker Haynes. Winterbottom's sides relied upon his vision and penetrative passing. Suffering with blistered feet, Haynes was a lacklustre presence in England's ineffectual attack. As in Brazil, England were eliminated at the group stage, this time after a play-off defeat by the USSR.

After winning the Jules Rimet Trophy, Brazilian skipper Hideraldo Luiz Bellini paid England an equivocal compliment, remarking, 'England gave us the hardest match. They were better than [finalists] Sweden, very good in defence, and played practical football.' Was 'practical football' the best we could muster? If this seemed like praise with a faint insult, it was probably fair. Helped by Bill Nicholson's shrewd defensive tactics, England had managed to blunt Brazilian brilliance in Gothenburg, achieving a creditable 0-0 draw. It was the only game in Sweden in which Brazil failed to win.

It seemed that the Spurs boss had learnt his Hungarian lessons well. Remembering how Hungary's Hidegkuti had been allowed to run amok at Wembley, he suggested that England could counter the threat from Brazil's deep-lying playmaker, Didi, by assigning Bill Slater to mark him closely throughout, also proposing that Don Howe should be moved from right-back to join veteran centre-half Billy Wright as a partnership in order to repel Brazil's centre-forwards, Mazzola (later known as Jose Altafini) and Vava. It was also agreed that the forceful wing-half Eddie Clamp should be shifted back to take care of their withdrawn 'fetch and carrying' outside-left Zagallo. Only left-back Tommy Banks was assigned a conventional defensive role. As well as the system worked, three times Mazzola broke past Wright but on each occasion, he was thwarted magnificently by goalkeeper Colin McDonald of Burnley. Only McDonald enhanced his reputation as an England player.

Like England, Scotland also fell at the first hurdle. Their normally reliable goalkeeper and skipper, Tommy Younger, was at fault for all three of Paraguay's goals in a 3-2 defeat in the opening group game. France were gifted the second match 2-1 after Scotland made a series of bewildering positional changes. These included consigning their best inside-forward, Bobby Collins, to the wing. Scotland finished bottom of their qualifying group with just one point. It was left to our underdogs, Northern Ireland and Wales, to fly the Union Flag with a flourish. Unexpectedly, both sides reached the quarter-finals.

Prompted by the midfield brilliance of Danny Blanchflower and Jimmy McIlroy, and the penetrative wing play of Peter McParland and Billy Bingham, Northern Ireland beat Czechoslovakia in a group play-off. Under Peter Doherty, they employed a canny 4-2-4 formation, but their brave fight was ended in the last eight by France in a 4-0 defeat. The Irish were already missing key players through injury. Their absurdly punishing itinerary did the rest. Having held France in the first half, spurning an excellent scoring opportunity, they eventually ran out of puff and were over-run.

Wales qualified for the quarter-finals after heroically defeating Hungary 2-1. There, they faced Brazil. Unfortunately, injury robbed them of the talismanic John Charles but thanks to Jack Kelsey's agility in goal, their plucky defence was breached just once, by Pelé, with fewer than 20 minutes remaining.

First Division table (May 1958)

	P	W	D	L	F	A	Pts	Goal ave
1. Wolverhampton Wanderers	42	28	8	6	103	47	64	2.2
2. Preston North End	42	26	7	9	100	51	59	2.0
3. Tottenham Hotspur	42	21	9	12	93	77	51	1.2
4. West Bromwich Albion	42	18	14	10	92	70	50	1.3
5. Manchester City	42	22	5	15	104	100	49	1.0
6. Burnley	42	21	5	16	80	74	47	1.1
7. Blackpool	42	19	6	17	80	67	44	1.2
8. Luton Town	42	19	6	17	69	63	44	1.1
9. Manchester United	42	16	11	15	85	75	43	1.1
10. Nottingham Forest	42	16	10	16	69	63	42	1.1
11. Chelsea	42	15	12	15	83	79	42	1.1
12. Arsenal	42	16	7	19	73	85	39	0.9
13. Birmingham City	42	14	11	17	76	89	39	0.9
14. Aston Villa	42	16	7	19	73	86	39	0.8
15. Bolton Wanderers	42	14	10	18	65	87	38	0.7
16. Everton	42	13	11	18	65	75	37	0.9
17. Leeds United	42	14	9	19	51	63	37	0.8
18. Leicester City	42	14	5	23	91	112	33	0.8
19. Newcastle United	42	12	8	22	73	81	32	0.9
20. Portsmouth	42	12	8	22	73	88	32	0.8
21. Sunderland	42	10	12	20	54	97	32	0.6
22. Sheffield Wednesday	42	12	7	23	69	92	31	0.8

33.

CHELSEA v WOLVERHAMPTON WANDERERS: FIRST DIVISION, 30 AUGUST 1958

IT WAS a day of swooning heat, a surprising interlude in a cold, grey, wet summer. The huge glass roof at Paddington station incubated the warmth of the sun and from the many copper chimney steam locomotives. Their wispy, shimmering vapours conveyed a mixed scent of sulphur, tar, and scorched oil.

Ruddy-faced men in open-necked shirts and flannels heaved strapped, swollen brown leather suitcases into the crammed chocolate and cream carriages. Meanwhile, intricately curled or pony-tailed women stood aside coolly issuing instructions. Some women wore flared floral skirts with broad black belts while others sported straight shift dresses. Many of these couples or young families were off to the Cornish Riviera – to St Ives, Newquay, or Looe. In 1958 the high-water mark of holiday rail traffic was reached. Thereafter many more families turned to the road.

London was bulging with tourists, many making for the parched parks where they could stretch out under the cooler canopies of the flaking plane trees. Despite the baking temperatures, Dad and I made for Lyons Corner House cafeteria where we joined the throng jostling with trays in search of elusive seats. It seemed that the protective metal covers provided for our fatty, soggy meals were as superfluous as any hope of taste or nourishment. Eating out in the '50s was generally a functional, joyless duty. The tube that rocked and rolled from Earl's Court to Fulham Broadway was packed, too, compressing the overpowering odour of tobacco. Every breath was worth 20 untipped. I felt like a laboratory beagle.

Outside the ground there were programme sellers, emphasising the second syllable in their hoarse cries for custom – proGRARMS! There were badge sellers, too, selling small, blue, star-shaped plastic brooches containing a selection of photographs of favourite players – Jimmy Greaves, Peter Brabrook and Ron Tindall. I chose one of Greaves sporting a crew cut. He was smiling mischievously. It was a prophetic pick.

In the programme, which I still have almost 62 years later, Ted Drake writes, 'Concern over British football seems to have been universal and has filled our minds during the close season [he was referring to England and Scotland's woeful World Cup performances]. The new campaign appears to have opened on the right foot. Regardless of the club results the goals have been coming. In the four league games I have witnessed this season the football has been thrilling with goals in abundance, and surely this is what the real soccer enthusiast wants to see.'

Here he was referring to Manchester United 5 Chelsea 2, Wolves 5 Nottingham Forest 1, Chelsea 4 Spurs 2, and West Ham 2 Wolves 0. Ted would not be disappointed with the outcome of this game, either.

Climbing up the steep stairwell on to the open western terraces, it was immediately obvious that there was a huge crowd here. It was recorded as being over 61,000. I had never seen so many people squeezed into such a limited space. Feeling the full force of the sun's glare, many found they were overdressed. Thick Harris tweed sports jackets were removed, ties were unfastened, and chests exposed but still the beady sweat trickled down so many purple faces. Someone tried to make a paper hat out of a newspaper. It was a poor effort attracting much good-natured ridicule.

On the public address system, they were playing a song from the popular musical, *My Fair Lady*. Stanley Holloway declaimed in a gruff, atonal, cockney voice, 'Wiv' a little bit of luck, wiv' a little bit of luck, someone else'll do the blinkin' work.' Chelsea had no need of luck or help on this scintillating afternoon. They murdered Wolves.

Greaves remembered, 'We didn't start well. Bobby Mason scored after only two minutes, but that did not bother me. I felt on this day everything would go my way. I knew I would score, and not just once.

The big occasions charged me up. My first touch of the ball was good. I felt in control. In our first attack, I corkscrewed past Ron Flowers and Gerry Harris before playing a one-two with our right-winger, Peter Brabrook. Though overshadowed by Bill Slater, when I got the ball back from Peter, I hit it first time. I had seen a gap just to the left of Wolves goalkeeper Malcolm Finlayson so I aimed for that. I did not need to belt it. It was enough to pass the ball in. Finlayson couldn't reach it and we were level.'

Although all of this happened 62 years ago, a sharp vision of Greaves remains; his speed of thought and movement and his precise finishing. He scored five times that day and each goal seemed to be a carbon copy of the one before. Time and again he latched on to a sharp pass, anticipating its weight and angle expertly, caressing the ball into his path, and drawing Wolves' defenders to him, only to flash past them with a shimmy and a dab of speed. Each time Finlayson advanced Jimmy was too quick, too astute and with meticulous timing and accuracy, he tapped the ball past him and into the net. Even at the age of nine, I recognised this was the hallmark of a master craftsman.

After half an hour Chelsea were 4-1 up. The Wolves defenders were not just red-faced on account of the heat. Billy Wright took unmerciful stick. He looked laboured and cruelly exposed, hardly a credible contender for England's most capped player. The young men around us were cooing 'Ooh Beverley' at him. He looked sheepish as if he could hear their banal jibes above the raucous commotion. He had recently married Joy Beverley, a member of a popular singing trio The Beverley Sisters. There was little fuss. He took a day off training. She took a few hours off her rehearsals. Just a few gathered at the Poole registry office. It was described as 'a quiet affair'. So, no Berkshire castle and hosts of angelic harpists. No tanker of pink champagne, and no celebrity magazine to pick up the tab.

Although Bill Slater reduced the deficit with a penalty before half-time, Chelsea seemed well out of sight. At the interval, Wolves manager Stan Cullis instructed Slater to mark Greaves instead. It made little difference. Greaves continued to exploit Wolves' square defence with his lightning reactions and only a spoilsport linesman denied him a double hat-trick. Cullis might have been the 'iron manager' but he was a consummate sportsman, too. He told the *London Evening News* reporter, 'What a player Greaves is. Someone's just said he doesn't run around enough; he wouldn't have to do that for me.'

Cullis may have been wedded to a long-ball game and his panzer assaults, but he knew class when he saw it. I was exulted. The drama of the magazine freeze frame had been trumped by the exhilaration of the moving picture. I had just seen a game with sudden changes of pace, rapid speed of thought and explosive acceleration. If I was less startled by Greaves's wonderfully honed technique this was because he made this look so simple.

As a postscript to this stunning victory, four days later Chelsea played at Spurs and lost 4-0. Any designs I might have had on becoming a glory hunter were knocked back into lugubrious shape. But anything else would have been an offence to karma.

In their next home game against Newcastle, Chelsea won 6-5. Chelsea completed this season in 14th place, having scored 77 goals and conceded 98. Their average home attendance of 40,850 received royal entertainment with 13 victories and 52 goals; so did their opponents' fans as Chelsea lost 14 games on the road conceding 61. Greaves scored 32 league goals, 42 per cent of Chelsea's total.

Although largely ignored in Britain, George Raynor from Barnsley coached a gold-winning Swedish side in the 1948 Olympics and another who reached the 1958 World Cup Final in Sweden. PA Images

'Eyes on the prize': Stanley Matthews takes on Bolton centre-half Barrass in the 1953 FA Cup Final. Blackpool won 4-3 after being 1-3 behind. PA Images

On 25 November 1953, Hungary tormented England with their passing, movement, and precise finishing. Here, Hidegkuti scores his hat-trick and Hungary's sixth goal, in a 6-3 rout. PA Images

Jimmy Hogan of Burnley, standing far left, coached the 1932 Austrian 'Wunderteam'. Hungarian manager, Sebes said after the rout at Wembley: 'We played football as Jimmy Hogan taught us'. PA Images

Leake of Third Division (North) Port Vale scored the only goal in an attritional FA Cup sixth round tie at Leyton Orient in March 1954 but lost to FA Cup winners, West Bromwich in the semi-finals. **PA Images**

Third Division (North) York City drew 1-1 with Newcastle United in the 1954/55 FA Cup semi-finals. Arthur Bottom narrowly failed to score here and Newcastle won the replay. **PA Images**

Gregg saves brilliantly in an FA Cup tie versus Ipswich, two weeks before the Munich crash. PA Images

Nat Lofthouse scoring the opening goal in a 2-0 win against Manchester United in an emotional FA Cup Final on 3 May 1958. Homegrown Bolton thrived in the top flight until the abolition of the maximum wage made it much harder for them to compete.
PA Images

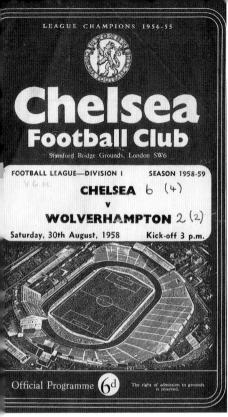

Jimmy Greaves (right) and Surrey county cricketer, Ron Tindall, were Chelsea's twin hit men in a 6-2 thrashing of Football League champions, Wolves on 30 August 1958. Greaves scored five goals.

Spurs goalie Hollowbread saves under pressure from Norwich's Terry Bly in an FA Cup tie on 14 February 1959. Jones's late equaliser saved Spurs' blushes but Norwich won the replay. PA Images

In his final season, Tom Finney helped Preston achieve a 4-1 win at Ewood Park in October 1959. PA Images

First Division champions elect Burnley beat Chelsea 2-1 at Turf Moor in January 1960.

Bolton 'hard man' Tommy Banks who turned the Manchester PFA meeting in favour of a strike, supporting Jimmy Hill's pursuit of the abolition of the maximum wage.

Burnley right winger, Trevor Meredith, substituting for injured John Connelly, scores the title-winning goal at Maine Road, Manchester on 2 May 1960. Jimmy McIlroy (right) looks on. **PA Images**

Afterwards, captain Adamson (left), Pointer, Blacklaw and Cummings celebrated in Burnley Town Hall.

Burnley Football League champions 1959/60. Back from left: Elder, Robson, Cummings, Blacklaw, Miller, Angus, Meredith. Front: Connelly, McIlroy, Adamson, Pointer, Pilkington. **PA Images**

'Double'-winning Spurs in 1961. Back left: Brown, Baker, Henry, Blanchflower, Norman, Mackay; Front: Jones, White, Smith, Allen, Dyson. **PA Images**

34.

NORWICH CITY: CANARY COMMOTION – CITY'S FAMOUS 1958/59 FA CUP RUN

THE 1953/54 season ended disappointingly for Norwich after a bright start. In early January they led Third Division (South) and were progressing well in the FA Cup, having eliminated a stubborn Hastings United in a third-round replay. This set them up with a prestigious tie at Highbury where they surprisingly beat Arsenal 2-1, after coming from behind. Thereafter league results were not quite as good, leaving them in seventh place at the end of the season and disappointingly losing to Leicester at home in the fifth round of the FA Cup. However, what happened in 1958/59 put them on a par with Port Vale and York City, two Third Division sides who almost reached the FA Cup Final.

Frequently, the poor state of '50s pitches during the winter months helped the underdog, allied to the supposed top dogs' lack of professionalism in training, tactics, and skills improvement. Nottingham Forest came perilously close to defeat in the third round on an ice-bound, rutted surface at Tooting and Mitcham on their way to winning the competition in 1959, while Liverpool, then a Second Division side, lost their balance on Worcester City's ice rink at the same stage. Non-league Boston United decimated promotion-chasing Derby County 6-1 at the Baseball Ground in 1955. Third Division Bournemouth eliminated both Spurs and Wolves in the 1956/57 competition, breaking one of Wolves' goalposts as well as their hearts, while Chelsea were humiliated 4-1 by Darlington in a 1957/58 third round replay. Afterwards, Ted Drake berated his players for over an hour in the dressing room, focusing on their wayward shooting and careless defending. As a result, they missed their return train.

The maximum wage cap and the feudal 'retain and transfer' system enabled smaller clubs to retain their most talented players for longer. After Third Division Southampton thrashed top-flight Manchester City 5-1 at Maine Road in the 1959/60 FA Cup, they kept their two wingers, who had created such mayhem – the tricky Terry Paine and tearaway John Sydenham. In time both proved they were talented enough to play at the highest level, with their parent club.

Norwich's 1958/59 cup run began inauspiciously. They were languishing in 16th place in the newly formed Third Division. Their manager Archie Macaulay, a distinguished former Arsenal and Scottish international right-half, was under intense pressure. Early in the season he barricaded himself in his office as disillusioned fans protested loudly in the street outside. In keeping with the dismal mood City struggled to beat amateurs Ilford, a lowly-placed Isthmian League side, at home in the first round. The Canaries were a goal behind at half-time and only secured victory late in the game through two goals from Brennan and one from Hill.

In the second round they drew at Swindon but then found themselves under the cosh in the replay. Worse still, goalkeeper Ken Nethercott was injured diving at the feet of a Swindon forward and had to leave the field. Instantly, adversity turned the crowd's disgruntlement into passion as they began bellowing their depleted side on. Revelling in the febrile atmosphere, the dapper, crew-cut Canadian Errol Crossan scored, putting City through for a home tie with Manchester United in the third round.

Despite taking merciless flak from the fans, the poker-faced Macaulay kept his nerve, managing to elicit a steely response from his previously under-performing side. Macaulay knew his team could play. He just needed to make them realise this. His shrewd positional changes helped. Ron Ashman, with over 400 senior games behind him, was converted from an underwhelming wing-half into a solid, thoughtful left-back. Here, he was partnered by the steady Brian Thurlow. Roy McCrohan was then shifted into the vacant right-half position, where he operated in a defensive capacity. Macaulay also restored the once twinkling Bobby Brennan to the left wing when most supporters thought he was finished. Meanwhile, on the opposite flank, Errol Crossan, nicknamed 'Cowboy' because of his Canadian roots, was encouraged to run with paralysing directness at opposing defences. The little Irishman, Jimmy Hill, was given licence to exercise his craft in midfield. In turn, Terry Allcock was instructed to partner the predatory Terry Bly. The tactical changes worked. Confidence began to sweep through the previously spluttering side. The alchemy may have been puzzling but no one at Norwich was complaining.

Manchester United did not cut any corners in their preparations. They fielded their strongest side, including expensive recruit Albert 'Golden Boy' Quixall, Bobby Charlton, Dennis Viollet, Bill Foulkes, Warren Bradley and Irish international goalkeeper Harry Gregg. Although Munich was still fresh in their minds, United's league form had recovered remarkably. They finished the season as First Division runners-up behind Wolves.

The afternoon was numbingly cold and 35 fans needed St John's Ambulance brigade assistance. Skipper Ron Ashman won the toss and invited United to face the low, dazzling winter sun. With a thin, crusty carpet of snow covering a rock-like surface, both sides had difficulty keeping their feet. Macaulay instructed his team to press United from the start and to sit tightly on their trio of forwards, Charlton, Viollet and Quixall.

Nevertheless, United made the better start. Fortunately, Charlton slipped when through on goal and Thurlow managed to clear another effort off the line. But thereafter Norwich seized control. United wing-halves Freddie Goodwin and Wilf McGuinness became bewildered by the skill and thrust of Hill and Allcock, while full-backs Carolan and Foulkes were undone by Brennan's sparkling footwork and Crossan's speed. The quality of Norwich's football was unbelievable. Only an outstanding display of goalkeeping from Gregg kept the final score down to 3-0.

The star was local-born centre-forward Terry Bly, who, on this shivering afternoon, simply roasted United centre-half Ronnie Cope. Macaulay commented, 'Using his speed and balance, Bly had all the room he needed in the middle and could have had half a dozen goals.' Bly had to settle for two. The first came after 31 minutes. Allcock's penetrative pass gave Brennan the opportunity to run to the goal line from where he sent a skidding centre into the United box. Bly's sprint proved too quick for the slipping and sliding Manchester defenders and without hesitation he blasted the ball past Gregg. Although a retaliatory attack resulted in Viollet heading wide, Norwich were deservedly in front at the break. Nethercott had only one save to make before half-time, when he dealt competently with Scanlon's curling shot.

Norwich were uncontainable after the break and United's defence became besieged. Bly's header hit the crossbar, releasing a shower of snow. Bobby Brennan's shot struck the post and Terry Allcock's effort was blocked on the line. Gregg was forced to hurl himself this way and that to keep the rampant Canaries at bay. It couldn't last and it didn't as on the hour, Bly beat Foulkes and raced down the left. Making an unaccustomed error, Gregg could only parry Bly's high delivery, allowing Crossan to head into the empty net.

Still Norwich poured forward. Gregg saved brilliantly from Bly. Allcock's shot fizzed past the post and a Crossan effort was disallowed. But with only two minutes remaining, Norwich added to United's humiliation. Having beaten the hapless Cope once again, Bly was left with a clear run on goal. He did not squander the chance, cutting in from the left and producing a searing drive which flashed past Gregg. Bly remarked, 'I only had a few touches, but each touch seemed to result in a goal.' The headline of the local *Pink 'Un* read, 'Bly, Bly Babes'. One female Norwich supporter made the mistake of wearing a red raincoat. Mistaking her for a United fan, a group of Norwich fans pelted her with snowballs throughout the game.

This was a personal triumph for Bly. He nearly gave up playing football during the previous season because of a serious cartilage injury. Former Norwich skipper and future manager Ron Ashman confessed, 'It's difficult to work out what happened to us. We were a struggling Third Division team lucky to be in the third round. Then suddenly we had this conviction we could beat anyone. You see it wasn't just that we had taken United to the cleaners. There were good players in our team, a lot of good players. We weren't a kick and rush side. It just needed something to set it off. Beating United did that for us. We were on our way. Home advantage is a tremendous thing in the FA Cup, but as time went on, we honestly believed we could win anywhere against anyone.'

A jubilant Macaulay remarked, 'They all laughed when I said we could beat United, but I knew our men were capable of winning. I planned two lines of defence. Right-half Roy McCrohan stayed back with centre-half Butler and the full-backs while left-half Matt Crowe operated in front. As soon as a Norwich move broke down, Terry Allcock doubled back with Crowe. This way we broke up most of their moves before they started. I reckoned full-back Billy Foulkes could be beaten so I told inside-left Jimmy Hill to stay on the wing with Bobby Brennan. That was where our goals came from. It worked to perfection.'

Norwich's next opponents were Cardiff City, heading for a top-flight return. They'd lost their top goalscorer, Gerry Hitchens, to Villa. Once again, Bly was the two-goal hero, chipping the Cardiff keeper for a second-half winner. Crossan was Norwich's other scorer. According to one supporter who had been on Christmas Island during the nuclear tests of 1957, the roar produced by the 38,000 crowd was louder than an H-bomb explosion. In a tough battle of birds, yellow had prevailed over blue with a 3-2 victory, setting up Norwich with a sterner fourth round tie, away at that old boiler of a cockerel – Tottenham Hotspur.

Spurs' boss Bill Nicholson was always meticulous in his preparations. He travelled to Carrow Road to examine Norwich's game plans, their strengths and weaknesses, making sure all his stars were fully briefed. He was a hard taskmaster. Nicholson expected the highest standards from his players on and off the pitch. He was also a shrewd tactician; one of the canniest around. In his first match in charge of Spurs, on 11 October 1958, visiting Everton were hammered 10-4, the call sign of TV detective Broderick Crawford in the popular series *Highway Patrol*. The spindly Tommy Harmer, Spurs' highly-strung, chain-smoking schemer, created most of the chances, which bustling centre-forward Bobby Smith put away. Captain Danny Blanchflower was not carried away, though, musing to Nicholson after this rout, 'It can only get worse.'

Nicholson knew he was right. He recalled, 'Too many silly goals were given away.' Spurs leaked 95 league goals during that season, relegation form. Ironically, Blanchflower was partly to blame. He tended to neglect his defensive duties while seeking to inflict damage at the other end. Having failed to heed his manager's instructions, Blanchflower was dropped for the Norwich game.

But Blanchflower's cavalier performances were not Nicholson's main problem. His whole team was misfiring. Cliff Jones, signed for a record fee from Swansea, looked more like an apprentice than the world-class winger he was about to become. As talented as he clearly was, Johnny Brooks performed fitfully at inside-forward – 'always better in a winning side', was Nicholson's terse assessment. Nicholson lacked a dynamic ball-winner in midfield. Hearts' Dave Mackay fitted that bill, but he would not arrive until March.

A more consistent goalscorer was needed to play alongside Smith but for now he had to make do with Dave Dunmore. Chelsea's Les Allen would become a better option, but he would not arrive until later in the year; the product of a shrewd swap, involving Brooks. Ultimately, Nicholson discovered that Jimmy Greaves would deliver the best solution, prompting him to ask his board to pay AC Milan £99,999 for him in 1961. The goalkeeping position was vulnerable, too. Nicholson did not rate either John Hollowbread or Ron Reynolds. Only Dundee's Bill Brown would satisfy his need.

While the task facing Norwich seemed enormous, Archie Macaulay was aware of Spurs' troubles. Despite their superior flair and technique, he knew their defensive organisation was shaky and their morale was fragile. He believed his team had a chance, particularly given the strength of support his team now commanded. Around 20,000 Norwich fans travelled to a grey, murky White Hart Lane; almost doubling the number that grumpily attended City's home games at the start of the season. Norwich was in the grip of cup fever with tickets at a premium and work schedules going haywire. There were hardly any locals unfamiliar with the mournful, yet oddly inspiring, lyrics of the Carrow Road anthem, 'On the Ball City'. The club dominated the front pages of the local paper for weeks.

Macaulay instructed his team to press Spurs – to get into their faces and force errors. He knew they had to stop the Londoners playing. It was not pretty, and his team's tackling was ultra-tough. Everyone defended, from back to front. But chances still arrived. Thankfully, Ken Nethercott was in excellent form, making three smart saves before the interval. Ron Ashman recalled, 'We had to keep things tight because Spurs had some outstanding individuals. They had to be pinned down, and in a cup-tie atmosphere you are bound to get rugged stuff. We needed a goal to settle us down.'

The Norwich players were buoyant at the interval. They had done half of their job well and Spurs had not hurt them. Their hosts seemed dispirited. Sensing this, Norwich seized the initiative straight after the break. They showed they could sting as well as tame. After 65 minutes Terry Allcock deservedly put them ahead. Much as Macaulay had hoped, Spurs began to fragment – drooping postures and resigned looks abounded. Jones's murderous pace deserted him. Like his colleagues he continually ran into blind alleys, wandering ineffectively along the left wing where he was barracked by the impatient home supporters.

With Spurs unravelling, Hill, Allcock and Bly had good chances to make the tie safe, but they spurned them. Time was almost up when Dunmore chased a loose ball on the left flank. He centred immediately. Hearing Jones's call to 'leave it', Bobby Smith dummied the cross, allowing the out-of-sorts Welsh winger to volley home the equaliser. Ashman was aghast, saying, 'It was the one defensive error we made. We never expected Dunmore to retrieve the ball after Jim Iley sliced a shot towards the touchline. But he did. I managed to get a hand to Cliff Jones's shot but I couldn't stop it.'

For the replay, Blanchflower was restored at inside-right in place of Harmer. Welsh international winger, Terry Medwin, came in for Brooks and Eddie Clayton took over from Dunmore. Norwich were unchanged. Carrow Road was like a cauldron as a further 38,000 crammed in. Blanchflower remarked, 'I have played all round the world in some of the world's greatest stadiums. But I have never experienced an atmosphere like that. The crowd is worth a goal start for Norwich. The anthems, the cheers are always in your ears. There is no way you can shut them out.' There was no way of shutting out Norwich's team, either.

Spurs almost went ahead through Smith, but Nethercott saved his shot superbly. 'At my age one good save a match is enough,' cracked the veteran goalkeeper. He was not troubled again. Roared on by a febrile crowd, Norwich swarmed all over Spurs and the crucial breakthrough came in the 63rd minute. Ashman chipped the ball in to the box, although he later conceded it was a miskick. The Spurs defenders were slow to react to a deflection. Finding indecent space, Bly unhesitatingly drove the loose ball past Hollowbread. The misty, night sky was rent with a thunderous roar, which might have been heard in Ipswich. City's rivals would never have admitted it, though.

At the final whistle, the delirious crowd poured on to the pitch. Still Ashman found enough space to dance an excited jig with a policeman whose sense of duty took second place to elation. Lugubrious yet sporting, Nicholson said, 'Norwich are a good side. They kept coming at us all the time. Good luck to them in the next round.' Norwich were drawn away at Sheffield United, then managed by Joe Mercer, Macaulay's former Arsenal colleague.

Wily Mercer had successfully introduced *Catenaccio* to Bramall Lane. The principal aim of this miserly defensive system was to bolt the back door securely before venturing forward. The priority was to ensure that each of the opposing forwards was picked up by a marker before they could intrude into the box. A 'sweeper' operated behind these markers, sealing any gaps and taking care of those breaking from deep positions.

Archie found that Blades right-back Cec Coldwell did not cover the centre-half as well as England's Graham Shaw did on the left. He decided, therefore, that Norwich should probe United's left flank to draw Joe Shaw over to that side and then attempt to exploit the greater space left by Coldwell on the Blades' right by launching long passes into the inside-left channel for Bly or Hill to latch on to. The move had to be played at pace and the passes executed with great accuracy. Also, the resulting crosses needed to be delivered far enough out to keep United goalkeeper Hodgkinson at home, but not so far out that the wing-halves could snuff out the danger.

Before the game plan could be implemented effectively, disaster struck. First, Norwich went a goal down as Billy Russell's deflected shot looped over a stranded Nethercott. Then, Norwich's goalkeeper dislocated his right shoulder after diving at the feet of United's winger. The sun shone brightly at Bramall Lane, yet City's hopes seemed eclipsed. Seeing how much pain Nethercott was in, Macaulay instructed him to come off, indicating that outside-left Brennan should replace him. Ashman over-ruled his manager, though, telling Nethercott, 'If you go off, we have no chance of equalising. You go back in goal, Ken, and we'll keep Sheffield out of your reach.'

Heroic Nethercott did as he was bid. Bert Trautmann had remained bravely at his post after being badly injured during the

1956 FA Cup Final. Nethercott's decision to remain was equally courageous if foolhardy. Nevertheless, one-armed Ken saw out the game. Ashman was as good as his word and with little time remaining Crossan equalised. Nethercott would never play for Norwich again, however, and Sandy Kennon replaced him in the replay.

Having jumped jail, Norwich grasped their chance to reach the semi-finals. At Carrow Road they surged into a 2-0 lead in the replay. Brennan opened their account, turning his marker before thumping a drive into the top-right corner. Then Bly seized upon a defence-splitting pass and dinked a delicate chip over the advancing Hodgkinson. However, the Blades reduced the deficit before half-time when the arch poacher 'Doc' Pace pounced after Kennon had fumbled Hamilton's low shot. After the break, Bly restored City's two-goal lead, blasting in from close range. Although Gerry Summers headed in from a late corner, causing a tense finish, Norwich held out for a 3-2 win.

In the semi-final at White Hart Lane, Luton were their opponents. Although Luton were then a declining First Division side, Norwich failed to rise to the occasion. Despite dominating the early play, they missed several gilt-edged chances. Allan Brown made them pay for their profligacy by heading the Hatters into a first-half lead from Billy Bingham's precise cross. Although Brennan equalised after the break with a scorching drive, capitalising upon a miscued header, Norwich could not make their superiority count. Kennon had been ill-at-ease in the Norwich goal, but City were indebted to his fine, acrobatic save which denied Luton a late winner.

In the replay at St Andrew's, Norwich again had the better of the early play but found former England goalkeeper Ron Baynham in international form. On the one occasion when a City forward managed to beat him, Brendan McNally cleared off the line. And once again Norwich were left to rue their negligence as Northern Ireland's World Cup hero, Billy Bingham, stabbed home a second-half winner.

At Wembley, Luton played poorly in losing to ten-man Nottingham Forest. The Norwich players and fans reckoned that they would have made a better fist of it. Instead, they had to console themselves with their unexpected celebrity status.

For almost three months they were the talk of the nation. Their heroics struck a positive note in a generally undistinguished time for British football.

First Division table (May 1959)

	P	W	D	L	F	A	Pts	Goal ave
1. Wolverhampton Wanderers	42	28	5	9	110	49	61	2.2
2. Manchester United	42	24	7	11	103	66	55	1.6
3. Arsenal	42	21	8	13	88	68	50	1.3
4. Bolton Wanderers	42	20	10	12	79	66	50	1.2
5. West Bromwich Albion	42	18	13	11	88	68	49	1.3
6. West Ham United	42	21	6	15	85	70	48	1.2
7. Burnley	42	19	10	13	81	70	48	1.2
8. Blackpool	42	18	11	13	66	49	47	1.3
9. Birmingham City	42	20	6	16	84	68	46	1.2
10. Blackburn Rovers	42	17	10	15	76	70	44	1.0
11. Newcastle United	42	17	7	18	80	80	41	1.0
12. Preston North End	42	17	7	18	70	77	41	0.9
13. Nottingham Forest	42	17	6	19	71	74	40	1.0
14. Chelsea	42	18	4	20	77	98	40	0.8
15. Leeds United	42	15	9	18	57	74	39	0.8
16. Everton	42	17	4	21	71	87	38	0.8
17. Luton Town	42	12	13	17	68	71	37	1.0
18. Tottenham Hotspur	42	13	10	19	85	95	36	1.0
19. Leicester City	42	11	10	21	67	98	32	0.7
20. Manchester City	42	11	9	22	64	95	31	0.7
21. Aston Villa	42	11	8	23	58	87	30	0.7
22. Portsmouth	42	6	9	27	64	112	21	0.6

35.

'NEVER HAD IT SO GOOD'?
BRINGING ON BACK THE
BAD TIMES

MATT BUSBY had flown to Madrid to persuade Real Madrid president Santiago Bernabeu to play two money-spinning friendlies with his team. But were United as penniless as he claimed? His club accounts for 1957/58 revealed an annual profit of £97,957 – the largest then in British football's history and worth around £4m in today's values.

Sunderland's relegation from the First Division in 1958 meant that they would taste second-tier football for the first time in their history. They were the architects of their own demise, having allowed their side to succumb to age and injury without securing adequate replacements. The club was also torn apart by an illegal payments scandal, anticipating the abolition of the maximum wage. While moral crusader Alan Brown cleaned up their act after taking charge in 1957, Sunderland would not recover their top-flight status until 1964.

Despite prime minister Harold Macmillan's confidence, Britain's consumer boom of the late '50s was not founded upon a strong, sustainable economy. Heavy reliance was placed upon traditional, heavy industries – steel, coal, shipbuilding, and car manufacturing. The textile industry was already in decline because of the strength of foreign competition. One by one, these heavy industries would follow suit.

As a reflection of our economy's growing vulnerability the jobless total rose by almost 500,000 in 1958 – the highest annual rise in ten years. The truth was that Britain was slipping down the international rankings – not only on the sports field but in commerce and industry. After its humiliation at Suez, Britain seemed more circumspect about churning out repetitious heroic war dramas, although the production of *The Battle of the River Plate* for a royal premier showing in 1956, just after the Suez fiasco, was badly off message.

Nevertheless, there were many Britons who were unprepared for the controversial 1959 British film, *Yesterday's Enemy*. For the film had the temerity to suggest that British armed forces were not always honourable in combat. The Oxbridge revue *Beyond the Fringe*, that would premiere in August 1960, went further, mocking stiff-upper-lipped heroism. *Beyond the Fringe* was appreciated more in London than in the provinces where there was a prevalent belief that Britain was always great and grateful.

In 1958 Britain re-tagged Empire Day as Commonwealth Day. Although Macmillan's 'Winds of Change' address to the South African parliament had yet to result in mass decolonisation, this was about to happen at breakneck speed during his 1959–64 administration. His Conservative government had realised that colonialism was no longer affordable. Although his government felt rightly compelled to meet their Commonwealth duties, allowing immigration from former and existing colonies, the growth in immigration escalated tensions in poorer areas where the competition for housing and jobs was more acute. This, plus sexual jealousy, was the background to the 1958 race riots in Nottingham and Notting Hill. Colin MacInnes, author of the 1959 novel *Absolute Beginners,* argued that he did not understand England anymore, questioning those who sought to exclude colonial immigrants when imperial Britain had formerly plundered their territories, arrogantly presuming a right of entry.

Racism was rife in the '50s as confirmed by Charlie Williams, Doncaster's mixed-race centre-half, whom I saw play at Reading on 6 September 1958. As a former coal miner, Williams said that he learnt to combat racial slurs with a martial art of humour. 'I've been left in the oven too long,' he would tell his detractors. So successful was he at comic self-deprecation that he eventually became a well-known TV stand-up comedian appearing alongside that bastion of political correctness, Bernard Manning, before hosting a game show, *The Golden Shot*. Whatever views we may hold about his choice of humour, he was one of very few professional footballers of colour during the

'50s, helping pave the way to wider acceptance of black and minority ethnic players during the ensuing decades.

While the '50s had featured a growth of more far-sighted coaches, prepared to question established truths, and propose new ways of playing, there were still glaring deficiencies in the organisation of English football, notably in arranging overseas tours and tournaments. Such shortcomings were evident during the 1950 World Cup and featured again in the organisation of England's summer tour of South America in 1959.

Walter Winterbottom and the FA failed to acclimatise the players in preparation for the blazing temperatures and high altitudes of Mexico and Peru. Consequently, the England team crumbled to humiliating defeats in both games, just as they had done in the intense heat of Belgrade, 12 months before, prior to the Sweden World Cup. The British press were unforgiving in their criticisms.

The following extract is from an anonymous report written by a journalist travelling with the 1959 FA party, 'The England players struggled to breathe in Mexico, a game played at high altitude. Wilf McGuinness was substituted after 30 minutes. He had to go to the dressing-room for an emergency intake of oxygen. Doug Holden was the next to leave after an hour. Ronnie Clayton's sunburnt back blistered so badly during the game that a Mexican doctor was summoned. Clayton and his colleagues were horrified when the doctor bathed his burns with methylated spirit.'

The Football Association had ignored Winterbottom's advice that the England team should always be accompanied by a team doctor and were rightly criticised for their negligence. The tour was a total fiasco. England lost all three internationals, 2-0 to Brazil, 4-1 to Peru and 2-1 to Mexico, and the accommodation provided was often shambolic with Ron Flowers once sharing a hotel room with six complete strangers. It was nine years on, yet nothing seemed to have been learnt from the 1950 World Cup.

After the wretched 1959 tour of South America, former England international and journalist David Jack concluded, 'Make no mistake this is crisis time for England. The game we gave to the world is no longer played with the required skill in these islands.' Jack blamed poor team selection, whereas Nottingham Forest's FA Cup winning manager, Billy Walker, blamed the lack of craft in the inside-forward and wing-half positions. Even Johnny Haynes, an inside-forward of Wayne Rooney's stature, was not excused. Walker complained that English coaches were suppressing individual flair. Charles Buchan, editor of *Football Monthly*, blamed England's failure to compete upon their tactical intransigence. He said, 'We will not accept the facts that long wing-to-wing passes and long kicks upfield by full-backs are useless. And that players trying to run, or dribble, round opponents are doomed to failure.'

Burnley and Northern Ireland playmaker Jimmy McIlroy shared Buchan's frustration. In 1960 Jimmy wrote, 'I wish I could interest every club in the country in FOOTBALL. I mean football, which does not include "getting stuck in", "fighting" or "belting the ball". Before Burnley leave their dressing room, the final instructions from manager Harry Potts are nearly always the same, "Play football but above all, enjoy your game." What a pity it is that other managers do not think the same way. Critics bewail the lack of ball players and so do I.

'Yet the blame rests entirely on the people who control the teams. What chance has a boy to concentrate on skill as he avoids crunching tackles and hard robust play? Why aren't defenders taught to win the ball in a tackle, instead of simply learning to "stop" an opponent? I believe skill and fight are opposites – the complete footballer possesses a blend of both – but the emphasis should be very much on skill. If we are to equal the best in continental football the tough stuff must be erased from our game, to make way for more subtlety, delicacy, and softness of touch. Like sheep, clubs follow the leader. When Wolves and Chelsea won the league the secret of their success was claimed to be hard fighting soccer, which led to many copying this method. My wish for the coming 1960/61 season is that Burnley's style of play becomes the fashion, because I'm certain English football will benefit from it.'

Writing in his book *One Hundred Caps and All That*, ex-Wolves and England captain Billy Wright concluded, 'Our whole approach to the game has marked time while the rest of the world, unfettered by a grand history and a ponderous league system, has galloped by at the double.' Wright played in the England sides twice thrashed by Hungary and, after watching his former club torn apart in both home and away legs by Barcelona in the European Cup of 1959/60, he commented, 'I used to think it was right for a team to go out and play their game naturally; to work things out as the game developed. That was until I met the crack continental sides. They showed football played to a highly organised plan. It is the big difference between English football and the best abroad.'

At home, football and cricket remained largely insulated from a world that was leaving Britain behind. Up until 1962, professional cricket staged an annual representative contest between the 'Gentlemen' and the 'Players'. The administration of the game epitomised the 'old school tie' ethos. England would not recover the Ashes until the early '70s and then, only after the appointment of a curmudgeonly professional, tactical leader in Raymond Illingworth.

At national and club levels, professional football was little different from cricket or indeed British politics and business. It was still gripped by what Anthony Sampson described, in his book *Anatomy of Britain*, as 'club-amateur' influences, characterised by complacency, insularity, nepotism and stale traditions. Even at national level, Winterbottom was not entitled to pick his team without the input of an FA committee, made up of the 'great and the good' but with no experience of managing professional football. Ultimately, English football would look to another ultra-professional tactician, Alf Ramsey, to change that practice and restore our international prowess.

In the 1959/60 FA Cup there were further surprises. Third Division Bradford City defeated Everton 3-0 in the Valley Parade slime. Fourth Division Watford eliminated Birmingham City thanks to goals from prolific pair Holton and Uphill and Second Division Rotherham overcame Arsenal after two replays. 'Arsenal Shamed'; 'Arsenal Flop'; 'Arsenal Quit'; 'No Skill, No Fight from Arsenal', shrieked the popular press. A celebrity carve-up was enjoyed then as much as it is now. Arsenal manager George Swindin vainly attempted to forestall the hanging party by making a pre-emptive admission of guilt. He solemnly announced, 'We were out-tackled, out-run, out-sped, out-played and out-thought by Rotherham.'

Even Spurs came close to a further embarrassment at Crewe, having been eliminated by Norwich City in the previous season. However, they escaped from Gresty Road with a 2-2 draw before inflicting bloody revenge in the replay. Crewe were decimated 13-2 with new striker Les Allen scoring five times. Ironically, Crewe left Euston from platform 13, arriving back at Crewe at platform two.

Alongside the successful Southampton smash-and-grab raid, one of the most astonishing results of the third-round ties in 1959/60 came at a frost-bitten, snow-covered Upton Park, where the pitch was pronounced fit for play only two hours before the Wednesday afternoon kick-off. Surprisingly, the victims were a leading, modern-thinking club. West Ham had drawn at Huddersfield and were expected to win the replay. On 13 January 1960, I inveigled Dad into excusing my school absence, and taking me to Upton Park.

36.

WEST HAM UNITED v HUDDERSFIELD TOWN: FA CUP THIRD ROUND, 13 JANUARY 1960

THERE WERE around 300 Terriers fans there who had travelled more in hope than expectation. Little did we know that a new star would be thrust before us. Improbably, he was on the side of the Second Division underdogs and even more improbably he took the form of a frail-looking 19-year-old. I heard the lad had earned his chance by scoring in the first game at Leeds Road. Now he proceeded to take his place in the limelight – if a hazy shade of winter grey could be so described.

As he limbered up, he looked as if he had duped his team-mates – a ball boy in the Huddersfield stripes. But if his slender physique suggested that he might be out of his depth, his technique instantly refuted this. From the first kick he was in the thick of the action. No nerves, no hesitancy, he was immediately on the money. Time and again he took on the slipping and sliding Hammers, retaining a mesmerising sureness of touch. With a feint here and a shimmy there he persistently bewildered his markers, deftly evading their lunging tackles and employing his darting pace to accelerate away from trouble.

Never selfish, he continually probed for openings which his team-mates could exploit, employing an expansive range of penetrative passes to ravage West Ham's jittery defence. His stamina was astonishing, pushing forward at lightning speed when the ball was won and tenaciously chasing opponents down when it was lost.

He never let the home defenders settle, constantly harrying and hurrying them, haring from one to another like a frisky sheepdog. His appetite for the ball seemed uncontainable, as he continually returned to the edge of his box to give his goalkeeper, Ray Wood, an attacking outlet.

Supremely confident but never arrogant, he seemed oblivious to the aggravation his precocious talent might be arousing. As it was, he had it his way – the chapped, foot stamping, ear tingling crowd was won over. Setting aside their partisan passions the home fans began to acknowledge his genius. If this was a 'ballet on ice' then its choreographer and leading performer was Denis Law.

As early as the 12th minute the young Scotsman had the ball in the net only to be frustrated by an offside flag. The reprieve was short-lived. Scampering around West Ham's midfielders, he released Ledger with a searing through ball. The right-winger seized his opportunity, flashing over a head-high centre for Massie to thump home an unstoppable header. In the 23rd minute Ledger was again the provider, lifting another centre into the West Ham box which keeper Dwyer failed to deal with, fumbling the ball that allowed left-half and captain Bill McGarry to tuck it away. Although West Ham reduced the deficit on 38 minutes through Musgrove, Huddersfield's two-goal lead was restored just before the break when Massie prodded in Jack Connor's pass.

Any hopes West Ham might have had of a second-half recovery were extinguished within a couple of minutes of the resumption. Seeing Ken Brown was having difficulty in controlling the ball on the tricky surface, Law struck instantly, dispossessing the West Ham centre-half and sending Connor clear. The visitors' centre-forward made no mistake finding goal with a crisp shot that evaded Dwyer's dive. With 20 minutes left, Connor doubled his account with an acute-angled shot that left Dwyer helpless. Grasping the 'if you can't beat them' mantra, the West Ham supporters began chanting 'we want six' while the ecstatic Huddersfield throng gave a full-throated rendition of their battle song 'Smile Awhile'. Law thought he had granted the ironic home fans' wishes but the referee played the party-pooper. Nevertheless, realising we had witnessed a performance of sublime skill, we gave Denis Law and his impressive team thunderous applause as they left the field.

For West Ham this was a further calamity as their promising season fell apart, while Huddersfield's glory was short-lived. Fewer than three weeks later, languishing Luton extinguished their mounting FA Cup ambitions with a solitary goal. Huddersfield had already lost their talismanic manager, Bill Shankly, to Liverpool. Soon they would lose their brilliant inside-right to Manchester City. The process whereby the richest talents flowed into the richest clubs was intensifying as the artificially level playing field, sustaining the archaic maximum wage and 'retain and transfer' systems, was about to be ploughed up.

In the meantime, fantasies of British dominance continued, as reflected in the huge popularity of Ian Fleming's 'snobbery with violence' fiction. Here we found superior British wit and courage confounding all, underpinned, even more improbably, by superior British technology. Fantasy was also at the heart of Keith Waterhouse's ironic novel *Billy Liar*, published in 1959, although a more sombre message lingers within Billy Fisher's serial escapism. It was as if fantasy was the sad refuge of bright, aspiring, young working-class men, frustrated by the class restrictions. These were the 'inbetweeners' who, unlike their forbears, did not have their identity defined by war, but were still too young to enjoy the better career opportunities and greater social mobility which the '60s conferred.

Perhaps *Billy Liar* served as a metaphor, too, for those who clung to the myths of Britain's past rather than facing up to the challenges of its present. Pathétically, the Crown chose to interpret one such challenge as a fight for decency by prosecuting Penguin books in 1960 for daring to print *Lady Chatterley's Lover*. Surely, the fustiness of Establishment thinking was no better exemplified than by the prosecuting counsel's summing up. He asked the members of the jury, 'Is it a book you would wish your wife or servants to read?'

At the beginning of the '60s, only two British teams threatened to challenge Real's supremacy in Europe: recently crowned First Division champions Burnley, and Bill Nicholson's Spurs. Ex-Busby Babe Eamon Dunphy reported, 'Burnley won the championship in 1960 playing cultured continental-style football under Jimmy Adamson, their captain, and Jimmy McIlroy, their gracious articulate schemer.'

Jimmy Greaves added, 'This Burnley team was brimming with outstanding individual players, and they were encouraged to play with emphasis more on skill than sweat and stamina. I loved playing against them because they put a smile on the face of football, and even in defeat I wanted to applaud their artistry. In an era when quite a few teams believed in the big boot, they were a league of gentlemen.'

PART TWO
1959/60

THE WATERSHED SEASON

1959/60
FACTS, FIGURES AND COMMENTARY

22 August 1959

Arsenal 0 Sheffield Wednesday 1
Birmingham City 0 Wolverhampton Wanderers 1
Blackburn Rovers 4 Fulham 0
Blackpool 3 Bolton Wanderers 2
Chelsea 4 Preston North End 4
Everton 2 Luton Town 2
Leeds United 2 Burnley 3
Manchester City 2 Nottingham Forest 1
Newcastle United 1 Tottenham Hotspur 5
West Bromwich Albion 3 Manchester United 2
West Ham United 3 Leicester City 0

August 1959 Match of the Month
Chelsea 4 Preston North End 4

Jimmy Greaves reckoned that specialist coaches and tacticians progressively took control of English professional football after this season. Neither Chelsea nor Preston had a coach and here it showed. Despite the scorching heat everyone piled forward at every opportunity. The wide spaces of Stamford Bridge left huge gaps to exploit. Greaves revelled in that space, scoring a hat-trick. England winger Peter Brabrook weighed in with another. But Tom Finney, in his last season before retirement, helped keep Preston in the game, scoring one and pulling the strings as a roaming centre-forward, while team-mates Derek Mayers, Tommy Thompson and future Manchester United manager Frank O'Farrell helped themselves. Both teams gave as good as they got as the game ended in an enthralling 4-4 draw. Preston's Scottish inside-left David Sneddon reflected, 'The rapid, first time passing confused me most of all when I came into English football. In Scotland, everything is much more deliberate, with forwards having time to carry the ball along before making their final passes. In England attacks are made so swiftly that the defenders hardly have time to ease up from one move to the next. I found this particularly true in this match. In the first few minutes the game seemed to be passing me by. Jimmy Greaves opened my eyes.

We have some bright young players in Scotland, but I have not seen a forward with so much potential brilliance as Greaves.' As for Greaves, he picked out Finney as his star of the show. He explained, 'Tom was so adept with either foot that I could never make up my mind which one was more effective when it came to shooting, passing, crossing, and dribbling. His body swerves and feints mesmerised countless defenders. He could beat any opponent, find the space to make a telling pass when under pressure, and he possessed a thunderous shot.'

25 August 1959
Birmingham City 4 Newcastle United 3
Bolton Wanderers 0 Blackburn Rovers 3
Burnley 5 Everton 2
Fulham 5 Manchester City 2
Leicester City 3 Leeds United 2
Luton Town 0 Blackpool 1
Manchester United 0 Chelsea 1
Nottingham Forest 0 Arsenal 3
Preston North End 1 West Ham United 1
Tottenham Hotspur 2 West Bromwich Albion 2
Wolverhampton Wanderers 3 Sheffield Wednesday 1

29 August 1959
Bolton Wanderers 2 Everton 1
Burnley 1 West Ham United 3
Fulham 1 Blackpool 0
Leicester City 3 Chelsea 1
Luton Town 0 Leeds United 1
Manchester United 3 Newcastle United 2
Nottingham Forest 2 Blackburn Rovers 2
Preston North End 1 West Bromwich Albion 1
Sheffield Wednesday 1 Manchester City 0
Tottenham Hotspur 0 Birmingham City 0
Wolverhampton Wanderers 3 Arsenal 3

29 August 1959	P	W	D	L	F	A	Pts	Goal ave
1. Blackburn Rovers	3	2	1	0	9	2	5	4.50
2. West Ham United	3	2	1	0	7	2	5	3.50
3. Wolverhampton Wanderers	3	2	1	0	7	4	5	1.75
4. Tottenham Hotspur	3	1	2	0	7	3	4	2.33

5. Blackpool	3	2	0	1	4	3	4	1.33
6. Burnley	3	2	0	1	9	7	4	1.29
7. West Bromwich Albion	3	1	2	0	6	5	4	1.20
8. Fulham	3	2	0	1	6	6	4	1.00
9. Leicester City	3	2	0	1	6	6	4	1.00
10. Sheffield Wednesday	3	2	0	1	3	3	4	1.00
11. Arsenal	3	1	1	1	6	4	3	1.50
12. Preston North End	3	0	3	0	6	6	3	1.00
13. Birmingham City	3	1	1	1	4	4	3	1.00
14. Chelsea	3	1	1	1	6	7	3	0.86
15. Leeds United	3	1	0	2	5	6	2	0.83
16. Manchester United	3	1	0	2	5	6	2	0.83
17. Bolton Wanderers	3	1	0	2	4	7	2	0.57
18. Manchester City	3	1	0	2	4	7	2	0.57
19. Everton	3	0	1	2	5	9	1	0.56
20. Luton Town	3	0	1	2	2	4	1	0.50
21. Nottingham Forest	3	0	1	2	3	7	1	0.43
22. Newcastle United	3	0	0	3	6	12	0	0.50

August 1959 Commentary

Blackburn were the early leaders with nine goals, four from Dobing. Cliff Jones scored three goals in Spurs' 5-1 win at Newcastle, as did Danny Clapton at FA Cup holders Forest. West Ham had begun the season in good form, too. Their 3-1 victory in Turf Moor's sizzling heat took them to second place. At the other end of the table, Newcastle had begun disastrously, losing all three opening fixtures and conceding 12 goals. FA Cup champions Nottingham Forest were scarcely better off. Both clubs were troubled by internecine squabbling. In a replay of the 1953 FA Cup Final, Blackpool defeated north-west rivals Bolton once again. Ray Charnley's brace was complemented by a goal from 1953 veteran, Jackie Mudie.

2 September 1959

Arsenal 1 Nottingham Forest 1
Blackburn Rovers 1 Bolton Wanderers 0
Blackpool 0 Luton Town 0
Chelsea 3 Manchester United 6

Everton 1 Burnley 2
Leeds United 1 Leicester City 1
Manchester City 3 Fulham 1
Newcastle United 1 Birmingham City 0
Sheffield Wednesday 2 Wolverhampton Wanderers 2
West Bromwich Albion 1 Tottenham Hotspur 2
West Ham United 2 Preston North End 1

5 September 1959
Arsenal 1 Tottenham Hotspur 1
Birmingham City 1 Manchester United 1
Blackburn Rovers 3 Sheffield Wednesday 1
Blackpool 0 Nottingham Forest 1
Chelsea 4 Burnley 1
Everton 0 Fulham 0
Luton Town 0 Bolton Wanderers 0
Manchester City 4 Wolverhampton Wanderers 6
Newcastle United 1 Preston North End 2
West Bromwich Albion 5 Leicester City 0
West Ham United 1 Leeds United 2

8 September 1959
Birmingham City 1 Chelsea 1
Bolton Wanderers 0 Arsenal 1
Burnley 2 Preston North End 1
Fulham 3 Wolverhampton Wanderers 1
Leicester City 1 Blackpool 1
Luton Town 1 Manchester City 2
Manchester United 6 Leeds United 0
Nottingham Forest 2 Sheffield Wednesday 1
Tottenham Hotspur 2 West Ham United 2
West Bromwich Albion 2 Newcastle United 2

12 September 1959
Arsenal 3 Manchester City 1
Bolton Wanderers 5 West Ham United 1
Burnley 2 West Bromwich Albion 1
Fulham 4 Luton Town 2

Leeds United 2 Chelsea 1
Leicester City 0 Newcastle United 2
Manchester United 1 Tottenham Hotspur 5
Nottingham Forest 1 Everton 1
Preston North End 3 Birmingham City 2
Sheffield Wednesday 5 Blackpool 0
Wolverhampton Wanderers 3 Blackburn Rovers 1

15 September 1959
Arsenal 2 Bolton Wanderers 1
Blackpool 3 Leicester City 3
Chelsea 4 Birmingham City 2
Everton 2 Blackburn Rovers 0
Leeds United 2 Manchester United 2
Manchester City 1 Luton Town 2
Newcastle United 0 West Bromwich Albion 0
Preston North End 1 Burnley 0
Sheffield Wednesday 0 Nottingham Forest 1
West Ham United 1 Tottenham Hotspur 2
Wolverhampton Wanderers 9 Fulham 0

19 September 1959
Birmingham City 3 Leicester City 4
Blackburn Rovers 1 Arsenal 1
Blackpool 3 Wolverhampton Wanderers 1
Bolton Wanderers 3 Fulham 2
Chelsea 2 West Ham United 4
Everton 2 Sheffield Wednesday 1
Luton Town 1 Nottingham Forest 0
Manchester City 3 Manchester United 0
Newcastle United 1 Burnley 3
Tottenham Hotspur 5 Preston North End 1
West Bromwich Albion 3 Leeds United 0

26 September 1959
Arsenal 2 Blackpool 1
Blackburn Rovers 3 Everton 1
Burnley 3 Birmingham City 1

187

Fulham 1 Chelsea 3
Leeds United 2 Newcastle United 3
Leicester City 1 Tottenham Hotspur 1
Manchester City 2 Blackburn Rovers 1
Nottingham Forest 2 Bolton Wanderers 0
Preston North End 4 Manchester United 0
Sheffield Wednesday 2 Luton Town 0
West Ham United 4 West Bromwich Albion 1
Wolverhampton Wanderers 2 Everton 0

September 1959 Commentary

One point separated four title contenders with Spurs in pole position. At the other end of the table, Leicester achieved a remarkable 4-3 win at St Andrew's having been 2-0 down inside 17 minutes. Preston avenged their 5-1 defeat at Spurs on 19 September by thumping Manchester United 4-0 a week later, including two goals from Finney in front of a 35,016 crowd. United's early form was erratic, losing 1-0 at home to Chelsea but winning the return game 6-3. They were thrashed 5-1 by Spurs at Old Trafford but beat Leeds 6-0.

Manchester City lost 6-4 at home to Wolves despite McAdams's hat-trick. Unreliable Chelsea then hammered title contenders Burnley 4-1, Greaves causing mayhem. Newly promoted Fulham beat champions Wolves 3-1 but lost the return game 9-0 with Deeley scoring four.

26 September 1959	P	W	D	L	F	A	Pts	Goal ave
1. Tottenham Hotspur	10	5	5	0	25	11	15	2.27
2. Wolverhampton Wanderers	10	6	2	2	31	17	14	1.82
3. Arsenal	10	5	4	1	17	10	14	1.70
4. Burnley	10	7	0	3	22	17	14	1.29
5. Blackburn Rovers	10	5	2	3	19	12	12	1.58
6. West Ham United	10	5	2	3	22	17	12	1.29
7. Preston North End	10	4	3	3	19	18	11	1.06
8. Nottingham Forest	10	4	3	3	11	11	11	1.00
9. West Bromwich Albion	10	3	4	3	19	15	10	1.27
10. Chelsea	10	4	2	4	24	24	10	1.00
11. Manchester City	10	5	0	5	20	21	10	0.95

12. Leicester City	10	3	4	3	16	22	10	0.73
13. Sheffield Wednesday	10	4	1	5	15	13	9	1.15
14. Blackpool	10	3	3	4	12	16	9	0.75
15. Fulham	10	4	1	5	17	27	9	0.63
16. Manchester United	10	3	2	5	21	24	8	0.88
17. Newcastle United	10	3	2	5	16	21	8	0.76
18. Leeds United	10	3	2	5	14	23	8	0.61
19. Bolton Wanderers	10	3	1	6	13	16	7	0.81
20. Everton	10	2	3	5	12	18	7	0.67
21. Luton Town	10	2	3	5	8	13	7	0.62
22. Birmingham City	10	1	3	6	14	21	5	0.67

September 1959 Match of the Month
Manchester City 3 Manchester United 0

Ageing City had made only two close-season signings: left-winger Clive Colbridge from Crewe for £10,000 and centre-forward Andy Kerr from Partick Thistle for £11,000. After three scoreless games, former star Bobby Johnstone was transferred back to Hibernian.

Both sides had made stuttering starts to the season. United were in tenth spot, seven places above City, but only two points ahead. Bristling with current and future internationals – Gregg, Foulkes, Quixall, McGuinness, Charlton, Viollet and Bradley – United had greater class but City made light of their disadvantage. Prompted by wing-half Ken Barnes, strikers Billy McAdams and Joe Hayes they set about the uncertain United defenders.

Stung by his omission at Luton, Hayes fired City into a two-goal lead within the first 11 minutes, taking advantage of sloppy United defending. With City centre-half McTavish dominating the dangerous Viollet, and their full-backs Leivers and Sear neutralising Scanlon and Bradley, the home side were comfortably in control. The 'man of the match' Hayes sealed United's fate with 20 minutes remaining, breaking free and setting up veteran playmaker George Hannah for a tap-in. Hayes liked derby games with ten goals in 17 of these encounters. Denis Law joined him up front in March 1960 when Law was bought from Huddersfield for £55,000, a British record.

City put too much faith in marquee signings rather than developing the whole team which was in dire need of new blood. Law soon realised his error – City's training was archaic and shambolic. It was scarcely better at United.

Lifted by this result, City completed five victories on the trot including a 5-1 win at PNE.

3 October 1959
Birmingham City 2 Leeds United 0
Blackburn Rovers 1 Preston North End 4
Blackpool 1 Manchester City 3
Bolton Wanderers 1 Sheffield Wednesday 0
Everton 3 Arsenal 1
Fulham 3 Nottingham Forest 1
Luton Town 1 Wolverhampton Wanderers 5
Manchester United 4 Leicester City 1
Newcastle United 0 West Ham United 0
Tottenham Hotspur 1 Burnley 1
West Bromwich Albion 1 Chelsea 3

10 October 1959
Birmingham City 0 Sheffield Wednesday 0
Burnley 1 Blackpool 4
Chelsea 0 Bolton Wanderers 2
Leeds United 3 Everton 3
Leicester City 2 Blackburn Rovers 3
Manchester United 4 Arsenal 2
Newcastle United 2 Nottingham Forest 1
Preston North End 1 Manchester City 5
Tottenham Hotspur 5 Wolverhampton Wanderers 1
West Bromwich Albion 2 Fulham 4
West Ham United 3 Luton Town 1

17 October 1959
Arsenal 0 Preston North End 3
Blackburn Rovers 3 Burnley 2
Blackpool 3 Leeds United 3
Bolton Wanderers 0 West Bromwich Albion 0
Everton 0 West Ham United 1
Fulham 4 Newcastle United 3

Luton Town 1 Chelsea 2
Manchester City 3 Leicester City 2
Nottingham Forest 0 Birmingham City 2
Sheffield Wednesday 2 Tottenham Hotspur 1
Wolverhampton Wanderers 3 Manchester United 2

24 October 1959
Birmingham City 2 Fulham 4
Burnley 4 Manchester City 3
Chelsea 1 Everton 0
Leeds United 0 Blackburn Rovers 1
Leicester City 2 Arsenal 2
Manchester United 3 Sheffield Wednesday 1
Newcastle United 0 Bolton Wanderers 2
Preston North End 4 Wolverhampton Wanderers 3
Tottenham Hotspur 2 Nottingham Forest 1
West Bromwich Albion 4 Luton Town 0
West Ham United 1 Blackpool 0

31 October 1959
Arsenal 3 Birmingham City 0
Blackburn Rovers 1 Manchester United 1
Blackpool 0 Preston North End 2
Bolton Wanderers 1 Leeds United 1
Everton 6 Leicester City 1
Fulham 1 West Ham United 0
Luton Town 1 Burnley 1
Manchester City 1 Tottenham Hotspur 2
Nottingham Forest 3 Chelsea 1
Sheffield Wednesday 2 West Bromwich Albion 0
Wolverhampton Wanderers 2 Newcastle United 0

31 October 1959	P	W	D	L	F	A	Pts	Goal ave
1. Tottenham Hotspur	15	8	6	1	36	17	22	2.12
2. Wolverhampton Wanderers	15	9	2	4	45	29	20	1.55
3. West Ham United	15	8	3	4	27	19	19	1.42

191

4. Blackburn Rovers	15	8	3	4	28	21	19	1.33
5. Preston North End	15	8	3	4	33	27	19	1.22
6. Fulham	15	9	1	5	33	35	19	0.94
7. Burnley	15	8	2	5	31	29	18	1.07
8. Arsenal	15	6	5	4	25	22	17	1.14
9. Manchester City	15	8	0	7	35	31	16	1.13
10. Chelsea	15	7	2	6	31	31	16	1.00
11. Bolton Wanderers	15	6	3	6	19	17	15	1.12
12. Manchester United	15	6	3	6	35	32	15	1.09
13. Sheffield Wednesday	15	6	2	7	20	18	14	1.11
14. West Bromwich Albion	15	4	5	6	26	24	13	1.08
15. Nottingham Forest	15	5	3	7	17	21	13	0.81
16. Everton	15	4	4	7	24	25	12	0.96
17. Blackpool	15	4	4	7	20	26	12	0.77
18. Newcastle United	15	4	3	8	21	30	11	0.70
19. Leeds United	15	3	5	7	21	33	11	0.64
20. Leicester City	15	3	5	7	24	40	11	0.60
21. Birmingham City	15	3	4	8	20	28	10	0.71
22. Luton Town	15	2	4	9	12	28	8	0.43

October 1959 Commentary

Burnley's John Connelly made his England debut having heard of his selection at Bank Hall Colliery, where he and several team-mates worked. Connelly opened the scoring against Sweden, but England lost (see opposite). Everton finally clicked into gear with a 6-1 trouncing of Leicester. Future World Cup star Gordon Banks recalled, 'It was like being back in Chesterfield's reserves. For all I conceded, I made telling saves late in the game.' Everton's joy was brief as humiliation awaited them on Tyneside. Manager John Carey was unabashed, saying, 'I am confident Everton can rise, so long as we play in an attractive manner.' He wanted a slow, sure build-up using flowing passes as Matt Busby did at Manchester United. He abhorred a 'wasteful' long ball game, believing this to be a gift to the opposition.

Champions Wolves won 5-1 at Luton but lost by the same score at Spurs with Bobby Smith scoring four times. Wolves beat Manchester United and Newcastle but lost 4-3 at Preston.

October 1959 Match of the Month
England 2 Sweden 3

The Football Association reluctantly agreed that Walter Winterbottom should select a younger side for games against Wales and World Cup finalists Sweden. The team included several England under-23 caps: Tony Allen, Stoke's full-back, John Connelly of Burnley, Brian Clough and Eddie Holliday who were both with Middlesbrough, and Birmingham centre-half Trevor Smith, who replaced the retiring Billy Wright.

This was possibly the youngest England team to represent the country. If a poor Welsh side, weakened by the absent Charles brothers, posed questions about England, the visiting Swedes rammed home some unpalatable truths. Sweden's team comprised a storekeeper, a fireman, a salesman, an electrician, a telephone worker, an engineer, a draughtsman, a businessman, two office clerks and a farmer. They won at Wembley without five of their stars: Hamrin, Gren, Liedholm, Skoglund and Gustavsson, who were needed by their Italian clubs. Just as English coach Jimmy Hogan of Burnley inspired two emphatic Hungarian victories against Winterbottom's side, another Englishman, George Raynor of Barnsley, masterminded a further humiliation here.

Raynor had helped Sweden achieve Olympic glory and World Cup success. He was revered in his country of employment but ignored by his country of birth. Snubbed here, he was given work as a Butlin's storeman and a part-time job with Skegness Town. Although a brilliant five-man move enabled Connelly to give England the lead, their players spent much of the game chasing shadows. The Swedes overwhelmed England with precise passing, constant movement, and sudden changes of pace. Smith could not hold Sweden's lithe, forceful centre-forward Agne Simonsson. Real Madrid were so impressed by Simonsson that they offered him a contract after the game. Sweden scored three times, Simonsson twice, creating a host of chances. England were out-thought, out-fought and out-played by a team with a superior tactical vision shaped by their self-taught coach. This was only England's second defeat by a foreign country on home soil. It was clear that the Hungary lessons had not yet been learnt. The Swedes, like the Hungarians, benefited from playing with a settled side. Raynor persuaded the Swedish club sides to play in a similar way to the national team. England's arcane, archaic, 'chop and change' selection process hardly helped Winterbottom in his attempts to establish continuity and stability. Brian Clough was much criticised for firing blanks. Once finding the ball nestling beneath him, he quipped, 'It was as if I was trying to hatch the bloody thing.' It would take a determined, Raynor-like tactician to sweep away the 'club amateur' fustiness and to develop a new way of playing. His name was Alf Ramsey.

7 November 1959
Birmingham City 1 Luton Town 1
Burnley 4 Wolverhampton Wanderers 1
Chelsea 3 Blackburn Rovers 1
Leeds United 3 Arsenal 2
Leicester City 2 Sheffield Wednesday 0
Manchester United 3 Fulham 3
Newcastle United 8 Everton 2
Preston North End 1 Nottingham Forest 0
Tottenham Hotspur 0 Bolton Wanderers 2
West Bromwich Albion 2 Blackpool 1
West Ham United 4 Manchester City 1

14 November 1959
Arsenal 1 West Ham United 3
Blackburn Rovers 3 West Bromwich Albion 2
Blackpool 2 Newcastle United 0
Bolton Wanderers 1 Manchester United 1
Everton 4 Birmingham City 0
Fulham 1 Preston North End 2
Luton Town 1 Tottenham Hotspur 0
Manchester City 1 Chelsea 1
Nottingham Forest 1 Leicester City 0
Sheffield Wednesday 1 Burnley 1
Wolverhampton Wanderers 4 Leeds United 2

21 November 1959
Birmingham City 2 Blackpool 1
Burnley 8 Nottingham Forest 0
Chelsea 1 Arsenal 3
Leeds United 1 Sheffield Wednesday 3
Leicester City 0 Fulham 1
Manchester United 4 Luton Town 1
Newcastle United 3 Blackburn Rovers 1
Preston North End 1 Bolton Wanderers 0
Tottenham Hotspur 3 Everton 0
West Bromwich Albion 2 Manchester City 0
West Ham United 3 Wolverhampton Wanderers 2

28 November 1959
Arsenal 2 West Bromwich Albion 4
Blackburn Rovers 2 Birmingham City 1
Blackpool 2 Tottenham Hotspur 2
Bolton Wanderers 3 Leicester City 1
Everton 2 Manchester United 1
Fulham 1 Burnley 0
Luton Town 1 Preston North End 3
Manchester City 3 Newcastle United 4
Nottingham Forest 4 Leeds United 1
Sheffield Wednesday 7 West Ham United 0
Wolverhampton Wanderers 3 Chelsea 1

November 1959 Commentary

Sheffield Wednesday were prospering under abrasive manager Harry Catterick. They hammered table-topping West Ham 7-0, Arsenal 5-1, and Chelsea 4-0. Former England centre-half Peter Swan recalled, 'Catterick made us practise going into goalies with our elbows. Keith Ellis our centre-forward did that with West Ham's Dwyer. Dwyer was looking for Ellis whenever the crosses came over. When Ellis went into him, he kept dropping the ball. A few goals came that way.' Some Owls fans dubbed Ellis as 'lino' as he was perceived to be 'limited on the ground'. After this mugging West Ham fell away badly. In an FA Cup tie with Sheffield United, Swan was told by Catterick to 'go straight through' the Blades' Derek Pace to stop him from holding the ball up and milking free kicks as he liked to do. In kicking Pace off the park, Swan earned himself the sobriquet 'Mucky Duck'.

28 November 1959	P	W	D	L	F	A	Pts	Goal ave
1. Preston North End	19	12	3	4	40	29	27	1.38
2. Tottenham Hotspur	19	9	7	3	41	22	25	1.86
3. West Ham United	19	11	3	5	37	30	25	1.23
4. Wolverhampton Wanderers	19	11	2	6	55	39	24	1.41
5. Fulham	19	11	2	6	39	40	24	0.98
6. Burnley	19	10	3	6	44	32	23	1.38
7. Blackburn Rovers	19	10	3	6	35	30	23	1.17
8. Bolton Wanderers	19	8	4	7	25	20	20	1.25
9. Sheffield Wednesday	19	8	3	8	31	22	19	1.41
10. West Bromwich Albion	19	7	5	7	36	30	19	1.20
11. Manchester United	19	7	5	7	44	39	19	1.13
12. Arsenal	19	7	5	7	33	33	19	1.00
13. Chelsea	19	8	3	8	37	39	19	0.95
14. Manchester City	19	8	1	10	40	42	17	0.95
15. Newcastle United	19	7	3	9	36	38	17	0.95
16. Nottingham Forest	19	7	3	9	22	31	17	0.71
17. Everton	19	6	4	9	32	37	16	0.86
18. Blackpool	19	5	5	9	26	32	15	0.81
19. Birmingham City	19	4	5	10	24	36	13	0.67
20. Leeds United	19	4	5	10	28	46	13	0.61
21. Leicester City	19	4	5	10	27	45	13	0.60
22. Luton Town	19	3	5	11	16	36	11	0.44

November 1959 Match of the Month
Newcastle United 8 Everton 2

Before this game, Newcastle had struggled to score more than a goal a game. Everton's return was not much better. Their away record was awful. Newcastle were beset with unrest, meaning Mitten had a hard task turning his side around. But he had two top inside-forwards with Allchurch and Eastham. Speedy Len White had ably replaced 'Wor'

Jackie Milburn, and helped by two flying wingers, Newcastle packed a strong punch. At the back were warriors Jimmy Scoular and Bob Stokoe and international full-backs Keith and McMichael. But his side was ageing, vulnerable to pace. This season they scored 82 goals but conceded 78. Carey had terrier-like Scottish midfield dynamo Bobby Collins, classy Scottish full-back Alex Parker, versatile Brian Harris, pacy Jimmy Harris and promising centre-half Brian Labone. But here his side took a hiding. Newcastle seized the initiative instantly. Nimble wingers Gordon Hughes and George Luke tore Everton's flanks to shreds. Both scored with rasping shots inside six minutes. Then White sprung Everton's ponderous offside trap, scoring a third. Before half-time, Eastham's trickery set him up for a fourth. There was no let-up after the break with White and Allchurch cashing in. Angered by this humiliation, Collins took the fight to his hosts, prompting, probing, and challenging. His aggressive industry set up two chances for Eddie Thomas which were taken. Allchurch and White reacted by inflicting a hateful eight. Hat-trick hero, White, also hit a post. It was a turning point for Newcastle, who won 13 and drew four of their next 26 games to climb into eighth place.

5 December 1959
Birmingham City 4 Manchester City 2
Burnley 4 Bolton Wanderers 0
Chelsea 0 Sheffield Wednesday 4
Leeds United 1 Fulham 4
Leicester City 3 Luton Town 3
Manchester United 3 Blackpool 1
Newcastle United 4 Arsenal 1
Preston North End 0 Everton 0
Tottenham Hotspur 2 Blackburn Rovers 1
West Bromwich Albion 0 Wolverhampton Wanderers 1
West Ham United 4 Nottingham Forest 1

12 December 1959
Arsenal 2 Burnley 4
Blackburn Rovers 6 West Ham United 2
Blackpool 3 Chelsea 1
Bolton Wanderers 4 Birmingham City 1

Everton 2 West Bromwich Albion 2
Fulham 1 Tottenham Hotspur 1
Luton Town 3 Newcastle United 4
Manchester City 3 Leeds United 3
Nottingham Forest 1 Manchester United 5
Sheffield Wednesday 2 Preston North End 2
Wolverhampton Wanderers 0 Leicester City 3

19 December 1959

Bolton Wanderers 0 Blackpool 3
Burnley 0 Leeds United 1
Fulham 0 Blackburn Rovers 1
Leicester City 2 West Ham United 1
Luton Town 2 Everton 1
Manchester United 2 West Bromwich Albion 3
Nottingham Forest 1 Manchester City 2
Preston North End 4 Chelsea 5
Sheffield Wednesday 5 Arsenal 1
Tottenham Hotspur 4 Newcastle United 0
Wolverhampton Wanderers 2 Birmingham City 0

25/26 December 1959

Blackburn Rovers 1 Blackpool 0
(*Last game to be played on Christmas Day*)
Arsenal 0 Luton Town 3
Birmingham City 2 West Ham United 0
Blackpool 1 Blackburn Rovers 0
Bolton Wanderers 2 Wolverhampton Wanderers 1
Chelsea 2 Newcastle United 2
Everton 2 Manchester City 1
Leeds United 2 Tottenham Hotspur 4
Leicester City 2 Preston North End 2
Manchester United 1 Burnley 2
Sheffield Wednesday 1 Fulham 1
West Bromwich Albion 2 Nottingham Forest 3

28 December 1959

Burnley 1 Manchester United 4

Fulham 1 Sheffield Wednesday 2
Luton Town 0 Arsenal 1
Manchester City 4 Everton 0
Newcastle United 1 Chelsea 1
Nottingham Forest 1 West Bromwich Albion 2
Preston North End 1 Leicester City 1
Tottenham Hotspur 1 Leeds United 4
West Ham United 3 Birmingham City 1
Wolverhampton Wanderers 0 Bolton Wanderers 1

28 December 1959	P	W	D	L	F	A	Pts	Goal ave
1. Tottenham Hotspur	24	12	8	4	53	30	32	1.77
2. Preston North End	24	12	7	5	49	39	31	1.26
3. Burnley	24	13	3	8	55	40	29	1.38
4. Blackburn Rovers	24	13	3	8	44	35	29	1.26
5. West Ham United	24	13	3	8	47	42	29	1.12
6. Wolverhampton Wanderers	24	13	2	9	59	45	28	1.31
7. Fulham	24	12	4	8	46	46	28	1.00
8. Sheffield Wednesday	24	11	5	8	45	27	27	1.67
9. Bolton Wanderers	24	11	4	9	32	29	26	1.10
10. Manchester United	24	10	5	9	59	47	25	1.26
11. West Bromwich Albion	24	9	6	9	45	39	24	1.15
12. Newcastle United	24	9	5	10	47	49	23	0.96
13. Chelsea	24	9	5	10	46	53	23	0.87
14. Manchester City	24	10	2	12	52	52	22	1.00
15. Blackpool	24	8	5	11	34	37	21	0.92
16. Arsenal	24	8	5	11	38	49	21	0.78
17. Everton	24	7	6	11	37	46	20	0.80
18. Leicester City	24	6	8	10	38	52	20	0.73
19. Nottingham Forest	24	8	3	13	29	46	19	0.63
20. Leeds United	24	6	6	12	39	58	18	0.67
21. Birmingham City	24	6	5	13	32	47	17	0.68
22. Luton Town	24	5	6	13	27	45	16	0.60

December 1959 Commentary

Bottom club Luton won 3-0 at Arsenal on Boxing Day with a brace from left-winger Tony Gregory, although they lost the return fixture

1-0. Despite Luton's dismal form, they beat title favourites Spurs 1-0 also drawing 1-1 at White Hart Lane helped by strapping centre-forward Joe McBride, a £12,500 steal from Wolves. McBride scored nine goals in 25 games for Luton in 1960. Had he been signed earlier Luton might have averted relegation. During his long career, McBride scored 217 at the top of Scottish football at a rate of two in three. The other major shock was Spurs' 4-1 home defeat by languishing Leeds on 28 December, having won 4-2 at Elland Road two days before. Burly Leeds centre-forward John McCole scored a brace in both games. Spurs' failure to pick up more points from lowly sides cost them the title. Blackpool and Blackburn players and fans had to forego festivities on Christmas Day and Boxing Day as home and away games with each other were scheduled on these two days. Blackburn won 1-0 at Ewood Park with a goal from Derek Dougan in front of a bumper 25,502 crowd, while Blackpool gained revenge on Boxing Day, winning by a solitary goal from Ray Charnley in front a of 30,071 crowd. We can only speculate about how this massed desertion went down with the family members left at home. Perhaps a vociferous demonstration was conducted at the Football League premises for this was the last occasion on which top flight football was played on Christmas Day. Wolves players and fans had a miserable Christmas after losing twice to Bolton. With Nat Lofthouse ruled out with an ankle injury that would prompt his retirement, Dennis Stevens deputised for him. His seventh league goal of the season enabled Bolton to win 2-1 at Burnden Park in front of their second best home attendance of the season, 36,039.

December 1959 Match of the Month
Preston North End 4 Chelsea 5

In high wind and sheeting rain, two brilliant artists were on show – Jimmy Greaves and Tom Finney. Both clubs were relegated after their departures – Preston in 1961 and Chelsea in 1962. Even in a mud bath Greaves and Finney could create and exploit space. This game was a fitting farewell to the '50s, and to an entertaining yet naïve style of play. Preston were top while Chelsea were flagging, having lost their previous four games. But Chelsea were quicker out of the blocks. After 14 minutes, Greaves latched on to a forward pass which skimmed across the gleaming mud. Without hesitation, he nudged the ball into his path, drawing Preston's central defenders to him, only to flash past them. Goalkeeper Fred Else advanced but Greaves was too quick, slotting the ball past him and into the net. But the lead lasted just one minute as prolific Tommy Thompson was quickest to a cross to equalise. Thompson then turned provider, setting up Sneddon to score from an acute angle. With half-time only three minutes away, Greaves turned the game on its head, scoring twice from close range, once brilliantly, to complete his hat-trick. After the break it was more of the same. Greaves was too nimble, too fast for the leaden Preston defenders. Having netted his fourth, John Sillett shouted at Greaves, 'Come on, Jim. Stop loafing about. One more will finish them off!' Greaves duly obliged. But prompted by Finney's pace and power and Thompson's striking prowess, Preston retaliated not once but twice. It was not quite enough, though.

Finney remembered, 'We were flying high as Chelsea arrived. They seemed ripe for a good hiding. It was gloomy, more like a night match with the floodlights on from the start, but the standard of play was electric. The ball was in one box or other for the duration. Ultimately, we had to doff our caps to Jimmy Greaves's brilliance, a hat-trick hero in the first meeting, this time he helped himself to all five. Tommy added another couple for his hat-trick, but we could not quite find the equaliser. The only disappointment was the size of the crowd. Just over 15,000 side-stepped the festive shopping expedition and braved the elements. The other 10,000 stay-aways really missed their way that day.'

2 January 1960

Arsenal 4 Wolverhampton Wanderers 4
Birmingham City 0 Tottenham Hotspur 1
Blackburn Rovers 1 Nottingham Forest 2
Blackpool 3 Fulham 1
Chelsea 2 Leicester City 2
Everton 0 Bolton Wanderers 1
Leeds United 1 Luton Town 1
Manchester City 4 Sheffield Wednesday 1
Newcastle United 7 Manchester United 3
West Bromwich Albion 4 Preston North End 0
West Ham United 2 Burnley 5

6 January 1960
Bolton Wanderers P Luton Town P
Burnley 2 Chelsea 1
Fulham 0 Everton 0
Leeds United 3 West Ham United 0
Leicester City 0 West Bromwich Albion 1
Manchester United 2 Birmingham City 1
Nottingham Forest 0 Blackpool 0
Preston North End 1 Newcastle United 2
Sheffield Wednesday 3 Blackburn Rovers 0
Tottenham Hotspur 3 Arsenal 0
Wolverhampton Wanderers 4 Manchester City 2

23 January 1960
Birmingham City 2 Preston North End 1
Blackburn Rovers 0 Wolverhampton Wanderers 1
Blackpool 0 Sheffield Wednesday 2
Chelsea 1 Leeds United 3
Everton 6 Nottingham Forest 1
Luton Town 4 Fulham 1
Manchester City 1 Arsenal 2
Newcastle United 0 Leicester City 2
Tottenham Hotspur 2 Manchester United 1
West Bromwich Albion 0 Burnley 0
West Ham United 1 Bolton Wanderers 2

January 1960 Commentary

The New Year began with a bang as Newcastle annihilated Manchester United 7-3, with Len White grabbing another hat-trick. The scale of this abject defeat prompted Matt Busby to sign West Bromwich Albion hardman Maurice Setters for £30,000, helping plug the huge gap left by the deceased Duncan Edwards. While he was a formidable stopper, under-23 international Setters was not in Edwards's class. Nevertheless, he did much to shore up a creaking back line, so much so that just 26 goals were conceded in United's final 17 league games, representing a 32 per cent reduction in their goals conceded. Arsenal welcomed back Mel Charles from injury for their home fixture with Wolves. Charles scored but the Gunners were indebted to Len Wills's late penalty in achieving a 4-4 draw. Luton sprung another surprise by whipping the Hammers 4-1 at Kenilworth Road with a goal from once prolific Gordon Turner. Burnley maintained their momentum by beating Chelsea 2-1 in the Turf Moor snow while Wolves' 4-2 victory over Manchester City meant that these two clubs had aggregated 16 goals from their two league meetings. In the FA Cup, Third Division Southampton savaged Manchester City, winning 5-1 at Maine Road with Derek Reeves scoring four times. Wingers Paine and Sydenham tore City apart. Meanwhile, Huddersfield Town humiliated West Ham in an FA Cup third round replay. However, neither side were able to capitalise upon their magnificent victories. After winning 4-1 at Spurs at the end of December, January was a productive month for relegation-haunted Leeds, taking five out of six points, including a 3-1 win at Stamford Bridge. Only 18,963 fans turned up, easily Chelsea's lowest gate of the season. This win took Leeds up to 17th place, just below Arsenal.

23 January 1960	P	W	D	L	F	A	Pts	Goal ave
1. Tottenham Hotspur	27	15	8	4	59	31	38	1.90
2. Burnley	27	15	4	8	62	43	34	1.44
3. Wolverhampton Wanderers	27	15	3	9	68	51	33	1.33
4. Sheffield Wednesday	27	13	5	9	51	31	31	1.65
5. Preston North End	27	12	7	8	51	47	31	1.09
6. Bolton Wanderers	26	13	4	9	35	30	30	1.17
7. Fulham	27	13	4	10	50	53	30	0.94
8. West Bromwich Albion	27	11	7	9	50	39	29	1.28
9. Blackburn Rovers	27	13	3	11	45	41	29	1.10
10. West Ham United	27	13	3	11	50	52	29	0.96
11. Manchester United	27	11	5	11	65	57	27	1.14
12. Newcastle United	27	11	5	11	56	55	27	1.02
13. Manchester City	27	11	2	14	59	59	24	1.00
14. Blackpool	27	9	6	12	37	40	24	0.93
15. Chelsea	27	9	6	12	50	60	24	0.83
16. Arsenal	27	9	6	12	44	57	24	0.77

17. Leeds United	27	8	7	12	46	60	23	0.77
18. Leicester City	27	7	9	11	42	55	23	0.76
19. Everton	27	8	6	13	43	50	22	0.86
20. Nottingham Forest	27	9	4	14	32	53	22	0.60
21. Birmingham City	27	7	5	15	35	51	19	0.69
22. Luton Town	26	6	7	13	32	47	19	0.68

January 1960 Match of the Month
West Ham United 2 Burnley 5

Upton Park resembled Agincourt. Mud, glistening in the floodlights' glare, stretched from end to end with only the flanks offering thin grass. Jimmy McIlroy was ruled out and replaced by Ian Lawson. The game was a reversal of the Agincourt result with Burnley's fleet-footed cavalry triumphing in the East End swamp. West Ham exerted brief pressure after Phil Woosnam's fortuitous 12th-minute equaliser, but for the most part Burnley were totally ascendant. Brian Pilkington and John Connelly left home full-backs Joe Kirkup and Noel Cantwell floundering in their spattering wake. Helped by a massive mud slalom, Ian Lawson slid in Burnley's first after 11 minutes. Brian Pilkington's brilliant run and chip in the 32nd minute put Burnley 2-1 ahead, atoning for Blacklaw's previous slip. Then Connelly's crisp shot gave Burnley a 3-1 interval lead. Lawson put the Clarets out of sight in the 75th minute when he converted Brian Pilkington's leaping header.

West Ham were gifted a penalty three minutes later, another mystifying decision from referee Stokes, but Burnley brushed aside their irritation as Connelly blasted a swerving drive past Noel Dwyer in the 89th minute to complete a 5-2 rout. Peter Kinlan of the *Sunday Pictorial* wrote, 'Who better than Burnley to end West Ham's run of seven home wins in a row? For this was brisk, business-like Burnley turning on a super show as they darted like demons across the mud to hit the Hammers well and truly on the head. Perky "Pilky" gave West Ham's right-back Joe Kirkup a rare runaround. "Crafty" Connelly put on a dazzling display, worthy of the international he is. So pulverising was the Connelly treatment of Eire full-back, Noel Cantwell that West Ham had to move him to their forward line in the second half. Accurate and artistic, the Burnley wing twins tore gigantic gaps in

West Ham's defence. If they go on playing like this, they'll soon have nobody above them.'

6 February 1960
Arsenal 5 Blackburn Rovers 2
Burnley 2 Newcastle United 1
Fulham 1 Bolton Wanderers 1
Leeds United 1 West Bromwich Albion 4
Leicester City 1 Birmingham City 3
Manchester United 0 Manchester City 0
Nottingham Forest 2 Luton Town 0
Preston North End 1 Tottenham Hotspur 1
Sheffield Wednesday 2 Everton 2
West Ham United 4 Chelsea 2
Wolverhampton Wanderers 1 Blackpool 1

13 February 1960
Birmingham City P Burnley P
Blackburn Rovers 2 Manchester City 1
Blackpool 2 Arsenal 1
Bolton Wanderers 1 Nottingham Forest 1
Chelsea 4 Fulham 2
Everton 0 Wolverhampton Wanderers 2
Luton Town 0 Sheffield Wednesday 1
Manchester United 1 Preston North End 1
Newcastle United 2 Leeds United 1
Tottenham Hotspur 1 Leicester City 2
West Bromwich Albion P West Ham United P

24 February 1960
Chelsea 2 West Bromwich Albion 2
Leicester City 3 Manchester United 1
Sheffield Wednesday 1 Bolton Wanderers 0
Wolverhampton Wanderers 3 Luton Town 2

27 February
Arsenal 1 Newcastle United 0
Blackburn Rovers 1 Tottenham Hotspur 4

Blackpool 0 Manchester United 6
Bolton Wanderers 2 Burnley 1
Everton 4 Preston North End 0
Fulham 5 Leeds United 0
Luton Town 2 Leicester City 0
Manchester City 3 Birmingham City 0
Nottingham Forest 3 West Ham United 1
Sheffield Wednesday 1 Chelsea 1
Wolverhampton Wanderers 3 West Bromwich Albion 1

February 1960 Commentary

Birmingham won a crucial relegation scrap at Leicester by 3-1. Leeds' 4-1 decimation by visiting West Bromwich helped them too. But while Birmingham were losing 3-0 at Manchester City on 27 February, their other rivals, Luton, and Everton, were winning. Everton leathered Preston 4-0 at Goodison, with new signing Roy Vernon, a Welsh international, grabbing a brace. Luton lost three in a row before beating Leicester 2-0 at Kenilworth Road. McBride was again on target. Manchester United trounced Blackpool 6-0. Bobby Charlton achieved a hat-trick. Blackpool then won their next five league games, scoring 15 goals, seven from beanpole centre-forward, Ray Charnley, whose hat-trick at Leeds set up a 4-2 win. This purple patch helped Blackpool secure safety despite taking only three points from their final seven games.

27 February 1960	P	W	D	L	F	A	Pts	Goal ave
1. Tottenham Hotspur	30	16	9	5	65	35	41	1.86
2. Wolverhampton Wanderers	31	18	4	9	77	55	40	1.40
3. Sheffield Wednesday	31	15	7	9	56	34	37	1.65
4. Burnley	29	16	4	9	65	46	36	1.41
5. Bolton Wanderers	30	14	6	10	39	34	34	1.15
6. Fulham	31	14	6	11	60	60	34	1.00
7. Preston North End	30	12	9	9	53	53	33	1.00
8. West Bromwich Albion	30	12	8	10	57	45	32	1.27
9. Manchester United	31	12	7	12	73	61	31	1.20
10. Newcastle United	31	13	5	13	64	62	31	1.03
11. Blackburn Rovers	30	14	3	13	50	51	31	0.98
12. West Ham United	30	14	3	13	58	62	31	0.94

13. Arsenal	31	12	6	13	53	62	30	0.85
14. Chelsea	31	10	8	13	59	69	28	0.86
15. Nottingham Forest	31	11	6	14	40	57	28	0.70
16. Manchester City	30	12	3	15	63	61	27	1.03
17. Blackpool	30	10	7	13	40	48	27	0.83
18. Leicester City	31	9	9	13	48	62	27	0.77
19. Everton	31	9	7	15	50	56	25	0.89
20. Leeds United	30	8	7	15	48	71	23	0.68
21. Birmingham City	29	8	5	16	38	55	21	0.69
22. Luton Town	30	7	7	16	36	53	21	0.68

February 1960 Match of the Month
Barcelona 4 Wolverhampton Wanderers 0 (European Cup quarter-final)

Barcelona had world-class performers in all positions. Leaving nothing to chance, French-Argentinian manager and coach Helenio Herrera went to Molineux to watch Wolves draw with Blackpool, making copious notes on every Wolves player, their style of play, their strengths and weaknesses, documenting Wolves' moves, tactics, dead-ball routines, successes and vulnerabilities. H.H., as he was known in Spain, discussed his findings with his team, inviting their comments. An agreed strategy was set out on a blackboard. Each player was clear about their team's game plan and their role within it. Wolves manager Stan Cullis was a command and control manager, reflecting his military background. Like Herrera, Cullis used a blackboard, putting each opponent under the microscope. Cullis was the English long ball king. He wanted to see the ball arrive in their opponents' penalty area with three passes or less, using the full width of the pitch. Cullis insisted his tactics were forensic and fair. Ken Jones of the *Daily Mirror* was unconvinced, describing one Wolves performance as 'crash-bang soccer with hardly a breath of imagination or intelligence to break the monotony of crash tackles and aimless passes.'

Cullis was unabashed, referring to Wolves' successes in friendlies against top European clubs. Barcelona knew better. They knew that Wolves' powerful wing-halves, Clamp and Flowers, liked to push up in support of their five forwards. This did not faze them. Wolves were allowed a free run to the edge of the Barca box, with all, but two or three forwards, behind the ball. Suddenly, Barca would close ranks, snuff out a Wolves attack and counter-attack at speed. With a sharp exchange of passes, Wolves' depleted defenders were by-passed. Forwards Martinez, Suarez and Evaristo revelled in the space created. Villaverde scored the first goal in the seventh minute. Then Hungarian Kubala added a second ten minutes later. Barca's third goal was exquisitely constructed. The Barca midfielders strolled forward, nonchalantly exchanging passes, evading any attempt at dispossessing them. Left-winger Villaverde pulled back from Stuart, positioning himself wide on the halfway line. A Barca midfielder fired the ball towards him. Instantaneously, Villaverde struck it down the inside-left channel where Brazilian centre-forward, Evaristo, seized upon the ball before Showell could close him down. Meanwhile, right-winger Martinez accelerated into the box leaving Harris in his wake. Spotting Martinez's run, Evaristo executed a sharp one-two with him, leaving the centre-forward to score with crisp shot before the Wolves defenders had grasped the danger.

Former Wolves and England captain Billy Wright observed, 'Each Barca player was always THINKING. Even goalkeeper Ramallets thought as if he was an extra full-back.' A Spanish critic stated, 'Once more the difference between artists and artisans was made clear. Wolverhampton, like all English teams, continue to play football that is 20 years behind the times. Against the English play, based on physicality, speed, hard shooting, the long forward pass and zonal play, the technical superiority of Barcelona was absolute.' Wolves lost the tie 9-2 on aggregate.

1 March 1960
Burnley 2 Tottenham Hotspur 0
Preston North End 5 Blackburn Rovers 3

5 March 1960
Birmingham City 4 Nottingham Forest 1
Burnley 1 Blackburn Rovers 0
Chelsea 3 Luton Town 0
Leeds United 2 Blackpool 4
Leicester City 5 Manchester City 0
Manchester United 0 Wolverhampton Wanderers 2
Newcastle United 3 Fulham 1
Preston North End 0 Arsenal 3

Tottenham Hotspur 4 Sheffield Wednesday 1
West Bromwich Albion 1 Bolton Wanderers 1
West Ham United 2 Everton 2

9 March
Bolton Wanderers 2 Luton Town 2
Leeds United 3 Birmingham City 3
Manchester City 2 Blackpool 3
West Bromwich Albion 3 West Ham United 2

12 March
Blackpool 3 West Ham United 2
Bolton Wanderers 1 Newcastle United 4
Everton 6 Chelsea 1
Fulham 2 Birmingham City 2
Luton Town 0 West Bromwich Albion 0
Nottingham Forest 1 Tottenham Hotspur 3

15 March
Arsenal 1 Leicester City 1
Wolverhampton Wanderers 3 Preston North End 3

19 March
Birmingham City 2 Bolton Wanderers 5
Burnley 3 Arsenal 2
Chelsea 2 Blackpool 3
Leeds United 4 Manchester City 3
Leicester City 2 Wolverhampton Wanderers 1
Manchester United 3 Nottingham Forest 1
Newcastle United 3 Luton Town 2
Preston North End 3 Sheffield Wednesday 4
Tottenham Hotspur 1 Fulham 1
West Bromwich Albion 6 Everton 2
West Ham United 2 Blackburn Rovers 1

26 March 1960
Arsenal 1 Leeds United 1
Blackpool 2 West Bromwich Albion 0

Bolton Wanderers 2 Tottenham Hotspur 1
Everton 1 Newcastle 2
Fulham 0 Manchester United 5
Luton Town 1 Birmingham City 1
Nottingham Forest 1 Preston North End 1

30 March 1960
Blackburn Rovers 1 Chelsea 0
Manchester City 3 West Ham United 1
Sheffield Wednesday 4 Manchester United 2
Wolverhampton Wanderers 6 Burnley 1

30 March 1960	P	W	D	L	F	A	Pts	Goal ave
1. Tottenham Hotspur	35	18	10	7	74	42	46	1.76
2. Wolverhampton Wanderers	35	20	5	10	89	61	45	1.46
3. Burnley	33	19	4	10	72	54	42	1.33
4. Sheffield Wednesday	34	17	7	10	65	43	41	1.51
5. Bolton Wanderers	35	16	8	11	50	44	40	1.14
6. Newcastle United	35	17	5	13	76	67	39	1.13
7. West Bromwich Albion	35	14	10	11	67	52	38	1.29
8. Blackpool	35	15	7	13	55	56	37	0.98
9. Preston North End	35	13	11	11	65	67	37	0.97
10. Fulham	35	14	8	13	64	71	36	0.90
11. Manchester United	35	14	7	14	83	68	35	1.22
12. West Ham United	35	15	4	16	67	74	34	0.91
13. Arsenal	35	13	8	14	60	67	34	0.90
14. Blackburn Rovers	34	15	3	16	55	59	33	0.93
15. Leicester City	34	11	10	13	56	64	32	0.88
16. Chelsea	35	11	8	16	65	79	30	0.82
17. Manchester City	34	13	3	18	71	74	29	0.96
18. Nottingham Forest	35	11	7	17	44	68	29	0.65
19. Everton	35	10	8	17	61	67	28	0.91
20. Leeds United	34	9	9	16	58	82	27	0.71
21. Birmingham City	34	9	8	17	50	67	26	0.75
22. Luton Town	35	7	10	18	41	62	24	0.66

March 1960 Commentary

Luton failed to win any of their five games in March, drawing three. Their 1-1 draw with Birmingham was a missed opportunity, although a decent result for the visitors who had already salvaged a critical point in the mud and pooled water at Leeds. Here 'the Blues' were indebted to a late Leeds own goal in taking a point. Wasteful Leeds twice threw away a two-goal lead, to the frustration of their goalscorers Don Revie and Billy Bremner and their 8,557 fans who had braved the foul weather to watch this dramatic game. Three defeats in March had tipped Forest into the relegation battle, too. With Wolves, Spurs and Burnley dropping points at the top, Sheffield Wednesday joined the title race.

March 1960 Match of the Month
Leeds United 4 Manchester City 3

Leeds had not won in five matches whereas Manchester City had won only once in seven games. With the prospect of the drop rattling them, City signed Denis Law for a British club record fee of £55,000, seeing off bids by Arsenal, West Bromwich, Everton and, ironically, Leeds. It was a dismal, cold day but 32,500 turned up to see Law's City debut. The autograph hunters were out in force. One boy in a thick coat and bobble hat doggedly ran after Law until the distracted star was persuaded to sign, prompting the lad to punch the air triumphantly. Law was already regretting his move. He said later, 'I genuinely felt that Huddersfield were a better team. I should have picked a team with better prospects.' The game began disjointedly, not helped by the rutted surface but Revie, surer of touch than swift in movement, set tiny Noel Peyton free to score the opener. The scores were soon level, though, as Archie Gibson carelessly misplaced his back pass, leaving Leeds goalkeeper Burgin stranded. Billy Bremner then restored Leeds' lead, exploiting loose City marking to smack a shot against the post and in. This was the cue for Law to excel. As was his habit, he picked up a ball from Ken Barnes deep in midfield. George Meek tried to arrest Law's progress, but the Scot's snazzy drag back, twist and turn confounded him. Law then brushed past Gibson and flicked a pass to Hayes on his left before racing into the Leeds box, anticipating a return pass, which he took in his stride. Law evaded Ashall's tackle and immediately clipped a low shot to the right of the wrong-footed Burgin. It was a sublime goal. In the 65th minute, Law made his presence felt again. This time his astute pass put Colin Barlow in on goal and the young right-winger tucked away the chance. As much as Leeds pressed for an equaliser, they were denied repeatedly by Bert Trautmann's agility. The former German paratrooper brilliantly turned aside close-range efforts by McCole and Revie while Cliff Sear and Branagan cleared shots off the line. However, despite Revie's intelligent probing, the game looked lost. That was until a diabolical penalty was awarded. With ten minutes remaining, McCole blasted Leeds level. Then, in the final seconds, Oakes impulsively handled Bremner's centre. McCole scored again and Leeds had two precious points. Afterwards, Law answered questions with brisk, breezy irony. The *Times* reporter described him as a 'quick-witted combatant disguised in a slim frame', adding, 'His value will only be felt when his colleagues learn to think as swiftly and as broadly as him.'

2 April 1960
Birmingham City 2 Everton 2
Burnley 3 Sheffield Wednesday 3
Chelsea 3 Manchester City 0
Leeds United 0 Wolverhampton Wanderers 3
Leicester City 0 Nottingham Forest 1
Manchester United 2 Bolton Wanderers 0
Newcastle United 1 Blackpool 1
Preston North End 4 Fulham 1
Tottenham Hotspur 1 Luton Town 1
West Bromwich Albion 2 Blackburn Rovers 0
West Ham United 0 Arsenal 0

6 April 1960
Sheffield Wednesday 2 Leicester City 2

9 April 1960
Arsenal 1 Chelsea 4
Blackburn Rovers 1 Newcastle United 1
Blackpool 0 Birmingham City 1
Bolton Wanderers 2 Preston North End 1

Everton 2 Tottenham Hotspur 1
Fulham 1 Leicester City 1
Luton Town 2 Manchester United 3
Manchester City 0 West Bromwich Albion 1
Nottingham Forest 0 Burnley 1
Sheffield Wednesday 1 Leeds United 0
Wolverhampton Wanderers P West Ham United P

11 April 1960
Wolverhampton Wanderers 5 West Ham United 0

15 April 1960 Good Friday
Arsenal 2 Fulham 0
Blackburn Rovers 0 Luton Town 2
Burnley 1 Leicester City 0
Chelsea 1 Tottenham Hotspur 3
Everton 4 Blackpool 0
Manchester City 1 Bolton Wanderers 0
Newcastle United 3 Sheffield Wednesday 3
West Ham United 2 Manchester United 1

16 April 1960 Easter Saturday
Birmingham City 3 Arsenal 0
Burnley 3 Luton Town 0
Chelsea 1 Nottingham Forest 1
Leeds United 1 Bolton Wanderers 0
Leicester City 3 Everton 3
Manchester United 1 Blackburn Rovers 0
Newcastle United 1 Wolverhampton Wanderers 0
Preston North End 4 Blackpool 1
Tottenham Hotspur 0 Manchester City 1
West Bromwich Albion 3 Sheffield Wednesday 1
West Ham United 1 Fulham 2

18 April 1960 Easter Monday
Birmingham City 1 West Bromwich Albion 7
Blackpool 0 Everton 0
Bolton Wanderers 3 Manchester City 1

Fulham 3 Arsenal 0
Leicester City 2 Burnley 1
Luton Town 1 Blackburn Rovers 1
Manchester United 5 West Ham United 3
Preston North End 1 Leeds United 1
Sheffield Wednesday 2 Newcastle United 0
Tottenham Hotspur 0 Chelsea 1
Wolverhampton Wanderers 3 Nottingham Forest 1

19 April 1960
Leeds United 2 Preston North End 1
Nottingham Forest 0 Wolverhampton Wanderers 0
West Bromwich Albion 1 Birmingham City 1

23 April 1960
Arsenal 5 Manchester United 2
Blackburn Rovers 0 Leicester City 1
Blackpool 1 Burnley 1
Bolton Wanderers 2 Chelsea 0
Everton 1 Leeds United 0
Fulham 2 West Bromwich Albion 1
Luton Town 3 West Ham United 1
Manchester City 2 Preston North End 1
Nottingham Forest 3 Newcastle United 0
Sheffield Wednesday 2 Birmingham City 4
Wolverhampton Wanderers 1 Tottenham Hotspur 3

27 April 1960
Birmingham City 0 Burnley 1
Blackburn Rovers 3 Leeds United 2

30 April 1960
Birmingham City 1 Blackburn Rovers 0
Burnley 0 Fulham 0
Chelsea 1 Wolverhampton Wanderers 5
Leeds United 1 Nottingham Forest 0
Leicester City 1 Bolton Wanderers 2
Manchester United 5 Everton 0

Newcastle United 0 Manchester City 1
Preston North End 2 Luton Town 0
Tottenham Hotspur 4 Blackpool 1
West Bromwich Albion 1 Arsenal 0
West Ham United 1 Sheffield Wednesday 1

April 1960 Match of the Month
Wolverhampton Wanderers 1 Tottenham Hotspur 3

Molineux was crammed with 55,000 supporters, most hoping for
a hat-trick of league titles and the elusive double of First Division
and FA Cup. Despite the burning heat, Danny Blanchflower calmly
conducted a team meeting in the middle of the pitch, ignoring the
Wolves fans' derision. It was mind games. He knew that Spurs were
probably out of the title race after a disastrous Easter programme.
But they were not there as king-makers, they had turned up as party
poopers. Manager Bill Nicholson was indisputably in charge at Spurs,
but wing-half Blanchflower was always his leader on the pitch.

Within two minutes Spurs made their point. Their flying
right-winger Cliff Jones laid the ball off to Blanchflower just inside
the Wolves half. Jones then made for the corner flag, taking two
defenders with him. Instead of supplying the expected return pass,
Blanchflower cut inside and from an oblique angle crossed quickly
and crisply towards the far post. Bobby Smith anticipated the move,
peeling away from his marker, Bill Slater. Right-back Showell was
too preoccupied with left-winger Terry Dyson to cover Smith's run.
Meanwhile, goalkeeper Malcolm Finlayson dithered in coming out
for the cross. Seeing his opportunity, Smith leapt with perfect timing,
heading the ball firmly into the top left-hand corner. Molineux
greeted the goal with stunned silence, with only the jubilation of the
Spurs supporters filling the void.

Having replaced injured Les Allen in number only, left-half
Dave Mackay added his combative strength to the Spurs midfield,
reinforced by the defensively inclined Tony Marchi. The supply line
to Wolves' voracious forwards was squeezed and neither Clamp
nor Flowers were able to push forward with customary menace.
Blanchflower was in majestic form, making a feint here, a turn there,
a succession of slick exchanges and probing passes dispatched to each
wing. Blanchflower was king.

A momentary lapse in concentration by Mackay allowed Clamp to race away to set up Peter Broadbent for an equaliser. But Spurs were not shaken and just before the break, Smith crossed for Mackay to make amends by heading firmly home. Wolves tore at Spurs after the break, but their 'punt and grunt' game was contained with ease. The action was at the other end where Finlayson was sorely tested, but he was helpless as Jones sealed the game with a diving header. The old gold standard had been lowered by the shock of the new and Burnley were its beneficiaries.

April 1960 Commentary

Bloomfield's hat-trick in a 5-2 win over Manchester United dug Arsenal out of trouble while Isherwood's brace against relegation-haunted Leeds halted Blackburn's fall. Birmingham's 7-1 home defeat by West Bromwich, with Ronnie Allen and Kevan scoring hat-tricks, put the Blues in grave danger of the drop until they won 4-2 at Hillsborough. A six-match unbeaten run got Everton off the hook, too, as did Forest's 3-0 victory over Newcastle.

2 May 1960
May 1960 Match of the Month – a personal memory
Manchester City 1 Burnley 2

I discovered that the BBC Light Programme was covering the second half. Bedtimes were a scarred war zone, so I had to smuggle the transistor into my bedroom, muffling it under heavy bedclothes. It was a dark wait of sweaty expectancy with dismal dance music filling the void, musty balm from another age and no longer in step. While waiting I was unaware that on a bald, bumpy pitch, Burnley had recovered their zest and taken a fourth-minute lead, after Bert Trautmann had fumbled Pilkington's cross-shot. City's response was immediate and ferocious. They threw themselves at Burnley as if contesting silverware, too. Play ebbed and flowed at a frantic pace, so I was told. With City throwing caution to the wind there were chances for Burnley on the break, but Trautmann made amends for his earlier error with some fine saves. The importance of this was underlined when Hayes blasted in from Denis Law's miscued flick. Back came Burnley and only Trautmann's brilliant fingertip save denied Robson. However, just past the half-hour tiny Trevor

Meredith struck Burnley's second goal, seizing upon a sliced clearance. All became clear when a plummy voice introduced commentator Raymond Glendenning. The claustrophobic tension of that night remains: wriggling under the covers; creating air conditioning from hell; straining to make sense of the play; the ambiguous crescendos; Law, a constant threat; yearning for reassurance; counting down the seconds too quickly. Football is always more frenetic on the radio. At last the final whistle; the volcanic roar; the toppling relief, euphoria and exhaustion and the hopelessness of sleep. England's smallest ever top-flight side were champions.

2 May 1960	P	W	D	L	F	A	Pts	Goal ave
1. Burnley	42	24	7	11	85	61	55	1.39
2. Wolverhampton Wanderers	42	24	6	12	106	67	54	1.58
3. Tottenham Hotspur	42	21	11	10	86	50	53	1.72
4. West Bromwich Albion	42	19	11	12	83	57	49	1.46
5. Sheffield Wednesday	42	19	11	12	80	59	49	1.36
6. Bolton Wanderers	42	20	8	14	59	51	48	1.16
7. Manchester United	42	19	7	16	102	80	45	1.28
8. Newcastle United	42	18	8	16	82	78	44	1.05
9. Preston North End	42	16	12	14	79	76	44	1.04
10. Fulham	42	17	10	15	73	80	44	0.91
11. Blackpool	42	15	10	17	59	71	40	0.83
12. Leicester City	42	13	13	16	66	75	39	0.88
13. Arsenal	42	15	9	18	68	80	39	0.85
14. West Ham United	42	16	6	20	75	91	38	0.82
15. Everton	42	13	11	18	73	78	37	0.94
16. Manchester City	42	17	3	22	78	84	37	0.93
17. Blackburn Rovers	42	16	5	21	60	70	37	0.86
18. Chelsea	42	14	9	19	76	91	37	0.84
19. Birmingham City	42	13	10	19	63	80	36	0.79
20. Nottingham Forest	42	13	9	20	50	74	35	0.68
21. Leeds United	42	12	10	20	65	92	34	0.71
22. Luton Town	42	9	12	21	50	73	30	0.68

End of Season Review

Arsenal (13th): Ravaged by injuries, Swindin constantly changed his team. A behind-the-scenes battle between him and chief assistant and coach Ron Greenwood did not help. David Herd scored 14 goals in 31 games but was oddly offered as a makeweight for Law.

Birmingham City (19th): But for the inadequacies of relegated Leeds and Luton, City would have gone down. Their manager, Pat Beasley, made over 100 failed bids for players.

Blackburn Rovers (17th): Despite a bright start and an FA Cup Final appearance, Rovers nosedived after Christmas, managing only three wins in their last 19 games.

Bolton Wanderers (6th): Jimmy Greaves said, 'I don't fear terrorism because I played against Bolton's Banks, Hartle, Hennin, Higgins and Edwards, the hardest players of the '50s.'

Burnley (1st): Their final-game win at Maine Road put them in top place for the first time in this season. They blew a 3-0 lead over Blackburn in the FA Cup, causing their double ambitions to vanish.

Chelsea (18th): Tommy Docherty said of the Chelsea defence, 'A jellyfish has more shape.' Their limitations were ruthlessly exposed by more physical sides such as Bolton, Sheffield Wednesday, and Wolves. Greaves's 29 goals helped the Londoners avoid the drop.

Everton (15th): Bobby Collins saved Everton from relegation. He said, 'Carey was not hard enough with the players and some took liberties. Top managers need a ruthless streak.'

Fulham (10th): Johnny Haynes said Macedo, Cohen and Mullery are outstanding players but Fulham depended on the England man himself, described by Pelé as the best passer of the ball he had ever seen.

Leeds United (21st): Let down by poor organisation, indiscipline, and shambolic defending. Ninety-two goals were let in, the highest in the division. Jack Taylor did not crack the whip enough.

Leicester City (12th): Crucially, Leicester managed to take points off their fellow strugglers. Defensive frailties prompted the selection of Gordon Banks, whose agility was sorely tested in a 6-1 defeat at Everton.

Luton Town (22nd): Luton's demise was attributed to a lack of bite in attack, post-Wembley blues after their defeat in the 1959 FA Cup Final and poor crowds but an ageing squad was a factor too.

Manchester City (16th): Bert Trautmann and Ken Barnes told their manager of the 'fallacy of relying upon frugal lower-division purchases'. The squad was ageing, morale was low, indiscipline festered, and manager McDowall was distant. Law was an expensive sticking plaster.

Manchester United (7th): The season was a switchback affair with crushing victories and humiliating defeats. While the attack had a surfeit of talent, the defence was often porous, hence the signing of Setters after the 7-3 debacle against Newcastle.

Newcastle United (8th): Media-savvy Mitten won over the disgruntled fans with attacking football. Gates rose by 11 per cent. He promoted young talent, including his own son, over fading stars. But his ageing squad needed fresh experience, too. Mitten persuaded the board to buy Ivor Allchurch, but not other targets Mel Charles, Law, St John, and George Herd.

Nottingham Forest (20th): Inside-right John Quigley said, 'The great thing at our club is the wonderful harmony from top to bottom.' But 12 months after Wembley most of the FA Cup-winning side was broken up as relations with manager Billy Walker soured. Forest struggled to score enough goals and nearly went down.

Preston North End (9th): Tommy Thomson said, 'Players were getting old together and there were no suitable replacements being bought or coming through the ranks. Tommy Docherty left and was never adequately replaced.' The same could be said of Tom Finney in his farewell season. Preston were relegated one year later.

Sheffield Wednesday (5th): Under Catterick's abrasive but shrewd professionalism Sheffield Wednesday prospered, challenging for the title until a 3-1 defeat at West Bromwich and an unexpected 4-2 reverse at home to Birmingham wrecked their chances.

Tottenham Hotspur (3rd): Spurs were title favourites but ultimately failed because of lapses against lowly sides like Luton, Leeds, Chelsea, Manchester City, Everton and Leicester. Crucially, Burnley took three points off them.

West Bromwich Albion (4th): Criticised by trainer Dick Graham for complacency but Albion were tough opponents. Up front they packed a vicious punch with tank-like Kevan and Ronnie Allen sharing 41 goals while their defence was generally solid. A strong showing in the second half of the season gave them an outside chance of the title, inflicting heavy defeats upon Preston (4-0), Leeds (4-1), Everton (6-2) and Birmingham (7-1).

West Ham United (14th): West Ham's season opened with verve and style yet ended in a rabble. They won only three and lost ten of their last 15 games. They were mugged 7-0 by Sheffield Wednesday, and thrashed 6-2 by Blackburn, 5-2 by Burnley and 5-0 by Wolves.

Wolverhampton Wanderers (2nd): This was a very disappointing season. Wolves pulverised Luton (5-1), Chelsea (5-1), Burnley (6-1), West Ham (5-0), Leeds (4-2) and Manchester City twice (4-2 and 6-4) but conceded too many careless goals. Spurs wrecked their hopes of a league hat-trick when they won 3-1 at Molineux, and Wolves were decimated 9-2 on aggregate by Barcelona in the European Cup. Even their 3-0 FA Cup Final victory over Blackburn was soured by the press verdict of it being a 'Dustbin Final'.

First Division leading scorers 1959/60 (all competitions)
32 Viollet (Man. U)
31 Murray (Wolves)
30 Greaves (Chelsea)
30 Smith (Spurs)
29 White (Newcastle)
29 Kevan (West Bromwich)
25 Connelly (Burnley)
25 Jones (Spurs)
23 Dobing (Blackburn)
23 Pointer (Burnley)
23 McCole (Leeds)
22 McAdams (Man. City)
21 Robson (Burnley)
21 Charlton (Man. U)
21 Finney (Preston)
20 Leggat (Fulham)
20 Barlow (Man. City)

Match of the Century
Real Madrid 7 Eintracht Frankfurt 3 (European Cup Final)
18 May 1960

On a dazzling evening in May, 135,000 people packed into antiquated Hampden Park to acclaim perfection as Real Madrid provided a sumptuous display of lithe, fluent, attacking football in what remains as one of the greatest matches of all time.

Real's forward line was the envy of the whole world: Brazilian right-winger Canario; Spanish schemer Del Sol; Spanish-naturalised Argentinian Di Stefano; Hungarian ace Puskas and flying Spanish winger Gento. Behind this glittering attack was a firm, dependable defence dominated by formidable centre-half Santamaria, and Dominguez, the Argentinian international goalkeeper.

Real had won the European Cup in each of its first five years, beating the best opposition that Italy, France, Germany, England, and Hungary could summon. They could produce sudden bursts of pulverising pressure that would sweep aside all opponents. As good as Barcelona were, having thrashed Wolves, they were unable to match Real's array of skill, swiftness of movement and explosive shooting. When they met in the semis, Real won 6-2 on aggregate.

Billy Wright described centre-forward Di Stefano as 'completely unorthodox, neither a striker in the traditional English mould of Lawton or Lofthouse, nor a deep-lying leader like Hidegkuti. He was both. He seemed to be in the thick of almost every action; one moment defending, the next, taking part in an audacious attack. He is supposedly a creator, but he is a predator too, who seizes upon half-chances.'

In this game Eintracht's goalkeeper was unable to hold Canario's drive. There seemed no immediate danger and yet Di Stefano materialised from nowhere to lift the ball over the prostrate keeper before anyone else had moved. Of Real inside-left Puskas, Wright said, 'He is a man of power and skill and among the greatest one-footed players of all time. Puskas can beat you with a half twist of his shoulders; his body always seems between you and the ball; his left foot, inside or outside, instep or studs, is always in control. But for all his skills, Puskas is not selfish. He will take and keep possession, if need be by screening and side-stepping until a colleague has found open space.'

Di Stefano scored three and Puskas four of Real's seven goals in this game.

Real allowed Eintracht to take a 19th-minute lead through Kress and yet 40 minutes later the Germans were 5-1 down. Real's third was a vintage Puskas goal. Taking a pass nonchalantly from Del Sol, Puskas jockeyed for position near the goal line and then, from a freakish angle, he blasted the ball over Loy in the Eintracht goal. And yet his fourth, scored in the 70th minute, surpassed this. He reached back for a pass that was straying, killed the ball instantly and, pivoting with astonishing speed, he shot high into the net from 16 yards.

But it was left to Di Stefano to score the best goal of the night. Having picked up the ball deep in his own half he ran down the middle exchanging a series of piercing passes, leaving a line of sprawling Germans in his wake before striking a searing low shot past Loy. Real had annihilated the 12-4 conquerors of Glasgow Rangers on the same bumpy surface blamed for the turgid 1-1 draw between England and Scotland. Real had speed, sinuous movement, fluid passing, dazzling tricks and devastating finishing. This was football for the space age whereas much of England's football was still in the age of steam.

Average gates in 1959/60 (population figures taken from 1961 Census)

	Average gate	population		Average gate	population
Spurs	47,864	250,000	Birmingham C.	27,689	550,000
Man. U.	47,137	330,000	West Brom. A.	27,310	330,000
Everton	40,788	370,000	Bolton W.	27,104	168,215
Chelsea	39,744	205,000	Burnley	26,869	80,559
Arsenal	39,508	228,345	Nottingham F.	26,000	155,000
Wolves	36,354	150,000	Leicester C.	25,389	275,000
Newcastle U.	35,751	320,000	Blackburn R.	25,061	108,000
Man. City	35,347	330,000	Preston N.E.	24,530	112,000
Sheffield W.	33,265	250,000	Blackpool	21,770	150,000
West Ham U.	28,245	270,000	Leeds U.	21,690	500,000
Fulham	27,830	210,000	Luton T.	16,423	130,000

Populations are calculated by reference to current municipal boundaries in which the teams are located e.g. Haringey for Spurs, Newham for West Ham, Islington for Arsenal. Where two teams are located within one municipal area, as in Manchester, Birmingham, Liverpool, Sheffield, and Nottingham the local population is halved for each of their two teams. Burnley's average gate as a per centage of its population was 33% whereas the First Division average was 12%.

Top shots: First Division 1959/60 and Premier League 2008/09

1959/60	Gls	Gms	Ratio	2008/09	Gls	Gms	Ratio
Dennis Viollet (Man.U.)	32	36	0.9	Anelka (Chelsea)	19	37	0.51
Jimmy Greaves (Chelsea)	29	40	0.7	Ronaldo (Man. U)	18	33	0.55
Jimmy Murray (Wolves)	29	40	0.7	Gerrard (Liverpool)	16	31	0.52
Len White (Newcastle)	28	40	0.7	Robinho (Man. City)	14	31	0.45
Derek Kevan (WBA)	26	42	0.6	Torres (Liverpool)	14	24	0.58
Bobby Smith (Spurs)	25	40	0.6	Bent (Spurs)	12	33	0.36
John McCole (Leeds)	22	33	0.7	Davies (Bolton)	12	38	0.32
Billy McAdams (Man. C.)	21	30	0.7	Kuyt (Liverpool)	12	38	0.32
John Connelly (Burnley)	20	34	0.6	Lampard (Chelsea)	12	37	0.32
Cliff Jones (Spurs)	20	38	0.5	Rooney (Man. U)	12	30	0.4

Thirty-six hat-tricks were scored in the 1959/60 season and six hat-tricks were scored in the 2008/09 season.

Top shots: Lower divisions 1959/60

	Gls		Gls		Gls
Holton (Watford)	48	O'Brien (Southampton)	27	Thomson (Villa)	22
Reeves (Southampton)	45	Curry (Brighton)	26	Massie (Huddersfield)	22
Clough (Middlesbrough)	40	Richards (Walsall)	26	Carter (Plymouth)	22
Stokes (Bradford City)	35	McParland (Villa)	25	Wheeler (Reading)	22
Uphill (Watford)	35	Hitchens (Villa)	25	Terry (Gillingham)	22
Hunt (Grimsby)	34	Philips (Ipswich)	25	Faulkner (Walsall)	22
Rowley (Shrewsbury)	32	Johnston (Orient)	25	Hickson (Liverpool)	21
Allan (Bradford City)	32	Bond (Torquay)	25	Summers (Charlton)	21
Francis (Brentford)	31	Biggs (Bristol R)	24	Sawyer (Rotherham)	21
King (Colchester)	30	Lawrie (Charlton)	24	Webster (Swansea)	21
Price (Southend)	29	Towers (Brentford)	24	Straw (Coventry)	21
Llewellyn (Crewe)	29	Rafferty (Grimsby)	24	Starkey (Shrewsbury)	21
Pace (Sheffield U)	28	Newsham (Notts County)	24	Fernie (Doncaster)	21
Bedford (QPR)	27	Hunt (Liverpool)	23	Clark (Hartlepools)	21

HOW MUCH HAS THE GAME CHANGED IN 50 YEARS?

A ROUGH STATISTICAL COMPARISON

1950s
Charles Reep (1950): 'Out of all the goals scored, one half precisely come from none to one pass, and 80 per cent come from not more than three passes.' (*Kicking & Screaming*)

Noughties – 2005/06
Jean Michel Benezet of FIFA (2006): '70% of all goals scored in the 2006 World Cup and UEFA Champions League tournaments were from attacks of no more than three passes and 90% from attacks with no more than six passes. 40% of goals came from quick breaks with 87% with three touches or less from the scoring player. 50% are scored with the scorer's first touch.' (*Trends in Modern Football*)

1950s
Bill Nicholson (Spurs manager – 1959): 'statistics have shown that between a third and a half of goals scored by a football team come from re-starts, corners, free kicks or throw-ins.'

Noughties – 2005/06
Jean Michel Benezet of FIFA (2006): '28% of goals are scored from set pieces and 72% from open play.' (*Trends in Modern Football*)

1959/60
Ray Simpson: 'In 64% of Burnley's 42 league games in 1959/60, the team scoring first won the game.' (*The Clarets Chronicles*)

Noughties – 2005/06
Jean Michel Benezet of FIFA (2006): 'In 75% of games, the team scoring first won the game.' (*Trends in Modern Football*)

1959/60
Glenda Rollin & Jack Rollin: '56% of league games in 1959/60 featured four goals or more with only 4% of games resulting in a 0-0 draw.' (*Rothman's Football Yearbook 2002-03*)

Noughties – 1999/2000
Glenda Rollin and Jack Rollin: '41% of league games in 1999/2000 featured four goals or more with 9% of games resulting in a 0-0 draw.' (*Rothman's Football Yearbook 2002-3*)

1959/60
'The average number of League goals scored by a First Division side at home was 2 compared with 1.5 for the away team.' (*Empire News Football Annual 1960-61*)

Noughties – 2007/08
'The average number of League goals scored by a Premier League side at home was 1.5 compared with 1 for the away team.' (*Sky Sports Football Yearbook 2008-9*)

1959/60	P	W	D	L	F	A	Pts	Goal ave
1. Burnley	42	24	7	11	85	61	55	1.39
2. Wolverhampton Wanderers	42	24	6	12	106	67	54	1.58
3. Tottenham Hotspur	42	21	11	10	86	50	53	1.72
4. West Bromwich Albion	42	19	11	12	83	57	49	1.46
5. Sheffield Wednesday	42	19	11	12	80	59	49	1.36
6. Bolton Wanderers	42	20	8	14	59	51	48	1.16
7. Manchester United	42	19	7	16	102	80	45	1.28
8. Newcastle United	42	18	8	16	82	78	44	1.05
9. Preston North End	42	16	12	14	79	76	44	1.04
10. Fulham	42	17	10	15	73	80	44	0.91
11. Blackpool	42	15	10	17	59	71	40	0.83
12. Leicester City	42	13	13	16	66	75	39	0.88
13. Arsenal	42	15	9	18	68	80	39	0.85
14. West Ham United	42	16	6	20	75	91	38	0.82
15. Everton	42	13	11	18	73	78	37	0.94
16. Manchester City	42	17	3	22	78	84	37	0.93
17. Blackburn Rovers	42	16	5	21	60	70	37	0.86
18. Chelsea	42	14	9	19	76	91	37	0.84
19. Birmingham City	42	13	10	19	63	80	36	0.79
20. Nottingham Forest	42	13	9	20	50	74	35	0.68
21. Leeds United	42	12	10	20	65	92	34	0.71
22. Luton Town	42	9	12	21	50	73	30	0.68

1968/69	P	W	D	L	F	A	Pts	Goal ave
1. Leeds	**42**	**27**	**13**	**2**	66	**26**	**67**	**2.54**
2. Liverpool	42	25	11	6	63	24	61	2.63
3. Everton	42	21	15	6	77	36	57	2.14
4. Arsenal	42	22	12	10	56	27	56	2.07
5. Chelsea	42	20	10	12	73	53	50	1.38
6. Tottenham Hotspur	42	14	17	11	61	51	45	1.20
7. Southampton	42	16	13	13	57	48	45	1.19
8. West Ham United	42	13	18	11	66	50	44	1.32
9. Newcastle United	42	15	14	13	61	55	44	1.11
10. West Bromwich Albion	42	16	11	15	64	67	43	0.96
11. Manchester United	42	15	12	15	57	53	42	1.08
12. Ipswich Town	42	15	11	16	59	60	41	0.98
13. Manchester City	42	15	10	17	64	55	40	1.16
14. Burnley	42	15	9	18	55	82	39	0.67
15. Sheffield Wednesday	42	10	16	16	41	54	36	0.76
16. Wolverhampton Wanderers	42	10	15	17	41	58	35	0.71
17. Sunderland	42	11	12	19	43	67	34	0.64
18. Nottingham Forest	42	10	13	19	45	57	33	0.79
19. Stoke City	42	9	15	18	40	63	33	0.63
20. Coventry City	42	10	11	21	46	64	31	0.72
21. Leicester City	42	9	12	21	39	68	30	0.57
22. Queens Park Rangers	42	4	10	28	39	95	18	0.41

First Division season	Goals scored	% annual change	First Division & EPL seasons	Goals scored	% decade change
1949/50	1247		1949/50	1247	
1950/51	1399	12.2%	1959/60	1618	29.8%
1951/52	1490	6.5%	1968/69	1213	-25.0%
1952/53	1508	1.2%	1978/79	1217	0.3%
1953/54	1626	7.8%	1988/89	1465	20.4%
1954/55	1572	-3.3%	1998/99	1060	-27.6%
1955/56	1529	-2.7%	2018/19	1185	11.8%
1956/57	1612	5.4%			
1957/58	1721	6.8%			
1958/59	1692	-1.7%			
1959/60	1618	-4.4%			
1960/61	1594	-1.5%			
1961/62	1582	-0.8%			
1962/63	1536	-2.9%			
1963/64	1571	2.3%			
1964/65	1543	-1.8%			
1965/66	1457	-5.6%			
1966/67	1387	-4.8%			
1967/68	1398	0.8%			
1968/69	1213	-13.2%			

Note: Premier League goals scored are extrapolated on the basis of a comparable number of games played (42). The 2018/19 figure is included above solely to give a present comparison.

English First Division 1959/60 hot shots (EFL & FAC)

1959/60	Goals
Dennis Viollet (Man U)	32
Jimmy Greaves (Chelsea)	29
Jimmy Murray (Wolves)	29
Len White (Newcastle)	28
Derek Kevan (WBA)	26
Bobby Smith (Spurs)	25
John McCole (Leeds)	22
Billy McAdams (Man C)	21
John Connelly (Burnley)	20
Cliff Jones (Spurs)	20

During the '50s there was a 30% increase in goals, supporting Jimmy Greaves's belief that this was a 'Golden Age' for strikers, and as he also indicated, goalscoring became progressively harder in the 60s particularly after the 1966 World Cup, although not for him apparently! Goals scored in the top flight fell by 25% during the '60s, reflecting a tightening of defences which began after the 1962 Chile World Cup and increased after the 1966 World Cup.

English First Division 1968/69 hot shots (EFL & FAC)

1968/69	Goals
Jimmy Greaves (Spurs)	32
Geoff Hurst (West Ham)	29
Joe Royle (Everton)	25
Jeff Astle (WBA)	24
Bryan Robson (Newcastle)	22
Ron Davies (Southampton)	22
Martin Peters (West Ham)	21
Frank Casper (Burnley)	21
Denis Law (Man U)	14

Attendances 1948/49 to 2017/18

Season	Matches	Total	Division One / Premier League	Division Two / Champ'ship	Division Three / League One	Division Four / League Two
1948/49	1,848	41,271,414	17,914,667	11,353,237	N/A	N/A
1959/60	2,028	32,538,611	14,391,227	8,399,627	5,739,707	4,008,050
1968/69	2,028	29,382,172	14,584,851	7,382,390	4,339,656	3,075,275
1985/86	2,028	16,488,577	9,037,854	3,551,968	2,490,481	1,408,274
2018/19	2,035	32,911,714	14,515,181	11,119,775	4,811,797	2,464,961

Division Three and Four were created in 1958/59 replacing Divisions Three (North and South).

Analysis of changing attendances 1948/49 to 2018/19

The decline in attendances between 1948/49 and the late '50s was probably a product of greater prosperity prompting the emergence of alternative attractions and pastimes. For example, TV and car ownership expanded significantly in the mid-'50s as did public enthusiasm for DIY. The birth of ITV in 1955 offered more choice of hearthside entertainment causing cinema attendances to fall sharply.

The decline after 1959/60 can probably be attributed to greater TV coverage of professional football (*Match of the Day* started in August 1964) and a declining economy in the second half of the '60s, which continued into the '70s and '80s. The 1966 World Cup success provided a temporary uplift which was lost after '70s industrial strife, the flurry of strikes by miners, rail staff and power workers, the three-day week, the 1973 oil crisis, and runaway inflation.

The 1985/86 figures were the lowest during this 70-year period reflecting the introduction of live TV coverage of top games, but also increasing disenchantment with a game scarred by hideous hooliganism, as occurred at Heysel stadium, Brussels, and St Andrew's, Birmingham, where there were losses of life.

The game was becoming unruly too with a new high of 219 dismissals in 1986/87. The cages introduced at football grounds to combat hooliganism were hated by many supporters, as were the promised identity cards. The caging measure also contributed to the 1989 Hillsborough tragedy. The tragic Bradford fire in 1985 drew attention to the dangers posed by decrepit stadia. Football was no longer attractive to many families.

The '80s was also a period of mounting unemployment. There were three million jobless at the start of the decade, principally in post-industrial areas in Scotland and the north, West Midlands, and South Wales. These were the worst figures since the Great Depression of the 1930s. Between 1983 and 1987 around 75 per cent of new jobs were in the south-east. In parts of Liverpool up to 90 per cent of young people were out of work.

In the wake of the Premier League's birth in 1992 and the implementation of the Taylor Report recommendations, football became appealing once more as reflected in the 2018/19 figure.

Total attendances in 2018/19 were one per cent up on the 1959/60 figure as were First Division/Premier League figures.

The old Second Division/Championship figure for 2018/19 was 32 per cent up on 1959/60. But the Third Division/League 1 number for 2018/19 was 16 per cent down on 1959/60.

The Fourth Division/League 2 total was 39 per cent down, indicating a significant movement of support to the top two divisions' sides over the last 59 years, but principally after the creation of the Premier League.

The above figures suggest that the biggest and the best, principally city clubs have attracted more fans at the expense and diminution of smaller, provincial, and local clubs.

In 1948/49 watching professional football was largely a working-class activity. That is no longer the case with the higher costs of admission favouring middle-class supporters with greater disposable incomes.

PART THREE
'The Shock of the New'

'YOU SAY YOU WANT A REVOLUTION'

38.

GLORY, GLORY HALLELUJAH: DOUBLE-WINNING SPURS

SOME THOUGHT the double of First Division and FA Cup was an impossible objective. Spurs manager Bill Nicholson felt otherwise, dismissing a journalist's scepticism with terse irritation just before the FA Cup was hoisted aloft. To be fair, since Preston North End became the first side to achieve this feat in 1889 and Aston Villa the second in 1897, no other English side had managed this in 60 years of the 20th century. During that time, Wolves had tried to achieve it and had twice failed as had Manchester United. Arsenal had three shots at this and missed on each occasion. Aston Villa had another go at winning both in 1912/13 and failed.

Other disappointed contenders were West Bromwich Albion, Portsmouth, Huddersfield Town, Sunderland, Newcastle United and Manchester City; 14 shots and 14 misses. The double had become akin to Excalibur or the four-minute mile until Roger Bannister broke that 'impossible' barrier in 1954. It was about time that the double hurdle was cleared too.

Spurs' eloquent captain, Danny Blanchflower, said about his side's achievement, 'Winning the cup and league double in this day and age, is a far more strenuous and exacting business than it has ever been. Neither Preston nor Aston Villa tackled anything as hard as the 49-match season programme that stood before Spurs and their great goal. There could not be a sterner test of a team's endurance.'

What Danny omitted to say was that Spurs achieved this feat with only 17 players. Moreover, they had the most wins (31) in First Division history, collecting 66 points to equal Arsenal's record of 1930/31, and they tied the Gunners' away record of 33 points.

Danny continued, 'Yet I always believed the double could be achieved even under modern stresses and that Spurs would have this distinction. I reminded the boys that you must believe in what you set out to achieve. My belief was never shaken either by the gloomy pessimists or by previous disappointments. Even if we had been beaten at Wembley my faith that this great prize still awaited us would have stood firm. We were not at our best at Wembley. At the end of a long hard race you cannot be at your peak.'

What Danny did not say here was that Leicester had only ten fit men for most of the final, a tedious further instalment of Wembley woes that the stubborn FA refused to rectify by permitting substitutes. But Spurs centre-forward Bobby Smith was also carrying a knee injury, unbeknown to Nicholson. Smith, who had enjoyed a splendid season, top scoring for his club with 33 goals and representing England with distinction, was so desperate to play at Wembley that he sneaked out of the team's hotel to obtain a pain-killing injection from a private doctor. Smith scored once and laid on the other for Terry Dyson in a 2-0 victory.

Blanchflower was the vital cog in Spurs' double-winning side. He was not blessed with pace but he had wiry strength. He read the game adroitly with an instinct for slipping into space at crucial moments, freeing himself from the restraints his opponents sought to apply. He had remarkable passing skills, too, that would change the point of attack and set up copious scoring opportunities.

To his great credit, Nicholson knew that Blanchflower could lead on the pitch. He never sought to over-ride him as some managers might do for egotistical reasons. He had implicit trust in Danny's judgement on tactical decisions made in the heat of battle. He recognised Danny's motivational skills, too. Fellow wing-half Dave Mackay remarked, 'Danny's midfield partnership with inside-right, John White, dictated the tempo of our games and he always found the right words to inspire us.'

Nicholson was once an integral member of Arthur Rowe's successful 'push and run' side. He acknowledged this influence when he said, 'In 1960/61, Spurs were renowned for their short passing, quick exchanges and constant movement off the ball.'

Arguably the game of that season was Spurs, champions elect, against Burnley, the current title-holders.

39

TOTTENHAM HOTSPUR V BURNLEY: FIRST DIVISION, 3 DECEMBER 1960

THE AUTUMN of 1960 was one of the wettest on record as wave after wave of Atlantic fronts drenched the British Isles. In Lewes, the Sussex Ouse flood waters reached platform level, forcing British Railways to bring back steam-hauled trains in place of electric ones. As autumn turned to winter there was no letting up. The White Hart Lane pitch was an oozing mud-bath, defying the best efforts of the ground staff with their sanding and forking. Could anyone manage to keep their footing in this quagmire?

Now over to BBC's Kenneth Wolstenholme for some vintage commentary, 'And with the rain pouring down the ground looks very muddy indeed. Spurs in the white shirts kick off against Burnley who have had to make one change after their European Cup match in Paris. Jimmy Adamson, their centre-half and captain, is not playing and is replaced by Tommy Cummings. Otherwise their team is at full strength after a great performance in Paris where they eliminated Reims 3-2 on aggregate.

'This ground is going to cut up badly. The covers were taken off this morning at ten and the rain has poured down on the pitch since. There are little pools of water everywhere. Now there is a great chance for Burnley's Robson, but his shot is blocked, and it runs out to Connelly who shoots ... ah, a great save from Brown but it is a Burnley corner. They are playing it short as they usually do. And there is another scramble in the penalty area and Joyce volleys wide.

'Burnley have made all the running here but here's Jones breaking away. He is flying over the mud! Now Blanchflower has it and with a quick turn he is free and plays a lovely square ball for the advancing Mackay. But Mackay misses it. He slipped and the ball ran away from him. It is so difficult for the players to keep their feet. But Mackay has retrieved it and he crosses and Norman heads in. As easy as that!'

Burnley had been dominant at the start, forcing four corners in quick succession. The Spurs fans could not be heard during a goalless first 18 minutes. Then their side scored three goals in three minutes and the place was bouncing.

Cliff Jones sped across the mud as if on a cushion of air. Years later he remarked, 'Once I had the ball, I could sense the crowd's expectation and I would respond. Sometimes I overdid the streaking runs, but I was aware of giving value for money. Besides, I loved having the ball at my feet, taking on defenders. I learnt how to hold on to the ball after playing in frantic 30-a-side games on the Swansea beach when I was a kid. If you lost possession you had a hard time getting it back. After playing on that wet sloppy sand, mud didn't bother me.'

Here, he beat the conditions twice in successive minutes to help Spurs open up a 3-0 scoreline and Dave Mackay added a fourth after 36 minutes, bowing flamboyantly to the home fans.

Most teams would have caved in at this point but not Burnley. On the brink of half-time, John Connelly reduced the arrears. Pilkington made inroads on the left and his pot shot was blocked but McIlroy was following up, crossing high to the far post. In a melee of players Brown's punch had no distance, allowing the alert Connelly to lash in the loose ball.

A calamity of errors early in the second half allowed Burnley to pull two more back. First, Spurs left-back Ron Henry became stuck in the mud with the ball at his feet. Jimmy Robson was quickest to react. Dispossessing the beached Henry, he prodded in Burnley's second. The Spurs fans became pensive, even more so after Maurice Norman made a similar error leaving blond Ray Pointer to take advantage and narrow the gap to one. Burnley had become masters of the mud and with 18 minutes left, they broke out of their penalty area, sending Connelly racing downfield. Spurs' defence was all over the place as he and Robson exchanged passes, allowing Connelly to smack in

Burnley's equaliser. White Hart Lane was stunned, and yet there was still time for John White to miss a sitter.

I only saw the highlights on BBC's Saturday night *Sports Special* programme, with Wolstenholme the commentator, but 60 years on it remains as one of my favourite games. Some 58,737 fans turned out in the cold rain to see this thriller. Bill Nicholson was less sanguine, however, shouting at his players, 'Tell me how we have scored eight goals and only drawn!' He thought his side were responsible for all eight goals. Spurs took their revenge on Burnley in the 1961 FA Cup semi-final at Villa Park. After riding their luck Spurs won 3-0.

40

ENGLAND'S SPECTACULAR, IF BRIEF, REVIVAL IN 1960/61

ENGLAND EMERGED from a dismal run to deliver a sequence of startling results during the 1960/61 season. They won seven and drew one of their nine internationals, scoring 45 goals and conceding 14. Whereas Spurs' glorious achievement was the product of two years of progressive improvement under Bill Nicholson's canny management, England's revival arrived in a sudden burst of brilliance. Spain were spanked 4-2 at a soggy Wembley in November and Italy were seen off 3-2 in the spring heat of Rome, with late goals from Greaves and Hitchens turning the game on its head, assisted by an enforced substitution of the Italian goalkeeper. In between these prestigious results, Scotland were hammered 9-3 and Mexico thrashed 8-0, avenging the 2-1 humiliation on the 1959 South American tour.

The inspiration for this unexpected revival appeared to be the adoption of a 4-2-4 system. Former England captain Billy Wright was an excited cheerleader of the new formation, believing it offered greater defensive solidity as well as greater attacking flair. But England's brief success with this style possibly owed more to the quality of the singers than to the merits of the song. The outstanding performer was midfield maestro Johnny Haynes. Haynes was an enigma. He practised his art with solemn dedication, reprimanding team-mates who did not share his studious work ethic. And yet he remained close to his joking, iconoclastic team-mate, 'Tosh' Chamberlain.

As gifted as Haynes was his talents seemed more appreciated in and around the capital than elsewhere in the country. His performances for England were variable at best but during that momentous 1960/61 season there was no disputing his class. Fulham chairman Tommy

Trinder had no doubt on that score, awarding Haynes a £100 weekly wage once the maximum wage was abolished.

Haynes was serious and thoughtful as if mulling over a move, like a chess grandmaster, before executing it. When on form, his 30-yard passes, struck with supreme accuracy and weight, were things of beauty. With the ball reaching its target and the receiver picking it up in mid-stride, the course of the game could be changed entirely. His leisurely manner was deceptive, for his ability to spot and exploit an opening was razor sharp. He rarely smiled and when not on the ball, he had an air of simmering impatience. Pelé described Haynes as 'the best passer of the ball I've ever seen'. Haynes was not only a hugely gifted playmaker; he was, at least before his career-threatening car crash in 1962, a regular goalscorer, also.

Prompted by his stellar performances, England prepared for the 1962 World Cup in Chile in good heart. Winterbottom's fluid team of Springett, Armfield, McNeil, Swan, Flowers, Robson, Douglas, Greaves, Smith, Haynes and Charlton combined pace, power, and ruthless opportunism. But England's choice of method was essentially vulnerable in that too much was expected of its midfield pairing, Bobby Robson and Haynes, who wore the number ten shirt. In Chile, a Yugoslavian coach observed, 'Number ten takes the corners! Number ten takes the throw-ins! So, what do we do? We put a man on number ten! Goodbye, England!'

It was Hungary rather than Yugoslavia, though, who exposed this weakness. They put Gyula Rakosi on Haynes, stifling him, consigning England to a toothless defeat. Jimmy McIlroy, then of Burnley, felt that Haynes's long, raking passes were less effective against foreign defenders, who had learnt how to curb his influence.

Burnley were also aware of how to neutralise Haynes. Jimmy explained, 'When we played Fulham, our left-half, Brian Miller, would be given the task of following Johnny Haynes all over the park. We didn't mind Brian not getting a kick providing Johnny didn't either.' In Chile, England's fitful performances caused Haynes to become prickly and sullen, confronting the critical British press with the accusation, 'You *want* us to lose.' England managed just one decent display, in beating a jaded Argentina, before Brazil eliminated them. England seemed as far away from World Cup success in 1962 as they were in 1950.

41.

FREEING THE
'SOCCER SLAVES'

THE 1960/61 season saw the abolition of the maximum wage for English professional footballers. Led adroitly by Fulham's 32-year-old inside-forward Jimmy Hill, the 2,700-strong Professional Footballers' Association (PFA) successfully challenged the feudal power of the clubs. The crisis came to a head in November 1960. The Football League tried to see off the mounting dispute by proposing that clubs raised the maximum wage from £20 to £30 per week and offered their players longer contracts. In 1960, each player was on a one-year deal. This afforded them and their families little security. Tom Finney remembered, 'The retained players were called in one by one and it would be something along the lines of, "Well, you've had a good season and we're offering you the same terms as last season, sign here," and he would sign a blank form and they would fill in the terms later.' The clubs held the whip hand.

In 1959, the average national wage was just over £11 per week but a top entertainer, such as Fulham's chairman Tommy Trinder, could earn £100 per week for compering the TV show *Sunday Night at the London Palladium*. While the leading professional footballers were able to earn substantially more than their predominantly working-class supporters, they were generally paid much less than other entertainers. Billy Wright, England's captain with over 100 international caps did better than most. He estimated that he earned around £2,000 per year from club and country alone. That amounts to around £50,000 per year in modern currency, which, of course, is less than most present Premier League players now earn in a week.

On top of that, Wright and other top players benefited from the commercial opportunities which emerged during the late '50s. For example, Johnny Haynes advertised Brylcreem, Tom Finney advertised Shredded Wheat and Jimmy Greaves advertised Bovril. Wright, too, had considerable earnings outside the game. Although the maximum wage created an artificially level playing field this did not mean that everyone earned the same, even at First Division level. Those differences sharpened down the divisions. For example, an average Third Division player in 1959 would earn about half of what Wright drew in basic wages alone.

Some clubs partially circumvented the wage restriction with the use of bonuses and 'under the table' payments, which caused a scandal when uncovered at Sunderland. Even before the wage cap was removed there were wage hierarchies, which were sometimes contested by players. Alan Mullery remembered that at the end of the 1958/59 season, Fulham's Maurice Cook went to see his manager, Frank Osborne, who told him, 'You've had a good season, we'll give you £18 in the season and £15 in the summer.' Cook replied, 'I'm not happy about that, Frank. Johnny Haynes has just been in, and he's on 20 and 17.' Osborne said, 'Yeah, but he's captain of the team and an England international and, to be honest, he's a better player than you.' Cook retorted, 'Not in the summer, he's not.'

To the astonishment of the Football League chiefs and the anger of the players, the Football League proposals were rejected by the clubs. Hill immediately summoned rallies in London, Birmingham, and Manchester. The players' attitudes hardened. They demanded a percentage of the transfer fees and an end to the enslaving 'retain and transfer' system, which enabled clubs to hang on to a player's registration after his contract had expired. This allowed clubs to bully players into staying on, as George Eastham found. It also meant that the club holding a player's registration could transfer its players when they saw fit, irrespective of the players' wishes.

Newcastle inside-forward Eastham went on strike after the Magpies refused to allow him to move to a club of his choosing even though his contact had expired. Burnley wing-half Bob Seith dug in his heels, too. Eventually, he forced his tough chairman, Bob Lord, into agreeing a transfer to his native Dundee because he had his chiropody qualification to fall back upon. Lord knew that if Seith walked away from football, Burnley would receive nothing for him. Eastham, too, had alternative work found for him while he fought his case. But most players were not so lucky.

Former Burnley outside-left Brian Pilkington vividly remembered the Manchester PFA meeting considering strike action. He recalled, 'We attended a big meeting in a hotel in Manchester about the proposed strike. All the players were there. We seemed to be of a similar mind but there was one dissenting voice. This chap said that he didn't think we should be telling the club directors their business. He went on about his father earning £15 per week for 44 hours' work at a local mine, so reckoned that £20 per week wasn't bad for 12 hours' work.

'But up gets Tommy Banks, the forthright Bolton full-back. In his typically blunt manner and broad Lancastrian accent, he retorted, "You can go back and tell thy father that he canna be much bloody good as a miner to be taking only 15 quid a week home. I'll come and do tha' dad's job and I'll make a bloody sight more than £15 a week – but can tha' dad come and do my job? How would he like to mark brother Matthews, here?" That did it. We were ready to strike.'

There had been threats of strike action before 1960 but now the players had a new weapon – the Football Pools. In the previous season, the Football League had sold its fixture rights to the Pools companies for over £250,000 a year. This contract was now in jeopardy. The public sympathised with the players, and so did the politicians – on both sides of the House. This was a fight that the clubs were destined to lose.

The clubs tried to win the propaganda war by publicising details of their players' earnings, including bonuses, in their matchday programmes. This was done in reaction to Danny Blanchflower's and Jimmy Hill's allegations, made on TV, of 'soccer slavery'. With the strike imminent, the clubs made one last vain attempt to sway public and professional opinion in their favour by emphasising the dire financial consequences facing the clubs if the wage restriction was ended.

Brighton manager Billy Lane wrote in his club's programme on 14 January 1961, 'I have always advocated that players should have better terms, provided the cash to cover increased wages comes through the turnstile. There are, in my opinion, 60 per cent of League clubs running at a loss. Now that the maximum wage scale may be abolished the Albion can no longer pay the maximum wage of approximately £25 per week to players playing in the League side although this has been the practice of the club during the past ten years.' In Brighton's case, this was not just shroud-waving.

But for all their protests, the clubs realised that the game was up. They had to give way. A consortium of clubs, led by West Bromwich Albion and a group from Lancashire, tried to revive the original Football League proposal and insert a new maximum wage of £30 per week. But by then it was too late as Fulham had already broken ranks. Trinder announced that he was going to pay Haynes £100 per week to keep him at Craven Cottage.

England was already losing its top players to Italy. Lured by the lustre of the lira, Denis Law, Jimmy Greaves, Joe Baker and Gerry Hitchens decided to follow John Charles's example and sample the Mediterranean sun. Jimmy McIlroy, Burnley's midfield magician, had also been attracted by the prospect, painting a vivid picture to his sceptical wife of a sumptuous lifestyle awaiting them. Being a Burnley lass through and through, she remained unconvinced, retorting, 'What do we want to leave Burnley for?' However, fearing that he might lose his prized asset, chairman Bob Lord stepped in and quickly offered Jimmy an £80-per-week contract.

There was much disquiet about Italian 'poaching' of England's leading players, even after the maximum wage was abolished. *News of the World* football correspondent Harry Ditton wrote in early 1962, 'Those saucy Italians are at it again! Latest news from the country where lira millionaires have cornered the soccer market is that Juventus want Dave Mackay and Cliff Jones of Spurs.'

Experience abroad suggested that better pay led to better football. But the abolition of the wage cap came when English gates were falling, and clubs were finding it harder to make ends meet. The clubs in the Third and Fourth Divisions were already leaning more heavily upon fans' contributions to keep their heads above water. During the 1960/61 season, supporter donations to Third and Fourth Division clubs totalled £370,000, about £9m today. Meanwhile, their total revenue from transfer sales was only £37,000. With transfer fees paid amounting to only a modest figure of £16,000, it was clear that lower-division football was heavily reliant upon supporters' patronage, particularly when reducing gate receipts were accounted for.

At Second Division clubs, such contributions were much less. Around £38,000 in total was received in 1960/61. Consequently, for them greater reliance was placed upon transfer fees and gate receipts to ensure solvency. The abolition of the maximum wage made it harder for the underdogs to hold on to their talented players. Thereafter, the lower-division sides needed to be more resourceful in attempting to overcome stronger opponents.

At the end of the 1960/61 season, 800 of the 2,800 registered players were released. The cost of increasing wages was met through greater redundancies. Ironically, one of the first players to be released was PFA chairman Jimmy Hill. He was given a free transfer by Fulham after struggling to recover from a knee injury, which restricted him to just 11 appearances in this ground-breaking season.

The abolition of the maximum wage began the shift of power from the autocratic clubs to the previously disenfranchised players. This trend was accentuated by a 1963 High Court judgement, which ruled that the 'retain and transfer' system was an unlawful restraint of trade. However, it would take the Bosman judgement of 1995 to complete the reversal of the pre-1961 balance of power.

With the abolition of the wage ceiling, top players began to develop a taste for the things that the extra money could buy. Although still far from being the plutocrats of today, many top players in the '60s became upwardly socially mobile. A cultural gulf was created between them and their supporters, at least in lifestyles. According to one sociologist, the late Professor Ian Taylor, a gradual process of gentrification took place among top footballers contributing to a re-emergence of football hooliganism.

Professor Taylor, an avid Sheffield Wednesday fan, set out his case in an article, 'Football Mad: a speculative sociology of football hooliganism' which featured in *Sociology of Sport: a collection of readings* edited by Eric Dunning (1971). He contended that working class fans believed they had a closer relationship with their heroes before the abolition of the maximum wage, thinking they were able to exert a greater control over club policies and the players, whom they met regularly around town, in local shops and pubs, or on buses that took both the players and them to and from home games. Professor Taylor argued that following the abolition of the maximum wage, this bond with the players was lost as the players adopted 'jet-setting, sports car-driving lifestyles' which separated them from their working-class roots.

His reasoning was that football hooliganism represented an attempt by young working-class fans to reassert a 'participatory democracy' which they believed they once had at their club and with its players. After their heroes began to move into more privileged circles, Taylor thought that hooliganism re-appeared as a 'working class resistance movement'. Put simply, the fans' shared identity with players whom they cheered on to victory was replaced with a separate identity as a member of a working-class gang that fought with opposing fans. However, it is difficult to believe that these fans ever thought they had any control over their club's policies, although the greater separation from the players they adored was regretted, notably the lost access.

The abolition of the maximum wage ended the contrived equality of pay between players. There were concerns whether this might undermine team spirit. Burnley players Ray Pointer and Trevor Meredith had no problem with the subsequent wage settlements. They thought that the higher amounts offered to the senior players was perfectly just. Ray said, 'I wasn't worried about the maximum wage issues or the possibility of a strike or the different pay-outs. Like others there, I pushed it all to the back of my mind and got on with playing. I had no problem with Jimmy McIlroy earning more. He was our best player.'

McIlroy recalled, 'When the maximum wage was abolished, our wages were doubled immediately but I was aware that Johnny Haynes had been awarded £100 per week, so I thought I should look for more. But I did not have Johnny Haynes's guts. I settled for £80 per week. To be honest, I felt tentative. I did not really feel I was worth that much. After all, it was such a massive increase. Looking back, I probably could have held out for £100 per week. Bob Lord may well have decided that I was worth it. I think he liked to show everyone how well we were paid at Burnley. It reflected well on him and the status of the club. Although there was now a difference between what we, as first-team players, were paid, there was no resentment among the players receiving less.

'We were close as a team. Although we had our separate friends, we all got on well together. I suppose it is because we were interdependent. We were reliant upon one another. It was the same when I played at Stoke and Oldham. Of course, success helps make that bond closer – the good results and reading good things about yourselves in the news. However, in those days, footballers did not have the celebrity status that they have now. The supporters may have held us in high esteem but among the wealthier residents of Burnley we were considered inferior. At this time, you were considered more important locally if you were a member of the Belvedere Tennis Club rather than being a professional footballer. It was quite a catch if you happened to be friendly with a girl from that club.'

Hill, the orchestrator in chief, assured all concerned that the increase in wages would be matched by an upsurge in playing quality. He said, 'I have made it clear to the players at every stage that they have to put their energies and enthusiasm into improving the game. We've told the League that we would back them 100 per cent in disciplining anyone who behaves badly or infringes the system.' Hill also made a personal appeal for better behaviour on the field. The experience from Spain, Italy, Argentina and Brazil was that there was a rise in standard following abolition of the maximum wage, but that this rise was often confined to the bigger clubs.

News of the World sports editor Frank Butler expressed regret that ageing or former stars missed out on this wage bonanza but had little sympathy for the clubs forced into paying up, saying, 'British clubs are grumbling. While I strongly disapprove of alien agents who are skimming the cream of British football, I do blame those old diehards of the Football League who fought and succeeded for so many years in pegging our greatest stars to a meagre maximum. Only after years of fighting by the Professional Footballers' Association was the maximum wage raised to £20 a week, before finally the players have won the day. I have the feeling that things would have worked out so much better for our clubs had the wage increase been given more willingly. The sudden tendency of making the sky the limit could work havoc with British football.'

George Best's take on the impact of the abolition of the maximum wage is salutary, 'I did not realise how massive the '60s were. There was the music, fashion, the hippie movement. I stepped over a line from being an athlete to becoming a personality, a pop thing. My friends were the Beatles and the Stones. It was frightening. I was getting hounded. A Benfica fan chased me with a knife. I thought he was going to kill me. He just wanted a lock of my hair! The media started asking me about politics. What did I know? I was 17!'

Francis Lee remembered, 'When I moved to Manchester City, I got a load of fan mail asking for photographs and things and I got a lot of letters from nutters. Every time there was a derby game, I would get 20 or 30 death threats.'

Bobby Keetch of Fulham found the publicity very wearing. He said, 'I had a taste of what George Best had. I gave up football for two years because of being captured in bars and restaurants.'

In London and other major cities, it became commonplace to see footballers out with film stars, artists, and writers. This was unheard of before the maximum wage was abolished and many traditionalists did not like it. It had drawbacks for the players, too, when they failed to perform and were instantly jettisoned by their so-called celebrity friends.

42.

WHAT THE 'SOCCER SLAVES' EARNED IN 1959

DURING 1959, Danny Blanchflower, captain of Spurs and Northern Ireland, and Jimmy Hill, Fulham's inside-right and chairman of the Professional Footballers' Association, appeared on British television claiming that their contracts and conditions of employment rendered them as virtual slaves to their 'masters', the Football League clubs. The clubs responded by presenting the following details of players' wages and entitlements in their matchday programmes.

Basic wages:
Maximum: £20 a week in the season; £17 a week in the summer
Minimum: For a full-time player of 20 years old £8 a week all year round

Friendly match:
£2-£3 an appearance plus £2 if the game is televised

League bonuses:
£4 a win, £2 a draw

FA Cup bonuses (half amounts paid in event of drawn matches):

First Round	£4	Fifth Round	£8
Second Round	£4	Sixth Round	£10
Third Round	£5	Semi-Final	£20
Fourth Round	£6	Final	£25

Talent money paid to First and Second Division clubs

First	£1,100	Fourth	£440
Second	£880	Fifth	£220
Third	£660		

Talent money paid to Third Division clubs and Fourth Division clubs

First	£550	First	£330
Second	£440	Second	£220
Third	£330	Third	£110
Fourth	£220	Fourth	£55

FA Cup prize money paid to clubs

Winners	£1,100	Defeated in Sixth Round	£440
Runners-up	£880	Defeated in Fifth Round	£220
Defeated semi-finalist	£660		

European Cup prize money paid to players for each appearance

First Round	£10	Fourth Round	£30
Second Round	£20	Semi-final	£40
Third Round	£30	Final	£50

Benefits:
£150 a year during the first five years and £200 a year for succeeding years of service with the same club

On tour:
£2 a day for out-of-pocket expenses

On transfer:
Removal expenses and a sum of up to £300 if transferred at the club's request

Provident fund:
A sum equal to eight per cent of a player's total earnings put aside each season and paid, free of income tax, in the first January following

his 35th birthday or following his retirement from league football, whichever is later

Vocational training:
The Football League pays whole or part of the expenses and fees of players studying for another trade or occupation

Coaching:
The FA pay fees to over 200 players who have qualified as coaches

Representative matches:
Fees are paid for appearances, up to £50 for a full international

Average wage in 1959:
£11 2s 6d

Rewards for top international players:
Billy Wright, England's captain with over 100 international caps, estimated that he earned around £2,000 per year from club and country alone

43.

'BEYOND THE FRINGE': DEFERENCE IN RETREAT

ALTHOUGH TOP footballers welcomed 1961 there was a growing malaise in the country. The run on the pound made nonsense of Harold Macmillan's boast that we had 'never had it so good' as he went cap in hand to the International Monetary Fund. Macmillan's repeated attempts at gaining EEC membership were refused. French president Charles de Gaulle feared that Britain would, as America's 'Trojan Horse', undermine the European project. He also thought our chronic deficiency in balance of payments made us a poor fit as did our tradition of obtaining cheap food from all parts of the world.

Although Macmillan's administration had brought about modernisation in the mines, the railways, schools, and universities and began large-scale decolonisation, he and his government seemed crusty and out of touch. There was a mounting urge, particularly among restless young adults that we should be shaking off the vestiges of staid British conservatism, with its 'club amateur' nepotism and embrace a sleek, shiny technological future, offering greater equality of opportunity. Anthony Sampson suggested as much in his seminal 1962 work *Anatomy of Britain*. Young people who had come of age as Britain emerged from post-war austerity enjoyed the late '50s consumer boom, and greater social and economic freedoms and increased educational opportunities. But this was not enough. Their frustrations helped satire become chic again in 1961.

A new satirical nightclub opened in London, called The Establishment. This attracted the controversial American comedian Lenny Bruce, who traded in edgy narratives on race. *Private Eye* produced its first scrappy editions and, much as it might appear tame now, the *Beyond the Fringe* revue scoffed at Establishment sacred cows, notably stiff upper lip heroism. But while Peter Cook, Dudley Moore, Jonathan Miller and Alan Bennett were criticised, particularly in the provinces, for trivialising a war from which they had been spared, this accusation could not be levelled at Joseph Heller, whose novel *Catch-22* first appeared in Britain in 1961.

Heller had served as a bombardier with the US Army Air Force flying missions over Nazi-occupied Italy, in support of the Allied invasion. His grotesquely funny satire savaged with nihilistic abandon the euphemisms, moral pretensions, and organisational chaos of war. In a year when Britain seemed to be declining and Cold War tensions mounting, perhaps gallows humour had more resonance.

Certainly, during 1961 and 1962 there were worrying escalations of global sparring – the Berlin Wall was erected, and the Cuban missile crisis intensified. Although its significance was not yet widely recognised in Britain, the US also reinforced its military presence in Vietnam. The worst of circumstances often provides fertile soil for satire. As the sordid details of the Profumo affair emerged in 1963, Macmillan was ridiculed with the Tory slogan 'Life is better under a Conservative' given a salacious twist, while 'We've never had it so often' mocked his 1957 boast and the prevalent sexual hypocrisy. Meanwhile, decolonisation attracted similar disdain as illustrated in a sketch from the mid-'60s featuring a spoof 'Prince Philip' at Kenya's independence ceremony. I was unable to track down the source. It went something like this:

'Why were you in Kenya, your Royal Highness?'
'I was there in a symbolic capacity.'
'What were you symbolising, sir?'
'Capitulation.'
'Did we not imprison Prime Minister Kenyatta, sir?'
'Yes, but we're good friends now. In fact, Mr Kenyatta gripped me warmly by the throat.'
'And what has happened to the imprisoned Mau Mau terrorists, sir?'
'An unfortunate misunderstanding. They were really freedom fighters.'

Just as the British Establishment had become a figure of fun, so had other guardians of sacred cows. Football was not exempt either with

Peter Cook of *Private Eye* inventing 'tight-lipped, ashen-faced Ron Knee', supremo of Neasden FC, and his 'bluff chairman Buffy Cohen', accompanied by their only supporters, 'Sid and Doris Bonkers'.

As the '80s TV satire show *Spitting Image* proved, daft and derisive publicity was more often welcomed by their targets than no publicity at all. But Macmillan felt demeaned by it.

44.

THE RISE AND FALL
OF IPSWICH TOWN
1961/62 – 1963/64

UNLIKE SPAIN, Italy, and South America, where a junta of powerful clubs cornered the honours, in 1962 it was still possible for a humble British outfit to achieve top-flight glory. Burnley had demonstrated this in 1960 although they were then an established First Division side, albeit not a wealthy one. By contrast, the rise and rise of Ipswich Town was Rocky-like. They had joined the Football League in 1938 and were still a Third Division club in 1957. Yet, come May 1962, they were First Division champions. They were only the second Football League club to win the First Division title at their first attempt and the first since Preston in 1888/89, although North End played only 22 league games in what was the inaugural Football League season.

It was quite by chance that Ipswich became a Football League club at all, let alone a successful one. The seed was sown during the mid-'30s after Arsenal chairman Sir Samuel Hill Wood suggested to his friend John Murray Cobbold that he might care to watch a game at Highbury rather than have a day at the races as was his wont. It was a Damascus-like experience for Cobbold. He enjoyed the occasion so much that he came away with the firm intention of turning his local amateur side, Ipswich Town, into the 'Arsenal of East Anglia'.

Cobbold took charge of the club and immediately put them on a professional footing, securing a place for them in the Southern League, then the strongest English non-league competition. Ipswich won the Southern League championship in their first season. Cobbold then set about campaigning for his club's election to the Football League. He was clearly a persuasive man because Ipswich began life in the Third Division (South) at the start of the 1938/39 season.

Cobbold enlisted highly experienced Scott Duncan as his manager. It was a wise decision as at the end of his first season in charge, Duncan had taken Ipswich to seventh place. After the Second World War had stopped play, Ipswich were forced to rebuild from scratch. During the austere post-war period, progress proved much slower. Although Ipswich finally won a Second Division place in 1954, their stay lasted for one year only. Then came the Alf Ramsey revolution.

Ramsey had re-invented himself. He came from a working-class background, enjoying a taste for jellied eels and the simple life. And yet he knew he had to smarten up his act if he was to advance his career prospects as a football club manager. It was not enough that he had enjoyed a glittering playing career.

Like John Major decades later, he encased himself in an elocution straitjacket. He needed to be credible within the social circles he was then expected to inhabit. At Ipswich this included the club 'aristocracy', the Cobbolds. The trouble was when Ramsey tried to 'toff it up' he sounded like Harold Steptoe. In the year Ramsey took over at Ipswich the national press was having a field day with Professor Alan Ross's study of 'U and non-U' linguistic conventions. It was a source of amusement to many and not only the 'plebs'. The aristocratic novelist Nancy Mitford had her tongue in her chic when she pronounced that it was non-U, that is, not 'upper-class', to use the term 'toilet' instead of 'lavatory'. Although absurd, the debate emphasised the strength of class divisions in post-war Britain.

Ramsey's diction was so formal, so clipped, so contrived that his use of the f-word, confined to journalists or players who crossed him, seemed shocking. He was not the only club manager to try to 'toff it up', at least while on duty. Take the stilted and florid prose adopted by Harry Potts at Burnley or George Curtis at Brighton. These were the strained attempts of working-class men at proving themselves in an elitist climate. With educational snobbery being rife in those times, they felt obliged to present themselves in refined tones. When alone with their teams they were much more relaxed and informal. In public they were constantly on guard. Ramsey once quipped that a crisis in the Cobbolds' boardroom was 'a shortage of sherry'. He knew where he belonged.

For all that, Ramsey was his own man. Although vastly experienced in domestic and international football, and shrewd in knowing what made a team tick, he was not sold on new coaching ideas. He was uninterested in obtaining coaching qualifications. It is possible that he had no wish to subject himself to formal examination. He seemed self-conscious about his rudimentary education. He was also a traditionalist when it came to training methods, too. Alf was not a tracksuit manager, either, despite sporting one at times when in charge of England's World Cup squad. At Ipswich he was quite prepared for his trainer, Jimmy Forsyth, to organise the fitness training – the weights, the sprints and long-distance running, supplemented with a bit of shooting practice and impromptu five-a-sides.

What singled Ramsey out as a brilliant manager was his use of tactics. He had an elephant-like memory of games played months before. He could recall the various runs his players made; the positions they took up; how they laid the ball off; which way they turned when challenged; how quickly and accurately they passed. Each of his players received feedback on their performances. He showed them how they might become better. He introduced voluntary skills sessions during the afternoons. These helped to sharpen up the accuracy of his players' short passing. He was never prescriptive, though. He did not direct his players – he made suggestions. His game plans were not a template. They were conceived in the knowledge of what his players could achieve. While his mantra was 'winning isn't everything, it is the only thing', he was pragmatic. But his pragmatism had room for professional development. Footballers who were once considered ordinary became better under Ramsey. Some became extraordinary, like Jimmy Leadbetter.

Although a private man, Ramsey fostered a close-knit team which championed his aims, methods, focus, determination, and self-belief. For a few years, Ramsey's Cinderella-like Ipswich side had a ball until the midnight chimes struck in the summer of '62, so soon after their crowning glory.

In 1960/61, Ipswich won the Second Division title with an average gate of 15,095, only slightly above average for the division then. The Cobbolds were comparatively well-off but their club was not rich and Ramsey had to make do with a collection of misfits and cast-offs. Typical of his captures was Leadbetter, the ploddingly orthodox inside-left. Leadbetter was nicknamed 'sticks' or 'Steptoe' on account of his wasted, geriatric appearance. In truth, he looked more aged than TV cop George Dixon. And Dock Green police had no concept of a retirement policy. Ramsey breathed new life into Leadbetter's spindly legs and deceptively frail frame.

Leadbetter was converted into an unorthodox left-winger who held back in the manner of Brazil's Zagallo. Having said that, Zagallo was much quicker – he could hardly have been slower – and was prepared to take up advanced positions. But like Zagallo, Leadbetter looked to pick up the ball deep inside his half. This enticed the opposing full-back into following him, allowing Leadbetter the chance to ping deadly long balls into the space left behind. The predatory central strikers Crawford and Phillips exploited these opportunities to the hilt. But this tactical innovation would not have worked without Leadbetter's skill in executing his passes so adroitly, consistently finding the right areas, at the right trajectory, pace, and height. Among Jimmy's previous clubs, neither Chelsea nor Brighton had any idea that he harboured such a lethal talent. Ramsey was proficient at spotting potential that others had missed.

Ramsey had a keen eye for bargain bin purchases. He signed left-back John Compton from Chelsea for £1,000, centre-half Andy Nelson from West Ham for £8,500, and outside-right Roy Stephenson from Leicester for £3,000. They hadn't become established first-team players at their previous clubs, but Ramsey knew better. It was a testament to his recruiting skills that no fewer than five Ipswich players collected Third, Second and First Division championship medals under his management – an unprecedented feat. These were goalkeeper Roy Bailey, left-half John Elsworthy, inside-left Ted Phillips, right-back Len Carberry and Leadbetter. His other buys were Ray Crawford, Portsmouth's disaffected, reserve centre-forward – an absolute steal at £5,000; Billy Baxter, a tough young Scottish defender snatched from junior football for a pittance; and inside-forward Doug Moran, bought from Falkirk for £12,300 after Ipswich won the Second Division title.

Ramsey's preferred system of play was a fluid version of a 4-2-4 formation which frequently morphed into 4-4-2 when the opposition had the ball. As Crawford pointed out, it took the players time to practise the tactic smoothly. He recalled that Leadbetter frequently covered the left post at a corner but was so slow in moving upfield, after the ball had been cleared, he played opponents onside. But once the teething problems were sorted out, the system worked like a well-oiled machine.

Tactically, Ipswich's success was founded upon a physically strong, quick covering defence, reinforced by its back-tracking wingers, Leadbetter and Stephenson. Like Mercer, Ramsey knew that success depended upon having a strong defence. He also adopted the mantra of his former boss Arthur Rowe in making it simple and fast. Like Stan Cullis, he wanted his team to move the ball quickly, attempting to reach their opponents' penalty area in no more than three passes. But he was no advocate of 'kick and rush'. These passes needed to be made with speed but also with precision. With Leadbetter and Stephenson, he had the right men.

Ramsey's plan also hinged on the powerful running and the ferocious shooting of Phillips and Crawford up front. They were entrusted with turning tactical advantage into goals. Crawford was a real handful for defences. He had strength, an alert eye for a half-chance and commanding aerial ability. But Phillips was more intimidating. Tall and wiry with a weathered complexion, he exuded hardness. You would not have expected to find Ted in a tanning studio unless it was of the hide-leathering sort. His blistering shooting was once timed at an incredible 94 mph, and that is with a ball that was much heavier than those used today. Even more impressively, Phillips could apply swerve to his shooting. So, if the opposing goalkeeper was not knocked senseless by his explosive shots, he was likely to be dumbfounded by their curve. Burnley's Adam Blacklaw recalled an evening game at Turf Moor, in August 1961, when he was first introduced to the power of Ted's shooting. Although Adam was a big, beefy lad, he remembered how Ted worked him over with a series of 30-yard thunderbolts that made the crowd gasp. Ted scored with one such effort. Adam did not see the ball until it was past him. He saw Phillips line up the shot. Then, wham, the ball was in the back of the net. Adam had not moved an inch. It was a breathtaking effort.

In 1960/61 Ipswich were promoted to the top flight having scored 100 league goals – Phillips scored 30 and Crawford 40. In winning the First Division, the pair scored a further 61 goals between them – Phillips 28 and Crawford 33 – in a team total of 93. Crawford was considered good enough to play for England. However, the strength of the side lay in its organisation, tactics, and self-belief. Their individual talents were less than their collective strength.

Arguably, their most prestigious achievement in winning the title was the two league defeats they inflicted upon 1961 double winners Spurs. The second game was played at White Hart Lane on 14 March 1962 and typified Ipswich's well-worked strategy. On a threadbare pitch, slick Spurs began by taking the game to their 'rustic' visitors. Wing-halves Blanchflower and Marchi pushed up in support of their voracious forwards. But this manoeuvre merely served Ipswich's purpose.

The 50,000 Spurs fans linked arms as they belted out their full-throated battle cry, 'Glory, glory hallelujah and the Spurs go marching on!' They were determined that their side should retain both Cup and League titles and avenge their surprising 3-2 defeat at Portman Road in October. But Crawford stunned them by giving Ipswich an eighth-minute lead. Stung by this slight, Jimmy Greaves equalised a minute later. It was a temporary setback.

The game marked a return to form for the out-of-sorts Phillips. Without Dave Mackay to close him down, Phillips ran riot in the spaces left in the Spurs defence, scoring twice with clinical shots. He had more to offer than just brute force. Spurs continued to press forward but found Elsworthy in outstanding form as their attacks foundered in front of Ipswich's tightly organised defence. Meanwhile, the visitors created havoc on the break and Stephenson and Moran both hit the bar as Ipswich completely dominated. Here was a side assembled for only £30,000 completely outplaying a team that cost over a quarter of a million. Spurs were reckoned to be one of the best clubs in Europe. Their narrow defeat by Benfica in the semi-final of the European Cup would prove that.

Ipswich's opponents were slow to combat Ramsey's tactical plan. This was partly because TV and video coverage were so limited then. Besides, there was not the depth or breadth of tactical scrutiny that there is today.

Spurs boss Bill Nicholson cottoned on quicker than most, as well he might. He had masterminded England's tactical response to Brazil in the 1958 World Cup. His plan then had similarities to that developed by him for the Charity Shield game in August 1962. Nicholson told his wing-halves to mark Leadbetter and Stephenson tightly, leaving the full-backs to tuck in alongside centre-half Norman, to repel Crawford, Phillips, and Moran. The innovation worked like a dream and Ipswich were thrashed 5-1. Arguably, Ipswich's game plan should have been sussed out much earlier, despite the lack of TV coverage. When Port Vale reached the FA Cup semi-final in 1954, their tactics were similar but those watching Vale then were more inclined to castigate than learn.

Defending champions Ipswich came perilously close to joining Leyton Orient on their instant return to the Second Division in 1963. Orient, like Northampton Town, shocked other English clubs with their 'Grand Old Duke of York' journeys, rising from bottom to top and back again. Carlisle and Swansea followed suit in the '70s and '80s. As in the '50s it was still possible for small, unfancied clubs to make an improbable splash in bigger pools.

Ramsey now had an ageing side and eight of his squad were aged 30 years or older. Their best days were behind them. But only one addition was made during the summer of 1962; 28-year-old Bobby Blackwood, a winger or inside-forward, signed from Hearts for £10,000.

Although Ipswich's average gate during their championship season was only 22,559, almost half that of Spurs, this should have given the club enough resources to strengthen the team. Perhaps Ramsey did not want to change a winning combination and all 28 players on the club's books were retained. As England's boss, Ramsey was prepared to chop and change. But at Ipswich, loyalty seemed to tie his hands. He appeared contorted by guilt at leaving Leadbetter out of a European Cup tie, having acknowledged his importance to Ipswich's championship success. Ramsey seemed to think that the heavy defeat inflicted by Spurs was due to individual failings rather than his outmoded or sussed tactics.

Only one point was taken from Ipswich's first three games in 1962/63 – a 3-3 home draw with Blackburn Rovers on a hot opening day. Although Blackpool were thumped 5-2 at home on Tuesday 28 August, league results stuttered. In fact, Ipswich's form was so shaky that after losing 3-1 to Arsenal, on a grey, late-November afternoon at

Highbury, they fell into the relegation zone and were just two points better off than bottom side Leyton Orient.

During that autumn they had suffered heavy home defeats by Birmingham (5-1) and Manchester United (5-3). Other teams followed Spurs' tactical lead and Ipswich's previously robust defence disintegrated. Goalkeeper Roy Bailey got the 'yips', making a string of costly errors. Meanwhile, at the other end the goals were drying up – Ipswich's final tally of 59 was almost 40 per cent down on the championship season. Their prestigious 2-1 victory over AC Milan, the eventual European Cup winners, four days after the Highbury defeat was entirely cosmetic as the first leg, played in an almost empty San Siro, had been lost 3-0. Ipswich's 14-1 thrashing of Floriana of Malta in the previous round counted for nothing.

It was not just age, form, and injury which were withering the champions. There was unrest over pay as Crawford and Billy Baxter held out for better terms. Crawford realised that his England team-mates were earning substantially more. While Ipswich were prepared to pay him £30 per week, Johnny Haynes was receiving over three times as much at Fulham.

On 25 October 1962, Ramsey decided to accept the England job. But he was stricken by divided loyalties and found it hard to let go of the team he had created. He found the separation so troublesome that he remained at Portman Road for a further six months, not moving on until the threat of relegation had been lifted. This made life difficult for his successor, Jackie Milburn, who could not strengthen the side until Ramsey left. This hiatus caused ructions in the Ipswich boardroom.

Long-serving director Ernest Steel was so incensed by his colleagues' prevarication that he resigned. He accused the other board members of being Ramsey 'yes men'. While Ramsey did not press for reinforcements, he told his successor that the team had little strength in depth and that the club had little money to rectify this deficit. Milburn had been handed a poisoned chalice. Although the team were the reigning champions, the club was organised like a Fourth Division outfit. After Bill Slater, the former Wolves and England half-back, turned down the Ipswich job, there were only two applicants: Milburn, and Stockport County's boss Reg Flewin. This said a lot about the club's standing in the football fraternity.

As the icy winter turned eventually to a chilly, soggy spring, Ipswich were still in big trouble. They had been beaten 3-0 at home by wealthy champions-elect Everton and 4-2 by Spurs, and they were thrashed 6-1 at West Bromwich. Their prospects of staying up seemed as bleak as Leyton Orient's. Ipswich's remaining fixtures included several four-pointers. They recovered a semblance of their championship form, winning six and drawing four of their final 12 games. It was just as well, as Ipswich were only four points clear of relegation on the final day of the season.

Two of those points were in doubt after *The People* alleged that their 2-0 home victory over Sheffield Wednesday on Saturday, 1 December 1962 was fixed. Three Wednesday players – centre-forward David 'Bronco' Layne, England centre-half Peter Swan and wing-half Tony Kay – admitted to placing £50 each on a fixed odds bet which would pay rich dividends if their team lost at Ipswich, York defeated Oldham and Lincoln won against Brentford. As it turned out, both Oldham and Brentford won. The ensuing court case led to all three Wednesday players being jailed and banned from playing football for life, although this ban was lifted later by the FA. Swan insisted that there was nothing out of the ordinary about either of Crawford's match-winning goals. As it was, Ipswich survived in the First Division for one more year only.

No provision had been made by Ramsey to replace the older members of his team. There was no youth policy at the club and no effective scouting network, so Milburn had to re-build from scratch. He was forced to sell Crawford – his only regular goalscorer – to finance essential replacements. He looked for cheaper acquisitions north of the border, but this was not a success. Billy Baxter said, 'Perhaps Milburn's biggest mistake was getting too many Scots together, for they started drinking and misbehaving and he couldn't do anything with them.' Crawford added, 'Jackie was a wonderful man, but as a manager he didn't have a clue. He'd turn up for training at 10am and you'd see him standing there with a cigarette in one hand and a cup of coffee in the other with his foot on the ball saying, "Good morning lads. We'll have a good day today," whereas Alf knew what he wanted. He got the players to play in a certain style. If you did not do what he wanted, you'd be out of the side.'

After scoring 100 league goals in their Second Division championship season of 1960/61 and 93 in winning the First Division a year later, Ipswich were relegated at the end of 1963/64 having scored 56 goals and conceded 121. Ramsey's triumph was a one-off. It would take Ipswich a further four years to regain their place in the top flight.

45.

THE CASE FOR THE
DEFENCE: 1962/63

A MAJOR topic of discussion in the 1962/63 season was the 'blanket defence'. Respected journalist Ivan Sharpe commented, 'Perhaps it was because defensive tactics played a prominent part of the 1962 World Cup games in Chile. This may have been the reason why English football developed this bugbear and menace last season. Perhaps it was because English league and cup honours have become so important. Whatever the cause, the trend was regrettable, especially as this dulling effect on the game as a spectacle arrived at an inopportune time.

'The sponsors of Manchester City's five half-backs formation denied that this was primarily a defensive system, but improved attack was not discernible in the team's actual performances. Such a system might prove attractive if the right type of player were available – mobile, nippy, versatile, able to advance or retire as the flow of the game demands, as might be expected of players with experience at forward and half-back. But this essential ability was not there when I watched the City.'

During the mid-'50s, Les McDowall's Manchester City were regarded as a stylish, innovative side, renowned for their successful introduction of the 'Revie Plan'. City goalkeeper Bert Trautmann said, 'We no longer had enough talented players.' Denis Law had left, meaning McDowall had to experiment with an ultra-defensive formation. He hoped that curmudgeonly tactics would compensate for a lack of potency. He deployed two backs to cover the centre of the defence while five half-backs sat in front of them. Bobby Kennedy and Roy Chatham wore inside-forward numbers on their shirts but assumed defensive duties only. City made do with three forwards – the veteran George Hannah, as an orthodox playmaker, plus two strikers in Peter Dobing and Alex Harley. Only Harley with 23 league goals reached double figures that season when only 58 goals were scored collectively, whereas 102 goals were conceded. There were repeated drubbings, 6-1 twice by West Ham, 8-1 at Wolves, 5-2 at Burnley, 5-1 by West Bromwich at home, 4-1 at Blackburn, Liverpool, and Sheffield Wednesday and 4-2 at Spurs.

Leicester found more success with their defensive tactics although it won them few friends. Members of the press were unimpressed when the Foxes shut up shop in the FA Cup semi-final, having taken the lead against Liverpool. One paper headlined with 'Leicester City's cul-de-sac'. Another sniped, 'A 10-1 system as sound as a castle dungeon.' Defeated Liverpool manager Bill Shankly carped, 'This can never be football. It is bad for the game and the best way of emptying the terraces.' Many agreed, but Leicester manager Matt Gillies shrugged off the criticism glibly, commenting, 'We have players, not forwards or defenders.'

Having secured a Wembley place he promised, 'You have my assurance that Leicester will go to the Final with the idea of showing just what they can do.' He need not have bothered. Manchester United's attacking flair made his pledge irrelevant. Gilles complained, 'We created a system but instead of playing to make it work we leaned upon it. That is why we failed. This has not changed my conviction that we are on the right path.'

Law was certainly on the right path. He performed at Wembley with immaculate style, vision, verve, and skill, yet shortly before the final, United were facing relegation. Two years later they would become First Division champions playing attacking football. The Potteries pair, Stoke City and Port Vale were criticised, too, for their defensiveness. Nottingham Forest had their detractors, as well, including many of their own supporters who took exception to manager Andy Beattie selecting an extra centre-half, Peter Hindley, instead of a centre-forward.

46.

SPURS CONQUER EUROPE:
EUROPEAN CUP WINNERS'
CUP 1963

SPURS HAD already reached the semi-final of the European Cup in
1962, where they were eliminated by Benfica. Having beaten Burnley
in that same season's FA Cup Final with Jimmy Greaves making his
customary impact, they qualified for the European Cup Winners'
Cup. Spurs' passage to the Rotterdam final was smooth, but as the
date came closer, Bill Nicholson had the wobbles. He fretted over the
sceptical press coverage but worried more about his side's late lapse
in form which had allowed Everton to steal the title. Moreover, his
enforcer Dave Mackay was struggling with an abdominal injury.
Danny Blanchflower had a niggling knee problem too. Mackay would
miss the final but despite constantly rubbing his troublesome knee,
Blanchflower made it. He knew his playing days were numbered and
was determined to go out with a bang.

Nicholson lugubriously listed the strengths of their opponents,
Atletico Madrid. It was a thorough, forensic examination but left his
players doubting their capacity to win. Blanchflower was not having
this. Providing an alternative briefing, he said, 'If their centre-half is
big and ugly, then Maurice Norman is bigger and uglier. If they have
a swift winger called Jones, then ours is so fast he can catch pigeons.'
Greaves said, 'We laughed so much, that all our concerns left us.' As
it turned out, Spurs' wingers Jones and Dyson were superior, tearing
the Atletico defence apart. Nicholson said afterwards, 'Dyson played
the game of his life, better than I've seen him play, better than I
thought he could play.'

Spurs struck the first blow in the 16th minute. Smith evaded a wild tackle from centre-half Griffa and released Jones, who flew down the touchline and crossed, low and fast, for Greaves to convert with typical aplomb. Sixteen minutes later, Spurs were two-up as Dyson found Smith who set up White for a measured finish.

The Spaniards flew out of the blocks on the resumption, forcing Henry to punch away a goalbound shot with Brown and his defenders in disarray and Spurs had to defend their narrow lead stubbornly as Atletico swarmed around them. The siege was lifted when Dyson escaped his gaolers and hung a hopeful, high cross into the Atletico box. The Spanish goalkeeper made a hash of it, fumbling the ball into the net, and Atletico were finished. Greaves rubbed salt into their wounds by volleying in Spurs' fourth while Dyson completed the rout with a 30-yard dash, a shimmy, a swerve and a rasping shot. It was the goal of his life.

Sadly, it was John White's final triumph for he would lose his life shortly afterwards following a lightning strike.

47.

CHRISTMAS CRACKERS: THE 1963 BOXING DAY GOAL RUSH

FOOTBALL WENT goal crazy on this overcast Boxing Day. In 39 Football League games 157 goals were scored, 66 of which came in the First Division. The declining trend in goals scored in the top flight since the 1957/58 season, when 1,721 goals were scored, was interrupted in the 1963/64 season in which 1,571 were scored, mainly because of this festive spree.

Having watched his side lose 10-1 at Craven Cottage, Ipswich chairman John Cobbold cracked, 'Only our goalkeeper was sober.'

Three First Division strikers bagged four goals each: Graham Leggat of Fulham, Andy Lochhead of Burnley, and Roger Hunt of Liverpool. Weirdly, several of these results were reversed in the return fixtures on 28 December. Jimmy Greaves's golden age of open, attacking football had not disappeared yet.

Blackpool 1 Chelsea 5
Burnley 6 Manchester United 1 (United won the return 5-1)
Fulham 10 Ipswich Town 1 (Ipswich won the return 4-2)
Leicester City 2 Everton 0
Liverpool 6 Stoke City 1 (Stoke won the return 3-1)
Nottingham Forest 3 Sheffield United 3
Sheffield Wednesday 3 Bolton Wanderers 0 (Bolton won the return 3-0)
West Bromwich Albion 4 Tottenham Hotspur 4
West Ham United 2 Blackburn Rovers 8 (West Ham won the return 3-1)
Wolverhampton Wanderers 3 Aston Villa 3

48.

PRESTON NORTH END v WEST HAM UNITED: FA CUP FINAL, 2 MAY 1964

PRESTON NORTH End's fortunes faded badly after Tom Finney's retirement in May 1960 and relegation to the Second Division came a year later. North End struggled, finishing tenth and 17th before improving in the 1963/64 season, rising to third and appearing in the FA Cup Final against West Ham.

Tommy Thompson, Finney's goalscoring partner, thought that Preston had neglected to plan for its future while still in its prime. In 1957/58, Thompson and Finney scored over half of Preston's 100 league goals as their club finished as runners-up to First Division champions Wolves. But when age and injury began to deplete their powers, Preston declined, although Finney regarded his final season as one of his best, despite enduring a persistent groin injury. Thompson blamed Preston's slide upon manager Cliff Britton for not buying better quality replacements. He also criticised the board for not developing better training facilities with which to attract talented youngsters. Preston's future Liverpool star Peter Thompson added that it was a lot easier to bring in good players when the team is winning.

He said, 'When we were close to winning the First Division championship that was when Preston should have pushed the boat out and bought better players. Cliff was tight. He used to inspect the club houses where the young players were staying and impose harsh limits on what we could spend on decorating. He was not popular. He was very defensively minded and imposed rigid rules about how we should play. If the full-back went over the halfway line, there was an inquest.'

Unlike Thompson, Finney was prepared to credit Britton as a 'master tactician'. Finney had reason to be grateful to Britton for helping revive his international career by converting him from a winger into a centre-forward. However, Finney despised Britton's man management which he described as 'ridiculously over-strict and unsympathetic', citing Britton's angry outburst at him for having a post-match drink with his team-mates. Finney was a model professional who drank only occasionally and always in moderation.

Britton was generally regarded as a dour man. One Preston player expressed the view that 'he would have been happier if his team comprised 11 teetotal, non-smoking puritans'. He was remembered by George Bray for castigating his Burnley team for sloppiness when they were winning 5-0. And yet as a player, Britton had been adventurous and creative, enabling Everton's Dixie Dean to plunder goals at will.

Britton might have pinned his hopes on his youth team delivering more first-team players of substance. Although Tommy Thompson was critical of Preston's training facilities, its youth team was good enough to reach the FA Youth Cup Final in 1960, having beaten Manchester United in the semis. Although Preston lost the final 5-2 on aggregate, this was to a strong Chelsea side, including Peter Bonetti, Terry Venables and Bobby Tambling. It was not as if the youth team failed to deliver. Four of its members became first-team regulars, which seems a fair return – pacy wingers Peter Thompson and David Wilson, inside-forward Alan Spavin and full-back George Ross. Thompson and young centre-half Tony Singleton progressed quickly enough to play regular First Division football in 1960/61.

Arguably, Preston's board might have been cautious about committing themselves to expenditure that was unlikely to be recovered through the gates. National attendances were continuing to drop after the 1948/49 high of just over 41 million. In 1957/58 when Preston finished second, that figure was about 33.5 million. Besides, Preston was the second smallest town or city in the First Division with just 112,000 residents. Cotton manufacturing, probably the town's most significant source of work, was in sharp decline. Moreover, Preston's annual attendance total for the 1958/59 season fell by 2,500, a ten per cent reduction.

Relegation in 1960/61 was a disaster. Not only did the club have to accommodate rising salaries following the abolition of the maximum wage, they had to withstand a 31 per cent loss in gate income in this relegation season. With the club's wage bill rising to £43,892, even the £21,278 profit generated from its FA Cup run could not avert an annual loss of £13,141. Although the FA Cup ties with Liverpool and Manchester United attracted large crowds, Preston's average league attendance in 1961/62 dropped to 13,000, representing a further fall in gate revenue of about 25 per cent.

In April 1961, Cliff Britton was replaced by his trainer Jimmy Milne, the father of England international wing-half Gordon, who served Preston and Bill Shankly's Liverpool with such distinction. Milne senior was known as 'Mr Preston' since he had been at the club for 30 years – as a skilful midfielder, trainer and, finally, as manager. Milne arrived at Preston in 1931 from his home city club, Dundee United. Although often in the shadow of Shankly and Andy Beattie, Jimmy became a first-team regular during the 1937/38 season. Unfortunately, he was denied a 1938 FA Cup winners' medal because of a collarbone injury sustained in the game before the final.

Milne was temperamentally different from Britton. Whereas Britton was inclined to be dogmatic and censorious, Milne was quietly encouraging, always urging his players to 'enjoy their game'. As Spavin recalled, even when confronted with the pressure of a Wembley final, Milne remained the same. When Milne picked up the reins, he knew it was time for some radical pruning. Out went a swathe of former stalwarts including defenders Joe Walton and Joe Dunne, forwards Tommy Thompson, Sammy Taylor and Derek Mayers, and goalkeeper Fred Else. Else was still good enough to play First Division football but Milne felt that the young Republic of Ireland international Alan Kelly deserved his chance.

Unfortunately, not all emerging talent blossomed. Alex Alston was a case in point. Finney had tipped Alston to be Preston's future centre-forward, but despite regularly leading the line for much of the 1960/61 season – Preston's last in the First Division – and topping the scoring charts with nine league goals, the 23-year-old failed to fulfil his promise and was transferred to Bury in 1963.

Sturdy and standing at more than six feet, Bristol Rovers centre-forward Alfie Biggs looked a better prospect. Biggs completed the

1961/62 season as Preston's top scorer, netting 21 league goals. But his stay was brief and after a barren start to 1962/63 he was transferred back to the Pirates. Biggs might have been discarded prematurely because he went on to net 211 league goals over a 16-year career.

Even with Biggs scoring regularly, Milne felt his attack was under-powered. So, in October 1961, he paid Manchester United £18,000 for their bustling, burly, dreadnought of a centre-forward, Alex Dawson. The heavily-jowled, warrior-like Dawson was invested as Preston's 'Black Prince'. He did all that was expected of him, notching 31 league goals in his first 59 appearances. But Dawson appeared to be carrying too much of the scoring burden during 1962/63. It seemed that if Alex did not score then no one else would.

There were other areas of the team that needed strengthening, too. Milne had imported full-back John Donnelly from Celtic and half-back Dave Barber from Barnsley but the mix still was not right. Milne, therefore, recruited three more to steer the ship and reinforce its hull. In came Nobby Lawton, a tough but cultured wing-half or inside-forward from Manchester United for an £11,500 fee. Doug Holden, a tricky, unorthodox former England winger, was recruited from Bolton. Finally, defensive wing-half Ian Davidson was signed from Kilmarnock. Lawton and Holden were recruited to add craft to a spluttering midfield while Davidson was expected to bolster a vulnerable defence. Milne was also fortunate in that young Howard Kendall was advancing so fast. The composed, elegant 16-year-old wing-half made his debut in a 2-2 draw at Newcastle on 11 May 1963.

Results continued to be erratic, though. Thumping victories, such as a Dawson-inspired 6-3 success over Swansea, were interspersed with abject defeats, the worst of which were a 7-1 humiliation at Plymouth in the second match of 1962/63 and a 6-2 thrashing by Cardiff at Deepdale a month later. By the end of that wintry season, Preston had dropped a further six places, and this time there had been no compensating FA Cup run. Promotion contenders Sunderland crushed them 4-1 in the third round at a wet, icy Deepdale. By May, apathy had set in, so much so that only 8,323 bothered to attend for the final home fixture. Alex Dawson's customary goal proved enough to defeat Derby County. Worryingly, the average gate had fallen by a further thousand to 12,000.

At the end of 1962/63, Preston parted company with their veteran Scottish full-back Willie Cunningham. The grizzled hardman was the last remaining regular from their successful side of the late '50s. He said, 'The great days were behind us and many of the players of the late '50s had gone. Whether a few should have been kept for their experience is a good point. For players like myself it meant a lot of responsibility and I think we rose to it. I played some good football at this time even though we were often not getting the results. There was always the hope that once the young side had settled, things would come right, but if we were to get back into the First Division it had to be quickly or we would be left behind with wages and transfer fees rising.'

Despite the adverse financial situation, Milne knew he needed further reinforcements, notably a goalscoring partner for Dawson. Northampton's powerful centre-forward Alec Ashworth seemed to fit the bill. He was signed during the summer of 1963 for £22,000. Scunthorpe striker Brian Godfrey was also signed later in the season. He would make his mark in the FA Cup sixth round tie with Oxford, putting Preston into an unbeatable 2-0 lead.

But to balance the books, Milne was forced into selling his prized asset: the fast and superbly skilful right-winger Peter Thompson. Preston were not short of takers. Juventus, Wolves and Everton all knocked at their door, but it was Bill Shankly who took Peter to Anfield in August 1963 for a fee of £40,000. Not frightened by hyperboles, Shankly told Thompson, 'If you come to Liverpool, you'll become the best player in the world; the fastest thing on two legs. You'll become the "White Pelé".' Thompson had to settle for less, although he quickly became the best right-footed left-winger in the country, winning two championships and one FA Cup medal. His sinuous skills, though, deserved better than just 16 England caps.

The first sign that Milne was getting the balance right came in the fifth game of 1963/64, at Southampton. A wonderful back-and-forth encounter ended in a 5-4 victory for Preston, with Lawton scoring a late winner. Howard Kendall had also impressed with a superb individual goal. Preston pushed Sunderland hard for the second promotion place but come April they were still six points short of overtaking the Wearsiders. Dawson confirmed his fearsome striking reputation with 30 league goals, equal second in the division's scoring charts alongside Manchester City's Derek Kevan.

This time, however, Dawson had someone to share the scoring with. Alec Ashworth, cast in a similar mould to Dawson, contributed 14 goals at a rate of almost one every two games. Flying right-winger David Wilson notched 11 as well. Importantly, the haemorrhaging of goals was staunched, with goals against reduced by 20. 'We had a good defensive system,' explained team captain Nobby Lawton, 'with five people at the back who did the tackling. They then gave the ball to the rest of us to play. It was a good mix of players.'

Those five at the back comprised full-backs George Ross and Jimmy Smith, who was a converted centre-forward, and half-backs Lawton, Ian Davidson or Howard Kendall, plus centre-half Tony Singleton. The Preston side of 1963/64 had a fine combination of pace, skill, defensive solidity, and striking power. This was almost their year.

Their FA Cup campaign started with successive away games at First Division Nottingham Forest and Bolton. Preston won both ties, albeit after replays. They nearly blew the Bolton encounter, though, after squandering a 2-0 lead at Burnden Park. Fourth Division promotion contenders Carlisle were beaten 1-0 at Deepdale in the fifth round, setting Preston up with a quarter-final against Fourth Division giant-killers Oxford United. Despite enduring some late Oxford pressure, Preston again won 2-1 to earn a place in the semi-finals. Fortune smiled in the draw as they were paired with Second Division Swansea. On a bog of a pitch at Villa Park, Preston prevailed thanks to Tony Singleton's speculative 30-yard shot which turned the game around and earned a 2-1 scoreline in their favour. It was his first goal in senior football. Preston were back at Wembley – ten years after their last appearance. Then, they lost 3-2 to West Bromwich Albion. This time, West Ham would be their opponents. The Irons had defeated FA Cup holders Manchester United 3-1 in the other semi-final.

West Ham were a progressive club. While Malcolm Allison, John Bond, Ron Greenwood and Noel Cantwell were frequently mentioned as movers and shakers, it was manager Ted Fenton who established 'the Academy', which spawned so many talented young players including Bobby Moore, Martin Peters, Ken Brown, Ronnie Boyce, Joe Kirkup, John Smith and Andy Malcolm. The youth teams that Fenton developed reached two FA Youth Cup finals in the late

'50s. With the help of his chairman Reg Pratt, Fenton encouraged his players to qualify for their FA coaching badges.

And yet West Ham began the '60s in disarray. Having led the First Division in November 1959, they hobbled to the tape in 14th place. Despite the abundance of young talent, only Brown and Moore were ready to step up. Centre-forward Vic Keeble's career was brought to an abrupt end because of a back injury and Scottish international John Dick seemed to lose form as well as fitness. Having no suitable reserves, Ted Fenton was forced to field his full-backs, Bond and Cantwell, as strikers. With goalkeeper Noel Dwyer's confidence frayed after his mugging at Hillsborough, Fenton's makeshift side struggled badly.

The 1960/61 season was no better. Taking their cue from the national team, West Ham became the first English club side to adopt the 4-2-4 system. But it availed them not as their final position of 16th was deeply disappointing, being two places lower than in their troubled 1959/60 season. Once again, their form fell away in the second half of the campaign and only 13 points were taken from their last 20 games. Their away record was awful, with just one win and six draws alongside 14 defeats with 57 goals conceded. Despite Billy Wright's championing of the 4-2-4 formation, West Ham found that the system was not a panacea for defensive frailty. Thankfully, Dick recovered his goalscoring powers to net 16 league goals while left-winger Malcolm Musgrove went one better. Former Spurs centre-forward Dave Dunmore contributed 14 goals, too, but seemed reluctant to impose himself upon his opponents.

Fenton's departure from West Ham in March 1961 has never been fully explained by the club. It was known, though, that he was unwell and that he had been under great strain on account of West Ham's poor form. He was succeeded by Ron Greenwood, a former Bradford Park Avenue, Brentford and Fulham centre-half who was also a member of Chelsea's First Division championship-winning side of 1954/55. Having obtained his FA badges, Greenwood was chosen to coach the England youth and under-23 sides, combining these duties with those of assistant manager at Arsenal, whom he joined in 1957. With his stay at Arsenal becoming increasingly fractious, he was ready to strike out on his own.

In 1961 Greenwood inherited a club on the slide. The average gate had fallen by 7,000, or over a quarter since their promotion to the top flight in 1958. Goalkeeper Brian Rhodes was gaining experience the hard way and the battle-hardened Cantwell had left for Old Trafford, meaning there was a big hole to fill at left-back. Bond's speed – never his strongest asset – was waning. The 1960/61 team lacked consistency and could not be relied upon to finish off apparently inferior opponents. This was underlined when relegation-bound Newcastle pulled back a 5-2 deficit to draw 5-5. Fourth Division Darlington also dumped them out of the League Cup.

Greenwood's team-building plans began with the signing of Scottish international goalkeeper Lawrie Leslie from Airdrie in time for the start of the 1961/62 season. Courageous and spectacular, Leslie soon became a big favourite with the supporters, as would Johnny 'Budgie' Byrne. Byrne was signed later in the season from Crystal Palace for £58,000, with the ill-fated Ronnie Brett returning to Palace as a makeweight in the deal. In November 1961, Byrne became one of only five players to be selected for a senior England side while playing in the third tier. However, Byrne took time to settle at West Ham. He did not score until his seventh game, helping secure a 1-1 Good Friday draw at Cardiff. This was when 18-year-old Martin Peters made his first team debut. Greenwood also swapped the under-performing Dave Dunmore for promising Leyton Orient youngster Alan Sealey. This would prove to be a good deal for both players, setting Sealey up for a European Cup Winners' Cup medal in 1965.

Greenwood did well in his first season in charge, guiding West Ham to eighth in the First Division, their best position since 1958/59. Dick headed the scoring chart with 23 league goals, followed by Musgrove (13) and new boy Sealey (11). West Ham's away form recovered, too. Six victories were achieved on the road including thumping wins at Sheffield United (4-1), Aston Villa (4-2) and Manchester City (5-3). The downsides were the 6-0 thrashing by a rampant Burnley at Turf Moor on 3 March and the surprising 4-0 home defeat by Manchester City. West Ham's 3-0 FA Cup third round exit at Plymouth was depressing, too. It was the first time that the club had been eliminated from the FA Cup by a lower-division side. Nevertheless, the team's revival was reflected at the turnstiles with the average gate rising by 4,000.

But the renewed optimism seemed premature as West Ham began 1962/63 calamitously. After losing 1-0 at newly promoted Orient on 1 September, West Ham were bottom with just one point from their opening five games. They had scored only three goals and conceded 15. In their first two home matches, Wolves (4-1) and Spurs (6-1) tore them apart. Thereafter, results improved dramatically. By the end of October, West Ham had risen to 13th on the back of a 6-1 thrashing of Manchester City at Maine Road and home wins over Liverpool (1-0) and Blackburn (4-0). Their earlier FA Cup exit at Home Park was avenged as they crushed Plymouth 6-0 in a home League Cup tie. Although Rotherham ended the Irons' interest in that competition, the FA Cup provided greater joy as victories over Fulham, Swansea and prospective champions Everton took Greenwood's team to the quarter-final round where they were unlucky to lose to a resurgent Liverpool.

Even the setback of Leslie's broken leg was overcome as Greenwood recruited a capable deputy in Jim Standen, a Luton and former Arsenal goalkeeper who was also an able Worcestershire pace bowler. Greenwood also managed to prise right-winger Peter Brabrook away from Chelsea for £35,000 after protracted negotiations. Brabrook was on target as West Ham put another six goals past relegation-bound Manchester City in the final game of the season. But this victory was only West Ham's eighth win at home and the deterioration in their home form resulted in a drop of four places.

Greenwood's side was in transition. Dick moved on to Brentford. Musgrove went to Orient and was replaced by young Tony Scott. Inside-forward Ronnie Boyce, another youth team product, came in for Phil Woosnam, who moved to Villa. Thanks to Greenwood's brainwave, Geoff Hurst was converted from an ordinary wing-half into a menacing, foraging inside-forward. Hurst proved to be a powerful front runner, strong in the air and adept at holding the ball up in advanced positions, helping bring his colleagues into play. He established a good partnership with the deeper-lying, creative Johnny Byrne. Hurst gave an indication of his future potential by leading the scoring chart with 13 league goals at a one-in-two ratio. Martin Peters enjoyed a long run in the first team, too. With Jack Burkett slotting in at left-back and Eddie Bovington adding defensive strength in midfield, the 1963/64 Wembley side was taking shape.

John Lyall, another former youth team player and future West Ham manager, made three appearances at left-back during the season. He remembered his days under Greenwood with great fondness, recalling that this was probably the most exciting and stimulating period of his career. He picked up phrases that Greenwood used daily such as 'simplicity is genius'. He came to realise that the best football, like that played by Liverpool in the '80s, is the simplest. Lyall said that Greenwood liked players with 'good habits', who consistently did the right things on the playing field. Greenwood told his players, 'You must leave the ball playable.' In other words, the receiving player had to be able to play the ball instantly. If the pass was made perfectly, the receiving player could play the ball, spin away from his marker and move into space to collect a return.

Greenwood felt that one of the most important arts of the game was improvisation. He recognised the value of the near-post cross used by the 1953 Hungarian team and embedded that into West Ham's attacking game. The central strikers anticipated the flight and timing of the cross and ran into the empty space as late as possible to head or volley the ball towards goal. Greenwood insisted that all players at all levels learned this move. Hurst perfected his dummy run, lingering on the edge of the box before making a decoy run. The marking defender would follow him, and Hurst would suddenly change direction and sprint into the space at the near post, arriving just in time to meet the ball from the wing.

Lyall believed that one of Greenwood's greatest strengths was his ability to spot the central problems every time, identifying where the problem lay and what was needed to fix it. Lyall said that Greenwood always put his ideas across in an intelligent and creative manner, adding, 'He taught us about life and how, as public figures, we should behave and handle ourselves. He taught us always to talk to the car park staff, to those who open the door for us or give us our match programme. He believed in respect and good manners. He was a kind, caring and thoroughly decent man who loved his job and football in all its aspects.'

Greenwood recalled, 'Malcolm Allison had moved on by the time I got to West Ham but had left his ideas behind which I welcomed. I considered it a priority to develop our youth players. There was a young player called Geoff Hurst who I had seen play as a left-half for the youth team. He was strong and good going forward, so we tried him at inside-left and he was a great success. Young Martin Peters was improving but was quite frail, and not always prominent. When we won the FA Cup in 1964, he did not play because he was going through a tough spell. Bobby Moore, though, was coolness personified. I always used to say to him, "Nobody seems to discover that you can't head a ball." He would compensate for this by positioning himself so he would catch it on his chest, or he would let the ball run and turn on it, but you rarely saw him head the ball. I didn't think he wanted to spoil his hair.'

Bobby Moore had already become England's youngest-ever captain. Now he was crowned Footballer of the Year. Captaining West Ham in the FA Cup semi-final against holders Manchester United, he gave due notice of the global glory to come. With 11 minutes to go in this fierce, mud-spattered game, Moore calmly chested the ball down, ten yards inside his own half. He advanced along the left flank, nonchalantly evading challenges from Charlton and Crerand. Then, perfectly judging his weight of pass, Moore slipped the ball across the cloying mud to find Hurst, who hammered it home to put West Ham 3-1 ahead. Wembley beckoned.

Hurst recalled the enthusiasm he and his team-mates shared in debating different ways of playing football. He explained that the Cassettari café was where they used to meet. Geoff spoke of the many happy hours he and others spent there, talking about the game and betting on the Pools. He reckoned that his wife could always tell when he had been at Cassettari. She told him that his clothes smelled of grease.

West Ham's 1963/64 league season was no more productive than the preceding one. Once more their home form was fragile. On the plus side there were emphatic home victories over Birmingham (5-0), Spurs (4-0), Stoke (4-1), West Bromwich and Everton (both 4-2) but on the minus side, there was a cataclysmic 8-2 home defeat by Blackburn on Boxing Day, avenged two days later with a 3-1 win at Ewood Park. There was also an unexpected 3-2 home defeat by relegation-bound Bolton. Once again, there were only eight home league victories to cheer. But at least Johnny Byrne found his shooting boots, scoring 33 goals in all competitions, 24 of which came in the league. Hurst added a further 14 league goals. But West Ham's cup form really turned heads. Victories over Charlton, Leyton Orient, after a replay, Swindon, Burnley and Manchester United, in the Hillsborough mud, took them to Wembley to meet Preston. Meanwhile, they progressed to the semi-finals of the League Cup, also, where they were beaten 6-3 on aggregate by eventual winners Leicester City.

Most pundits had Greenwood's side to win hands down. It seemed not to matter that Preston had performed creditably as Second Division promotion challengers while West Ham's top-flight form had been as erratic as ever. Many reckoned this would be the most one-sided final in years. The more scorn that was poured upon Preston's prospects, the more I rooted for them. As if Preston did not have enough to contend with, it was reported that their Scottish wing-half Ian Davidson had gone missing. Apparently, he told the club that he had to attend a relative's funeral. But according to team-mate Alan Spavin, 'Ian went to Scotland and apparently took some drugs and didn't make it.' So, 17-year-old England youth international Howard Kendall was selected in his place. Kendall was then the youngest player to feature in an FA Cup Final. But as young as he was, Kendall was not fazed by his unexpected selection. Unlike Spavin who hardly slept a wink, Kendall spent a relaxed night before his big day.

Saturday, 2 May dawned overcast and wet. When the BBC began its televised lunchtime build-up, Wembley was clad in a clammy, gruel-like mist. The players' tentative pre-match stroll suggested that the bowling green turf might be moist and slippery.

The pre-match entertainment was the same as ever – a military brass band blaring out brash versions of popular tunes. This time the combined bands of the Coldstream and Irish Guards were on duty. The only concessions made to the supposed 'swinging' era were their renditions of Joe Meek's 'Telstar', Lennon and McCartney's 'Can't Buy Me Love', and 'World Without Love', a recent hit for Peter and Gordon. As a mark of respect to the finalists, Preston were graced with 'Lassie from Lancashire' and West Ham, inevitably, with 'I'm Forever Blowing Bubbles'. The community singing followed, featuring that saccharine hymn 'Abide with Me'. Before the adapted terrace chants and anthems, the Wembley crowd sang obediently to order, orchestrated by a conductor who would throw his arms all over the place, and an oompah military band.

At half-time, there were more military bands. This time the Scots and Welsh Guards marched up and down the verdant Wembley turf. When Harold Macmillan made his famous 'Winds of Change' speech in 1960, heralding the dissolution of the British Empire, his message was not heard at Wembley. Here, imperial pomp and splendour reigned supreme as if the days of the Raj had not ended. It was a relief to get down to business.

Jimmy Milne had no intention of allowing West Ham to settle into their stride. His lads pressed their First Division opponents immediately, crowding them and avidly snapping into the tackle. West Ham were rattled. Errors abounded. Even the ultra-cool Bobby Moore seemed ill at ease.

Preston centre-forward Alex Dawson had the features of a heavyweight boxer. Barrel-chested with chiselled features, he looked well up for a scrap. He was so muscular he seemed steel clad. Being an old-school warrior, he shrugged off the knocks as he threw himself into the fray. It did not take long for him to impose himself, bumping and grinding, and boring into the heart of the West Ham defence. Inside the box he jostled for space, heaving himself above the West Ham centre-backs to contest the high crosses. From the off, he led a tank-like assault on the Irons' goal, well supported by his burly partner Alec Ashworth.

Strong, determined, and direct, Ashworth caused consternation too among West Ham's overworked defenders. Behind this rugged, 'rugger'-like spearhead was a midfield cavalry unit with craft and speed. Preston's tearaway right-winger David Wilson found he had the beating of his marker, Jack Burkett, forcing Moore to provide protective cover. Meanwhile on the opposite flank, Doug Holden played a more patient game, happily exchanging short passes with the inventive Spavin as he jockeyed for space.

With his colleagues using their guile and strength to pull the West Ham defenders around, Lawton revelled in the resulting freedom to home in on goal. Such was Preston's early domination that young Kendall could push up from his defensive berth, displaying an impressive range of elegant passes. In fact, Kendall began the move which led to Preston's opening ninth-minute goal. West Ham managed to clear the ball but right-back George Ross returned it, pumping the ball high into the box where Ashworth won the aerial challenge to present Dawson with an awkward shooting chance. Dawson scuffed his shot, but the bouncing ball squirmed out of Standen's grasp, presenting the alert Holden with a tap-in.

Preston's lead was short-lived. Two minutes later, Moore dispossessed Ashworth, who had dwelt on the ball. Moore loped forward before releasing young left-winger Sissons with an inch-perfect pass. Sissons ran directly for goal, executing a sharp one-two with Byrne, before beating Kelly with left-footed cross-shot. Lifted by this equaliser, West Ham raised their game. Byrne volleyed negligently high and wide from Brabrook's header after Singleton had failed to clear his lines.

But with bright sun now piercing the gloom, Preston began to recover. Brown's desperate tackle deflected Ashworth's effort just over the top and then two neat wall passes put Lawton in, only for Standen to push away his goalbound shot. Kendall's sizzling drive was unluckily blocked by Dawson and Brown put his body in the way of Ashworth's effort, much to the relief of Standen.

Although a fierce shot from Hurst stung Kelly's left palm, it was Preston who deservedly regained the lead five minutes before half-time. Holden jinked this way and that on the left flank, finally finding enough space to send a lofted pass in the direction of the advancing Kendall. The youngster shot immediately but the ball was deflected wide by Moore. However, from the subsequent corner, Wilson found Dawson's head. With both Standen and Brown slipping on the greasy surface, Dawson had all the time and space he needed to plant a simple header into the back of the net. The advantage was almost doubled moments later as Dawson headed wide from Spavin's centre.

BBC TV commentator Kenneth Wolstenholme described the Preston formation as 4-2-4 but it seemed more fluid than that. Although Preston pushed forward in numbers, Lawton, Spavin and Holden were quick to help their defence when the ball was lost. Also, while Wilson operated as an orthodox winger who looked to hit the goal line and cross, the right-footed Holden did not. He frequently wandered into central midfield, exchanging a series of short, tippy-tappy passes. During the first half, Preston played with two out and out strikers, Dawson and Ashworth, and three confirmed defenders, Ross, Singleton and Smith. The others seemed to have flexible roles, exercising collective attacking and defensive duties. However, after the break, a more conservative approach was taken. Kendall stayed closer to centre-half Singleton as Milne attempted to protect his team's slender advantage.

West Ham's first-half formation did not seem to be a straightforward 4-2-4 line-up, either. Because of the pressure that Preston applied, West Ham seemed to be operating more of a 4-5-1 system. Boyce retreated, Bovington helped Moore in defence, Hurst was left to operate as a lone striker while Byrne, Sissons and Brabrook made runs from deep, remaining ready to track back when possession was lost.

Greenwood used the break to make important tactical changes. He explained, 'We had been giving Lawton and Spavin too much room. The pitch is so spacious that normal marking systems can be wrecked by the extra yards. So, we decided to pitch Bovington against Lawton, Boyce against Spavin and pull Bobby Moore up to take on Ashworth. For the first time we were playing 4-2-4.'

Certainly, West Ham began the second period employing a higher defensive line, enabling them to press Preston in the Lancastrians' half. Centre-back Brown was also given licence to push up at set pieces to provide greater aerial strength. This proved crucial. Just seven minutes after half-time, West Ham won a corner on the right. Brown out-jumped Dawson to head Brabrook's delivery goalwards. Hurst instantly flicked the ball on with his head. Kelly was wrong-footed. The ball looped from Hurst's forehead on to the underside of the bar, whereupon it bounced down. Kelly made a despairing backward dive but could only push the ball gently over the line.

As hard as Preston tried to restore their lead, through efforts by Dawson, Ashworth and Lawton, West Ham grasped the initiative. Byrne hesitated fatally when put through on goal, Hurst failed to convert a sizzling low cross from Byrne, and then Sissons's shot missed the post by a whisker. Nevertheless, it was heartbreaking that Preston's brave fight should be ended by Ronnie Boyce's injury-time header. They deserved better.

After the game Jimmy Milne – three times a loser at Wembley – sportingly commented, 'We don't grumble. You can only do your best. I am pleased the lads put on a good show.'

Captain Nobby Lawton couldn't conceal his disappointment, though, saying, 'It's nice to know you have played well ... we could have had a couple of penalties but that's how it goes in football. Twice it looked very much like hands ... I suppose I'm expected to say we were beaten by a great side but, honestly, I don't think they were great. They couldn't stop us from creating far more chances than they did.'

As for Bobby Moore, he gave an equally downbeat assessment of his side's performance, 'We'd been magic against Manchester United. Wembley should have belonged to West Ham. We simply played badly. We were lucky to beat Preston and bloody lucky that Preston were no better than they were.'

Arguably, young Howard Kendall was the man of the match. He performed immaculately, displaying a level of maturity well beyond his years. Like Moore, he seemed so much at ease, pushing the ball around with calm authority, always alert to what was happening around him, anticipating threatening situations so astutely, timing his tackles precisely, rarely diving in, and always looking for a constructive pass. It was obvious that this lad had a glittering future ahead of him. He did not disappoint, later becoming a key member of Harry Catterick's championship-winning Everton side. However, he never represented England at a senior level – an inexplicable omission.

After the game, Kendall commented, 'I was a bit edgy before the game but once I got out there, I relaxed. My job was to cover the West Ham strikers – sometimes I was stuck with Byrne, sometimes Hurst.'

The next morning, the national papers were lavish in their praise of Preston but cool in their appreciation of West Ham. How we love a plucky loser. West Ham goalkeeper Jim Standen begged to differ. He griped, 'We expected to wake up next day as heroes but Wembley, it seemed, belonged to the losers. It was a real sickener.' Standen had no need to feel so churlish as just 12 months later he and his team-mates became national heroes. Although he might not have anticipated this, West Ham's FA Cup victory provided them with a perfect springboard for greater success. In May 1965, they would emulate Spurs' triumph by winning the European Cup Winners' Cup. Moreover, it was a success achieved with so much style. For a while longer West Ham could be relied upon to serve up attractive football. While occasionally flirting with relegation, they would remain as a First Division side for a further 13 seasons.

The immediate future proved less bright for Preston, though. In the following season they fell back nine places. Three years later, they would lose their talisman Alex Dawson after a spat over terms. Preston's loss would become Bury's and Brighton's gain, and they would not challenge again for a top-flight place until the turn of the century. When I caught up with them again, at the end of the decade, I found a club in a state of advanced decay. The Third Division beckoned and despite recovering from a worse fate, the top flight still eludes them.

49.

LIVERPOOL v ARSENAL: FIRST DIVISION, 22 AUGUST 1964

THE 1964/65 season opened with the newly created *Match of the Day* TV progamme covering a cracking game on a sparkling summer afternoon at Anfield. Liverpool ended the previous season as First Division champions while their visitors finished eighth. BBC commentator Kenneth Wolstenholme welcomed us to 'Beatleville' with the Swinging Blue Jeans' hit song 'Hippy, Hippy Shake' playing on the Anfield PA. He explained that Liverpool were depleted with St John recovering from appendicitis and sharp-shooter Alf Arrowsmith still unavailable with a leg injury that would ultimately end his Liverpool career. The hosts lined up in a conventional 2-3-5 formation as did Arsenal. Liverpool were quicker out of the traps with their right-footed left-winger Peter Thompson roasting Arsenal's England right-back Don Howe at will. Determined not to allow Thompson to humiliate him, Howe treated the sinuous flank man with the upmost disrespect, incensing many in the packed crowd.

The 21-year-old had been signed from Preston North End in 1963 for a club record fee of £40,000. Having played in all 42 matches in Liverpool's title-winning season, he was at the top of his game. For the first 45 minutes he was unstoppable, setting up the opening goal in the 11th minute with a mazy run and high cross to Callaghan on the right touchline. Callaghan instantly looped the ball into the Arsenal box where Roger Hunt hooked it in with a high volley. The quiet Anfield crowd were stirred into life, chanting 'Liverpool, Liverpool!'

Shankly's men then proceeded to swarm over and around the increasingly besieged Arsenal defenders, relishing the wide-open spaces they were allowed. But having grasped the whip hand, over-confidence crept in, giving Arsenal a rare counter-attacking opportunity with England international centre-forward Joe Baker given a free run at goal. Neither left-back Moran nor centre-half Ron Yeats were anywhere to be seen as Baker lined up his shot. Luckily for them, the Arsenal spearhead pushed the ball just wide of Lawrence's right-hand post. Baker soon had another shot that struck the woodwork and Liverpool needed to tighten up. However, they reached the interval with their narrow lead intact.

Liverpool recovered their early momentum upon the resumption with Stevenson, Milne, Wallace and Chisnall having the upper hand in midfield. Callaghan was once again the instigator as he stood up a high cross for inside-forward Wallace to head emphatically past Arsenal goalkeeper Furnell. Arsenal had 40 minutes left to mount an improbable comeback, but to their great credit that is what they did. Their inspiration was playmaker George Eastham who suddenly sprung into life, pulling the strings in central midfield. It was his one-two that set up Geoff Strong for a thumping shot on goal which Lawrence could not stop. Demonstrating admirable sporting spirit, the Liverpool fans warmly applauded this magnificent goal.

Arsenal were back in the game with 24 minutes left and just two minutes later, right-winger Armstrong crossed strongly for Baker to produce a twisting header which flashed into the roof of the net at the near post. With Eastham continuing to boss the central midfield with his nifty twists and turns and probing passes, Arsenal seemed to be likely winners. Eastham combined with re-invigorated left-winger Anderson to set up a gilt-edged chance for the onrushing Armstrong. With the whole goal at his mercy Armstrong hammered a shot on target. Somehow, Lawrence managed to flick the stinging drive over the bar. Eastham then wriggled to the goal line and cut back an inviting opportunity for one of his colleagues, but the resulting shot was blocked. Sneddon also wasted a clear shooting chance, blasting the ball over the bar.

With only two minutes to go, and Arsenal on the attack, Anderson's first touch let him down, allowing right-back Gerry Byrne to break away at speed. His diagonal pass was seized upon by

Callaghan who set up Wallace to drive home Liverpool's winner from 18 yards. Undeterred, Arsenal immediately went on the attack but a team-mate blocked Baker's powerful shot on goal. Arsenal were left to rue their luck having raised their game so impressively.

Nevertheless, it was a magnificent match, one of the best I have seen. With the *Match of the Day* coverage stretching to around 50 minutes, it was possible to have a valid grasp of the game. The danger was, of course, that televised football of this quality might deter many from supporting their local clubs, particularly those in the lower divisions or in non-league. It was this fear that prompted domineering Burnley chairman Bob Lord to reject TV coverage of his club's games at Turf Moor. He insisted, 'Television is not for professional football. It will damage and undermine attendances as it did with American baseball. It is a menace because it keeps folks at home. TV does not see the real thing. You only see snatches of play. It is bitty and misleading. It is something for nothing and "all laid on". If Real Madrid are put on TV, the public will become dissatisfied with what is on offer here.'

Despite his reputation for bigotry. his concerns here were justified.

50.

YOUTHQUAKE: 'MY GENERATION', 1964

IF THE popular press were to be believed, the summer of 1964 was scarred by seaside violence, perpetrated by warring gangs of Mods and Rockers. The moral panic aroused was largely without justification, although the bold Mod and Rocker youth cultures did challenge restrained middle-class society. The cessation of National Service was a significant factor in their growth as was an extended period of full employment. Baby Boomers, notably those from working-class families, benefited enormously from greater disposable income and the resulting freedoms denied to previous generations.

Mod and Rocker cultures were defined by contrasting choices of fashion, music, and wheels. With her eye-covering fringe and long hair, Cathy McGowan of *Ready Steady Go!* was a Mod role model. Other Mod girls had short cuts like model Twiggy. Shift dresses with round collars were the rage, worn with white stockings and stack-heeled shoes, although tights replaced stockings once mini-skirts became fashionable. Make-up was minimal and lipstick was out.

But Mod guys were equally fastidious. Mod boys liked a middle parting with puffed-up, lacquered tops and backs, their girlfriends supplying the lacquer. If you can remember Steve Marriott of the Small Faces, you will know the look. Many were fond of small-brimmed blue beat hats. As for the rest of the gear, it was not cheap. Ivy League suits – three buttons, narrow lapels, and two vents – cost £30, more than £600 today. To get the picture, watch the video footage of The Righteous Brothers singing 'You've Lost that Lovin' Feelin'' or The Zombies performing their breathy, jazzy single, 'She's Not There'. Then there were the trousers with 17-inch bottoms and imitation crocodile or python shoes with rounded toes, although many of the cheapskates settled for desert boots. Blue suits were popular too. For Mods who could afford wheels, this meant a Lambretta or Vespa scooter, bristling with lamps and wing mirrors. Scooter wear was an olive-green Parka with a fur-trimmed hood.

Then there was the music. Blue beat, rocksteady artists like Prince Buster were Mod favourites until abrasively energetic bands like The Who and the Small Faces emerged. The Who's centrepiece was 'My Generation', completed with a frantic trashing of their instruments.

As for Rocker fashion, this was strictly retro, caught up in the '50s beat – driving rock 'n' roll, grease, leather gear and roaring bikes. The Rocker girls wore leathers too, with flat shoes, lacquered bouffants and thick make-up. They were keen on Elvis pendants. While Rockers remained faithful to the jive and the Twist, the Mods were strictly Blue Beat, knees stiff, arms flailing all over the place.

There was a third youth movement, too. The first skinheads were largely lower working-class youths based in the East End of London. They felt no association with more prosperous, middle-class Mods. Instead they celebrated their blue-collar, working-class status, hence their shaven or closely cropped hair, their Ben Sherman button-down shirts and braces, sta-Prest or straight 501 Levi jeans, shiny army boots or Doc Martens, and Crombie overcoats. This was manual labour chic. At the outset many of them were friendly with their British Jamaican neighbours ('rude boys') whose families had emigrated to Britain to meet their mother country's desperate need of post-war reconstruction work. These original skinheads shared the rude boys' fondness of reggae, the heavy, repetitive rhythms of dub and ska and rocksteady. They helped Jamaican music to enter the mainstream, as with Desmond Dekker and the Aces' 1969 hit single, 'Israelites'.

The notorious reputation that skinheads subsequently acquired was occasioned by a declining British economy in the late '60s and '70s. With their manual job prospects declining, as exemplified by the containerisation of the East End docks, these skinheads sought to place the blame on so-called 'aliens', hence their hostility towards Asian immigrants. Homosexuals were targeted, too, as was anyone who challenged their sense of masculinity such as 'hippies' or students. From around 1967, this aggressive strain of skinheads was commonly associated with disorder at or outside football grounds, raiding, occupying and defending stadia ends such as Chelsea's Shed or West Ham's North Bank, also fighting over territories outside perceived to be home ground. This was a troubled situation which far-right and neo-Nazi groups sought to exploit. Despite their racist attitudes, these aggressive skinheads retained a penchant for Jamaican music and Tamla Motown.

However, the original skinheads disassociated themselves from such unruly and racist behaviour, establishing a counterculture of S.H.A.R.P. – Skinheads Against Racial Prejudice. From these roots emerged a healing '70s movement which sought to bring together blacks and whites in a shared love of reggae, ska, punk, and new wave as illustrated by the 2 Tone bands such as The Specials and the 1976 'Rock against Racism' movement.

51.

ALF RAMSEY'S WORLD CUP WINNING FORMULA

ALF RAMSEY'S boast that England would win the World Cup sounded like absurd bravado after his side's disastrous showing in the mini tournament in Brazil during the summer of 1964. Ramsey gave no instructions for marking Pelé. Instead he told his players to try to stop the ball getting through to him, directing that the man closest to Pelé should pick him up.

The plan appeared to be working tolerably well in the first half. Although Brazil had taken the lead through left-winger Rinaldo England seemed to be still in the game. Johnny Byrne had a shot cleared off the line and Jimmy Greaves missed narrowly. But after Greaves levelled the score midway through the second half, Pelé overwhelmed them.

In a magical five-minute spell, Pelé took Brazil out of sight. Twice he danced through England's defence juggling the ball sensationally before being impeded. Both ensuing free kicks swerved past Waiters and England were suddenly 3-1 down. Then Pelé nutmegged both Bobby Moore and Maurice Norman before blasting the ball past Waiters from 25 yards. Pelé was running England ragged, so much so that they failed to pick up Diaz running from deep to score Brazil's fifth with two minutes left. Byrne said, 'Pelé's speed was deceptive. It was only when we were chasing him that we realised we were competing with an Olympic sprinter with the ball at his feet!' The two remaining games were dispiriting, also. England achieved a mediocre 1-1 draw with Portugal and were then defeated 1-0 by an under-strength Argentinian 11.

The 1965 spring tour was more encouraging: a 1-1 draw with Yugoslavia in Belgrade followed by single-goal victories over West Germany and Sweden. Although the performances hardly quickened the pulse, Ramsey was still sifting through the candidates for his best side. This did not necessarily include his most talented performers, as Jimmy Greaves would soon discover. Along the way Ramsey had to contend with some behavioural challenges. He dealt with these decisively, signalling, 'If you don't do as I say, you won't play.'

If the Battle of Waterloo was won on the playing fields of Eton, then England's World Cup victory was rehearsed on the playing field of Madrid. On 8 December 1965 England met the previous year's European Championship winners, Spain, in a friendly at Real Madrid's Bernabeu Stadium. It was a bitterly cold evening. With the Bernabeu's frosty surface glistening in the glare of the floodlights, it was obviously too cold for most Spanish supporters – a thinly sprinkled crowd of 25,000 came to watch a stupendous England performance. Here, Ramsey revealed his blueprint for World Cup success.

Most pundits were sceptical of England's chances after their shambolic showing in the 1964 South American tournament. But here Ramsey unveiled a new winning gameplan. Ramsey knew he had neither Brazil's creative brilliance nor Argentina's sophisticated technique. As at Ipswich, he knew he needed a superior game plan executed by committed, disciplined and technically proficient players, if a better team was to be beaten.

For the previous 18 months Ramsey had persisted with a 4-2-4 formation that was largely successful against Home Nations Championship and European opposition but unconvincing against the might of Brazil and Argentina. Ramsey explained, 'A vital requisite for a 4-2-4 system is a pair of attacking wingers with the ability and speed to take on defenders, to get past them, take the ball to the goal line and pull it back. This always presents the biggest problem for goalkeepers. It became apparent to me that we did not have the wingers who could do this because of the way that defences had tightened up. If the winger did get past a full-back, he was always confronted by another covering player. We had to think of something else.'

That something else was a 4-3-3 formation, although Ramsey's World Cup-winning version was a flexible 4-4-2 set-up. He denied that Argentina's performance in 1964 had prompted his thinking. Ramsey pointed out, 'The Argentines usually played with at least five, and sometimes more, players crowding the middle of the field. Their object seemed mainly to avoid defeat. Mine has always been to win.'

His idea did not emerge as a year zero, Damascus-like brainwave. The Brazilians had flirted with this tactical plan in winning the 1958 World Cup in Sweden. But Ramsey first realised its winning potential after successfully experimenting with the system in a practice match between the England seniors and his under-23 side in June 1965. Unbeknown to the under-23s, Ramsey instructed the seniors to adopt the 4-3-3 formation while their juniors were told to play their natural game. The upshot was that the senior midfield trio of Bryan Douglas of Blackburn, Johnny Byrne of West Ham and George Eastham of Arsenal over-ran the youngsters. The under-23s were bewildered as to how they might counter their opponents' total control.

Nevertheless, Ramsey proceeded cautiously. During the 1965 summer tour, he continued to select two orthodox wingers: Terry Paine of Southampton and Derek Temple of Everton against West Germany, a game which was won 1-0; and Paine and John Connelly of Manchester United against Sweden which was won 2-1. England's subsequently poor performances: against Wales, a 0-0 draw; Northern Ireland in a 2-1 win; and a 2-1 defeat to Austria; forced a more radical change.

In Madrid, Ramsey went for broke. He announced in typically strained diction, 'The numbers my men will wear are nothing more than a means of identifying them for the spectators.' Ramsey's back four of George Cohen of Fulham, Jack Charlton of Leeds, Bobby Moore of West Ham and Ray Wilson of Everton seemed reassuringly tight. His midfield comprised George Eastham, Nobby Stiles and Bobby Charlton of Manchester United. They combined artistry, ball-winning and powerful probing. The forwards – Alan Ball of Blackpool, Joe Baker of Arsenal and Roger Hunt of Liverpool – not only hunted as a pack but also defended from the front, continually hounding and harrying the Spanish when possession was lost, interrupting their distribution.

The Spanish full-backs were thrown by the absence of wingers to mark. Consequently, they were lured into uncertain areas, causing their defence to lose its shape. The emerging gaps on the flanks were then ruthlessly exploited by England's fast, overlapping full-backs. Meanwhile, Ball ran here, there, and everywhere, foraging in advanced positions, taking on the perplexed Spanish defenders, pulling them out of position and creating space for others to plunder.

Here, Ball gave notice of his amazing show of stamina and skill that would shine in the World Cup Final. As early as the eighth minute, Wilson crossed to the far post for Baker to nip in and nod the ball past Spanish goalkeeper Iribar, one of five survivors from the 1964 European Championship Final team. Even when an injury to Baker forced a reshuffle, with Hunter replacing Bobby Charlton in midfield, there was no disturbance to England's devastating fluency. The Spaniards were left chasing phantoms. Just before the hour, Roger Hunt emphasised England's total superiority by scoring their second goal, having benefited from some sharp interplay between the liberated Moore and the fleet-footed Cohen.

The Spanish manager said afterwards, 'England were phenomenal, far superior in the experiment and their players.' And yet despite this resounding endorsement, Ramsey still clung on to his wingers – Connelly, Paine and Ian Callaghan of Liverpool played one game each in the three dull World Cup group games. England's performance against Argentina in the quarter-finals was unimpressive also. Had it not been for Antonio Rattin's self-destruction, Argentina might well have won. In the end Ramsey was indebted to Ron Greenwood's inventive near-post drills as Geoff Hurst's flicked header, from Martin Peters's pinpoint cross, gave England a narrow victory against their depleted opponents.

It was not until the semi-final against Portugal that England displayed the proficiency they had shown in Madrid. The rest is of course history. Certainly, England benefited from being the host nation and in playing their games at Wembley, but this was still a victory against the odds. There were stronger nations in this tournament. Notwithstanding the world-class credentials of Bobby Charlton, Gordon Banks, and Bobby Moore, an enterprising tactical plan was necessary to achieve supremacy.

Jimmy Greaves thought that England's success spawned many imitators. He contended that suddenly clubs were playing the 4-3-3 way with an emphasis upon defence. He claimed that it made life harder for the goalscorers, such as himself, having to cope with frequently packed penalty areas. He believed that the lifeblood of the game was being diminished, criticising the new jargon, 'work-rate'; 'the overlap'; 'tackling back'; 'running off the ball'; 'centre-backs'; 'sweepers'; 'midfield anchor men' and so on. The coaches were said to be in charge and their tactics started to 'squeeze the goals out of football just as I had seen in my brief spell in Italy'.

Yet while there were 25 per cent fewer First Division goals in the '60s, Greaves's haul was slightly higher in the 1968/69 season with 32 in all competitions compared with his 29 in 1959/60.

52.

NOTHING IS REAL: 'TOMORROW NEVER KNOWS', 1966

BY JULY 1966, British pop music sat alongside Alf Ramsey's 'wing-less wonders' at the top of the world. Inspired by Dr Timothy Leary's mantra, 'Turn on, tune in and drop out', The Beatles recorded their first 'trippy' song, 'Tomorrow Never Knows'. Fewer than three years previously, the mop-haired Fab Four were still peddling soppy love songs such as 'I Want to Hold Your Hand', but by 1966 they had become beaded, bearded hippies intrigued by notions of cosmic love and metaphysical meanderings. In 'Tomorrow Never Knows' a spectral-sounding John Lennon emerges from a droning swirl of instrumental distortion, agonised seagull-like cries and a pounding Indian drumbeat, to insist it was time to leave reality behind and drift listlessly downstream. The narcotic age of pop had arrived.

'Tomorrow Never Knows' set the pace for a swathe of psychedelic compositions from both sides of the Atlantic, as exemplified by Jefferson Airplane's 'White Rabbit', The Jimi Hendrix Experience's 'Purple Haze', The Velvet Underground's 'Heroin', Pink Floyd's 'See Emily Play' and, of course, The Beatles' later composition, 'A Day in the Life'. It was left to the iconoclastic Kinks to deconstruct the venal vapidity of mid-'60s pop culture, mocking Carnaby Street-style narcissism in 'Dedicated Follower of Fashion', scorning parvenu decadence in 'Sunny Afternoon', graphically itemising grinding poverty in 'Dead End Street', and satirising fond sentiments of imperial glory in 'Victoria'. Hogarth might well have been impressed. Meanwhile, in his sardonic 1966 film *Blow Up*, Italian film director

Michelangelo Antonioni scoffed at the vacuity of Swinging London values.

With British manufacturing in retreat, the Labour government faced a huge imbalance of payments which soon led to devaluation. The country, particularly the industrial areas of Scotland and Northern Ireland, Northern England, the West Midlands and South Wales, remained sullied by slum, derelict and shabby prefabricated housing. Too many people were without basic amenities, adequate shelter being the most pressing need. BBC Wednesday play *Cathy Come Home* would ram that point home better than any government inquiry. Beneath the vapid gloss of 'Swinging Britain' there was a grim, grimy reality, much nearer to the abject poverty of *The Whisperers* than the atavistic preening of *Darling*, closer to the austerity of *Z Cars* and *Softly Softly* than the cosiness of *Dixon of Dock Green*.

While the froth of Swinging Britain suggested a thriving UK, its economy was far from sound. In *Anatomy of Britain Today*, esteemed political commentator Anthony Sampson wrote, 'It is hard to see how Great Britain can quickly break out of its supine contentment without the challenge of the Common Market. Its quasi-aristocratic society has difficulty in generating dynamic movement. Much of its current energy comes not from the English but from the immigrant, particularly in the fastest growing industries – electronics, television, hire purchasing and advertising. This monopoly must be broken if Britain is to make proper use of her brains and her energy. The public schools and richer colleges not only perpetuate an anachronistic class system, they project a view of Britain which is out-of-date and often irrelevant.'

Britain's productivity was being outstripped by former Axis adversaries. While the country was constructing its final steam locomotive, *Evening Star*, in 1960, Japan was developing its ultra-swish, much faster 'Bullet Train'. No wonder the people consoled themselves with preposterous James Bond tales of British supremacy.

Embattled Prime Minister Harold Wilson was keen to extract the feelgood factor of a World Cup victory. His government was in disarray, beset by petty jealousies and Machiavellian intrigues. Wilson's Cabinet failed to grapple with urgent problems at home and abroad. Because hard-up Britain was so reliant upon American economic support, Wilson felt obliged to maintain unaffordable commitments east of Suez to underpin President Lyndon B. Johnson's toxic involvement in Vietnam. British handling of the Rhodesian Unilateral Declaration of Independence was inept as was its response to mounting insurgency in Aden, leaving British Army soldier Colin Campbell Mitchell – 'Mad Mitch' – to reoccupy Aden's crater district.

Wilson's handling of the national seamen's strike was no better. Constrained by Johnson's insistence that the pound should remain at its current value to protect the American dollar, Wilson refused to accept the inevitability of devaluation. Instead, there was a mandatory six-month freeze of pay and prices; cuts in public spending; increases in petrol and excise duties and heavy restrictions on hire purchases. Much to George Brown's chagrin, economic planning was junked. This flurry of activity smacked of knee-jerk expediency as we doffed our caps towards Washington. The socialist Michael Foot railed, 'We share the guilt for the infamy of Vietnam.' It was as if the country's national pride hung upon the achievements of Ramsey's men and The Beatles.

53.

'THE LISBON LIONS': STYLE VERSUS STERILITY, EUROPEAN CUP FINAL 1967

CELTIC MANAGER Jock Stein reckoned, 'The best place to defend is in the other team's penalty area.' Stein worked on basic principles. He believed that supporters wanted to see adventurous, attacking football but he also knew that to deliver this successfully his team needed to be supremely fit. He made sure that each of his outfield players were capable of lasting 90 minutes of scurrying and scrapping.

He insisted that the man on the ball must be constantly supported. There had to be progressive options in all areas of the park. Intelligent running off the ball was mandatory. Everyone was expected to hunt hungrily for space. The full-backs were expected to overlap, and the midfielders were urged forward to find menacing attacking positions. Meanwhile, his wingers were required to track back and continually harass their opposite numbers. It was work, work, work. There was to be no letting up. The product was lovely to watch but punishing to play.

Stein said, 'The difference between a really good side and a great side can often be the touch of the unpredictable. Call it a flash of genius if you like. Or flair.' His team certainly had men with flair. There was 'jinking' Jimmy Johnstone, the flame-haired right-winger who could turn full-backs inside out. There was muscular midfield architect Bertie Auld with an immaculate range of penetrative passes. There was Bobby Murdoch who combined power with finesse in his playmaking role, deft in his touch but possessing a ferocious shot.

And then there was buoyant bhoy Tommy Gemmell, a roving turret at left-back. With players of this calibre, Celtic could upset their vaunted opponents.

On 25 May 1967, Celtic became the first British club to reach a European Cup Final. They had got there in style, trampling on Zurich 5-0 on aggregate; sweeping aside Nantes 6-2; squeezing past Yugoslavian champions Volvodina by the odd goal in three; and disposing of Dukla Prague 3-1 in the semi-final. Reflecting Stein's insistence on playing 'total football', the goals were shared around. Centre-forward Steve Chalmers led the rest with five but Gemmell chipped in with three; all scored in the two Zurich games.

Celtic's opponents on that serene spring evening in Lisbon were Inter Milan. Italian football had reigned supreme in continental competition since the Spanish and Portuguese giants had been deposed in the early '60s. But success had been achieved by eliminating the prospect of defeat. The Italian gold standard was a clean sheet, although Inter Milan's boss, Helenio Herrera, vehemently rejected the accusation that his side had focused upon erecting walls to the point of sterility. Herrera accepted that *Catenaccio* – four defenders and a sweeper – was his invention but maintained, 'The problem is that most of those who copied me, copied me wrongly. They forgot to include the attacking principle. I had Picchi as sweeper, yes, but I also had Facchetti, the first full-back to score as many goals as a forward.' Although this was an exaggeration, Facchetti was renowned for his attacking thrusts along Inter's left.

However, Celtic were determined to teach Inter a better way of winning. Stein remarked before the game, 'It is important for Celtic's players to think they can win every match but if it should happen that we lose to Inter Milan, we want to be remembered for the football we have played.'

For Stein, style and substance went hand in hand. To demonstrate his point, he showed his players a film of Real Madrid's masterclass at Hampden Park in May 1960. The fluidity of Real's shape and the fluency of their passing and movement were mesmerising. Stein insisted, 'The formation is not as important as the attitude. Attack should be in the mind.'

Only once had Celtic departed from this principle in the preceding rounds, when they decided to shut up shop in Prague, having won the home leg 3-1. All this did was to confirm they were better off sticking to their strength, attack.

Whereas Celtic approached the final in a relaxed frame of mind, the Inter players were stewing with nervous tension having been incarcerated for three days in a seafront hotel that Herrera had cleared of other guests. Centre-back Burgnich complained, 'None of us could sleep. All we did was obsess over the match and the Celtic players. Facchetti and I would stay up and listen to our skipper, Armando Picchi, vomiting from tension in the next room.' The hothouse atmosphere incubated the players' fears and paranoia, a situation hardly helped by Inter's disintegrating Serie A form. To make matters worse, they were without the injured Jair and Suarez, depleting them of their counter-attacking potency. Moreover, Mazzola, their other forward of note, was suffering with flu.

Nevertheless, Inter stuck by their normal gameplan. This comprised attacking their opponents from the off to try to secure an early lead, and then tenaciously defend it. Mazzola almost gave Inter the perfect start when he headed against the veteran Ronnie Simpson's legs in an opening raid. But Mazzola did not have long to wait for a better opportunity. He started the move which resulted in Corso finding centre-forward Cappellini with a defence-splitting pass. Craig felt obliged to bring him down and Mazzola wrong-footed Simpson from the spot. It was an enterprising start by the Italians but having gained the lead they reverted to type, pulling all but two forwards back.

Rejoicing in the acres of space Inter had conceded, Celtic proceeded to swarm all over them. Celtic had adopted a 4-2-4 formation. Their twin centre-forwards, Stevie Chalmers and Willie Wallace, took turns in dropping deep, trying to draw out Inter Milan's central defenders. The two wingers, Jimmy Johnstone and Bobby Lennox, were encouraged to drift inside, creating space for the attacking full-backs Craig and Gemmell. Celtic were going to attack with everything in their power.

Inter Milan's Burgnich recalled, 'We just knew, even after 15 minutes, that we were not going to keep them out. They were first to every ball; they just hammered us in every area of the pitch. It was a miracle that we were still 1-0 up at half-time ... we knew we were doomed.'

Sarti performed magnificently, producing one of the greatest goalkeeping displays in the history of the European Cup. He took hits from all directions but still managed to keep his goal intact with his astounding agility. However, he was indebted to the crossbar for denying blasts from Gemmell and Auld. With Celtic committing everyone to attack and Inter defending so deeply, the Italians were not able to pick up everyone, particularly those breaking from deep positions. And that's how Celtic's equaliser came about on the hour.

Murdoch's pass invited Craig to advance quickly down the right flank. With the Italians expecting a lofted centre towards the far post, the Celtic right-back swept a low pass into the path of his opposite number, Gemmell, who unhesitatingly hammered a shell-like shot into the top corner. Inter were played out. They could muster no response, other than punting high and hopeless clearances which were immediately seized upon by the voracious Scots.

Sure enough, with just six minutes remaining, Chalmers deflected Murdoch's scuffed effort past Sarti and Inter were undone. The might of Italy had been toppled by a relatively unknown team from Scotland. This unfancied side had become the first British team to lift the European Cup. In crushing *Catenaccio* Stein had prospered where Cullis had foundered. But while the tactic was now a bit peaky it was not yet dead.

After the game, an enthralled Bill Shankly sought out his victorious compatriot. As Shankly entered the Celtic dressing room, he boomed, 'John [using Jock's given name], you've just become a bloody legend.' Not as far as Prime Minister Harold Wilson was concerned, though. While he proposed that Stanley Matthews, Alf Ramsey, and Matt Busby should receive knighthoods, Stein was ignored. Scottish heroics seemed to count for less. No wonder the Scots enjoyed their 3-2 Wembley win over the World Cup winners in April 1967.

54.

BLUE MOON RISING: SPURS v MANCHESTER CITY, FIRST DIVISION, 4 MAY 1968

DURING THE late '50s and early '60s, Manchester City remained in the shadows of their richer, slicker but ill-fated neighbours. The gap between the two sides grew, particularly after City's relegation in 1963, a fate that United only narrowly averted that same year. But having jumped jail, United made a spectacular revival, winning the FA Cup at the end of that troubled 1962/63 season.

By 1965, United's championship year, Maine Road was a sorry sight. Even in their relegation-haunted seasons of the late '50s and early '60s, City had managed to draw an average crowd of 32,000 plus. And yet only 8,015 deigned to turn up for their Second Division home game with Swindon on 16 January 1965. One of their players remarked, 'I've never felt as depressed in all the time I've been a professional footballer. It was ghastly playing a first team match in front of all those vacant spaces.' Things were about to change, though.

Seven months after the Swindon 'no show', Joe Mercer was appointed as City's manager. He was possibly not in the best of health, having suffered a stroke 12 months previously. This setback forced him to relinquish his previous post at Aston Villa. Despite his wife's attempts at dissuading him, Mercer believed he was ready for the fray. He knew he could no longer be a tracksuit manager. He needed someone to do the running; someone who could knock his new team into shape. Mercer decided Malcolm Allison was his man so he gave the ebullient coach a call.

Allison's playing days had been cut short by tuberculosis, but he had put aside his grief by committing himself wholeheartedly to developing his coaching skills, acquiring a full range of FA badges. He quickly established a reputation as a physically demanding, original and sharp tactical operator. Allison cut his teeth at West Ham where, according to a young Bobby Moore, he taught him everything he knew. Allison then managed Southern League Bath City before moving to Plymouth Argyle. Mercer intervened as Allison was considering a coaching position with Raich Carter at Middlesbrough. Mercer persuaded him to come to Maine Road instead.

Allison believed that it was England's slaughter by the Hungarians in 1953 that alerted him to the possibilities of coaching. Almost 50 years later, he told the *Observer* journalist Jon Henderson, 'What was amazing to me was how the Hungarians, by changing positions, made such a difference. Herbert Chapman's "W-M" formation – the full-backs and half-backs arranged in a W and the five forwards in an M – lasted for more than 25 years. Everyone copied this formation, so when the Hungarians changed their tactics and played with a deep centre-forward, they destroyed England. Okay, they might have had some great players, but they were not that much better than us, not 6-3 and 7-1 better. Ramsey was at right-back and nearly all the goals came down that side. He could not handle the winger who was too quick for him. So, when Ramsey became England manager, he adopted two deep wingers, as he did at Ipswich, to protect the full-backs so they couldn't get chased like he had been. He developed the 4-4-2 formation which was the 1966 World Cup winning line-up. It got me thinking, too, that it was more about formations, about the way you played, than about great players.'

Mercer and Allison faced a huge challenge upon their arrival at City in July 1965. They found a squad of just 21 players made up of seasoned professionals and largely untried youngsters. City had completed the previous season in the Second Division in 11th place. Allison believed that City needed to be tighter at the back. Mercer agreed. Allison's irrepressible enthusiasm and energy left an indelible mark upon his new squad. Former forward Neil Young said, 'Under previous regimes the training sessions were basically run, run, run. There was no variation and we hardly saw the ball until the next game. Now we still ran but there was much more emphasis upon ball work. We played a lot of five-a-side games and attack against defence. The sessions were shorter and faster. Joe would walk around taking in every detail. Later, Joe would say to Malcolm, "Why don't you try that?" "What about this?"

'Joe was really a father figure to us. Nothing was too much trouble. Joe and Malcolm encouraged me to shoot more often, the theory being that goalkeepers were used to saving shots, but only from certain areas and anywhere else could cause them problems. Another thing we would do in training was head tennis. We won an FA tournament against teams like Arsenal and Chelsea. I think Malcolm was about 20 years ahead of his time. Malcolm was especially good as a psychologist. He used to make each one of us think we were the best in the world.'

Nevertheless, City needed better players. Some of the existing squad were no longer good enough. Mercer brought in Mike Summerbee, a direct right-winger or centre-forward from Swindon for £35,000; Ralph Brand, a prolific scorer with Rangers; George Heslop, Everton's reserve centre-half for £20,000; and, just before the March 1966 transfer deadline, midfielder Colin Bell from Bury for £45,000. Allison had set his heart on Bell. He was impressed with his stamina, speed, and skill. Neil Young later observed, 'Bell could make 20-, 30-, 40-yard runs, and defenders couldn't pick him up.' Allison played a canny game in landing Bell, bogusly emphasising his shortcomings to rival scouts to end their interest.

Meanwhile, several seasoned professionals departed. Out went powerful inside-forward Derek Kevan to Crystal Palace, centre-forward Jimmy Murray to Walsall, and full-back Dave Bacuzzi to Reading. Mercer and Allison inspired an immediate and startling change in City's fortunes. At the end of their first season in charge, City were promoted as Second Division champions.

On 18 December 1965, I watched City overpower Crystal Palace at a boggy Selhurst Park. It was an indomitable display of muscular professionalism. The star of the show was Mike Summerbee. Allison said, 'When I saw Summerbee playing in practice matches he was playing too deep for an outside-right. I encouraged him to play further forward.'

On this dark, wet, December afternoon, Summerbee took this advice to heart. He was the fulcrum of City's devastating counter-attacks. He was so quick and strong, versatile, too, confident about taking on the Palace defenders unaided. On this saturated surface, he showed astonishing sureness of touch. Time and again he collected the ball deep inside City's half and proceeded to run with intimidating directness at the Palace goal. The home defenders attempted to close him down, but he had the quickness of feet and surge of acceleration to continually confound them. And while he created mayhem in Palace's defence, gaps appeared for his team-mates to exploit. Twice, midfielder Mike Doyle broke through to finish what Summerbee had set up. Palace had one of the meanest home defensive records in the division, but City were in a different league.

City's first season back up in the top flight was one of stability. They might have hoped for more because they got off to a sensational start. But having faltered, Allison looked for further reinforcements. He persuaded Mercer to fork out £17,500 on Tony Book, his talismanic full-back from Plymouth. Book had played for Allison at Bath and Plymouth but was then 31 years old. Too long in the tooth, feared Mercer but Allison knew better. Having finally won his partner over, it did not take Book long to assuage all doubts. Young concluded, 'Not many players got the better of Tony Book.' Allison experimented by using Book as a sweeper, an innovation that Mercer had used when at Sheffield United, but one that had been hardly employed in English football. Book was ideally suited to the role with his uncanny positional sense, his sharp reading of the game, his physical strength and accurate distribution.

Allison then caused his partner further consternation by bringing in a left-winger, Tony Coleman, from Doncaster, a cocky lad with a Beatles-style mop top covered in tattoos, for £12,350. Even Allison described him as a 'parole officer's nightmare'. Before the 1969 FA Cup Final, Coleman famously asked Princess Anne 'how's your mam?' But Mercer conceded that despite Coleman's waywardness, the lad could play. The late Mark E. Smith, formerly the grouchy leader of the waspish Fall, and lifetime City fan, reckoned that Coleman was the only City player he could write a song about.

During 1967/68, goalkeeper Ken Mulhearn was brought in from Stockport. He had established a reputation as an excellent shot stopper. But undoubtedly City's signing of that triumphant season was Francis Lee – captured from Bolton for £60,000. Allison knew that Lee's dynamic speed over the first five yards and his bustling directness would hurt opposing defences. He was not wrong.

The campaign began slowly – a 0-0 home draw with Liverpool was followed by two away defeats, 3-2 at Southampton and 3-0 at Stoke. A brace each from Bell and Young put paid to the Saints with a 4-2 scoreline in the return fixture and then Summerbee and Coleman felled Forest for a 2-0 success. The winning streak extended to five games as City beat Newcastle 2-0 and Sheffield United 5-2 at home, and Coventry 3-0 at Highfield Road. Stan Bowles scored two against the Blades on his league debut having snatched a brace against Leicester in a League Cup game. Ultimately Bowles would make his name at Loftus Road having left a lasting memory at City, not only of his extravagant talent, but his suspect temperament, too.

Just as City were moving through the gears, they took three hits in succession. A 2-1 home defeat in a feisty Manchester derby featured a scrap between Bowles and Kidd which the police had to quell. Francis Lee made his debut on 14 October, helping his new club to gain a 2-0 home win against Wolves. He opened his account a week later as City scored four second half goals to defeat struggling Fulham 4-2 at Craven Cottage. Don Revie's Leeds then came to Maine Road and were beaten by Bell's header four minutes from time. After City and Everton shared the spoils at Goodison in a 1-1 draw, Leicester were thrashed 6-0 at home with Young and Lee both scoring twice. Lee added two more in City's 3-2 victory at West Ham while Coleman followed suit a week later in a brilliant home display to see off Burnley 4-2.

After being pegged back to 1-1 by John Fantham's injury-time equaliser at Hillsborough, it was time for the 'ballet on ice' as Spurs were well beaten 4-1 in front of the *Match of the Day* cameras. A Spurs player remarked, 'It was extraordinary. City moved like Olympic speed skaters while we were falling around like clowns on a skid patch.' It was clear then that City were strong title contenders. An ensuing 1-1 draw at Anfield and another thumping 4-2 home win over Stoke underlined their candidature. But West Bromwich spoiled City's Christmas with back-to-back victories. City recovered with two 3-0 away wins, at Forest and Sheffield United, but visiting Arsenal arrested their momentum by grabbing a deserved 1-1 draw. Successive 1-0 victories were achieved at home against Sunderland and away at

Burnley, before Coventry were beaten 3-1 in a bad-tempered affair that saw Coleman dismissed along with Coventry's Bruck.

Although City reached the fourth round of the League Cup before being surprisingly beaten 3-2 by bottom side Fulham, the FA Cup did not cause them to tarry long. After City had beaten Reading 7-0 in a third-round replay, Leicester eliminated them 4-3 in the next round, also at the second attempt. The Reading victory featured a hilarious incident involving the maverick Coleman. As Francis Lee prepared to take a penalty, Coleman hared in and blasted the ball over the bar. When confronted by the incensed Lee, Coleman replied, 'I just felt like it.'

The 5-1 demolition of Fulham on 16 March put City in pole position, albeit on goal average. Young was twice on target. However, a 2-0 defeat at Leeds a week later put them back to third. City then recovered strongly by beating their Manchester rivals 3-1 at Old Trafford. It was a superb performance which left Mercer crying with joy. Frustratingly, a stinker followed as City lost 1-0 at lowly Leicester, which returned them to third. The Easter programme featured two home victories, 1-0 over Chelsea and 3-0 against West Ham, but also an unfortunate 1-0 defeat at Stamford Bridge. When City drew a blank in a draw at Wolves the following Saturday, Mercer conceded that their chances were fading. But two successive home victories – a jittery 1-0 win over Wednesday, thanks to an own goal, and a more comfortable 2-0 win over Everton – put them back on top, if only with a slender advantage over Manchester United. Leeds and Liverpool were not out of the race, either. This was the situation as City came face-to-face with Spurs at White Hart Lane on a warm, overcast Saturday, 4 May. It was a game I was fortunate to see.

After lifting the FA Cup in May 1967, Spurs lost their shine in the following season. Jimmy Greaves said that 1967/68 was one of the unhappiest he had ever experienced. The tremendous team spirit Spurs had shown had deserted them. Spurs had enjoyed a great win over Manchester United in the FA Cup but had then lost at Liverpool in a replay to relinquish their grip on the trophy. Greaves scored 23 goals during 1967/68, plus three in the FA Cup, but complained of feeling tired and jaded. He realised his appetite for football was fading, causing him to contemplate retirement. He thought that Spurs manager Bill Nicholson was aware of his malaise because he bought Southampton striker Martin Chivers for a club record fee of £125,000. Chivers replaced Alan Gilzean with Alan Mullery reverting to a deeper role behind Chivers and Greaves. Although Greaves's partnership with Chivers seemed to work, he admitted that he was not experiencing the fire of old. He believed that deficiency applied to the whole team, underlined when former stalwarts Dave Mackay and Cliff Jones were sold to Derby and Fulham respectively.

Greaves's downbeat mood was reflected in Spurs' matchday programme. In its 'Comment' section was written, 'Last season we won the FA Cup and finished third in the Football League. This year we can make no such claim. In spite of our long unbeaten home record, extending from November 1966 until December 1967 – a sequence of 27 league and FA Cup matches – we missed our way in the autumn when we were knocked out of the European Cup Winners' Cup by Olympic Lyonnaise. That game can only be described as a "Spurs disaster". This experience deflated everyone at the club.'

Had Joe Mercer or Malcolm Allison read these notes before the game, they must have taken heart from them.

Spurs lined up with Pat Jennings in goal; Phil Beal and Cyril Knowles as the full-backs; Mike England and captain Dave Mackay as the centre-backs; Jimmy Robertson, Alan Mullery, Terry Venables and Alan Gilzean in midfield; Greaves and Chivers up front. Greaves and the departing Jones were the only Spurs goalscorers to reach double figures in this season.

City were unchanged with Mulhearn in goal and Book and Pardoe as full-backs. The last time I had seen the strapping Pardoe he scored four goals in an England Schoolboys international on my first visit to Wembley in 1961. In his 17 years at City he played in every position bar goalkeeper and centre-half. Powerful centre-back Heslop was partnered by tough-tackling Michael Doyle and the penetrative pass master Alan Oakes. Up front, City had an impressive array of marksmen, comprising winger Tony Coleman (8 goals), midfielder Colin Bell (12), versatile centre-forward Summerbee (12), striker Neil Young (17) and wide-man Franny Lee (15).

At first it was nip and tuck. Spurs created openings through Chivers, Greaves and Gilzean without troubling Mulhearn unduly or Heslop. At the other end City were showing greater potency with Coleman and Lee continually stretching the full-backs while Summerbee put himself up against England, pulling the centre-half one way and another with his wiry twists and turns, creating gaps for the foraging Bell. Not that Bell needed much space in which to thrive. He made a succession of blind-side runs, carving out even wider corridors that Young and others could exploit.

The Spurs defenders seemed dumbfounded by the dazzling movement of the City players, particularly Bell. Even when they seized upon a loose ball, Bell and colleagues immediately hemmed them in, forcing hurried, wayward clearances. Bell never stopped running. His energy level was incredible. With Spurs at sixes and sevens, City advanced their defensive line with Doyle supplementing the incessant assaults on the home goal. From an even beginning this game began to resemble siege warfare. Spurs looked like beleaguered defenders of a holed fortress. Greaves was frantic with frustration while Chivers was merely ornamental. It seemed inconceivable that City would not score. Yet Doyle, Young, Coleman and Lee failed to put away excellent opportunities. With the Spurs fans silenced, the raucous City chants filled the ground.

Although Spurs made periodic advances these were so hesitant and lacking in conviction that they were easily stemmed by the City defenders. But just as it seemed as if Spurs might reach half-time unscathed, City struck. Five minutes before the break, a slick exchange between Book, Summerbee and Coleman enabled Bell to latch on to the ball at pace, glide past Mackay and find goal with a sweetly struck, low drive that gave the diving Jennings no chance. Almost from the restart, Jennings made a brilliant save to deny Young.

As the downcast Spurs players sauntered off the field, the excited City men exchanged fist pumps with their baying supporters. The Spurs fans could only hope that Nicholson would gee their lads up for a better second half. But they were disappointed as the second half started like the first had ended and City were immediately at Spurs' throat. City's second goal came less than a minute after the restart. Knowles had managed to keep out Young's snapshot, but the ball ricocheted to Bell who rifled it low into the net at brutal velocity.

With their position now apparently hopeless, Spurs somehow found their feet. Not that City were much troubled by Spurs' lame forays and 15 minutes from time Summerbee's skewed shot beat

Jennings to seal the game, securing two vital points. Greaves reduced the deficit with a penalty with seven minutes left but City could have added two more as Lee blazed over when well-placed and Young's shot clipped the top of the crossbar. Spurs' humiliation had been as great as in December's 'ballet on ice'.

Allison said afterwards, 'The game at Tottenham was a brilliant tactical success. The plan was to isolate the ageing Dave Mackay in the centre of the Spurs defence. Francis Lee's task was to pull Cyril Knowles wide on the right while Mike Summerbee would do the same with Mike England. This would leave a huge gap in the middle for rampaging Colin Bell to run at Mackay. The plan worked beautifully. Dave Mackay told me after moving to Derby, "I've never been so insulted in my life as I was on that day. You absolutely slaughtered us in that match. That was the reason I left Tottenham."'

After Leeds lost their midweek game at Arsenal, the City boys knew they needed only to win at Newcastle to take the title they had last secured in 1937. After a tense first half, City duly achieved their goal, winning in style after a 4-3 encounter. Although United lifted the European Cup, ten years after the Munich tragedy on a night of high emotion, City were rightfully the club team of the season. Reflecting upon his two spells at Maine Road, Malcolm Allison told Jon Henderson of *The Observer*, 'The first time Joe and I were at City it was because the club was doing badly. Everything I asked the players to do, they did. When I went there for the second time in 1979 there were a lot of successful players there who did not want to work. They did not want to train, they moaned, and they dodged. They were non-professional.'

55.

'PAINT IT BLACK': A CHANCE ENCOUNTER IN A DIVIDED LAND, 4 MAY 1968

ON THE train to White Hart Lane I offered my seat to a young black woman who seemed uncomfortable pressed into this carriage scrum. It was only at my insistence that she took my place, though. Coming from a town then with very few people of colour, I was unaware of the sensitivity of her situation. I assumed her discomfort was due to shyness. It was only afterwards, when I recalled how uneasily she had cast her eyes around in response to my offer, that I thought there might have been a more sinister explanation for her anxiety.

We had exchanged places just weeks after Enoch Powell's infamous 'rivers of blood' tirade. Powell's startling volte face on the issue of immigration had stoked the fires of segregation and racism, particularly among the white inhabitants of declining heavy industrial areas in the West Midlands and the north. Although Powell's remarks had caused his political career to collapse as dramatically as Ronan Point, he received messages of support from hundreds of sympathisers. After his dismissal from Ted Health's Shadow Cabinet, some workers in Reading, Norwich and Southampton went on strike in support of him. As in Smethwick, many local white inhabitants regarded their black and Asian neighbours with suspicion, an aversion which intensified with declining job prospects.

Not that the Windrush generation and other immigrants were made welcome during the late '40s and early '50s when shortages of cheap labour threatened to disrupt Britain's reviving economy.

Then the country was still producing goods that the rest of the world wanted. Racial animosity was the background to Patrick Gordon-Walker's controversial electoral defeat in 1964.

Although Johnny Speight and Warren Mitchell, script-writer and lead actor, in the TV sit-com *Till Death Us Do Part*, lampooned the casual racism which was rife in the '60s, the satire was lost on many viewers who readily identified with Alf Garnett's racial bigotry. The team that the fictitious Garnett supported was West Ham. It was ironic then that 'his club' was the first to play three black footballers in the same 11, when on 1 April 1972, Clive Charles, Ade Coker, and Clyde Best were selected to face Spurs. I remember the West Ham fans chanting at Clyde Best, 'We bought Clyde Best and we covered him with chocolate.'

It was an adaptation of a Cadbury's advert and was clearly meant affectionately but did the chant also carry an implication that Best's blackness was merely superficial, an honorary white, therefore? Although many players of colour now represent English teams, the problem of racism has yet to be fully eradicated at home and abroad. While this process of inclusion took far too long the selection of these three black West Ham players was an important step in the right direction.

56

MANCHESTER UNITED'S FAMOUS 1968 EUROPEAN CUP VICTORY IN QUOTES

'We are professionals. We cannot let emotion take over. We have lived with it [the legacy of the Munich tragedy] for so long. This time we must do it.'
Munich survivor Bobby Charlton before the Wembley final.

'I want to win for the boss.'
Nineteen-year-old Manchester United striker Brian Kidd before the final.

'For me it is like the World Cup Final all over again.'
Manchester United defender Nobby Stiles before the final.

'You're throwing the game away with careless passing, instead of continuing with your football. You must start to hold the ball and play again.'
Munich survivor Matt Busby before the start of extra time.

'I didn't want to listen. I didn't want to think. I just wanted to get it over with, one way or another.'
Munich survivor, centre-half Bill Foulkes.

'No lads, this is your day.'
Having refused to receive the European Cup, **Matt Busby** calmly walked away alone, concealing the emotion he must have felt, disappearing inside the Wembley tunnel.

57.

'STREET FIGHTING MAN': FOOTBALL DISORDER IN THE '50s AND '60s

PROFESSOR IAN Taylor believed that the re-emergence of football hooliganism in the middle part of the 20th century began at Roker Park, Sunderland, when the home side equalised against Spurs in an FA Cup tie. Apparently, the equaliser prompted a mass invasion of the pitch by young Sunderland fans.

However, there had been disturbances at Football League games during the '20s, '30s and '40s, albeit in small numbers. For example, 35 incidents of spectator misconduct at Football League games were reported to the FA during the four seasons of the '40s. In the '50s there were 103 such reports, mostly due to missile throwing. The missiles included teacups, coal and clinker, stones, nails, a piece of iron and a potato.

The clubs attempted to redress the falling gates of the '50s by attempting to draw in a more middle-class clientele. This was possibly the first step in the re-gentrification of the game which the abolition of the maximum wage hastened.

The clubs and better-behaved fans were alarmed by this apparent deterioration in supporters' behaviour at games, fearing that the Football League might cage grounds, as happened in the '80s. But there was even greater concern about misbehaviour outside grounds. Initially Liverpool and Everton fans were considered most culpable. A *Times* report in March 1956 itemised the damage done by Everton supporters to carriages carrying them to a game at Manchester City.

The list included smashed windows and bulbs, destroyed luggage racks and a door pulled off.

With a rise in prosperity during the late '50s, many former fans needed little persuasion to abandon the terraces in favour of family outings on Saturdays. As television ownership increased, more former fans were content to watch game highlights on *Sports Special*, a forerunner of *Match of the Day*. With the England World Cup coming closer, there was some anxiety whether continued hooliganism might threaten the tournament. In this febrile atmosphere, the *Sketch* adopted an ironic tone in reviewing the damage done on a football weekend in November 1963, 'What no darts? No invasions? No sending offs? No fights on the field? No protests? No menacing mobs awaiting the exit of referees? What is British football coming to?'

After a lull during the World Cup the moral panic was stoked up again by the press during the aftermath. The press attempted to outdo one another with panicky hyperboles such as 'Soccer Marches to War!', 'War on Soccer Hooligans!' and 'Soccer Thugs on the Warpath!' The winner, though, was a measured headline, 'What Next? Napalm?' During the 1966/67 Football League season the first references were made to hooligan gangs inside and outside the grounds. Previously, concern focused on ad hoc alliances on the day. With largely skinhead gangs occupying and defending their ends while also attempting to invade their opponents' turf, segregation measures were taken, with lines of policemen to maintain the separation of fans inside and immediately outside the ground. This raised the stakes in fans attempting to capture one another's territory. Hunter Davies, eminent author of *The Glory Game*, wrote about this activity, having spent an afternoon with some aggressive Spurs fans at Coventry.

Davies observed that their infiltration and seizure of their rivals' territory gave them as much, if not more, satisfaction than causing harm. 'WE'VE GOT THE WEST STAND IN OUR HANDS!' they bragged loudly. He sensed, too, their adrenaline rush when the prospect of a violent confrontation was imminent. He watched their alpha male gesticulations, remarking it is 'like something out of *The Naked Ape*'. Although frustrated by the raised Spurs scarves, stretched across his eyeline, blocking his view of the game, he became intoxicated by their booming chants, suggesting 'they had taken over'. Yet when he removed to the relative calm of the main stand, those same chants seemed 'puny' and perhaps risible. Yet he learnt much about the key features of hooligan culture – shared pride and identity, masculine posturing and approbation, and the adrenaline rush of potential combat.

Combat can arouse exhilarating excitement. Former soldiers, such as Philip Caputo (author of *A Rumor of War*) have referred to its addictiveness, leaving many yearning for a return to action, irrespective of countervailing fears of death and disability. This is the central theme of the film, *The Hurt Locker*. The prospect of violence can also confer a sense of power on those prepared to use it. The bigger the occasion, the greater that sense of power and excitement is likely to be. Football has helped create the occasion with its vast pulling power. The media has perhaps widened the platform. English hooligans abroad have a further incentive of 'flying the flag', indulging in a grotesque parody of patriotism, fuelled perhaps, not just by booze- or drug-related bravado, but by a preposterous desire to rectify Britain's dwindling status.

In his book *Among the Thugs*, American journalist Bill Buford graphically documented the pernicious nature of gang culture in shaping attitudes and behaviour. Having 'gone native' he described how the brutality of gang life infiltrated his urbane sensibilities, temporarily converting him from a well-mannered, considerate adult into one who ruthlessly pushed aside and barked thuggishly at a dithering older couple.

Explaining the class component of football-related gang behaviour is a lot trickier. Despite the media claims about 'designer hooligans' – 'thugs' who supposedly double as estate agents and bankers – the reality is that most football 'firms' or 'crews' comprise largely white, youngish, lower working-class men, who seem keen to exercise their warrior-like masculinity. That is not to say that economic status does not matter – it does. It is reflected in the gangs' bragging rights. During the '80s, the London-based 'firms' frequently derided their less well-off rivals in the north by flaunting their Pringle sweaters and Calvin Klein underwear. It has not always been about denim, Doc Martens and building site chic.

Football hooliganism was not a new phenomenon in the mid-'60s. Football-related disorder not only preceded the '60s, it preceded the 20th century. But there is little doubt that it took root and spread widely during the latter half of the '60s. It is doubtful, however, that John and Yoko had football 'aggro' in mind in their plea for peace.

58

'THIS IS THE MODERN WORLD': COACHING, TRAINING, AND TACTICS AT TWO '60s CLUBS

AS WALTER Winterbottom's assistant in the 1962 Chile World Cup, Player of the Year Jimmy Adamson saw how defensively-minded the international sides were, Brazil apart, recognising that new methods were needed to beat them. He impressed Bobby Charlton with his tactical acumen and was duly offered the England manager post. He refused, deciding to continue his august playing career with Burnley. Jimmy then became his club's coach and eventually its manager. Three former players gave this assessment of his capabilities as a coach.

Burnley midfielder Arthur Bellamy said, 'Jimmy Adamson was perhaps one of the first new tacticians, the first modern day coach and teacher. Harry Potts was a great manager, but he was not a great coach. He was a smoother of troubles. He gave players confidence. However, Jimmy Adamson taught me to do things I did not know I could do like playing sweeper. Gradually Jimmy became responsible for the training. It became more planned and technical under Jimmy. The man from the next era was replacing the man of the old.'

His club colleague Martin Dobson had good reason to be grateful to Adamson, who had rescued his career after being rejected by Bolton. Dobson said, 'Jimmy had us practising set plays for hours on end. Each time we erred, he hauled us back and we would start again. The delivery had to be spot on, the positioning had to be exact, the runs needed to be timed perfectly. Jimmy wouldn't accept anything less than perfection.

'After spending a year as an apprentice at Bolton I could see life at Burnley was different. Everyone trained with a ball, the international players, and the younger ones. There was two-touch and "shadow" football going on. Players were going through pass and move drills. What impressed me was much of the training centred on developing ball skills. There was instruction in what to do, in technique, in making runs, positioning and so on. I had never seen anything like this at Bolton.

'At the heart of this activity was Jimmy Adamson. He seemed to know exactly what he wanted from his players – blowing his whistle to stop the play when the exercises were not being executed as he wanted, praising the players when they got it right and demonstrating what was missing when they did not. He was outstanding. He commanded so much respect. Everyone knew what he had achieved as a player. He had been the national Player of the Year in 1962. So, they listened closely to what he said. Adamson was steeped in modern tactical thinking.'

Utility player Geoff Nulty added, 'What impressed me was the training sessions were well planned. Jimmy Adamson and his assistant, Joe Brown, worked out the training schedules in advance. This was unlike what I had experienced as a young player at Stoke where only the first team received real attention from the coaches and even their training sessions did not seem well prepared. The reserves were largely left to their own devices. But at Burnley the senior players, the reserves and youth team players trained together, at least for most of the week.

'Jimmy Adamson and Joe Brown would divide us into mixed groups and, typically, these groups would be made up of four first team players, four reserves and four apprentices. Jimmy wanted everyone to be inducted into the Burnley style of play, so that when anyone stepped up, say from the youth team to the reserves or from the reserves to the first team, they were ready to make that transition.

'The mixed group training took place on Mondays, Tuesdays and Wednesdays. There was always a strong focus on ball work. But on Thursdays we trained in our team units in preparation for the Saturday games. As first-teamers we practised "shadow football".

This is where we played against imaginary opponents. This really helped to tighten up our positional sense and interplay. Jimmy also organised a routine whereby the first team would be reduced to four defenders and a midfielder.

'They would be tasked with taking on a full reserve side. The only concession was that everyone on the reserve side was expected to fulfil their normal roles. The defenders could not become extra attackers. This exercise helped improve our defending. We had to play as one. It helped sharpen up our defensive instincts and organisation, our ability to cover for one another. We learnt how to spring the offside trap more effectively as a group. We became better attuned to one another. Having no attacking outlet, the defence was under constant pressure. This helped in getting organised. By doing this, we found we could keep the reserve sides out for some time.

'We also used this other routine designed to improve our wing play. Burnley had a string of great wingers – John Connelly, Ralph Coates, Willie Morgan, Dave Thomas, Leighton James and so on. It was a key part of the club's success over many years. To make the most of these assets, Jimmy Adamson devised practice matches comprising 15 players per side with no goalkeepers. We could only score with our head. To get goals we first had to work the ball wide, so this became instinctive. We scored a lot of goals from headers in League and Cup games. I am sure these practice sessions helped us in co-ordinating our attacks. When, say, Leighton James was attacking down one flank, the opposing defenders would be drawn over to his side to deal with the threat, so we then pushed up our full-back on the other flank to help exploit the gaps that this left.'

Dobson added, 'There was much practising of building attacks from the wing. Once again, Jimmy was meticulous about the type of cross to be supplied from the wings. We would go through a series of routines involving whipped or hanging crosses, say. He paid so much attention to detail, which, of course, paid off. I recall the intense repetition of practising flicked-on corner kicks at the near post. It involved performing decoy runs to create gaps so that the player concerned could arrive at the near post at the exact moment he was required to flick on a corner. The leap had to be right, too, so that the ball just kissed the top of his head.'

Nulty concluded, 'I felt well looked-after at Burnley. They found me digs near to the ground. It did not matter that some of the senior players were big names. They treated the younger players like themselves.'

Like Burnley, West Ham was a 'go-ahead' club with their manager Ron Greenwood giving leading edge coaching which brought about an FA Cup victory in 1964 and a European Cup Winners' Cup a year later. Here, England World Cup hero Geoff Hurst provides an insight into Greenwood's coaching methods, 'We worked hard on our near-post strategy. We spent hours crossing balls, not only forwards or midfielders but defenders, too, so whoever got in this position was able to deliver the ball to the near post with the accuracy required.'

Greenwood added, 'The ball had to drop roughly between the six-yard line and the near goal post. We did that to perfection time and time again, involving Johnny Sissons, Alan Sealey, Martin Peters, the full-backs, everybody.'

Hurst recalled, 'Against Newcastle, we had a big centre-half to contend with. I went to the far post taking this big guy with me. Alan Sealey delivered the ball to the near post. I was ready. In a flash I raced to the near post to flick the cross into the net with my head. The Newcastle centre-half was dumbfounded. It was incredible the number of times we scored with that move.' It certainly helped England to win the World Cup.

59.

NORTHERN EXPOSURE: THE DECLINE AND FALL OF BURNLEY

THIS CHAPTER describes the plight of Burnley, a small northern town and football club with an illustrious past, brought low by industrial recession and reduced competitiveness, a legacy of the 'winner takes all' scenario following the abolition of the maximum wage. It was a fate shared with other north-western clubs such as Preston, Bolton, Blackburn, and Blackpool.

Burnley's economy 1911 to 2011

The industrial revolution converted Burnley from a small, quiet, out-of-the-way market town into the world's largest single producer of cotton cloth. Its typically damp atmosphere was conducive to the manufacture of cotton fibre, which quickly displaced wool as the nation's number one textile when British colonial markets opened a massive export trade for light cloth. The ready availability of local coal – by 1800, there were a dozen pits in the town centre alone – meant Burnley was ripe for rapid industrialisation. Its population grew from 10,000 in 1801 to 21,000 in 1851 before expanding prodigiously to 106,322 by 1911.

The town's football fortunes reflected its increasing economic prosperity, with its premier team capable of attracting the best talent in the country in the early 20th century. In 1914, Burnley won the FA Cup for the first and only time, thus far, defeating Liverpool 1-0 at the Crystal Palace ground. Shortly after the First World War, Burnley won the First Division for the first time. However, the tide of prosperity had begun to ebb by the time that hostilities ended in 1918. With the textile trade and coal mining stuttering during the inter-war depression, the town's population fell by almost 20 per cent between 1921 and 1939.

In 1959, when Burnley were winning the First Division title, the town was caught up in a dilemma about how it should sustain its economic future. Reflecting national misgivings about shifting from a heavy manufacturing base, there were concerns in Burnley about relinquishing those industries which had made the town successful – textiles and coal. In this regard, Burnley was comparable with other nearby mill towns, including Preston, Blackburn and Bolton, First Division competitors when the maximum wage was abolished.

There were certain industrialists and local politicians who thought that the cotton trade could still be salvaged through new technology and increasing specialisation. There were morale-boosting lectures about the continued importance of coal. There seemed to be a strong belief that alternative manufacturing (aircraft components, fridges, tyres etc.) could be made to work despite growing evidence that many items could be produced more cheaply abroad. When new employers were courted to replace the closing mills and mines, greater faith was placed in specialist manufacturing than in service industries.

Helped by post-war modernisation in both the mills and the pits, there was a brief recovery during the early '50s, with almost full employment, but even the introduction of cheap labour, recruited from the Indian subcontinent from the early '50s onwards, could only defer but not prevent the abdication of 'King Cotton'. Ultimately, there was no way of competing with low-cost Far-Eastern competition. Consequently, the town's population continued to decline, falling by a further five per cent between 1951 and 1961.

Nevertheless, the economic decline was slowed during the first part of the '50s. In fact, there was a shortage of labour in the mills with school-leavers seeing little long-term prospect in the trade. Those who remained in the town tended to opt for apprenticeships at the new manufacturers such as Lucas components, which had moved some of its Birmingham-based operations to Burnley during the war and had retained its business here on account of the lower wage costs. Young apprentices at Lucas knew they could transfer their accredited skills to areas such as Birmingham where higher earnings could be gained.

Therefore, the mills were required to recruit employees from outside the Burnley area. Not only were Asian immigrants encouraged to move into Burnley but also unemployed Londoners, too. Inducements were offered in the form of council housing, for example.

It would be wrong to give the impression that the town was resting upon its laurels and not embracing change. A variety of new manufacturers had been successfully attracted to the area besides Lucas. These included Mullards electrical components, Belling electric cookers, Michelin, Rolls-Royce at Barnoldswick, and Rover at Clitheroe. Moreover, cotton manufacturers consolidated, diversified, and specialised to meet the new economic climate, also taking over the production of man-made fibres. Qualitex was an example of a local firm re-establishing itself in specialist production. Regrettably, this did not last after Qualitex was taken over by a larger competitor, ICI. Nevertheless, there was hope that a slimmed-down, modernised, diversified and specialist textile business might still be made to work.

In 1959, arguments raged back and forth in Burnley about what should be done. Attempts were made to enlist government assistance in attracting new industry to the town, but the government would not act while the employment figures were so high. While the present employment statistics gave hope that things were not as bad as some claimed, it was clear to the local MPs that these figures falsified the true situation. Mills were closing rapidly but to honour outstanding orders, some would run double shifts staffed with temporary labour.

The high rate of closure was encouraged by the government's Cotton Industry Act which sought to rationalise the cotton industry, providing financial inducements to owners to scrap their looms and 'weave out'. However, new jobs were not being created at the speed at which old ones were being lost. The temporary employment arrangements were merely disguising that fact. Places such as Burnley were once the crucible of the industrial revolution whereas by the later '60s and early '70s, they resembled its casket.

Seen from the heights of its surrounding moors in 1959, Burnley seemed to be still thriving. As supporter Lester Davidson recalled, 'In 1960 you could still see at least 14 mill chimneys in Burnley in any direction you cared to look.' This was no museum. An industrial pall still hung over the town with fumes belching from the mill chimneys. The new factories hummed and clattered with activity and hoppy aromas from Massey's Brewery still scented the Burnley air. Meanwhile, panting, clanking coal trains still struggled up Copy Pit, their hoarse whistles echoing across the valley, as they had done for 100 years.

As much as the local paper talked up the brighter prospects ahead, there was no denying the fact that the town's traditional industries were in various stages of retreat and its new ones stamped with a limited life span. With Burnley positioned precariously away from the main national transport networks, new trade was difficult to attract. The town's hopes and fears, warnings, and reassurances about its economic future, were played out week by week in the local press. That dialogue intensified on account of the General Election taking place in October 1959. But oblivious to the growing economic threats the town's football team continued to progress towards their prestigious prize, the First Division title.

Many manufacturers which moved into Burnley after 1959 disappeared, with the last deep coal mine, at Hapton Valley Colliery, closing in February 1981. Cotton went as well with the last steam-powered mill, Queen Street Mill, Briercliffe, closing in 1982. Over the ensuing decades, Burnley's two largest manufacturers both closed their factories: Prestige in July 1997 and Michelin in April 2002.

The town has struggled to recover. Its employment growth between 1995 and 2004 placed it 55th of England's 56 largest towns and cities and as of 2007 it was the 21st most deprived local authority (out of 354) in the United Kingdom. At the end of the noughties, almost 100 years after the town was at its peak, the largest employment sector was public administration, education and health (31.2 per cent), followed by manufacturing (21.9 per cent). Key manufacturing employers at the end of the noughties were in highly specialised fields: Gardner Aerospace, Safran Aircelle Unison Engine Components (aerospace components) and TRW Automotive (automotive components). In 2004, the Lancashire Digital Technology Centre was established on land formerly occupied by the now-closed Michelin factory to provide support and incubation space for start-up technology companies.

Burnley FC 1960 to 2020

Before the mandatory wage cap and the feudal 'retain and transfer' system were removed in the early '60s, a talented, tactically astute

'David', like Burnley or Ipswich Town, could defeat richer, more fancied 'Goliaths' over the long, rugged haul of a First Division football season. But even then, money screamed. As with Ipswich's championship in 1961/62, Burnley's victory in 1959/60 was a triumph against the odds. Thereafter, those odds grew ever longer for a team like Burnley. Situated in a small, secluded, declining area, Burnley's team, like its town, required more resources than it could muster by its own productivity to thrive. The abolition of the footballers' maximum wage in 1961 not only disturbed the balance sheet, it also meant that the team could no longer rely upon attracting the best young talent.

That talent would go increasingly to the highest bidder. As a small-town club with limited means greater efficiencies needed to be found while facing increasing competition from richer clubs. Following the consumer boom of the late '50s football had rival leisure attractions to contend with. And as that boom unravelled during the '60s with British manufacturing becoming less competitive, leading to a worsening imbalance of trade, Burnley FC was forced to consider how it should market itself within the confines of a declining local economy. Its 'sell to survive' policy was born in this climate. Regrettably, that policy could only work while the club remained in the top flight and was seen to give its talented youngsters an earlier opportunity to shine on the big stage. By so doing, Burnley could still hope to compete with and confound the more lucrative enticements offered by larger clubs.

However, it needed its youth policy to deliver at a consistently high rate of productivity to plug the gaps left by its departing stars. By the mid-'60s Bob Lord, Burnley's blunt, autocratic, yet canny and far-sighted chairman, had been forced to sell at least one of his stars each season for a high return in order to offset annual revenue losses and the wincing cost of ground improvements. Once the likes of John Connelly (£40,000), Gordon Harris (£70,000), Willie Morgan (£117,000), Ralph Coates (£190,000), Steve Kindon (£100,000), Brian O'Neil (£75,000), Dave Thomas (£165,000), Martin Dobson (£300,000) and Leighton James (£310,000) had departed, the 'sell to survive' policy faltered.

With Burnley's bumper harvests of young talent disappearing, its team strength eroded, and its support fell away. With the law of diminishing returns biting ever deeper into its prospects, the club slid steadily, but ultimately rapidly, downwards to that traumatic day in May 1987 when the club was poised precariously on the brink of oblivion. Other once-famous northern clubs, including Bolton, Blackburn, Preston and Huddersfield, have suffered similar fates in the mid-20th century as recession and poverty gripped these post-industrial towns.

60.

BURNLEY v WEST BROMWICH ALBION: FIRST DIVISION, 21 MARCH 1970

IT WAS a foul day. Dirty, ragged clouds rolled in from the Irish Sea, dragging with them curtains of rain. Stepping out on to a greasy cobbled street, a blustery wind propelled stinging, spiteful rain into our screwed-up faces. All around us were the scars of industrial blight: the derelict mills, the oily canal, the empty unwanted housing, earmarked for demolition, and the rusted, weed-strewn marshalling yards. Yet in this secluded valley, beneath the drab and rain-darkened moors, the stone-terraced housing that survived appeared welcoming. The inviting light falling from their latticed windows, the flickering front room fires, did not mock our discomfort. Almost perversely, it gave us a sense of how homely it was here. So did the Burnley fans with their jaunty gallows humour.

The football club, like its town, was a declining force. A newly constructed, all-seated stand had been built at the western end, but the southern flank was a cordoned-off demolition site. Post-war austerity characterised the remaining parts of the ground. Rusted roof girders dripped with the penetrating rain, pools of grubby water gathering in the holed concrete and tarmac. In step with their surroundings, the kids exuded nonchalant toughness. It was not so much their Bovver Boots or their scuffed scarves, tied tightly to their wrists. None of them wore coats.

They seemed oblivious to winter's late riposte. I was deeply impressed.

Harry Potts was no longer in charge. He had been pushed 'upstairs' as general manager, allowing former captain, coach and favourite son Jimmy Adamson to take over team affairs. Harry's move was made to keep Adamson at the club. After all, Adamson had an impressive reputation as a coach. Bobby Charlton rated him. He had been schooled for the England job, to follow Walter Winterbottom, but turned it down.

Chairman Bob Lord thought that the Potts–Adamson partnership was his dream ticket, pairing Potts's impressive managerial track record with Adamson's vaunted coaching skills. Besides, as manager and skipper, they had complemented one another so well during the club's glory years. In 1963, Adamson still thought so highly of Potts that he recommended him as a part-time adviser to new England manager, Alf Ramsey. But after Adamson was appointed as first team coach one year later, it was not long before their relationship became strained.

Adamson was steeped in modern tactical thinking. Potts was more of an old-school thinker, wedded to what had worked well for him in the past, not appreciating, perhaps, that he no longer had the surfeit of talent which could make up for any tactical deficiencies. Whereas the excitable, enthusiastic Potts rarely gave detailed instruction about how he wanted his team to play, the ostensibly cooler Adamson was much more specific about what he wanted from his players, using training ground drills and blackboard diagrams to make his points.

But it was not just a clash of ideas that was the problem. With the club's fortunes fading and its average attendances falling to 16,072, the lowest in the top flight, Burnley had to sell to survive. The growing pressure on the bottom line caused the cracks to widen in the Potts–Adamson relationship. Their differences in personality and style started to grate. From rubbing along famously they began to rub one another up the wrong way.

One-club man Brian Miller was a Potts fan. In fact, he based his later managerial style upon Potts's way. He was aware of Harry's tactical limitations, though. Brian remembered suffering a heavy defeat at Ipswich in 1961. Potts attributed it to the humid conditions, failing to recognise how Ramsey had out-thought him. Brian added, 'There was no inquest or fuss made by Harry, it was simply "ah well, let's get on with the next game".'

Former left-back Les Latcham became a first-team regular in 1967, following the transfer of Alex Elder to Stoke. He told Burnley writer Dave Thomas how the atmosphere gradually soured between Potts and Adamson. Les said, 'It became increasingly clear that the partnership was not working, and that Adamson wanted sole control. This was not an unnatural ambition. He had his own theories, tactics, and aspirations. It meant, however, that there was growing confusion about exactly who was in charge. If there is one thing that footballers want it is clarity. But this was becoming blurred and the happy club was splitting into pro-Adamson and pro-Potts camps as loyalties were divided.

'Burnley's ace midfielder, Ralph Coates remembered Jimmy Adamson promising him that he would start the next game, after playing well in a previous one. However, Potts over-ruled this. Willie Irvine also recalled that Adamson had decided he would not feature in one of the Fairs Cup games. It was Potts who informed him, though, and when Irvine asked why he was not playing, Potts replied it was Adamson's decision and nothing to do with him.'

Clearly, this divisive situation was not helping anyone, least of all the team's prospects.

In February 1970, the change was made. Lord appointed Adamson as team manager and Potts was 'pushed upstairs'. Surprisingly, it came about after Nottingham Forest had been thrashed 5-0 at home, Burnley's fourth win in a five-match unbeaten run. It was clear, then, that this had been a planned decision, although Potts had not been consulted. Potts graciously acknowledged Adamson's accession, saying, 'I could not hand over to a better fellow.' But he was devastated to be excluded from the Gawthorpe training ground. Potts never lost his love of the place, rubbing his hands on icy mornings, excitedly exclaiming, 'It's just like Switzerland.'

Potts found it hard to adjust to the role of general manager. He had been a father figure to many of his younger players, having rescued Steve Kindon after he had been thrown out by his landlady; and comforting Ralph Coates during a family bereavement. According to Thomas, Harry's wife Margaret harboured a grudge about the affair, feeling that her husband had been stabbed in the back. When she and Harry were denied a top table place at the club's annual dinner, she had no hesitation in speaking her mind. What had been a happy, close-knit club began to fragment.

It was not just the club management which was in a state of flux. The team was changing markedly. Only full-back John Angus remained from the 1959/60 championship-winning side. By then, goalkeeper Adam Blacklaw had moved on and central defender Brian Miller had retired hurt. But still young hearts ran free. Wingers Kindon and Dave Thomas (not the writer by the same name) were the newish kids in town, complementing established home-grown stars like Coates and midfield enforcer Brian O'Neil, plus astute signings like striker Frank Casper and attacking midfielder Martin Dobson. Kindon and Thomas had graduated from the youth team that had won the FA Youth Cup in 1968. In his programme notes for the Albion game, Potts purred about Adamson's gifted youngsters, who had done him proud in the 3-3 midweek draw at Old Trafford.

Potts wrote, 'Congratulations to Jimmy Adamson and his team on a fine performance. We have a most promising set of players. Next season looks likely to be an important, exhilarating one for this club and its supporters. Two-up after five minutes and 3-1 ahead at the break, it certainly seemed to be our night. It was just our luck that Manchester United pulled one back midway through the second half and grabbed another in the final minutes.'

Potts picked out Kindon and Thomas as his men of the match. Kindon hammered in the first goal from 25 yards while Thomas's quick feet accounted for the other two. 'Breathtaking footwork,' said Potts.

Not that Potts's pre-match euphoria inhibited West Bromwich. A skidding strike from midfielder 'Bomber' Brown gave the visitors a 21st-minute lead. This was a nasty setback, for Burnley were still in relegation trouble in 18th position. That midweek point at Old Trafford had been a good result but did little to ease their worries about the drop. Stung by the early blow, Burnley set about wresting control from the Baggies, who were two points better off. Gradually, the collective industry of flitting Coates, twinkling Thomas, terrier-like O'Neil and dogged Bellamy forced their West Bromwich counterparts to concede the soggy centre ground. Increasing pressure was placed upon Albion's suspect defence.

Kindon was in 'runaway wardrobe' mode. Making light of the heavy conditions, he powered in from the left, uninhibited by surface water, spattering mud and despairing tackles, launching muscular assaults on Osborne's goal. Warming to his efforts, the home crowd set aside their groaning and moaning, and threw themselves wholeheartedly into the fray. Belligerently bellowing their side on, they were suitably rewarded in the 36th minute when Kindon's powerful running enabled him to break through the left side of the Baggies' defence. Not stopping to take aim, from 18 yards he lashed home a fierce, rising drive that screamed into the net. Albion goalkeeper Osborne hardly saw the ball, let alone attempted to save it. The visceral force of Kindon's shot unleashed a leaping tumult on the Longside terracing. The sullen away support was treated to their jabbing gestures of derision.

The rain grew in intensity as a premature dusk descended. The glare of the floodlights flashed and twinkled in the muddy pools appearing all over the pitch. As the second half progressed, the game became, quite simply, a trial of strength. It was a challenge that Burnley's youngsters were determined to win. By the time that Bellamy's slithering long-range effort had evaded a thicket of legs and found goal, there was only five minutes left. Neat football had been abandoned. The main objective was to propel the ball as far forward as possible and set off after it in dogged pursuit. Hacking it clear of the mud and puddles seemed to require Herculean power. We felt exhausted by association.

The crowd continued to urge Burnley forward, hurling encouragement and invective in equal measure, but the Clarets could not find another way through. It did not matter. By then, West Brom had lost their way. Little did I realise, but a claret and blue potion had been injected into my veins on that foul afternoon. Life would never be the same again.

Burnley stayed up that season. The two points they took off West Bromwich meant that only two more were required from their final six fixtures. Two more victories, 1-0 over Newcastle and 3-1 against Chelsea, plus a hat-trick of 1-1 draws, made that task a formality. Adamson crowed, 'We have a wonderful set of young players at Turf Moor and although we haven't won any senior honours we are soon going to. Mark my words. Our potential is better than that of all other clubs and I do mean all. Some First Division managers would give their right arms for our teenagers.'

Adamson was so confident in his young guns that he paraded them en masse in the 1-1 Good Friday home draw with Stoke. Coates, at 23, was the oldest in that line-up. Despite Adamson's faith, his emerging stars could not live with Eddie Gray's master-class in the penultimate game of the season as Leeds triumphed 2-1 at Elland Road.

A year later Burnley were relegated, 11 seasons after their title triumph, joining their once famous north-west rivals in the Second Division. By the end of the '70s Burnley's average gate had fallen below 10,000 as they dropped to the bottom of the table. By the mid-'80s Burnley were in the lower reaches of the Fourth Division with gates of under 2,000 for midweek games.

Hope was in short supply with their survival as a club dependent on a win-or-bust game against Orient. At last fortune smiled in front of over 15,000 fans. A year later they met Wolves in the Sherpa Van Trophy at Wembley watched by more than 81,000, and a miraculous recovery began. Twenty-one years later Burnley reached the Premier League and despite experiencing two relegations have managed to remain there for five seasons and possibly more, too, a remarkable feat for such a small club and town.

Falling support at north-west clubs 1957/58 to 1966/67

NW clubs' average gates	57/58	58/59	59/60	60/61	61/62	62/63	63/64	64/65	65/66	66/67	change 57/58 to 66/67	% change
Preston	24908	22400	24530	16894	13077	12000	18821	15621	14022	14350	-10558	-42.4%
Blackpool	21402	20859	21770	18528	18617	18361	16540	18641	16185	17187	-4215	-19.7%
Bolton	22080	27658	27104	21669	17518	19298	16830	14649	11837	13235	-8845	-40.1%
Burnley	22251	23745	26869	24442	27125	25518	19755	15739	19950	20350	-1901	-8.5%
Blackburn	22640	30500	25061	19300	15908	16000	21543	16109	13513	14720	-7920	-35.0%
Total	113281	125162	125334	100833	92245	91177	93489	80759	75507	79842	-33439	-29.5%

Preston were relegated in 1961, Bolton in 1964, Blackburn in 1966, Blackpool in 1967, and Burnley in 1971.

61.

'WORLD CUP WILLIES' 1970

WITH ENGLAND expected to do well in the Mexico World Cup, prime minister Harold Wilson hoped to trade on the feelgood factor. He planned a General Election after the quarter-finals.

Alas, it was to end in tears for both Ramsey and Wilson. Alf Ramsey's class of '70 was touted as his strongest but England's form had not been startling. Having lost to Yugoslavia in the 1968 European Championship, England weren't even the best team in Europe, let alone the world. During 1968, their record had been unremarkable – inferior to both West Germany and Czechoslovakia. Although England progressed through the final group stages on the back of dull 1-0 victories over Romania and Czechoslovakia, their 1-0 defeat by the brilliant Brazilians underlined how difficult it would be for them to retain their crown.

But it was not the sublime Pelé and his superb team who caused England's downfall, it was that durable old enemy, West Germany. With bad luck, crucial goalkeeping errors and a mistaken substitution contributing to their loss, having been 2-0 ahead, it was not only England's hopes that evaporated in the searing heat of Leon.

Harold Wilson's chances of electoral victory faded too. Ramsey was a bust flush. England were eliminated from the 1972 European Championship at the qualification quarter-final stage by a vastly superior West German side. Having lost the first leg 3-1 at Wembley, Ramsey's side for the second leg seemed set up to defend that deficit. They also failed to qualify for the next two World Cup finals.

After Poland held England to a 1-1 draw on 17 October 1973, meaning they proceeded to that summer's tournament at their hosts' expense, Ramsey's days were numbered. On 1 May 1974 he was sacked and replaced by Joe Mercer. However, it would take England until the Italy World Cup in 1990 to make a credible bid for honours; 1966 had been just a brief spell in the Wembley sun.

While England's national side'has continually failed to add to its 1966 silverware, English clubs have acquitted themselves successfully in European competitions during the '60s, '70s and '80s. Manchester United won the European Cup in 1968 while Leeds won the Inter-Cities or European Fairs Cup twice, in 1968 and 1971, with Newcastle, in 1969, and Arsenal, in 1970, following suit. This was before this competition was re-branded as the UEFA Cup after the 1970/71 season when Chelsea emulated Spurs, West Ham and Manchester City in winning the European Cup Winners' Cup. These successes helped establish a glorious era during the '70s and '80s, when Liverpool won the European and UEFA Cup on multiple occasions, when Nottingham Forest won successive European Cup finals, and Aston Villa had their solitary taste of European Cup glory. Meanwhile, Spurs won the UEFA Cup twice and Ipswich once, and Everton lifted the UEFA Cup Winners' trophy in 1985. This is a clear measure of how the international competitiveness of English clubs improved dramatically after the '50s.

62.

ALAN BROWN: 'A MAN FOR ALL SEASONS'

AS A football manager, mainly during the '50s and '60s, Alan Brown's style and personality divided opinions among those he managed.

For many he was a charismatic innovator, a frank modernist among countless anachronists. His disciples regarded him as a tough, censorious, yet compassionate man, a shrewd tactician dedicated to recruiting and developing promising young players. He was a captivating coach, an evangelist of the coaching gospel preached by FA head of coaching Walter Winterbottom. He urged his players to follow his example and obtain their coaching certificates, not only to spread the word, but to broaden their competencies for a life beyond playing.

For some, though, Brown was regarded as a dogmatic tyrant who would brook no argument. According to Stan Anderson, author of *Stan Anderson: Captain of the North*, written with Mark Metcalf, he and Brown did not get on. Anderson had been Sunderland's captain under Brown. He was loyal to the club he had supported as a boy. As a player, Anderson racked up 402 senior appearances for Sunderland in an 11-year stay. He was popular with his team-mates and the Roker fans, but was summarily transferred to Newcastle in November 1963, much against his wishes, after he attempted to persuade Brown to adopt a different way of playing. After Sunderland had crushed Preston 4-1 in an FA Cup tie in early 1963 with a 4-2-4 formation, Anderson tried to persuade Brown to stick with this set-up. Brown took exception to this. The altercation that followed festered, souring their relationship. Anderson explained some years later: 'Playing for the team I supported was always a privilege and a pleasure for me.

I never wanted to leave Sunderland but eventually Browny bombed me out. I knew there would be trouble if I swapped stripes. I was in a family of dyed-in-the-wool red and whites!

'Was Brown a difficult man? That was like asking if the sun was hot?' Anderson told Sunderland fan and author, Mark Metcalf: 'Brown was the *boss* and he would not have any truck with anyone challenging his authority. He thought I was too big for my boots. I was not trying to take his job off him. I was quite prepared to work under him.

'At Newcastle, manager Joe Harvey was like a breath of fresh air. He was prepared to listen. Browny was not.'

Brown admitted, 'I think everywhere I've been I've been viewed at the start with distaste.' As a member of the international Moral Re-Armament movement, he came over as a fierce and ascetic moral warrior. Some of those who played alongside Brian Clough at Roker Park during the early '60s, remarked that Clough only listened unquestioningly to two people in his life – his mother and Alan Brown. The first time Brown met Clough he told his young striker, 'You may have heard people say that I'm a bastard. Well, they're right.' He prided himself on his commitment to his work saying, 'I get an hour's work out of an hour's time. I think I'm known for that.'

When a cruciate knee ligament injury ended Clough's playing career, Brown encouraged him to seek a career in football management. When Clough graduated to the dugout, he often said, 'I wish I had Alan Brown beside me.'

Brown remained as Clough's mentor, even during the glory years at Forest. Sports author and former Nottingham journalist Duncan Hamilton once told me that whenever Brown arrived at the City Ground, Clough treated him like royalty. Brown's belief that football was God's gift resonated with Clough, who was convinced he was God's gift to football.

Brown was the son of a painter and decorator and was sent to Hexham Grammar School as a child. Brown had an insatiable appetite for knowledge. While at Hexham Grammar School he developed an ambition to become a teacher. However, this was during the Great Depression of the 1930s. He was a member of a large working-class family. His parents could not afford to pay for his further education.

Brown's other passion was football. He described it as 'one of the biggest things that happened in Creation'. However, at Hexham, the school only played rugby, so he had to play as a stand-off half for the school team on Saturday mornings and as a centre-half for a local youth football team in the afternoons. Brown's cousin, Austin Campbell played as a half-back for Huddersfield Town and Blackburn Rovers. He was also an England international. Brown also joined Huddersfield in 1933, at the age of 16. Brown was persuaded by his cousin, Huddersfield's captain, to sign as a trainee. Brown hoped that the club would sponsor his further education, although he was soon disappointed. Unable to settle, he left and spent the following two and a half years as a policeman. Brown's love for football eventually led him to leave the police force, rejoining Huddersfield, and appearing in 57 matches prior to the Second World War.

After the war, Brown was given a transfer and moved to Burnley. Although he was 32 years old when the 1946/47 season began, new Burnley manager Cliff Britton recognised Brown's abilities, both as a tough, uncompromising but thoughtful centre-half, and as an inspirational and authoritative leader capable of motivating his fellows and organising an 'Iron Curtain' defence. With Brown alongside fellow defenders Reg Attwell, George Bray, Arthur Woodruff, Harold Mather, and goalkeeper Jimmy Strong, Burnley earned promotion from the Second Division at their first attempt, conceding just 29 goals. This figure is still a club record low in a 42-game season. Brown played in every game. The club also reached the FA Cup Final in this long, arctic season, losing 1-0 to Charlton Athletic after extra time.

Another good campaign followed in 1947/48 with Brown missing just six games and Burnley managing to finish third in the top division, with only goal average separating them from Manchester United in second. The defence was again an integral part of Burnley's success, conceding just 43 goals despite the promotion to a higher division. Only champions Arsenal conceded fewer.

After Brown had played in ten games of the 1948/49 season, Burnley accepted an offer of around £15,000 from Notts County for him. Brown was still club captain and a first team regular. This was a huge fee then, worth about £15m today, for a 34-year-old defender. His stay at Notts County was only short, though, with Brown retiring from professional football three months later, having played in only 13 games. He moved back to Burnley and opened a restaurant while also obtaining coaching qualifications.

This persuaded Stanley Rous, secretary of the Football Association, to suggest to Brown that he should return to the game as a full-time coach. In 1951, Brown joined Sheffield Wednesday in this capacity. He remained at Hillsborough for three and a half seasons before being appointed as Burnley's new manager in 1954, Frank Hill having left to join Preston North End. Brown's arrival back at the club was not well received by some of the senior players who were unhappy being managed by a man of fierce, moral integrity. Undeterred by the potential backlash, Brown set about instilling into his players the values of righteousness, hard work and honesty that he held dear. Bob Seith, Burnley's 1959/60 championship-winning right-half, was hugely impressed by Brown.

I met Bob a few years ago in his native Dundee. He told me, 'Let me be clear about who was the architect of that title triumph in 1960. It was not Harry Potts who took us over the line. It was Alan Brown, who preceded him. Brown devised the array of dead ball routines that proved so successful. He introduced short corners when our forward line was too small to benefit from lofted crosses. It was him who brought in "shadow play", where the forward line attacks without defenders to impede them, to sharpen our rhythm, movement and passing accuracy. He was inspirational. He was exacting, though.

'I remember a pre-season game in which he was constantly urging our left-winger, Brian Pilkington, to run faster. In the first half he was continually urging him on, running along the cinder track beside him shouting, "Go! Go! Go!" Brian slumped in the dressing room at half-time, saying, "Well at least that bastard won't be able to get at me in the second half." The dugout was on the opposite flank. But Brian reckoned without Brown's tenacity. Brown switched sides for the second half, so Brian got another earful.

'Alan Brown was a stickler for high standards in everything he and his players did.'

But Bob discovered his softer side during a time of family bereavement. He recalled, 'I was so upset I didn't think I could play. Alan Brown was superb. He placed no pressure on me to turn out, but said, "If you do choose to play, think of your lost loved one. Play for her." That did it. I resolved to play and had a great game. That was down to Brown's thoughtfulness.'

Bob credited Brown with initiating the club's youth policy which resulted in hundreds of talented young players being recruited under the noses of the bigger clubs which ensured that Burnley remained as a force during the '50s and for much of the '60s. He said, 'Alan Brown persuaded chairman Bob Lord to buy some land adjacent to Gawthorpe Hall to develop it as a training ground. Many top clubs then did not have their own training facilities. Many used the cinder car parks or the areas underneath the stands. It was so primitive, but our own training ground which we helped build in the summer of 1955 was a state-of-the-art construction. It was a warm summer, but Alan led us in digging the foundations and trenches for the brickies, plumbers, and electricians to finish the job. That was really hard work but fun. Alan did not flinch. By the end I was so fit it was frightening.'

Towards the end of Bob's successful football career with Burnley and Dundee, he returned to Lancashire in 1968, to manage Preston North End. Bob found a once famous club in steep decline. True to his mentor, Alan Brown, Bob tried to instil good professional standards. He said, 'I needed to be tight on discipline because the players had not grasped good habits. I remember laying the law down to a group of them, emphasising how important it was that they looked after themselves, if they were to make the most of their short careers. I knew full well how privileged I had been to be a professional footballer. However, I am not sure that all of them cottoned on. I remember saying to them, "For the brief time that you play this game you must be prepared to live like monks!" I could hear Alan saying this!

'The casual attitude of some of the players irked me. I recall a time when Archie Gemmill was on our bench. During the pre-match warm-up he was shuffling around with his hands in the pockets of his tracksuit. I immediately asked the laundry staff to sew up the pockets of each player's tracksuit. Malcolm Allison also referred to a decline in players' personal standards during the '70s when the hunger of old had eroded in more prosperous times.

'I wouldn't tolerate long hair, either. This did not go down well. Some players complained that George Best could have long hair, to which I replied, "When you can play like him your hair can be as long as you like." As tough as I needed to be, it must have had some positive impact. One of my signings was Willie Irvine, from Burnley. He later remarked that though I was strict, I was always fair and well respected by the players. That's nice to know.' Bob was right. Willie Irvine speaks of Bob with great fondness and admiration.

Brown's legacy rolls on. Brown influenced Clough who in turn influenced a young Forest apprentice by the name of Sean Dyche, who at Burnley is now practising modern versions of the set play moves that Brown initiated at the club in the mid-'50s. Talk about 'Dead Ball Descendants', with apologies to The Fall for adapting one of their song titles.

Former Burnley striker Jimmy Robson began his professional football career in 1956 under Alan Brown. He told me, 'Alan Brown was good to me. A no-nonsense fella with a "they shall not pass attitude" but he did not coach that way. He wanted us to pass the ball. He was tough and strongly principled but did not impose his moral standards upon us. He led from the front as a tracksuit manager.

'I remember a time when we were playing away, and he got the train times wrong, leaving us with a long wait at Preston. He just laughed it off and got out a pack of cards to while away the time. It was wrong to say he did not have a sense of humour. He was a canny psychologist. He knew how best to handle us when we were struggling against a better side. He was very good, too, when my grandmother died. He got me on the train back to County Durham that evening. He was far-sighted as well, arranging summer games against strong European opposition.

'He did not like Germans, though. I suppose it was a legacy of the war. We were due to play in Essen on one summer trip. The weather was foul. It was bitter with icy rain. But Alan insisted we trained on the pitch doing press-ups and sit-ups before the game. We were absolutely soaking. We were due to play a West German select XI. It was a strong team, but we won 3-1. I am sure we were made to go through that pre-match fitness routine so he could show the other team how tough we were. We could not wait to get into the hot showers at the final whistle.

'Those foreign games were good for us. We learnt to play against a sweeper system, for example. Sometimes we had to endure ten-minute periods when we were denied possession but did not lose focus. Alan Brown did a lot for Burnley, expanding our horizons. Several of us followed his example and obtained our coaching badges. Unfortunately, he fell out with chairman Bob Lord and left us in 1957.'

Brown was appointed as Sunderland manager at a time when the club was awash with scandals over illegal payments to players. The club was struggling at the bottom of the First Division table, not helped by the internecine squabbling between the players. Brown saw the appointment as an opportunity to 'clean up' the club that he had supported as a child.

It was a time when parents were often bribed to get their sons to sign for a club. Brown refused to comply with this practice which breached FA and Football League rules. Brown recalled, 'On two occasions parents have said to me, when I came to the point of signing their lads, "Well, what about a bit of so and so?" My reply was, "Look, you can take your boy home if you like, but you won't get anything illegal here." Then they said, "Well, what about a suit of clothes for the lad?" I replied, "If and when he goes abroad with us, he'll get his blazer and flannels like everybody else."'

Brown inspired fear, even in Clough. He set strict club rules including fining players for minor indiscretions. He ordered the senior players to be ball boys for the youth team and yanked Clough off the touchline for talking to a friend during training. According to Duncan Hamilton, Brown 'dressed him down, like a schoolboy caught with matches in his pockets'. His training drills were tough too, as in the arctic winter of 1962–63 when he arranged sessions in the freezing North Sea. He allegedly used golf balls for heading practice, too.

Despite Brown's arrival, Sunderland were relegated in 1958 for the first time in their history. It was not a great start to his time at Roker Park. But in succeeding years Brown gradually turned the club's fortunes around while also ridding the club of corruption.

Ex-Sunderland left-back Len Ashurst recalled, 'Brown arrived at Roker Park in July 1957 having had a successful period in charge at Burnley. He had a no-nonsense approach and a firm belief in building his teams with younger players. He was ahead of his time as a football innovator as well as being highly thought of at the Football

Association as a forward-thinking coach. As at Burnley, he gained his chairman's approval to create a training ground at Cleadon.

'This was a masterstroke. And yet after he got us back in the First Division at the end of the 1963/64 season, having endured the heartache of two close calls in 1961/62, when we were pipped by Leyton Orient, and in 1962/63, when Stoke and Chelsea triumphed instead of us. When we went up, Brown was denied a £1,000 bonus that we, the players, received. So, he resigned. He was not even granted the dispensation to buy his club house at the original price as most of the senior players were. He must have made enemies in the boardroom. It was a difficult pill for us to swallow. He was our guiding light, the driving force behind our success.'

Instead, Brown was lured to Sheffield Wednesday. Hillsborough was then regarded as the most sumptuously appointed stadium in the land. Before the start of the 1964/65 season the Wednesday board targeted Brown as their next manager with the aim of cleaning up the club in the wake of the match-fixing scandal that had scarred the club, with three of their former players being jailed. Brown was well respected among the players and quickly restored pride in the club. Against expectations, Brown led the club to the FA Cup Final in 1966, their first final in over 30 years. His assistant at Hillsborough was Lawrie McMenemy, later becoming a successful manager at Southampton.

Lawrie told me, 'I first came across Alan Brown when he was at Sunderland. I was then a coach at Bishop Auckland. I asked Alan for a pre-season game. I was delighted when he brought a strong team. Bishop Auckland had been a successful amateur side, winning the FA Amateur Cup at Wembley on several occasions. But by the mid-'60s, it was living off its former glories. Anyway, I stayed in touch with Alan afterwards. In 1965, when he had moved to Sheffield Wednesday, he contacted me to say that he was coming up to Newcastle and asked to see my wife and I at Low Fell, Gateshead. I was not sure why he wanted to see both of us, but we went along with his request.

'I was surprised when he asked to speak with my wife first. He was very charming. My wife did not have a problem with this. I remember the time clearly as our second child had just been born. Apparently, he wanted to know from my wife whether she was prepared to leave the North East. My wife told him she wanted to move away from the area.

'He then explained that he was changing his staff and would like me to become his assistant. I was delighted to do this. I shared the first team coaching with Ian McFarlane, formerly of Bath City. We alternated the responsibility.

'Alan was a terrific man to work under. He led by example, teaching us things without knowing it. I knew he had been the architect of the Washington training ground while at Sunderland. He had an incredible attention to detail. He had a heart of gold, too, but did not want to show it. When one of his players was involved in a car crash in which his girlfriend died, he immediately went to see him at home.

'There was sometimes tension between Alan and general manager Eric Taylor. They did not always see eye to eye. But it was a good move for me. He introduced shadow training at Hillsborough, as he had done elsewhere. He also encouraged us to go to Lilleshall where we could hear the views of visiting coaches from abroad which improved our knowledge. Alan was so dedicated. He arranged Sunday morning training with the kids which included Gary Megson, Don's son. Every boy had a ball to work with.

'What stands out in my mind about him was the canny psychology he used during a home game with Chelsea. During the mid-'60s, Docherty's Chelsea were a terrific side, scorching pace, darting movement, and crisp exchanges of passes. They packed a strong punch up front with Osgood and Tambling. Well, they were at their best on that evening and by half-time they were ahead. Our players came in looking downcast. Alan did not yell at them. He was very calm and measured, saying quietly to them, "Chelsea are a good team, better than I thought they would be. Can you suggest how we might be stronger?" Because he did not destroy them with criticism and instead put himself alongside them, the players felt freer to suggest potential remedies like "I could get a bit tighter to x" and so on. This was brilliant. The players went out re-empowered and performed a lot better.'

Although the 1966 FA Cup Final was not expected to be an attractive game, it turned out to be one of the best, a wonderful back-and-forth contest. Everton had reached Wembley without conceding a goal while Wednesday had won every match away from home at the first attempt. Wednesday dominated for the first hour, taking a 2-0 lead, but Everton mounted a comeback with a brace of goals from unexpected selection Mike Trebilcock, and went on to win 3-2 after Derek Temple had capitalised on Gerry Young's slip.

Brown remained at the club until February 1968 at which point he rejoined Sunderland. Sadly, it was not a wise move.

Brown was relegated with Sunderland again in the 1969/70 season, and after two failed attempts at regaining promotion he resigned in November 1972 after the club had stalled in extending his contract. With home gates dropping below five figures, Brown was forced to work with a tight budget and rely increasingly upon home-grown youth, which the *Sunderland Echo* correspondent, 'Argus', complimented him upon. Argus wrote: 'The production lines have already filled key positions in the team and there is a wave of talent coming along which promises more exciting progress.'

Commanding centre-half Dave Watson was shocked by Brown's resignation. He said: 'I felt sorry for the man; he wanted to sign a few more players but the club would not give him the money.' On the contrary, Brown was forced to sell his highly accomplished centre-back, Colin Todd, to Derby for £175,000. Brown must have been seething when Sunderland chairman, Collings, announced, after appointing Bob Stokoe as his successor, 'Money will be made available for Mr Stokoe, if he requires it.'

Billy Hughes was one of several Sunderland players who clashed with Brown, believing him to be too much of a sergeant major. He claimed that when Browny became angry the vein in his neck used to stick out. He said: 'That was the time to back off.' However, Hughes saw another side to Brown shortly before Brown's resignation. Hughes had reproached Brown for frightening the young players. Instead of angrily dismissing this accusation Brown welled up, claiming that the young players 'were not footballers, they were his family'. Ritchie Pitt, one of Brown's young players appreciated him, remarking: 'Alan Brown would stick with you even if you had a bad game. I had a few of those although I learnt quickly, and he could see that. He was strict. He gave you a role and you were expected to stick with it. I thought he was an excellent manager.' Having been given his debut by Brown when only 17, Pitt would acquit himself splendidly in the 1973 FA

Cup Final when Sunderland shocked the English football fraternity by beating Leeds. The team that Bob Stokoe led out at Wembley was largely fashioned by Brown.

After leaving Sunderland Brown spent time coaching in Norway before assisting Plymouth Argyle. He then left the game completely and spent a sad retirement blighted by grief and ill health. When Roker legend Len Ashurst visited Brown in Devon, he found that his respected former boss had fallen upon rough times but Brown would not dwell on his misfortune. Instead, he said to Ashurst, 'Come here, see those flowers? Brian Clough sent them. And see this cheque? He sent me this as well.' To his credit Clough never forgot his trusted mentor.

63.

LEEDS v EVERTON: FIRST DIVISION, 23 NOVEMBER 1968

THE PERSISTENT morning rain had turned to drizzle by the time my girlfriend and I arrived at a heavily overcast Elland Road. There was a huge crowd there, later revealed to be 41,716 strong, only 8,000 below full capacity. Leeds had progressed well under Don Revie, since returning to the First Division in 1964, coming within a whisker of taking the title in 1965 when Manchester United had pipped them on goal average. Having lost a turgid FA Cup Final to Liverpool in that same year, Leeds were keen to add domestic silverware to the Inter-Cities Fairs Cup which they had recently won in a two-legged tie with Hungarian side Ferencvaros.

Apart from a blip at Turf Moor where they were torn apart 5-1 by Burnley's vibrant youngsters, they were well-placed in third position coming into this game. They were unbeaten at Elland Road during 1968/69 and had not conceded a goal in their six games since the Burnley debacle on 19 October. Their visitors Everton were one point and one place better off but with one extra game played. Everton had not been defeated in 16 games. Liverpool were then top on goal average.

Both sides lined up with a 4-3-3 formation. The Leeds side comprised: Sprake; Reaney, Charlton, Madeley and Cooper; Bremner, Hunter and Giles; O'Grady, Jones and Eddie Gray. Lorimer was their substitute. Everton had West in goal; Wright, Labone, Hurst and Brown; Kendall, Harvey and Ball; Husband, Royle and Morrissey with Ray Wilson as substitute. The opening was highly combative with possession quickly won and lost in a blitz of scrapping melees and ruthless tackling. Initially, Leeds relied upon long balls pumped into the visitors' box while Everton counter-attacked progressively, using the full width of the pitch. Cooper gave Leeds greater purchase with two dangerous left-wing forays. The first resulted in Kendall fouling him, prompting home chants of 'Animal! Animal!' Cooper's second advance released Giles who skipped past Wright and crossed, but too high for Charlton to convert.

In the sixth minute Madeley was caught in possession by Husband who instantly found Morrissey in the inside-left channel. He in turn offloaded to Kendall who had made a penetrative run into the box. But before Kendall could pull the trigger, alert Sprake raced off his line to thwart him. Two minutes later, Leeds took the lead. After a short interlude of head tennis outside the Everton box, the ball ran free. As Wright attempted to deal with the loose ball, it bounced up and struck his arm. A penalty was awarded which Giles calmly put away. A volcanic roar went up.

Everton were not deterred, though, persisting with their quick, forward thrusts with crisp exchanges of passes. Even the loss of Morrissey did not impede them. The breakthrough came in the 22nd minute when a sloppy pass from Bremner was intercepted by Kendall who moved infield before releasing the ball to Alan Ball on the right. The World Cup winner moved towards the Leeds box before curling a near-post cross around Madeley for 19-year-old Royle to nudge past Sprake with a diving header. It was a magnificent goal, although arguably Madeley allowed Ball too much space and Charlton and Reaney failed to block Royle's charge. The Everton fans in the 'Scratching Shed' behind Sprake went wild with joy. Right on cue, the glowering clouds parted with the Leeds box bathed in brilliant sunshine. Everton continued to dominate after their equaliser although O'Grady wriggled free on the left flank, requiring a cluster of Everton defenders plus goalie West to stop him. A posse of Leeds players immediately besieged the referee demanding a penalty be given but he summarily waved them away.

Despite the cloying mud that impeded the ball's passage, the second half was played at a frantic pace. Charlton pushed up more, giving the previously shackled Jones more space in and around their opponents' box. Although Everton continued to attack brightly with their incisive passes and zipping movement, Leeds were threatening the Everton goal more often. With both Charlton and Madeley using their physical strength to jostle the Everton defenders, goalie West became increasingly jittery, twice dropping the ball under pressure. As Leeds became more commanding, Reaney joined their advance, finding Jones with a crisp cross, but the centre-forward's fierce header was grasped well by West.

Gray was now playing with greater freedom on the left flank, challenging Wright severely with his pace and trickery. Cutting inside, the Everton goal suddenly came within Gray's range, but his blistering cross shot was superbly turned aside by the diving West. Leeds were so preoccupied with attack that they neglected to bolt their back door. A long Everton clearance found Royle in oceans of space. The young centre-forward quickly made for goal, beating the solitary defender in his way, only to prevaricate, allowing Sprake to snatch the ball at his feet. Husband was wasteful, too, spurning a couple of inviting chances.

Then in the 75th minute the winning goal came, fashioned initially by an exchange between Bremner and Giles who were working closer together in central midfield. Seeing Charlton racing forward yet again, Giles fed him the ball. Sheer strength got Charlton past the first defender, followed by a nutmeg of the second, but with other Everton defenders rushing to block his way, Charlton momentarily lost control of the ball. Attempting to rectify this Charlton flew into a tackle, studs showing, but with the referee unconcerned, the ball ricocheted upwards in the direction of the leaping Madeley inside the Everton box. The ball brushed his hair before falling to Gray who unhesitatingly volleyed it into the net at heat-seeking velocity. Game over!

Having re-visited the extended *Match of the Day* coverage on YouTube over 50 years later, I am gratified to see this game was as good as I remembered. No doubt Michael Oliver would have sent off half of the participants using modern rules for there was an abundance of hideous tackles, but there was superb, exciting, attacking football, too, on a farmyard surface. Brilliant football did not stop at the 1959/60 season, Jimmy. I think you know that.

Some years later, Johnny Giles gave this tribute of Don Revie, 'Don was brilliant. If we lost a bad goal on a Saturday, we'd be out first thing on Monday morning, assessing what went wrong and working out how to put it right. Whereas when I was playing under Matt Busby, he wasn't great on the tactical side. We did not have a good team when I was at Old Trafford. But I don't remember us ever being out on the training ground early on a Monday putting right a technical or tactical flaw. It was, "Okay lads, we'll start on Wednesday."

'When Don started as a manager, he did not have the same luxury as Matt to pick the best schoolboys. Leeds had to make the most of what they had, kids like Paul Madeley, Norman Hunter, Paul Reaney, and Terry Cooper. When I went to United in 1956, those players would not have got in on ability, but because of coaching that brought out their ability, and their dedication and will to work, they became great players. Don built a fantastic side albeit one that went too far with fierce tackling, although this was often a response to other sides getting stuck into us. That was the culture of the game back then. I am aware of the things that have been said which purport to tarnish his reputation. I am speaking here about a manager whom I rate as one of the best.'

Jack Charlton added, 'Don made it clear that we weren't there to enjoy the game, we were there to get results.'

Billy Bremner said, 'He would talk about our opponents and point out their strengths and weaknesses. He gave each of us a dossier with a run-down on the team we were about to play but he never told us how he wanted us to play. He left that up to us.'

Norman Hunter remembered, 'Don never lost his temper with us, but you knew when he was unhappy. I used to get carried away at times and try to nutmeg opposing players. He would make it clear that was not to happen again. He'd say, "Win the ball and give it to those who can play!"

'We turned games into tough, physical contests when we probably did not need to. He admitted he wished he could let us play more. That was probably a fault, but he was still a great manager.'

As a Spurs player, Bill Nicholson won the First Division title in 1951. As their manager he won 'the double' in 1961, the FA Cup in 1962, the European Cup Winners' Cup in 1963, the FA Cup in 1967, the League Cup in 1971 and 1973 and the UEFA Cup in 1972.

'Northern Exposure'. Burnley in 1959. A new hotel is being constructed hailed fancifully as the 'Claridges of the North' but despite the thicket of mills, Cotton was in fast retreat as in Bolton, Blackburn, and Preston.

Ipswich's incredible 1961/62 First Division title winners. Back left: Compton, Baxter, Nelson, Bailey, Elsworthy, Carberry. Front: Stephenson, Crawford, Phillips, Moran, Jimmy Leadbetter. **PA Images**

Denis Law opens the scoring in the 1963 FA Cup Final against Leicester. Manchester United narrowly avoided relegation in this season, but this stylish victory set them on their way again, winning the First Division title in 1965 and 1967 and the European Cup in 1968. **PA Images**

After an enthralling 1964 FA Cup Final West Ham won with a late goal from Ronnie Boyce. Here Sissons levels for West Ham after Preston scored first. **PA Images**

Gordon Wallace outjumped Arsenal centre-half, Ure, to head Liverpool into a 2-0 lead in August 1964. This was the first match covered by Match of the Day. *Liverpool won this thriller 3-2.* **PA Images**

Martin Peters puts England 2-1 up against West Germany in the 1966 World Cup Final. **PA Images**

The pride of Lisbon's lions: Tommy Gemmell turns away in jubilation after lashing in an equaliser against Inter Milan in the 1967 European Cup Final. Celtic deservedly won 2-1. PA Images

'Ballet on Ice' at Maine Road. City beat Spurs twice on their way to the league title in 1967/68. PA Images

*Roger Smart opens the scoring for Third Division Swindon against Arsenal in the 1969
League Cup Final which Swindon won 3-1, after extra-time.* PA Images

*Osgood equalises late in normal time in the Chelsea v Leeds FA Cup replay 1970.
Chelsea came from behind to win 2-1 in an ugly game littered with reckless challenges.*
PA Images

Eddie Gray of Leeds was a highly gifted attacking player, capable of making defenders look foolish. He was often a target for rough treatment, as Everton's John Hurst shows.
PA Images

Jimmy Adamson's self-styled 'Team of the Seventies'. Burnley were Second Division champions in 1972/73. Back: Jim Thomson, Colin Waldron, Alan Stevenson, Jeff Parton, Keith Newton. Middle: Mick Docherty, Doug Collins, Alan West, Geoff Nulty, Harry Wilson, Dave Thomas, Leighton James. Front: Billy Ingham, Frank Casper, Paul Fletcher, Martin Dobson, Eric Probert, Paul Bradshaw.

Burnley hammered champions elect, Leeds at Elland Road in 1974, 4-1, helped by Paul Fletcher's spectacular scissor kick.

*Burnley chairman, Bob Lord, a self-styled 'John Bull' of English football, (left),
celebrating the 1959/60 triumph with the town mayor Edith Utley and vice-chairman,
Reg Cook.*

*By the late 60s the traditional North Western industries were in full retreat, not only
cotton but coal and steam too, impacting upon its towns' football fortunes. Here a coal
train crosses Burnley viaduct.*

64.

LIVERPOOL v WOLVERHAMPTON WANDERERS: FIRST DIVISION, 5 APRIL 1969

LEEDS'S MAIN rivals during the 1968/69 season were Liverpool. On 5 April 1969 *Match of the Day* covered Liverpool's home fixture with Wolves and thanks to YouTube a substantial segment of the highlights remains. It was a day of brilliant spring sunshine. The Anfield pitch looked in a terrible state, rutted, bald and uneven in large areas. The ball bobbled badly. The game was certainly not a classic. BBC commentator Kenneth Wolstenholme began by introducing the sides.

I knew something about each of the Liverpool players having watched them frequently on *Match of the Day* and on the TV coverage of the disappointing 1965 FA Cup Final. There was burly Scottish international goalkeeper Tommy Lawrence, dubbed affectionately, 'the flying pig'. With Liverpool playing a flat back four, he had to be on his toes, often dashing from his goal to block a player penetrating the back line. He was huge, brave, alert, and reliable.

Chris Lawler was at right-back; a no-frills, dependable defender who managed to score 61 goals almost unobtrusively. At centre-half was the mountainous Ron or 'Rowdy' Yeats. After signing him from Dundee, Shankly invited the journalists present to 'take a walk around my centre-half'. His nickname was taken from the TV western, *Rawhide*. In this game, Tommy Smith partnered him, an aggressive ball-winner with excellent distribution about whom a BBC commentator, possibly David Coleman, once claimed, 'He was not born but quarried.' At left-back was Gerry Byrne, a nondescript defender until Shankly helped him realise his great talent. Byrne was renowned for his bravery having played 117 minutes of the 1965 FA Cup Final with a broken collarbone.

With Emlyn Hughes out injured, utility player Geoff Strong filled in capably. Ironically, Strong left Arsenal because he was not getting enough game-time up front where he had a one in two strike-rate. Ian Callaghan had begun his career as a direct right-winger, having played under Ramsey in that role in the 1966 World Cup. But by this time, he was operating successfully as a central midfield general. Former Scottish international striker, Ian St John, had been playing well in a more withdrawn capacity but was then recovering from appendicitis.

Up front was modest, hard-working, predator Roger Hunt. When confronted by a journalist who had a poor opinion of Hunt, Ramsey replied, 'Roger Hunt scores 25 goals in a season, *every* season. Yes, Roger Hunt is a poor player.' Accompanying Hunt was perky young striker Alun Evans, full of cute tricks and razor-sharp movement. Finally, jinking, swaying, right-footed Peter Thompson played on the left wing.

The Wolves side was largely made up of combative grafters who had done well to keep their side out of relegation trouble. But they did have a pair of dangerous strikers with showman Derek Dougan, an eloquent Northern Ireland international, and the mercurial Peter Knowles, who was both skilful and reckless. Knowles would cast away his hugely promising career to join the Jehovah's Witnesses as a door-to-door evangelist. In a strange BBC interview, he explained that he would damage a fellow player for life if he remained as a footballer.

Wolstenholme told us that Liverpool had not given up their ambition of overtaking Leeds and winning the title, although they had recently thrown away a point in a 1-1 home draw with Arsenal. Liverpool had clobbered Wolves 6-0 at Molineux in September 1968 and were hoping for a repeat display. However, they started poorly. The opening exchanges were scrappy. It was Wolves, though, who moved the ball with greater confidence.

Dougan was a constant menace, notably in the frequent aerial skirmishes while Knowles flitted here and there combining well with right-winger Farrington in pacy counter-attacks. Seizing upon the second balls, Knowles had two good chances. His first shot flashed over the bar while his second forced Lawrence to dive to his right to parry the ball away. Liverpool were indebted to Smith for repelling danger and sweeping up. Meanwhile, Liverpool struggled to assert themselves, relying too much on hopeful lofted punts, which the tall Wolves defenders Holsgrove, McAlle and Munroe dealt with easily. Then out of the blue Callaghan put his foot on the ball and floated a teasing right-wing cross towards the far post. Munroe unaccountably missed it, allowing Hunt to slip behind him, chest the ball down and smack it against the top of the bar at point-blank range. Goalkeeper Phil Parkes took a deep breath. Hunt did not often spurn such simple chances, although he had managed to score only two goals at home this season.

Gradually, the tide turned with Liverpool getting more players into the Wolves box to the increasing consternation of their defenders, but it took an unnecessary foul to supply the opening. Smith took the free kick quickly from the halfway line, lofting the ball towards the right apex of Wolves' penalty area. Hunt was culpably ignored as he pounced on the ball, brought it under control and stabbed it into the net without any defender attempting to impede him. It was his 300th career goal. Hunt would move on to Second Division strugglers Bolton Wanderers during the following season.

After Hunt's goal, the game returned to a bump and grind contest with the ball squirting off at unexpected angles from the crunching challenges. It was no surprise that Liverpool were scoreless in four of their final seven fixtures. Meanwhile, Leeds won four and drew three of their final seven games to take the title, six points ahead of Liverpool.

When Leeds arrived at Anfield on Monday 28 April the Liverpool players and fans generously applauded them much to the appreciation of Billy Bremner who wrote, 'The Anfield Kop cheered and chanted and sang their tribute to the league champions. I stood on the pitch with a lump in my throat as I waved to them. In a marvellous moment of sportsmanship, the Kop gave Leeds the treatment they usually reserve for their Liverpool idols.'

On that magical evening in Liverpool on 28 April 1969 the superb reception Leeds received suggested the English game was still in a good place.

Leeds amassed 67 points (worth 94 today), losing only twice. For the next five years they vied principally with Shankly's Liverpool and double winners Arsenal for the title. Meanwhile, Manchester United, having won the European Cup in 1968, amid much high emotion, began a post-Busby decline that ultimately led to their relegation in 1974.

65.

CITY SLICKERS v COUNTRY BUMPKINS: LEAGUE CUP FINAL, 15 MARCH 1969

ONCE AGAIN, the League Cup Final threw up another startling feat. The competition had began with Fourth Division Rochdale reaching the first final in 1961/62, although admittedly many leading clubs did not take part back then. Norwich beat Rochdale 4-0 on aggregate to lift the new trophy but 'Dale' were rightfully proud of their efforts.

Five years later, Third Division Queens Park Rangers won the League Cup when there was full representation. They beat First Division West Bromwich Albion 3-2 at Wembley, after coming back from a two-goal deficit. But the third surprise was the most astonishing one when third-tier Swindon Town overpowered First Division Arsenal just two years before the Gunners achieved the double.

The Swindon team included Rod Thomas, an intelligent, tough-tackling Welsh international full-back. Their resourceful midfielder John Smith had made little progress at West Ham and Spurs, having Bobby Moore, Danny Blanchflower and Dave Mackay in front of him. But at Swindon he shone as a midfield general who fired out pinpoint passes for his forwards. Geordie Peter Noble was a versatile, ball-playing inside-forward who was strong in the air and a deadly finisher. He had scored the winning goal in the semi-final replay with Burnley; a club he would later serve with distinction.

But the Robins' outstanding player was winger Don Rogers, a former England youth and under-23 international. Half a dozen First

Division clubs were buzzing around 23-year-old Rogers in 1969, making bids of £100,000 upwards for his services. The Swindon board members were unmoved. They would not consider parting with their maestro whose repertoire included bewildering swerves, explosive acceleration, tight control, and ruthless finishing power. He scored five goals in the 1968/69 League Cup competition alone. This season concluded with Swindon's promotion to the Second Division behind champions Watford. Rogers's tally was 108 goals in 268 league appearances, a spectacular strike-rate for a winger. Some suspected that Rogers was too much of a small-town boy, a home bird, to do the business in the glare of the big city lights. On 15 March 1969 he forced his critics to eat their words.

But if Rogers was Arsenal's extra-time assassin, goalkeeper Peter Downsborough was Swindon's normal-time saviour. After Arsenal centre-half Ian Ure had gifted Roger Smart a 36th-minute opener, the heroic Downsborough repelled the Gunners for almost an hour. Time and again he plunged into the muddy melees to grasp the greasy ball, also snatching it from the feet of Bobby Gould and John Radford on countless occasions. He commanded his area with elastic invincibility, defying everything that Arsenal could fire at him. But, with only four minutes remaining, Downsborough made his first error. He had timed his dashes from goal to perfection, making nine successful interceptions inside a frantic ten-minute spell in the second half. But with his tenth he guessed wrongly. Gould was quick to take advantage, tapping the ball into the empty net and Swindon were expected to wilt in extra time.

Rogers defied that expectation. He took heart from the exhausted state of the Arsenal players, half of whom had their socks rolled down. They looked spent. The crucial goal came at the end of the first period of extra time. As the ball ran loose in the Arsenal box, Rogers kept his feet better than any of the slithering, sliding Arsenal defenders. His goal was described as 'Puskas-like'. Side-stepping one lunging tackle after another Rogers found he had only goalkeeper Bob Wilson to beat, which he did, unhesitatingly, with a crisp, close-range shot.

With fatigue and desperation creating ever-widening gaps, Rogers revelled in the greater freedom. His second goal came shortly before the end with Arsenal committing everyone, bar Wilson, to a desperate attack. Picking the ball up on the halfway line, he drove towards goal, shoulders hunched, his stride lengthening, the ball remaining under control despite the sludgy, sanded surface. Upon reaching the penalty area, Rogers swerved expertly around the helpless Wilson, and planted the ball into the empty net.

Swindon manager Danny Williams described his side's victory as 'a triumph of fitness and attacking football'. This was a gloss. While Swindon were certainly the fitter side in the energy-sapping swamp, Arsenal did most of the attacking. Put simply, Arsenal ran out of puff in extra time, not helped by having half of their team recovering from flu. But make no mistake, Swindon were a good side. They had deposed of First Division4 Coventry and Burnley on the way to the final. Their semi-final victory over Burnley was a testament to their skill, stamina, and resilience.

Ironically, this magnificent triumph benefited beaten Arsenal more than victorious Swindon. After the game, Arsenal coach Don Howe said sourly, 'This was a match that we should have won by half-time. We won't take too much notice of it.' That was just a raw reflex response though. He and manager Bertie Mee reflected long and hard upon this unexpected defeat.

It was Arsenal's second successive League Cup final failure. They realised that if their side were to have any hope of winning honours again, having spent too long in the doldrums, radical changes had to be made. They realised they required a centre-half, who was less impulsive, less inclined to dive in than Ure. They decided, too, that midfielder David Court had to be replaced by someone with sharper vision and better distribution. Thirdly, they realised that Gould was not reliable enough as a striker. Fourthly, they wanted someone with the strength and flair of Rogers. And finally, Frank McLintock needed to curb his over-adventurous sorties because they left big gaps behind him.

During the late '50s and early '60s, Arsenal had placed excessive faith in individual superstars, hoping that they would turn the team around largely of their own accord. This expensive fallacy was exposed in the signings of Mel Charles, George Eastham, and Joe Baker, for example. Mee and Howe looked to develop a team by investing in Arsenal's rich crop of talented youngsters. The Swindon defeat prompted the inclusion of Charlie George, Ray Kennedy, and Eddie

AN END OF INNOCENCE

Kelly in their subsequent sides while Frank McLintock was converted into a disciplined centre-half. The 1971 double-winning side began to take shape. A year after their defeat by Swindon, Arsenal won the Inter-Cities Fairs Cup. A year after that, Arsenal won both the First Division and the FA Cup. Honour had been restored.

As for Swindon, they settled for mid-table in the Second Division. But after Rogers's departure, to First Division Crystal Palace, Swindon returned to the Third Division.

In 1990 they were back at Wembley to beat Sunderland in the Second Division play-off final only to have their elevation to the top flight overturned after they admitted breaching Football League finance rules.

Three years later they were there once more under player-manager Glenn Hoddle and triumphed again, this time earning a place in the Premier League and top-flight football for the first time in their history. But that success was short-lived, too, and just two years later they found themselves back in the third tier after successive relegations.

66.

A ROUGH GUIDE TO UNRULY ENGLISH FOOTBALL IN THE '60s

DURING THE '60s there was increasing concern about unruly behaviour on the pitch as well as off it. This concern was aroused after the shocking 'Battle of Santiago' in the 1962 World Cup fixture between Italy and hosts Chile. BBC TV commentator David Coleman introduced a highlights programme thus, 'The game you are about to see is the most stupid, appalling, disgusting and disgraceful exhibition of football, possibly in the history of the game.'

English referee Ken Aston ordered Ferrini off inside eight minutes for a second wild challenge. The Italian's reluctance to walk delayed the match for several minutes before armed policemen helped Aston bundle him off the pitch. Two players were sent off, numerous punches were thrown, and police intervention was required four times. Aston, who later invented yellow and red disciplinary cards, said, 'I wasn't reffing a football match, I was acting as an umpire in military manoeuvres.' Although alarmed, most of us put it down to the 'Latin temperament'.

Then came the 'Battle of Goodison' in 1964, as Everton took on Leeds in a game that saw a player sent off in the fourth minute, two players felled after a clash of heads and fans warned for spitting at players. The *Guardian* reporter present stated, 'Such was the hostility, the referee, in a first for an English league game, marched both teams off the pitch so that the players and fans could cool down. When the enforced ten-minute break ended, a tannoy announcement warned that any further crowd trouble could see the game abandoned.'

Although this First Division match was completed – Leeds winning 1-0 – mounted police had to disperse angry fans from the streets around Goodison. The FA disciplinary committee suspended Everton's Sandy Brown for two weeks for his sending off having punched Leeds's John Giles in the fourth minute. The FA also punished Everton for the behaviour of their fans. Leeds came out unscathed. The FA's judgement came with a promise that it would be taking a firmer line with player discipline. It also threatened to close grounds if clubs didn't tackle 'rowdy' behaviour. Both teams were said to have form. Another view suggested it was the competitive nature of both teams that was to blame.

Less than a year earlier, an FA Cup fourth round match between the two at Elland Road ended in a fractious 1-1 draw. Writing about the Elland Road game for *The Guardian*, Eric Todd noted, 'Leeds committed the first misdemeanour, and this was followed at regular intervals by fouls of subtle, flagrant, and sometimes cruel variation on both sides. By the time the two met again at Goodison in November, Leeds, managed by Don Revie and marshalled on the pitch by dogged competitors like Jack Charlton, Billy Bremner, and Norman Hunter had furthered their reputation as an uncompromising team; this was largely the same team that had been promoted the year before with a terrible disciplinary record. But Leeds could also play attractive football, as this match report showed.'

However, when interviewed in 1969, Don Revie dismissed these concerns about rough play, saying, 'You will always get some conflict between players, particularly at the start of the season when they are really keyed up. Once the midweek games are over the normal pattern will return. I do agree, though, that the First Division has become more physical in recent years, although this is not yet excessive. Players put a lot more into the game now than they did in the days when I was playing. There is quite a lot more bodily contact. Naturally, this limits skill, but I believe in the next few years the players with real skill will learn to use this at greater speed. As defenders become quicker to tackle, forwards will have to become quicker in evading them.'

The Inter-Continental Cup, contested by the winners of the European Cup and the South American Cup holders, tended to be a brutal contest, too. Celtic were the first British side to compete. The tie went to a play-off match in Montevideo, Uruguay. The game was a shambles exacerbated by Racing Club's cynical fouling, Celtic's loss of composure, and discipline, and the incompetence of the Paraguayan referee who was clearly out of his depth. Riot police had to intervene on the pitch several times as six players were sent off; four from Celtic and two from Racing Club. Celtic's Bertie Auld refused to leave the field, though, after being sent off and still played for the whole game! Racing Club scored the only goal in the second half through Cárdenas, winning 1-0 and becoming the first Argentinian holders of the trophy.

A year later Manchester United were beaten in this competition by Estudiantes. Players were sent off in both legs, Nobby Stiles being dismissed for United in the first leg, and George Best and José Hugo Medina after a scuffle towards the end of the return match.

67.

CHELSEA v LEEDS UNITED: FA CUP FINAL, 11 APRIL 1970

SHORTLY BEFORE the final, Leeds were pursuing the First Division championship, the European Cup, and the FA Cup, but their ambitions quickly turned to dust. Everton accelerated to take the title. Jaded after three FA Cup semi-final tussles with Manchester United, Leeds lost 1-0 at home to Celtic in the European Cup semi-final first leg. Yet they arrived at Wembley in fighting form.

The pitch was a disgrace after the Horse of the Year Show contestants had ripped it apart. Hundreds of tons of sand had turned it into a sticky, bumpy, soggy beach. Johnny Giles said with disgust, 'It was the worst I have ever known. You didn't need boots, you needed hooves.' The surface cut up immediately, the ball bobbled badly and, crucially, there was no bounce – a factor which played a vital part in two of the goals scored. Quite frankly, it was miraculous that these two sides produced such an enthralling performance.

BBC TV commentator, Kenneth Wolstenholme, opened proceedings with customary hyperboles, 'Here we have two of the greatest sides in modern football. And two of the most professional managers, Dave Sexton and Don Revie.' He told us that Leeds were without right-back Reaney who had broken his leg in a league game at West Ham. The versatile Madeley substituted. Hardman Hunter had recovered from a knee injury. Chelsea were without Hudson, so Baldwin replaced him with Houseman shifted into midfield alongside Hollins. Harris was said to have recovered from a pulled thigh muscle. Harris explained later, 'It took a lot to keep me out. I had an injection two days before and managed to play for most of the game although the pitch did not help.' David Webb played in Harris's usual position at right-back. He was in for a difficult afternoon against Eddie Gray. The first ten minutes' play was nip and tuck, with Chelsea making a couple of useful sorties and Bonetti having to grab a couple of crosses under pressure. He then made a terrific save to deny Lorimer's typical piledriver, tipping over for a corner. At the Leeds end Madeley dived to head away a threatening left-wing cross from Houseman. Burly Hutchinson followed this up with a misplaced header from Cooke's centre.

In the 20th minute Leeds won a corner on their right flank. Gray crossed high into the penalty area where Charlton out-jumped Dempsey and Bonetti to nod in the opening goal. Harris and McGreadie were guarding the line but both players were confounded by the ball's lack of bounce. Leeds appeared to be in control, yet Osgood and Baldwin combined well to set up Houseman whose header flashed wide. A better opportunity came in the 38th minute when Hollins crossed from the left for Hutchinson to head up into the air, and with the Leeds defenders momentarily bemused, he headed again, this time into the path of Osgood whose stinging shot was blocked brilliantly on the line by gymnastic Charlton.

In the 41st minute the sub-standard pitch evened things up. Houseman's speculative effort deceived Sprake with the absence of bounce, the ball squeezing under his body. It remained 1-1 at the break. Three minutes after the resumption Bonetti clung on to a fierce drive from Gray, who had been making a fool of Webb. Back came Chelsea with Sprake making amends by stopping two point-blank efforts from Hutchinson and one from Osgood. Play continued to switch from end to end, although Leeds had more possession and better chances. Gray then slammed a shot against the Chelsea bar after dazzling footwork set him up. Not to be outdone, Houseman fed Baldwin whose flicked header made Sprake make a sprawling stop. Then in the 81st minute Houseman dragged a shot wide when well-placed inside Leeds's box.

That looked to be a costly miss when, three minutes later, Clarke headed against the bar and Jones drove in the rebound, the ball whistling past helpless Bonetti and finding the left-hand corner. This looked like being Leeds's day, but Chelsea refused to be subdued. With two minutes remaining, Leeds were penalised for obstruction on the left of their area. Hollins fired in a centre towards the near post for Hutchinson to lose his markers and power a towering header into the left-hand corner. Chelsea were exultant while culpable Charlton bowed his head with frustration. There was still time for Hutchinson to muscle into the Leeds box once more to meet a cross from Houseman but under pressure he was forced to head wide. Thirty minutes of extra time could not separate the sides. Webb saved on the line to deny Jones, Clarke again headed against the bar, Osgood's header was deflected wide, Bonetti grabbed another effort from Jones and Houseman forced Sprake to make a diving save. This was a terrific display by both sides on a sandy swamp. If Gray was deservedly the man of the match with his searing wing play, Bonetti was a worthy runner-up with a succession of brilliant saves.

The replay at Old Trafford on 27 April was a grave disappointment, not helped by a scarred pitch on which the ball bobbled badly, popping up when one of the many divots was struck, and bouncing high and erratically. The game was full of ugly challenges, quite possibly as a result of the unpredictable run of the ball or the uncontrolled adrenaline rushes. Players clattered into one another all over the pitch, with a litany of dangerous play incidents that were not penalised by indulgent referee Jennings. In the second minute, Gray's run at goal was stopped dead in its tracks by Webb's shin-high, flying tackle. While shortly before the end of normal time, Bremner's head was almost taken off by McCreadie's kick boxing routine. Jennings was unperturbed by either incident, waving on play.

Esteemed *Observer* journalist Hugh McIlvanney wrote, 'At times, it appeared that Mr Jennings would give a free kick, only on production of a death certificate.' Webb recalled, 'Every time the referee went for his pocket, and you thought he was going to book someone, he pulled out his hankey, blew his nose and said, "Get on with it, will you?"'

Both sides had little control with possession frantically won and lost. Consequently, the ball was constantly lumped forward more in hope than expectation and pursued with ferocious intensity. Two moments of skill beamed out of this morass of clogging, bump, and grind. First, there was a magnificent 35th-minute goal from Jones, who collected Clarke's pass and drove determinedly through a succession of lunging tackles to smash the ball past a statuesque

Bonetti, who had been hurt by Jones's prior charge. Second, with only a few minutes left of normal time, there was an exquisite late riposte by Osgood who deftly headed in Cooke's wonderful, curling chip which evaded a posse of Leeds defenders.

The winner came late in extra time when Hutchinson's prodigious throw from the left touchline was flicked on by Dempsey's head for Webb to bundle in. It was difficult for Leeds to swallow this defeat. They were clearly the better side and the winner was scored by one of Chelsea's hardmen who had helped nobble their Wembley star, Eddie Gray. However, the challenge that left Gray hobbling was made by Harris. Gray went to ground in great pain, clutching the back of his knee. It reduced Gray to a virtual passenger. Years later, Harris met Gray at an after-dinner speaking event. Harris tapped Gray on the shoulder and asked, 'Can I have my studs back?'

This game bellowed a mantra attributed to Alf Ramsey, 'Winning is not everything, it is the only thing.' English football was about to develop a harder edge, as epitomised by a remark made by ex-Burnley centre-forward Paul Fletcher. Speaking of '70s football, he said, 'We used to say it's not a foul unless the referee sees it.' So much for Corinthian values.

Chelsea's Ron Harris, dubbed 'Chopper', insisted his reputation was overblown, saying, 'I was only sent off once, at Brighton, in the FA Cup, when I broke my usual vow of silence and got involved in some verbals with Eddie Spearritt, a notorious stirrer.'

Former Premier League referee David Elleray said he would have shown six red cards in this game after watching a video of the final replay in 1997. Current top-flight official Michael Oliver looked at it in 2020 and decided upon 11. This perhaps reflects how much the English game and refereeing has changed, but let's not forget how brutal this decider was.

A BBC article suggested that the ill-feeling between the sides was indicative of a clash of cultures, pitting Chelsea, the showbiz side, the King's Road slickers, against Leeds, the gritty, unpretentious northerners with a penchant for carpet bowls and working men's clubs. However, the author of the article did not buy this caricature, stating, 'The two sides were more alike than they would have been willing to admit, both being a blend of brute force and brilliance, each driven and on the way up.'

However, that was not either club's story. Having beaten Real Madrid in the 1971 European Cup Winners' Cup Final, Chelsea ran up substantial debts after constructing a new cantilever stand and in 1975 they were relegated to the Second Division. Their later revival was hard-won until flooded with Roman Abramovich's riches.

Leeds, too, ran into difficulties after Revie left, and despite winning a First Division title just before the birth of the Premier League, and briefly 'living the dream' as the 1990s became the 2000s, only in 2020, 16 years after last playing top-flight football, did they manage to join the elite once again.

68.

THE STATE OF ENGLISH FOOTBALL DURING THE '60s FROM TEN PERSPECTIVES

'On the continent the play is more elaborate, and the individual ball play is often dazzling in its skill, but this would cut little ice in our League football when both conditions and crowds demand that the ball be transferred rapidly from end to end. The result is usually 90 minutes of thrilling cut-and-thrust, and I doubt if you can find a more exciting or attractive spectacle.'

England manager Alf Ramsey, 1965.

'Tactics are forced upon us to a large extent and we follow the leading exponents. But in copying, we must modify a system of play according to the players we have at our disposal. To play purely defensive football is easy, and it is equally easy to play attractive short passing favoured by the continentals or even kick-and-run. What we need is a winning blend of all those styles. Tradition is a wonderful friend but a dangerous enemy.'

Manchester City's Joe Mercer, 1965.

'There are many world stars in Italian league football who are capable of playing this delicate game. The tragedy is that despite this, team tactics out there are producing only negative football. The biggest danger is that the British game will follow a similar line.'

Manchester United's Denis Law, 1965.

'Northampton Town's promotion to the First Division was a miracle, a greater triumph against the odds than England's World Cup victory.'
Joe Mercer, 1966.

Note: Under Joe Mercer's former Arsenal team-mate Dave Bowen, Northampton rose from the Fourth Division in 1961 to the First Division in 1965, an incredible ascent spanning just five years, whereupon they returned to the Fourth Division at a similar speed, and were subsequently forced to apply for re-election to the Football League.

'Three vital developments have transformed football – air travel, floodlighting and television. We were shaken out of our insularity by the arrival of overseas star teams and by England's defeats. The Austrians started it with "scientific play", then Spain, Italy and the South Americans reached high standards of play. British coaches like Jimmy Hogan of Burnley showed them the way, and they really WORKED at it. Air travel and intermingling with foreign methods have shown new scope.

'Take the "Revie Plan" for example. The sooner we get a Premier League the better. This will bring back the missing millions we hear about. If there was less tension through fear of relegation, clubs would be less frightened of experimenting with new ideas in match play ... Floodlighting opened new rooms for progress. The lights enhance the spectacle and male supporters can bring their families. But television is a menace. It's good for the fireside but how much have those who run it contributed to the costly upkeep of their local Football League club?'
Burnley chairman Bob Lord, 1963.

'Football pundits like Malcom Allison and Brian Clough attacked the clinical defensive system of Ramsey. I do not want to join their bandwagon, but I never gave England a real chance in the 1970 Mexico World Cup. In 1966, we had home advantage. We were also lucky to have the referee on our side when we beat Argentina in a rough game. We did not find any championship form until we beat Portugal and West Germany. But we were far from being an entertaining side. In fact, in the last four years I have found our displays efficient but not entertaining. Ramsey's system made our football dull and we failed to produce many goals ... Now we are out of the 1970 World Cup, I hope Ramsey will not stubbornly insist his tactics are infallible. We need attack and imagination. And let's not forget that football should still be an entertainment and not a bore.'

News of the World **sports editor Frank Butler, 1970.**

'Most people say we are a more attractive team now than we were a season or so back. But I reckon we're going to have to work out a compromise between playing it tightly and playing it brightly.'

Leeds United's Paul Reaney, 1970.

'Ron Greenwood taught me everything about playing at the top level. He was a great coach, knowledgeable about English and world football. He saw how the Hungarian successes could improve our game. He took the best parts of football abroad and added these to the best of the English game. Ron wanted us to play against opponents abroad. We played in a pre-season tournament against Mexican, Brazilian, Scottish, German, Polish and Czechoslovakian teams. At West Ham Ron focussed upon improving our technique – on the ball, in our movement, where and how to run. Ron helped us to become top international players.'

Geoff Hurst of West Ham United, England's hat-trick hero in the 1966 World Cup Final.

'I always wanted creative football. I wanted method. I wanted to manage the team as I felt players wanted to be managed. I wanted a more humane approach than there was when I was playing. The first team hardly recognised the lads underneath. There never seemed to be enough interest taken in players. I tried to make the smallest member think he was part of the club.'

Manchester United manager Matt Busby, 1968.

'Don Revie was always in touch with his players' families. He sent birthday cards to the wives and children and boxes of chocolates to the wives on their birthday. He always looked upon the family as part of the success.'

Leeds United first team coach Syd Owen, 1970.

'At Chelsea I drank with Richard Harris, Michael Caine, Michael Crawford, who was an ardent Chelsea fan, and Peter O'Toole.'
Chelsea player Tommy Baldwin talking about the '60s showbiz culture at Stamford Bridge.

LAST WORDS

DESPITE THE falling attendances, English club football delivered many exciting goalfests in the '50s just as Jimmy Greaves claimed. There did seem to be greater freedom to attack then, as Jimmy Greaves argued and others confirmed, such as Jimmy Robson of Burnley. Based on goals scored, if Greaves thought that the 1959/60 Division One season was the watershed between prolific goalscoring and defensive parsimony, he might have chosen the 1957/58 season instead, the year of the Munich tragedy. It was then when the highest number of post-war goals were scored in the top flight. This peak was followed by a steady decline thereafter, as shown in the chart on page 227. But as shown on page 228, Greaves's goalscoring was equally prolific in the 60s. However, Greaves is correct in regarding the 1959/60 season as being on the brink of enormous change in English football, not in terms of how the game was played but in how it was run. In 1961 the maximum wage cap was abolished. This was a momentous event because it signalled the beginning of a shift in power from club to player. This shift was given extra impetus when the High Court pronounced in 1963 that the feudal 'retain and transfer' system was an 'unlawful restraint of trade'. The clubs had used this to restrict player movement. The 1995 Bosman judgement then accelerated the shift in power markedly.

According to sociologist Professor Ian Taylor, the abolition of the maximum wage contributed to the re-emergence of hooliganism. He claimed that the hike in wages tipped top players into a more privileged class, thereby accelerating the gentrification of football, with players becoming less accessible and wrapped up in a glitzy world of remote celebrities. In Taylor's view hooliganism represented a working-class revolt against such gentrification. There may be something in his theory but, as discussed in this book, the issue of hooliganism is a complex subject and its causes are probably multifarious.

Whether the game as played in the '50s was a time of innocence is open to conjecture as the copious amounts of goals conceded often impeded victory. In this sense these times could be described as ones of naivety, complacency and insularity in that alternative ways of winning as practised abroad seemed not to have been considered, until the new thinkers like Arthur Rowe, Joe Mercer and Malcolm Allison emerged, basing their playing styles on continental sides. It was ironic that two English coaches – Hogan and Raynor – influenced the growth of these ideas, notably in Hungary and Austria for they were largely ignored in Britain.

Also, did this supposed innocence extend to the game's administrators and managers? If we look at some of the actions and inactions of the FA and the Football League, during this period, 'culpability' might be a more apposite term. For example, the FA's preparations for the 1950 World Cup were shambolic, undermining the capacity of the England team to compete effectively in an alien climate with substandard facilities. It seems incredible that the FA passed the responsibility for team selection to an FA chairman who had never played professionally, rather than to the manager it had recently appointed. In 1959, the FA declined to accept this manager's recommendation that a qualified doctor should be present on a summer tour of South America. Given the extremities of heat and altitude the players had to bear, this seemed at best negligent. As for the Football League, its secretary took it upon himself to attempt to dissuade two league champions from participating in the new European Cup. Chelsea capitulated to his 'Little Englander' will, but thank goodness Sir Matt Busby was made of sterner stuff.

Esteemed political, social, and economic analyst Anthony Sampson coined a term 'club amateur' to describe those who obtained power through privilege and nepotism rather than by merit, who had neither the experience nor qualifications to make the executive decisions required of them, leading to 'backward, inefficient and unambitious' practices whether in politics, commerce, industry or manufacturing. In many cases the 'old school tie' influence prevailed. Sampson found repeated examples of this in his research, possibly explaining why Britain's productivity during the '50s lagged far behind that of former Axis nations. Arguably, 'club amateurs' exercised undue influence in first-class cricket, too, but many of these had at least played the game at a high level. In English top-flight football management, there were 'club amateurs', too. At three First Division clubs in the '50s, directors attempted to influence team selection or choice of tactics or assume sole charge of player purchases.

And yet, English football in the '50s featured significant innovations, too. There was Matt Busby with his ground-breaking accent on youth. Bill Nicholson at Spurs, who like his former boss, Arthur Rowe, made it 'simple' and made it 'quick', and, importantly, made it entertaining, too. There was abrasive Harry Catterick at Sheffield Wednesday who brought forensic tactical analysis and detailed player instruction to the game. There were the West Ham luminaries, headed by Malcolm Allison, who with their manager's blessing debated new ways of playing with unflagging intensity. At Burnley Alan Brown became renowned for his array of dead ball 'scams'. Vic Buckingham's two-pronged attack at West Bromwich Albion also extended the 'push and run' strategy developed by Arthur Rowe. There was Joe Mercer's experimentation with the Italian *Catenaccio* tactic at Sheffield United and Aston Villa. And there was 'tinker man' Les McDowall at Manchester City who fostered the introduction of the 'Revie Plan'. This was not a dormant or anachronistic decade.

Although Jimmy Greaves claims that '60s football was strangled by defensive tactics, it did not impede his goalscoring. Also, many of the matches covered in this book suggest that there were plenty of high quality, exciting games in the '60s, despite an increasing emphasis upon defensive solidity. The ideas put forward by the '50s theorists about how the game should be played continued to be influential in the '60s, when new names joined the high table debate including Bill Shankly, Don Revie, Alf Ramsey, Tommy Docherty, Ron Greenwood, Brian Clough, Dave Sexton, and Jimmy Adamson among others.

Although this book is largely concerned with football played in the English First Division, for that was the level at which Greaves played, it also looks at notable giant-killers, considering how they overthrew their mighty opponents. Without the element of surprise, this game would lose its attraction. And despite the Football League's initial Euroscepticism, by the '60s British clubs began to enjoy success in Europe. Celtic's pioneering triumph in the European Cup in 1967 opened the door to other such feats, just as Spurs' victory in the European Cup Winners' Cup in 1963 did that for this competition.

The issue of televised football is still debated hotly between the haves and have nots. The views of controversial former Burnley chairman Bob Lord 60 years ago have relevance today. As to whether football is too rough, I doubt whether many current players would want to return to the refereeing standards of the '50s and '60s, after seeing the 1957 and 1970 FA Cup finals.

I am grateful to Jimmy Greaves for arousing such an interesting debate. Football in these two decades, like life outside, featured such rapid changes despite implacable conservatism.

Tim Quelch
2020

REFERENCES

Football books and journals consulted:

Adamson, Richard: *Bogota Bandit: The outlaw life of Charlie Mitten*: Mainstream (2005)

Anderson, Stan with Metcalf, Mark: *Stan Anderson: Captain of the North*: Sportsbooks (2010)

Andrew, Henry: *Today's the Day*: Birmingham City Football Club: Britesport (2002)

Arsenal Football Club Handbook 1960-61 (1961)

Ashurst, Len: *Left Back in Time, the Autobiography of Len Ashurst*: Know the Score Books (2009)

Banks, Gordon *Banksy*: the autobiography: Penguin (2002)

Batty, Clive: *Kings of King's Road: The Great Chelsea Team of the 60s & 70s*: Vision Sports Publishing (2007)

Berry, Mike (ed) Backpass magazine: issues 1-50: PCP: (2007-2020)

Bingham, Billy: *A Biography of Billy Bingham*: Robert Allen: Viking (1986)

Bowler, Dave: *Winning isn't everything...: Biography of Sir Alf Ramsey*: Orion (1998)

Bowler, Dave & David Reynolds: *Ron Reynolds: the life of a 1950s' footballer* Orion (2003)

Brown, Tony (Ed.) *The Football League: Match by Match 1959-60*: SoccerData (2007)

Bruford, Bill: *Among the Thugs*: Arrow (1992)

Butler, Bryon: *The Football League: 1888 – 1988*: Macdonald Queen Anne Press (1987)

Cawley, Steve & Gary James: *The Pride of Manchester: A history of Manchester derby matches*: ACL & Polar Publishing (1992)

Charles Buchan's Football Monthly magazines: 1956–1969 Charles Buchan's Publications

Charles Buchan's Soccer Gift Books: 1957-8–1968-9 annuals: Charles Buchan's Publications

Charlton, Sir Bobby: *The Autobiography: The Manchester United Years*: Headline (2007)

Cooke, Charlie with Martin Knight: *The Bonnie Prince: Charlie Cooke – My Football Life*: Mainstream (2007)

Crambie, Geoff R. & Nathan D. Lee: *The Greatest Burnley Team of All*: M.M. Publishing Corp. (2004)

Davies, Hunter: *The Glory Game*: Mainstream (1972)

Delaney, Terence & Maurice Edelston: *Masters of Soccer*: Naldrett Press (1960)

Delaney, Terence: *A Century of Soccer*: Heinemann (1963)

Docherty, Tommy: *My Story: Hallowed be thy game*: Headline (2006)

Doherty, John with Ivan Ponting: *The Insider's Guide to Manchester United*: Empire Publications (2005)

Dougan, Derek & Patrick Murphy: *Matches of the Day 1958–1983*: Dent (1984)

Dunning, Eric, Patrick Murphy, and John Williams: *The Roots of Football Hooliganism: An Historical and Sociological Study*: Routledge (1992)

Dunphy, Eamon: *A Strange Kind of Glory: Sir Matt Busby and Manchester United*: Aurum (2001)

Eastham, George: *Determined to Win*: Sportsman's Book Club (1966)

Edwards, Gary: *Paint it White: Following Leeds Everywhere*: Mainstream (2004)

Edwards, Gary: *Leeds United: Second Coat:* Mainstream (2005)

Empire News and News Chronicle Football Annual: 1958-1972 annuals: Thomson & Co.

Fenton, Ted: *At Home with 'The Hammers'*: Kaye (1960)

Ferrier, Bob: *Soccer Partnership: Walter Winterbottom and Billy Wright*: Heinemann (1960)

Ferris, Ken: *The Double: The inside story of Spurs' triumphant 1960-61 season*: Mainstream (1999)

Finney, Tom: *My Autobiography*: Headline (2003)

Fox, Norman: *Prophet or Traitor: The Jimmy Hogan Story:* Parrs Wood Press (2003)

Francis, Tony: *Clough: A Biography:* Stanley Paul (1987)

Gardner, James: *Johnny Haynes: Portrait of a Football Genius*: Pitch Publishing (2017)

Giller, Norman: *Footballing Fifties*: JR Books (2007)

Glanville, Brian: *The Sunday Times History of the World Cup*: Times Newspapers Ltd. (1973)

Glanville, Brian *England Managers: The Toughest Job in Football*: Headline (2007)

Goldstone, Phil & David Saffer: *Champions: Manchester City 1967/8*: Tempus (2005)

Gordos, Steve: *Peter Broadbent: A Biography*: Breedon Books (2007)

Gray, Andy with Jim Drewett: *Flat Back Four: the tactical game*: Boxtree (1998)

Greaves, Jimmy: *Greavsie: The Autobiography* Little, Brown Books (2003)

Greaves, Jimmy: *The Heart of the Game* Little, Brown Books (2005)

Greaves, Jimmy with Norman Giller: *The Sixties Revisited*: Queen Anne Press (1992)

Green, Geoffrey: *Soccer in the Fifties*: Ian Allan (1974)

Hadgraft, Rob: *Ipswich Town: Champions of England 1961-62*: Desert Island Books (2002)

Hamilton, Aidan: *An Entirely Different Game: British Influence on Brazilian Football*: Mainstream (1998)

Hardy, Lance: *Stokoe, Sunderland and '73: The Story of the Greatest FA Cup Final Shock of All Time*: Orion books (2009)

Hill, Jimmy: *Striking for Soccer*: Peter Davies (1961)

Holden, Jim: Stan Cullis*: The Iron Manager*: Breedon Books (2000)

Holgate, Mike: *The Rivals: Blackburn v Burnley*: Tempus Publishing Ltd. (2005)

Hopcraft, Arthur: *The Football Man:* Aurum (2006)

Hunter, Norman: *Biting Talk*: *My Biography*: Hodder & Stoughton (2004)

Inglis, Simon (Ed.): *The Best of Charles Buchan's Football Monthly*: English Heritage & Football Monthly Ltd. (2006)

Imlach, Gary: *My Father and Other Working Class Heroes*: Yellow Jersey Press (2006)

Irvine, Willie with Dave Thomas: *Together Again*: Sports Books (2005)

Jeffs, Peter: *The Golden Age of Football: 1946 – 1953*: Breedon Books (1991)

Kelly, Stephen F. (Ed.) *A Game of Two Halves*: Mandarin (1992)

Law, Denis: *The King: My Autobiography* – Bantam/Transworld Books (2003) Reprinted by permission of the Random House Group Ltd.

Lawson, John: *Forest: 1865–1978*: Wensum Books (1978)

Leatherdale: Clive England: *The Quest for the World Cup: A Complete Record*: Two Heads Publishing (1994)

Lee, Edward & Simpson, Ray: *Burnley: A Complete Record*: Breedon Books Sport (1991)

Lord, Bob: *My Fight for Football*: Stanley Paul (1963)

The Luton News *Luton Town Football Handbook 1960-1961*: published in association with the Green 'Un (1961)

Lyall, John: *Just Like My Dreams: My Life with West Ham*: Penguin (1990)

McKinstry, Leo: *Jack and Bobby: A story of brothers in conflict*: Collins Willow (2002)

Mackay, Dave with Martin Knight: *The Real Mackay: The Dave Mackay story*: Mainstream (2005)

Matthews, Stanley: *My Autobiography: The Way It Was*: Headline (2000)

Matthews, Tony: *The Wolves: An Encyclopaedia of Wolverhampton Wanderers*: Paper Plane Publishing Ltd. (1989)

Matthews, Tony: *West Bromwich Albion: The Complete Record*: Breedon Books (2007)

McIlroy, Jimmy: *Right Inside Soccer*: Nicholas Kaye (1960)

Mercer, Joe: *The Great Ones*: Sportsman's Book Club (1966)

Metcalf, Mark: *Charlie Hurley: the greatest centre-half the world has ever seen*: Sports Books (2008)

Morris, Peter: *West Bromwich Albion*: Sportsman's Book Club (1966)

Mourant, Andrew: *Don Revie: Portrait of a footballing enigma*: Mainstream (1990)

Mullery, Alan with Tony Norman: *Alan Mullery: the autobiography*: Headline (2006)

Mullery, Alan & Paul Trevillion: *Double Bill: The Bill Nicholson Story*: Mainstream (2005)

Nawrat, Chris & Steve Hutchings: *The Sunday Times Illustrated History of Football*: Hamlyn (1994)

Nicholson, Bill: *Glory Glory: My Life with Spurs*: Macmillan (1984)

News of the World Football Annual: 1965-1995 annuals: Thomson & Co. / Invincible Press

Osgood, Peter with Martin King & Martin Knight: *Ossie: King of Stamford Bridge*: Mainstream Sport (2002)

Penney, Ian: *Manchester City: The Mercer-Allison Years* Breedon Books / DB Publishing (2008)

Prestage, Mike: *Blackpool: The Glory Years Remembered*: Breedon Books / DB Publishing (2000)

Prestage, Mike: *Bolton Wanderers: The Glory Years Remembered*: Breedon Books / DB Publishing (2000)

Prestage, Mike: *Burnley: The Glory Years Remembered*: Breedon Books / DB Publishing (2000)

Prestage, Mike: *Preston North End: The Glory Years Remembered*: Breedon Books / DB Publishing (2000)

Ponting: Ivan: *Liverpool: Player by Player*: Crowood (1990)

Potts, Margaret & Dave Thomas: *Harry Potts – Margaret's Story*: Sports Books (2006)

Prole, David *Football in London*: Sportsman's Book Club (1964)

Pringle, Patrick *The Boys Book of Soccer*: 1958–1963 annuals: Evans Brothers Ltd.

Quelch, Tim: *Never Had It So Good: Burnley's Incredible 1959/60 League Winning Triumph*: Know the Score Books (2009) / Pitch Publishing (2015)

Quelch, Tim *Underdog! 50 Years of Trials and Triumphs with Football's Also Rans*: Pitch (2011)

Rothman's & Sky Sports Football Yearbooks 1973-2020: Macdonald's & Jane's / Headline

Rowlands, Alan: *Trautmann: The Biography*: Breedon Books (2005)

Saffer, David: *Bobby Collins: The Wee Barra*: Tempus (2004)

Sharpe, Ivan: *Soccer Top Ten*: Stanley Paul (1962)

Simpson, Ray with Darren Bentley, Wallace Chadwick, Edward Lee and Phil Simpson: *The Clarets Chronicles: The Definitive History of Burnley Football Club 1882 – 2007*:

Simpson, Ray: *Burnley Football Club 1882-1968: Images in Sport*: Tempus Publishing Ltd. (1999)

Simpson, Ray: *The Clarets Collection 1946–1996: A Post-War Who's Who of Burnley Football Club*: Burnley Football Club (1996)

Smith, Martyn *Match of the Day: 40th Anniversary*: BBC Books (2004)

Signy, Dennis & Norman Giller: *Golden Heroes: Fifty Seasons of Footballer of The Year*: Chameleon (1997)

Soar, Phil & Martin Tyler: *The Official Illustrated History of Arsenal*: Hamlyn (1997)

Swan, Peter with Nick Johnson *Peter Swan: Setting the Record Straight*: Stadia (2006)

The Big Book of Football Champions: 1954–1969 annuals: Purnell

The Sportsview Book of Soccer: 1958–1963 annuals: Vernon Holding & Partners Ltd.

Taylor, Rogan & Andrew Ward: *Kicking and Screaming: an oral history of football in England*: Robson Books (1996)

Thraves, Andrew (Ed): *The Daily Mail History of the Wembley FA Cup Final*: Weidenfeld & Nicolson (1994)

Thomas, Dave: *No Nay Never: A Burnley FC Anthology*: Dave Thomas (2004)

Thomas, Dave: *No Nay Never: A Burnley FC Anthology Volume 2*: Burnley Football Club (2008)

Thomas, Dave: *Jimmy Adamson: The Man Who Said No To England*: Pitch (2013)

Thomas, Dave & Smith, Mike: *Bob Lord of Burnley: The Biography of Football's Most Controversial Chairman:* Pitch (2019)

Topical Times Football Book: 1960–1963 annuals: Thomson & Co.

Turner, Dennis: *Fulham: The Complete Record*: Breedon Books / DB publishing (2007)

Tyrrell, Tom *Manchester United: The Official History*: Tom Tyrrell & David Meek: Hamlyn (1988)

Ward, Andrew and John Williams: *Football Nation: Sixty Years of the Beautiful Game*: Bloomsbury (2009)

Watts, Derek: *Football's Giant Killers: 50 Great Cup Upsets*: Book Guild (2010)

Wheeler, Kenneth (Ed.): *Soccer the British Way*: Sportsman's Book Club (1965)

Widdows, Richard (Ed.): *Book of Football: 60 Memorable Matches*: Golden Hands / Marshall Cavendish (1973) Rights acquired by Eaglemoss Publications Ltd.

Winterbottom, Walter: *Training for Soccer: An official coaching manual of the Football Association*: Heinemann (1960)

Wiseman, David, *'Up the Clarets!': The Story of Burnley Football Club*: R. Hale (1973)

Wiseman, David: *A Case of Vintage Claret: Fifty of the best Burnley footballers of all time*: Hudson & Pearson (2006)

World Sports magazine March 1959, May 1962, March 1963

Wright, Billy: *One Hundred Caps and All That*: Robert Hale (1962)

Young, Percy: *Football in Sheffield*: Sportsman's Book Club (1964)

Young, Percy: *Bolton Wanderers*: Sportsman's Book Club (1965)

Plus football match reports and additional material from: *Burnley Express, Daily Mail, Daily Mirror, FourFourTwo, Backpass, The Guardian, The Independent, Lancashire Evening Post, News Chronicle, Mail on Sunday, News of the World, The Times, The Observer, Observer Magazine, Sunday Express, Sunday Times, Daily Sketch, Daily Herald, When Saturday Comes*, club programmes and websites: Tony Scholes at Burnley's Up the Clarets website; Phil Whalley of Clarets Archive; Leeds 'Mighty Whites' site; York City South supporters' website (www.yorkcitysouth.co.uk); YouTube footage.

Non-football reference works consulted:

Caputo, Philip: *A Rumor of War*: Pimlico (1999)

Chronicle of the 20th Century: Longman (1998)

Hodgson, Geoffrey: *The People's Century Vol. 2*: BBC Books (1996)

Marr, Andrew: *A History of Modern Britain*: Macmillan (2007)

MacInnes, Colin: *Absolute Beginners*: MacGibbon & Kee (1959)

Marwick, Arthur: *The Sixties*: Oxford (1998)

Nuttal, Jeff: *Bomb Culture*: MacGibbon & Kee (1968)

Patrick, James: *A Glasgow Gang Observed*: Eyre Methuen (1973)

Sampson, Anthony: *Anatomy of Britain*: Hodder & Stoughton (1962)

Sampson, Anthony: *Anatomy of Britain Today*: Hodder & Stoughton (1965)

Sandbrook, Dominic: *Never Had It So Good: A History of Britain from Suez to The Beatles*: Little, Brown (2005)

Sandbrook, Dominic: *White Heat: A History of Britain in the Swinging Sixties*: Abacus / Little, Brown Books (2006)

Thomas, Peter: *The Golden Years of Burnley*: True North (1998)

Waterhouse, Keith: *Billy Liar*: Penguin (1959)

OTHER PITCH BOOKS BY TIM QUELCH

Never Had it So Good
Burnley's Incredible 1959/60 Title Triumph

'A superb book' *Trevor Meredith Burnley's title-winning goalscorer in May 1960*

Underdog!
Fifty Years of Trials and Triumphs with Football's Also-Rans

'This is a major work, erudite, keenly observed. It is dripping with authentic atmosphere. I was captivated.' *Ivan Ponting: Backpass magazine*

Bent Arms & Dodgy Wickets
England's Troubled Reign as Test Match Kings during the Fifties

'Once we thought of the 50s as a golden age. We now look back and find snobbery, imperial arrogance, and racial prejudice. For looking at history differently Tim Quelch should be applauded.' *The Cricketer*

Stumps & Runs and Rock 'n' Roll
Sixty Years Spent Beyond a Boundary

'Tim's descriptive powers regarding players are a treat.' *Andrew Roberts CricketStatistics.com*

From Orient to the Emirates
The Plucky Rise of Burnley FC

'Burnley's inspirational, never-say-die recovery from the cusp of oblivion to once more competing against the top flight's big guns. To call the intervening 30-year journey a "roller-coaster" is an understatement. An abundance of comments from fans, players, newspaper reports and other contemporaneous accounts. An uplifting formula.' *SportsBookoftheMonth.com*

Good Old Sussex by the Sea
A Sixties Childhood Spent with Hastings United, the Albion and Sussex County Cricket

'Few have the skill of Quelch in describing the spirit of the times. He has also interwoven a commentary on current affairs and pop music to remind readers that sport was not the only activity changing fast. He ends with a few pen portraits of players he particularly liked. His quirky, highly personal book is an unexpected delight.' *Sussex Life magazine*